CITIZENSHIP

AND THOSE WHO LEAVE

STUDIES OF WORLD MIGRATIONS

Donna R. Gabaccia and Leslie Page Moch, editors

A list of books in the series
appears at the end of the book.

CITIZENSHIP
AND THOSE WHO LEAVE

THE POLITICS OF EMIGRATION
AND EXPATRIATION

EDITED BY
NANCY L. GREEN
AND FRANÇOIS WEIL

UNIVERSITY OF ILLINOIS PRESS

Urbana and Chicago

1 2 3 4 5 C P 5 4 3 2 1
♾ This book is printed on
acid-free paper.

Library of Congress Cataloging-in-
Publication Data
Citizenship and those who leave : the politics
of emigration and expatriation / edited by
Nancy L. Green and François Weil.
p. cm. — (Studies of world migrations)
Includes bibliographical references
and index.
ISBN-13: 978-0-252-03161-8 (cloth : alk. paper)
ISBN-10: 0-252-03161-x (cloth : alk. paper)
ISBN-13: 978-0-252-07429-5 (pbk. : alk. paper)
ISBN-10: 0-252-07429-7 (pbk. : alk. paper)
1. Emigration and immigration—History.
2. Emigration and immigration—
Government policy.
I. Green, Nancy L. II. Weil, François.
III. Series.
JV6021.C57   2007
325'.2—dc22   2006017846

CONTENTS

PREFACE

Donna R. Gabaccia
Leslie Page Moch

Citizenship and Those Who Leave is the second volume in the "Studies in World Migrations" series, following Leo Lucassen's *Immigrant Threat*. This volume was chosen for the series because it casts an eye to emigration and expatriation worldwide—from the Americas and Europe to India, China, and Israel. Like the emerging field of migration studies, the perspective is interdisciplinary; although most contributors are historians who have read widely in the social sciences, other contributors bring the expertise of sociology and political science to their contributions.

This volume, like the series, appears at a time of transition from methodological nationalist paradigms (such as case studies of immigration to the United States) to global and border-crossing scales of analysis. Scholars are producing more comparative studies, adopting global or world perspectives, and experimenting with transnational studies. A present danger, then, is losing sight of the still-significant power of nation-states to guard their borders. This power may be peaking currently; certain national laws governing immigration and emigration continue to frame a concrete reality for people on the move. This volume keeps the influence of the national state firmly in view even as it reverses our paradigms from immigration to emigration and offers comparisons that show how states in most world regions have sought to regulate their mobile populations.

The key questions embedded in these chapters include: How successful has the state been in controlling departures? What is the administrative structure that shapes emigration policy, and what are its concerns? How do the politics and the bureaucracies of nations conceive of and attempt to control the costs of emigration? How are potential emigrants viewed by their home state? Do nation-states actually seek to learn from policies implemented elsewhere as they face the mobile millions they call their subjects or citizens? Answers to complex questions such as these are never simple or straightforward. Still, it is our hope that by asking such questions, we will encourage our readers to develop a more balanced approach to the study of international migration and that future scholarship will devote as much analytical attention to issues of emigration as scholars over the past half-century have devoted to related issues of immigration.

ACKNOWLEDGMENTS

Most of the chapters in this volume originated at a conference entitled "Citoyenneté et émigration," held at the École des Hautes Etudes en Sciences Sociales on December 7 and 8, 2001. The meeting brought together an interdisciplinary group of migration scholars to look at the other side of the migration process from a comparative perspective. We would like to thank all of the participants, including the discussants, Marie-Claude Blanc-Chaléard, Catherine Collomp, Ambassador Richard Kauzlarich, and Patrick Weil. Rebecca Fite gave invaluable assistance in helping the conference take place.

We are also grateful to the following French institutions for their support throughout this project: the École des Hautes Etudes en Sciences Sociales, the Centre de Recherches Historiques, the Centre d'études nord-américaines, the Mission Recherche (MiRe) of the Ministère de l'Emploi et de la Solidarité, the Ministère des Affaires étrangères, the Commissariat général au Plan, and the Ministère de la Recherche.

Our special thanks go to Donna Gabaccia and Leslie Page Moch, fellow migration scholars, for accepting this book into their series.

CITIZENSHIP

AND THOSE WHO LEAVE

INTRODUCTION

Nancy L. Green and François Weil

Exit, like entry, has helped define citizenship over the last two centuries, yet little attention has been given to what could be called the politics of emigration. Most of the migration literature of the last few decades, as seen from the major countries of arrival, has been resolutely a literature of *im*migration. As immigration studies took off during the ethnic renaissance of the 1970s and 1980s, and as immigration remains front-page news, it is not surprising that most migration history is written from where we are: the countries of immigration, past and present.

Indeed, immigration has come to be seen as a litmus test for how nations define themselves. The expanding field of citizenship studies has raised fundamental questions about hospitality and sovereignty from the perspective of the state, focusing on admissions policies, the integration of foreigners, the acquisition (or not) of rights and eventually political citizenship, and the definition of foreignness as perceived by host countries. All of these issues have to do with perceptions of the Other, and with defining the nation itself.

We propose here to reverse this perspective in order to examine how nations also have defined themselves by their attitudes toward those who leave. Surprisingly little attention has been given to the history of policies and attitudes of the state with regard to departure. How have countries impeded or facilitated leave-taking? How have they perceived and regulated those who leave? What relations do they seek to maintain with their citizens abroad, and why? Citizenship is conceptualized not just through entry but through exit as well.[1]

The emigration perspective is important for two reasons. First, emigration is intimately related to immigration. This has been recognized for the migrants, with repeated calls for better integrating the stories of their past with stories of their present.[2] However, the recent debates and historical scholarship on citizenship have been framed almost entirely within the perspective of the countries of immigration.[3] We can look to the history of migrations past—even before the "invention of the passport"[4]—in order to re-examine the ways in which countries have perceived those who left.

A study of the politics of emigration could range in time from colonial policies of the nineteenth century to taxation regimes for business expatriates in the late twentieth century. Emigration can be a strategy encouraged in the name of imperialism, or it can be perceived as a loss of labor or a "brain drain." At one extreme, countries have expelled their citizens for political or religious reasons; local potentates have sold their subjects into slavery. At the other, totalitarian regimes have prohibited their citizens from leaving, creating everything from administrative barriers to physical walls.

We concentrate here between the extremes, on free movement during the mass migrations of the nineteenth and twentieth centuries. We ask how voluntary leave-taking—motivated, as we know, by a combination of economic, demographic, political, religious, and individual factors, and often with the intent (if not the reality) of return—was conceptualized by the sending countries. The material reasons for departure have been documented, but the political perceptions of departure have never been studied in a comparative perspective. In what ways did the state accompany, encourage, or impede exit?

With this volume, we argue for the importance of a multifaceted study of emigration, from the laws governing departure and the formal ties that bind citizens (from military service to consular services), to research into society's attitudes about departure and about those left behind. Emigration may be encouraged or discouraged by the sending societies. It may be seen as a form of diffuse ambassadorship—the spread of civilization or the avant-garde of investment abroad—or it may be lamented as a drain of resources or feared as treason.

FREEDOM OF MOVEMENT

The right to exit is not a historical given, and, over the last two centuries, the limitations on internal and external mobility have been many. Until the end of serfdom, after all, the first impediment to movement was internal: people were bound to the soil; voluntary leaving was proscribed. Interregional movement or internal colonization was often regulated, if not organized, by the state. In chapter 1, John Torpey dates the modern notion of free departure to the French Revolution, arguing that the freedom to leave has corresponded to a free labor market. He contrasts these norms, which spread throughout Western Europe, with the Soviet Union and with internal and external Chinese restrictions on movement, while pointing out how the United States combined freedom of movement for European immigrants with restrictions on movement for blacks.

This modern freedom of departure was facilitated by an "exit revolution" (as Aristide Zolberg calls it in chapter 2), which overturned many mercantilist assumptions. Agricultural, economic, and demographic change combined with new ideas about leave-taking. Contrasting British and French attitudes and comparing the German, Belgian, and other European cases, Zolberg shows how the political economy of Europe led not just to the "push" of emigration but how state policies contributed by reducing restraints on movement. Like Marx or Polanyi (*The Great Transformation*), Zolberg sees the nineteenth century as a veritable revolution of globalization, in which the allowing of emigration was one of its new systemic attributes.

NATION BUILDING AND THE ADMINISTRATIVE FRAMEWORK

The nineteenth century was not simply a new period of increased movement; perhaps even more important, it was a time when states started to problematize this movement, shifting from a presumption of stability to one integrating mobility.[5] Emigration became a particularly sensitive issue for nations in the process of inventing themselves while simultaneously large numbers of their subjects/citizens were leaving. In chapter 3, Donna Gabaccia, Dirk Hoerder, and Adam Walaszek look at the language of emigration in Italy, Germany, and Poland, examining how emigration was variously regarded with suspicion, controlled, or even encouraged. These countries (and particularly their nationalist elites) were concerned with "consolidating the homeland" by protecting their citizens abroad and promoting policies they hoped would strengthen the links between those who had moved away and their country of origin. Defining emigrants was thus part of a larger process of defining citizens (and their obligations), national character, as well as the notion of a cultural nation.

Caroline Douki argues in chapter 4 that Italian emigrants even helped the modern Italian *État gestionnaire* (the managerial, or administrative, state) come into being. Even as a nationalist discourse was reflecting alarm at the great increase in the numbers of emigrants circa 1900, those distant citizens became one of the first groups to benefit from state aid. As the state attempted to count those abroad and became concerned about their welfare, the perception of the Italians overseas shifted from marginal to central in debates about social policy. Ultimately, the construction of the modern

Italian state came about through the debates about social legislation undertaken with the emigrants in mind.

Yet even an older country such as France was concerned about the meaning of emigration for the state. Contrary to the usual image of France as a country of little emigration (and the concomitant paucity of historiography on the subject), François Weil shows (in chapter 5) how different levels of the French state were concerned with the issue and how public debate as well as administrative reforms reflected and affected emigration from the 1820s through the Second Empire. State ministers and statisticians as well as local prefects and mayors all took part in creating an increasingly specialized administrative apparatus concerned with French citizens and other nationals who left via French ports.

THE COSTS OF EMIGRATION

Emigration is a highly political issue, but it is also closely connected to economic concerns and discussions over things financial and fiscal. While Britain's early nineteenth-century attitude toward emigration as a solution to the Irish problem has often been cited, David Feldman and M. Page Baldwin argue in chapter 6 that in spite of Robert Wilmot Horton's 1826 report in favor of "shoveling out paupers"—especially to the empire—few measures were actually undertaken. Fiscally conscious opponents to such a policy objected that state-sponsored emigration was simply too expensive, while radicals argued that it was a conspiracy against the poor. Malthusian pessimism thus confronted the imperatives of good fiscal virtue. In the end, Feldman and Baldwin argue, few people actually left as a result of direct subsidies; the vast majority departed under their own steam, and it was not until after World War I that the British state actually actively supported emigration, in spite of Treasury objections, to the empire.

The economics of emigration frame the question in more ways than one. In examining the Dutch case (chapter 7), Corrie van Eijl and Leo Lucassen offer the example of emigration to a nearby destination that was directly linked to domestic issues concerning welfare. The Dutch saw emigration as a way to export unemployment to Germany, yet both countries had to negotiate the issue of financial responsibility when a migrant applied for poor relief. The debate over emigration reflected fears about the mobile unemployed, yet at the same time the Dutch government wanted to maintain good ties with Germany and with Dutch citizens there. Ultimately, the result was strengthened poor-relief measures on behalf of citizens living abroad.

Similarly, in tracing how attitudes toward emigration changed in the German lands, Andreas Fahrmeir emphasizes (in chapter 8) how there have historically been competing concerns over emigration. Like other countries, the German states shifted over time from a mercantilist attitude against emigration toward a more favorable policy toward leave-taking in the hope of resolving pauperism. Emigrants who left with no intention of returning lost their citizenship, insuring that they did not later return penniless, seeking aid. But ethnic ties with Germans abroad (particularly in eastern Europe) became paramount to National Socialist ideology, while today the Federal Republic has returned to a more balanced consideration of ethnic and economic issues concerning emigration/immigration.

BORDERS AND THE LINKS BETWEEN IMMIGRATION AND EMIGRATION

As three chapters (9, 10, and 11) dealing with North America show, the links between immigration and emigration occur on several levels, from international relations to border-crossings to asymmetrical power relations. Dorothee Schneider (chapter 9) has studied European emigration as viewed by U.S. policymakers. In an effort to limit the volume and improve the quality of immigration, the American government sought to intervene at the source by affecting emigration policies in the countries of origin. The U.S. government sent investigators to Europe to study administrative and legal procedures there and tried (not very successfully) to get the sending states to revise their free-to-leave policies. Not surprisingly, the more authoritarian governments of this period met with the greatest approval by U.S. immigration officials. In the end, however, it was the business interests—the shipping companies—that bore the brunt of responsibility as regulatory agents at the ports of embarkation.

The connections between immigration and emigration concerns are even more acute in the Canadian example. Like François Weil, Bruno Ramirez (chapter 10) brings to light a heretofore under-studied migration, one that again involves emigration to a nearby location: from Canada to the United States. Canada (like France and the United States) has primarily been a country of immigration, but it has also been one of emigration, serving in large part as a sieve, or what could be called a *lieu de passage*.[6] Labor market shifts have caused immigrants to come to Canada and then to move on, looking for better opportunities south of the border.[7] Consequently, the Canadian government has worried about who enters and who exits, at times to the extent of seeing emigration as desertion and sending repatriation agents to the United States to try to convince citizens to return home.

In the case of Mexico (chapter 11), the government also tried initially to discourage its citizens from moving northward. But by the mid-twentieth century, the number of Mexican citizens in the United States led Mexico to enter into negotiations in order to improve conditions for its citizens abroad, under what became known as the *braceros* programs. However, from 1965 to 1990, as Jorge Durand shows, the Mexican government once again took a passive role in an asymmetrical power relation, while the United States initiated regimes of regulation and surveillance. Since 1990, however, and particularly since the election of Vicente Fox in 2000, the Mexican government has become more active in setting up programs for its citizens abroad and in attempting to negotiate better conditions and rights for them.

NAMING EMIGRANTS

While we can chart the political and economic emigration debates—once we look for them—we have to admit that the actual definition of the emigrant is often itself in flux. How do we tell an emigrant, in the absence of official papers, from an ordinary traveler? The size of his or her baggage? Is departure permanent or temporary? Intent is a slippery concept, since projects of return may take years to finalize. Indeed, nineteenth-century emigrants have been called by different names, sometimes corresponding to different destinations. Van Eijl and Lucassen have suggested the following typology: long-distance, (largely) transatlantic emigrants; colonial emigrants; and emigrants who went to neighboring countries (intra-European). In Britain, one imperial enthusiast argued that the term "emigration" should refer only to going to a foreign country, not to a colony; migration within the empire should simply be termed "overseas settlement" (Feldman and Baldwin). Italians, Germans, and Poles all used different words to differentiate between the more worrisome overseas and "permanent" emigrants, and the intra-European or intraregional, supposedly temporary, ones (Gabaccia, Hoerder, and Walaszek).

Yet we can look at three cases of emigration in the twentieth century in which specific terms have been used to describe different relationships to the country of origin: the "Overseas Chinese," the "brain drain" from India, and the *yordim* of Israel. In each case, the country of origin has constructed a complex relationship of dismissal/need with its citizens abroad.

The genesis of the category of Overseas Chinese (chapter 12) can be traced to the nineteenth century, when emigration carried a doubly negative connotation: rebellion against the emperor and desertion of one's ancestors. By the late nineteenth century, however, the state began to be aware of its emigrants, largely due to alarming reports on the conditions of coolies. A nationality law of 1909 was elaborated in the context of increasingly urged protection, especially for Chinese merchants abroad. Sun Yat-Sen saw "Overseas Chinese" as integral parts of the nation, to be controlled on its behalf, a position that was continued by the Communist regime. Although emigration was forbidden during the Cultural Revolution, and internal and external departures were still controlled thereafter, Carine Pina-Guerassimoff and Eric Guerassimoff show how, since 1978, the Overseas Chinese have been reconceptualized as a specific economic and cultural category, important to the homeland.

The Indian case (chapter 13) provides an example of an elite emigration, one which continues to be in the news as a function of Western technological needs. However, in retracing the origins of the Indian "brain drain" (the terms dates back to the emigration of Indian doctors to the United Kingdom in the late 1950s and early 1960s to fill the vacuum created by the emigration of British doctors to the United States), Binod Khadria emphasizes the importance of understanding the supply-side production of emigrants. India's expansive education policy of the last half century, with its stated goal of universal elementary schooling, nonetheless ultimately created a top-heavy system leading to an overabundance of unemployed college graduates. As Khadria concludes, what had been perceived as a wealth drain to Britain when India was a colony has been paralleled by a brain drain to the United States since Indian independence.

Finally, the story of Israeli emigration (chapter 14) is perhaps the starkest example of the conceptualization of the emigrant as traitor. For a country explicitly founded on the ideology of ingathering, constructed against the Jewish Diaspora, there could be no stronger opposition than that between *aliyah* ("going up")—the process of immigration —and "going down," emigrants being derogatorily referred to as *yordim*. Yet, as Steven Gold shows, policies and attitudes that disparage emigrants have ultimately shifted in recent years from condemnation to outreach. Israeli consulates, which at one time cared to have little contact with their citizens abroad, have turned to helping Israeli citizens abroad in pragmatic recognition of the quantity and quality of those who have left.

As Donna Gabaccia has suggested, "We can write the story of nations from their borders." If this has been increasingly achieved through the lens of immigration, we propose here to look at it from the inside out. "Studying emigration seems to hold special promise as a way to understand how nations and states and identities are constructed, not just ideologically or linguistically, but socially, administratively, and juridically."[8]

The questions we ask and begin to answer here benefit from the comparisons over time and place that are possible among scholars. David Feldman and M. Page Baldwin, and Aristide Zolberg, provide somewhat different views of the British attitude toward emigration (from the nineteenth to the twentieth century, from politics to finances, from ideology to practice), while John Torpey focuses on the Maoist period of emigration restrictions, and Carine Pina-Guerassimoff and Eric Guerassimoff explain how the construction of a specific legal category of Overseas Chinese and their families was constructed both before and after the Cultural Revolution. Dirk Hoerder and Andreas Fahrmeir address different moments of expression of the German nation with regard to those who leave, while Donna Gabaccia and Caroline Douki both clearly situate the *italiani all'estero* within a problematic of nation building.

The question of the state's response to emigration implies continuing research on at least two fronts: further analysis of state measures with regard to leave-taking, but also questioning the importance of the role of the state. How did state encouragements and discouragements, ideological and fiscal worries, financial aid, and cultural concerns affect individuals in emigrants' decisions to leave? Perhaps a lot, perhaps a little, but the migration process cannot be fully understood without questioning the administrative, political, and ideological forces surrounding that move.

Above all, we have begun to chart the importance of a historical look at emigration. It is a complex concept, and one that, as we clearly see, changes over time, in conjunction with state policy and the migratory movement itself. States promote and regulate, but they also respond to the movements of their citizens. They too are actors in the migration drama. Emigration, like immigration, needs to be understood at the intersection of structural and individual agency.

1. For an important exception, see, for example, the writings of Dirk Hoerder and of Klaus Bade on Germany, Jose Moya on Spain (*Cousins and Strangers: Spanish Immigrants in Buenos Aires, 1850–1930* [Berkeley: University of California Press], 18–25), and some of the older work on Hungary (Julianna Puskàs) and on Italy (Robert F. Foerster; Dino Cinel). For an elaboration on the "exit" focus, see Nancy L. Green, "The Politics of Exit: Reversing the Immigration Paradigm," *Journal of Modern History* 77, no. 2 (June 2005): 263–89.

2. See, for example, Frank Thistlethwaite's call for a less American-centered migration history, "Migrations from Europe Overseas in the 19th and 20th Centuries," in Comité international des Sciences historiques, *XIe Congrès International des Sciences Historiques, Rapports*, vol. 5, *Histoire Contemporaine*, 32–60 (Gothenburg, Swed.: Almqvist and Wiksell, 1960) (reprinted in Herbert Moller, ed., *Population Movements in Modern European History*, 73–92 [New York: Macmillan, 1964]); and, more recently, Abdelmalek Sayad, *La double absence: Des illusions de l'émigré aux souffrances de l'immigré* (Paris: Seuil, 1999). Rare today is the immigration history that does not begin with a chapter on "the old country."

3. Sune Akerman, "From Stockholm to San Francisco: The Development of the Historical Study of External Migrations," in *Commission internationale d'histoire des mouvements sociaux et des structures sociales*, 8–45 (Uppsula, Swed.: Almqvist and Wiksell, 1975); Thistlethwaite, "Migrations." Marcus Lee Hansen called for a better integration of the migration stories in his article "The History of American Immigration as a Field for Research," *American Historical Review* 32, no. 3 (April 1927): 500–518, and in his book *The Atlantic Migration, 1607–1860* (1940; repr., New York: Harper, 1961).

4. John Torpey, *The Invention of the Passport, Surveillance, Citizenship, and the State* (Cambridge, Eng.: Cambridge University Press, 2000).

5. This point was made by Leo Lucassen during the conference "Citoyenneté et émigration," Paris, December 7–8, 2001; see also Caroline Douki (chapter 4) in this volume. On earlier migrations and the notion of a continuum, see Leslie Page Moch, *Moving Europeans: Migration in Western Europe since 1650* (Bloomington: Indiana University Press, 1992); Charles Tilly, "Migration in Modern European History," in *Human Migration*, ed. William McNeill and Ruth Adams, 48–72 (Bloomington: Indiana University Press, 1978); Yves Lequin, ed., *La mosaïque France: Histoire des étrangers et de l'immigration* (Paris: Larousse, 1988); and Daniel Roche, *Humeurs vagabondes: De la circulation des hommes et de l'utilité des voyages* (Paris: Fayard, 2003).

6. Nancy L. Green, "Trans-frontières: Pour une analyse des lieux de passage," *Socio-anthropologie* 6 (2nd semester 1999): 33–48.

7. See also François Weil, *Les Franco-Américains, 1860–1980* (Paris: Belin, 1989).

8. Donna Gabaccia, "Citoyenneté et émigration" conference, December 7, 2001.

PART I

FREEDOM OF MOVEMENT

1

LEAVING: A COMPARATIVE VIEW

John Torpey

In the early stages of the French Revolution, the Constitution of 1791 promulgated the norm in liberal democratic societies that citizens were to be permitted to leave their homes in pursuit of better opportunities elsewhere. Although most of us have come to take this norm for granted, its prominent place in the catalog of revolutionary freedoms signaled a major innovation. Freedom to depart was a matter of the greatest importance to vast numbers of people who confronted one or another form of restraint on their mobility, whether in France or elsewhere. Indeed, the freedom to move about internally or to emigrate beyond the borders of one's country has remained a matter of the greatest significance in political struggles down to our own day.

In contrast to what we might regard now as their more usual function of regulating entries, passports and related paperwork have frequently played an important role in regulating departures as well. These documents merit attention because, beyond the mere adoption of strictures, they are among the papers that have been crucial to implementing restrictions on movement by helping to establish identity. And they reflect an essential but largely unstudied aspect of modern states: namely, their efforts to construct and enforce durable identities that facilitate their "embrace" of their own subjects/citizens, and the states' resulting ability to establish, maintain, and enhance their control over particular territories.[1] The use of passports and similar pieces of paper to constrain departure is closely connected to the history of "unfree labor," but such documents may also be employed when states seek to restrict mobility in order to undermine what they view as political or other kinds of opposition or unruliness.

As Aristide Zolberg has noted, the relative relaxation of constraints on departure was crucial to the surge of migration that created the modern world, as Europeans poured across the Atlantic in a growing stream during the nineteenth century.[2] Prior to this "great Atlantic migration," paradoxically, millions of Africans traversed the "middle passage" without escaping severe limitations on their movements. Their contribution to the peopling of the Americas had little to do with emigration in the sense of individual decisions to move in search of improved life chances. They came as slaves and, having arrived in the New World in chains, remained largely immobilized. Despite the trend toward a loosening of restrictions on leaving, the persistence of constraints in many parts of the world during the nineteenth century helped to determine the composition and timing of other elements of the migrant streams generated during the advance of modern industrial societies. Those kept from leaving—who might have contributed substantial numbers—would have to await the coming of the twentieth century before they began to move in large proportions.

THE FRENCH REVOLUTION AND THE FREEDOM TO DEPART

Constraints on departures, including passport requirements, were an important fact of life for the vast majority of the subjects of prerevolutionary France. The battle to abolish passport controls in the late eighteenth century was thus part of the larger struggle against what the revolutionaries regarded as the ancien régime's tyrannical grip on French society. In this regard, the revolutionaries objected to a 1669 edict of Louis XIV that had forbidden his subjects to leave the territory of France, and they objected to related requirements that those leaving the kingdom be in possession of a passport.[3] The matter of passport restrictions on movement appeared among the many complaints regarding royal government that were presented to the estates general convened at Versailles in 1789.[4] These protests led to a relaxation of controls on movement immediately after the fall of the Bastille on July 14. The result of this relaxation of restrictions, according to a historian of the revolutionary emigration, was that "Frenchmen were free to go and come as they pleased" during the initial revolutionary period of 1789–1792.[5]

As the leaders of the revolution came to feel more besieged, however, they sought measures to curtail this extensive freedom to move about. The situation in France changed dramatically with the flight of the king on June 21, 1791. In a state of shocked alarm at the king's attempted escape, France's National Assembly mandated a complete halt to departures from the kingdom.[6] Yet just a week later, the assembly decreed that foreigners and French merchants would be free to leave only if they were in possession of a passport supplied by the ambassador from their own country or by the French ministry of foreign affairs.[7] The insistence on strict control over movement for military purposes would soon reveal itself as a central motif of those advocating the reintroduction of passport restrictions.

As calm returned following the uproar sparked by the king's unexpected flight, the National Assembly took up the business of writing a new constitution from September 3–14, 1791. The matter of controls on movement quickly came to occupy the center of attention; the very first "natural and civil right" the Constitution guaranteed was the freedom "to go, to remain, [and] to depart."[8] Indeed, this article preceded the Constitution's enumeration of the rights of freedom of speech and assembly.

The French parliament further specified its defense of the freedom of movement on September 13. During that day's deliberations, the Marquis de Lafayette proposed—and the Assembly adopted by acclamation and to sustained applause—the abolition of all controls, including passports, on the movements of Frenchmen, as well as an amnesty eliminating all penalties on (noble) émigrés imposed in the June 21, 1791, decree barring departure from the realm. The parliamentary records make plain that the French revolutionaries believed they were making a major contribution to the cause of human freedom when they eliminated passport controls on the movements of the French people,[9] controls that nonetheless returned in varying degrees of severity and for various periods throughout the course of the revolutionary wars. Sometimes these restrictions were a reasonable response to threats of counterrevolutionary activity both foreign and domestic, and sometimes they were a part of what became (in 1792) a hysterical and pervasive suspicion of enemies.

Opponents of the resurrection of passport controls regarded the reinstitution of a mechanism of social control characteristic of the ancien régime as harmful to the newfound liberty proclaimed by the revolution. They feared that such constraints would undermine popular support for the revolutionary project more than they would bolster security.[10] In response to a new passport law introduced in early 1792 with the aim of thwarting potential threats to the revolution, one critic pleaded in the National Assembly against the law: "A nation that claims to have a constitution cannot enchain the liberty of its citizens to the extent that you propose. *A revolution that commenced with the destruction of passports must insure a sufficient measure of freedom to travel, even in times of crisis.*"[11] Certainly not all would agree with this characterization of the beginning of the revolution, but the statement suggests the importance that at least some of the deputies ascribed to the passport question and to its significance for the revolution. Others felt, reasonably enough, that without passport controls on those entering the country and on those moving around within it, the revolution was doomed.

When the Napoleonic Wars finally came to an end—and despite the fact that the movements of workers and the "lower orders" were frequently troubled by an increasingly professional gendarmerie that might still demand "papers, please"—the norm gradually became established that French citizens should be free "to go . . . and to depart" without requiring leave from the government in order to do so. As the ripples of the French Revolution moved outward, the norm of untrammeled departure was gradually extended. But the norm did not yet apply to everyone, nor was it accompanied by any corresponding freedom to *enter* other domains.

THE END OF SERFDOM AND ITS CONSEQUENCES
FOR EMIGRATION IN GERMANY

As has often been noted, the French Revolution (and its older sibling, the American Revolution) had powerful effects in many quarters beyond France. In continental Europe, the bonds of serfdom that had tied peasants to the land hereditarily were gradually shattered by the revolution, in an arc running from west to east.

The liberation of the peasants in early nineteenth-century Germany foreshadowed an extensive loosening of restrictions on movement for the lower strata, always the chief target of such constraints. With Napoleon's defeat of Prussia at Jena in 1806, the Holy Roman Empire of the German Nation met its final demise. The Prussian king, Frederick William III, responded with measures designed to bring into existence a coherent body of subjects "with a sufficient stake in their nation so that they would be willing to fight and die for it." The so-called October Edict of 1807 freed the Prussian peasantry from hereditary servitude, traditional labor obligations and dues, and seigneurial limitations on their ownership of land. Many occupations were opened to all comers, stripping the guilds of their power to regulate access to employment. These measures were the first strides down the road to a free market in labor. At the urging of the Prussian reformers, halting steps were also taken in the direction of popular participation in government.[12]

Once the Napoleonic menace had been put to rest, a new Prussian passport law sought further to enhance the internal mobility of Prussians. According to the 1817 law, Prussians moving about within the country required no passport from the police, "but may travel freely and unhindered without one."[13] Despite this liberalization, not all inhabitants of Prussia escaped the requirement of carrying a passport for internal movement. Among the nonexempt groups were noncitizen Jews and certain types of journeymen.

Exit from Prussia was another matter entirely, however. Technically, no one—whether native-born or foreign—was permitted to leave the country without a passport authorizing departure. Exemption from these restrictions was provided for those not requiring a passport for entry and those who arrived from abroad with acceptable foreign passports, though a visa had to be affixed to these by the police in the Prussian town from which they were returning to their country of origin. In contrast to the situation with regard to entry passports, however, those for exit were not to be issued by local police officials, but only by authorities at the provincial level or higher.

The Prussian situation was typical of the broader German one. Despite some encouragement of emigration to open lands in Russia immediately after the Congress of Vienna, into the 1830s most of the German states denied passports to their departing subjects unless they could demonstrate that the destination country would admit them. The result was that an early version of the visa system as we know it today began to operate, as prospective emigrants went to the relevant foreign consulate to obtain the documents affirming that they would be accepted on arrival in the destination country. Only then did the German governments give dispensation to leave the country.[14]

The situation began to change decisively in the 1840s. New laws on internal migration guaranteed freedom of settlement in all Prussian towns and cities to all but the currently indigent. These laws limited the right of communal bodies to deny entry to such persons—a right which until then had been an important feature of their control over poor relief.[15] These statutes deprived Prussian municipalities of their earlier authority to close their doors to those they merely *feared* might become public charges.[16] Taken together, these laws comprised a major contribution to the construction of a labor market that was truly "national" in scope.

It was likewise during the decade of the 1840s that Prussia openly accepted the emigration of its subjects beyond its own borders. With the exception of those who owed military service, Prussia affirmed the right of its subjects to emigrate.[17] Despite this insurgent liberalism in emigration policy, however, the ascent to the French throne of Louis Napoleon after his "Eighteenth Brumaire" alerted German rulers to the fact that they might soon need to muster the troops again. They therefore sought to keep young men from leaving indiscriminately, efforts that were stepped up as the Crimean War of 1854–56 approached.

These formal restrictions notwithstanding, the actual difficulties of departure depended to a considerable extent upon where and by what means of transport one sought to leave. In the estimation of the noted migration historian Marcus Lee Hansen, "passport formalities were more or less perfunctory" in France, making it relatively easy for those wishing to slip across the Rhine to escape their military obligations. In contrast, embarkation in Hamburg or Bremen was complicated by strict official supervision of steamship passengers, owing to these cities' concern to remain on good terms with interior states anxious to retain potential soldiers.[18]

Eventually, the Passport Law of 1867 of the North German Confederation confirmed the drift toward liberalism with respect to departure and emigration.[19] The law abolished passport and visa requirements for subjects of the states of the Confederation as well as for foreigners, irrespective of whether they were leaving, entering, or moving about within the territory comprised by the Confederation's member-states. With this law, freedom to travel—unhindered and without explicit state authorization—was established as the law of the land. The Confederation deepened its commitment to such liberty only three weeks later when the Reichstag adopted a law guaranteeing freedom of settlement (*Freizügigkeit*) to its subjects. The law provided for the right of subjects of the Confederation's member-states to settle and to acquire property anywhere within the territory, irrespective of religion or lack of previous municipal or state membership. Moreover, subjects of the Confederation were to be at liberty to practice any trade, whether sedentary or itinerant, under the same conditions as those to which the indigenous residents were subject.[20] With regard to the physical mobility of its subjects, the restrictive regime in Germany was in headlong retreat. Indeed, this shift bore witness to a broader transformation of the population from rightless subjects to right-bearing citizens. The liberal 1867 passport law remained the principal legislation in this area until the end of the Weimar era.

FROM SERFDOM TO STATE FEUDALISM IN RUSSIA AND THE SOVIET UNION

The end of serfdom arrived later and more uncertainly in Russia than it had in Western Europe. The legal code of 1649 had originally consolidated the Russian pattern of serfdom, the very essence of which lay in controls on peasant movements, though these were by no means entirely successful in achieving their aim.[21] In the early eighteenth century, Czar Peter the Great promulgated a series of decrees further regulating the domicile and travel of Russian subjects. An edict of 1719, for example, required anyone moving from one town or village to another to have in his (or less likely her) possession a pass from his superiors.[22] The use of documents as mechanisms of control made serfdom's legal restrictions on peasant movements and residence easier to enforce.

The terms of the emancipation decree of 1861 ended the right of landowners to own their serfs' "souls." Yet the circumstances of emancipation were widely regarded as doing little to improve the circumstances of the average peasant. The relatively favorable terms of emancipation for the Russian *pomeshchiki* (planters) resulted from the fact that the abolition of serfdom was widely accepted by the Russian elite and was worked out with their interests in mind. In contrast, slavery in the southern United States remained at this time a comparatively vibrant undertaking and had to be violently subdued if it was going to be eliminated.[23] While the quasi-aristocratic American South appeared from a Northern perspective to have become a beachhead against industrialization and the advance of "free labor" that had to be pried open with force, there was little inclination to transform Russian society into an industrial power, and the end of serfdom did relatively little to change power relations in Russia.

Paradoxically, just as serfdom was being abolished, the czarist government reiterated long-standing constraints on the movement of its populations. Reflecting the broader process of the "state monopolization of the legitimate means of movement,"[24] these restrictions shifted control over the peasantry from the (mostly absentee) planters to the state. In an extensive "Collection of Statutes on Passports and Runaways" of 1857, the government reinforced its commitment to fixing persons to places and requiring them to have official permission to depart. In contrast to the liberalization that was taking place in Germany during these years, the Russian government reasserted its insistence that persons moving about the territory of the empire seek government authorization to do so. Regulations concerning departure remained severe. "Subjects of the empire," as one commentator has tersely put it, "did not have the right to travel or reside abroad."[25] Moreover, the terms of the emancipation decree left ordinary Russian subjects under a variety of obligations—not the least of which was military service (for males, at least)—that diminished their freedom to depart. It was not until the last decade of the nineteenth century and the first decade of the twentieth that the passport system was relaxed so that "the majority of the population, [though] not everyone, finally acquired freedoms characteristic of more advanced western societies."[26]

Despite the demise of the formal restrictions on movement associated with serfdom, Russians remained relatively immobilized with regard to departure from the country, and relatively few people left Russia. The main emigrants were Jews fleeing anti-Semitic pogroms and constraints on their livelihoods, followed by Poles. Despite the persistence of a general desire on the part of the Russian state to hold onto population, the Russian elite tended to view these two groups in a rather unfavorable light, and hence their departure could be counted as something of a blessing. Of an estimated 2.36 million emigrants from the Russian Empire between 1899 and 1913, some 70 percent were Jews and Poles, and no other group comprised as much as 10 percent of the emigrant flow.[27] Despite the emancipation of the serfs in 1861 and a somewhat greater formal freedom of *internal* movement, there was, in short, relatively little freedom of departure for—and therefore relatively little emigration of—Russians during the last centuries of the czarist autocracy.

It remained for the October Revolution to complete the task of liberalizing "exit." Soon after taking power, the Bolsheviks sought, with the Declaration of the Rights of the Working and Exploited People of January 1918, to sweep away the remaining restrictions on freedom of movement and domicile associated with czarism. At the same time, however, the fledgling regime announced the creation, "literally from scratch from amidst a war-weary population no longer amenable to nationalist appeals,"[28] of a Socialist Red Army of Workers and Peasants. The task of building this new army, which became increasingly urgent with the onset of the Civil War, necessitated the reintroduction of conscription among a largely unwilling populace. In order to stem evasion and desertions, the government introduced a variety of registration procedures; failure to comply with these regulations could result in prosecution.[29] Military pressures on the fragile Communist state were used to justify a retreat from some of its more liberal early inclinations.

The Soviet experience would largely recapitulate that of the French revolutionaries, who zigged and zagged on the matter of restrictions on movement in response to threats to the revolution. The major difference was that the early liberalism of the revolution was not vindicated in the Soviet Union, which soon came to operate as if living in a permanent state of emergency. That sensibility, along with entirely realistic fears of peasant rebellion, led the Soviet regime in 1932 to reinstitute an internal passport, this time for good. The document was designed primarily to keep peasants in the countryside despite the fact that the regime was requisitioning food for the cities at the expense of the farm regions that produced it—a policy that had tragic consequences for the Ukraine, in particular.[30]

The internal passport and its allied residence permit (*propiska*) became "one of the main levers of social and political control in the USSR"[31]—"the heart of police power."[32] Under the Soviets, the rural population experienced a brief period of sympathy and concern under the "New Economic Policy (NEP)" of the early 1920s, only to end up in a "second serfdom." After collectivization, farmers were officially condemned to life on the land, consigning them to a form of "state feudalism."[33] In reality, peasants had a variety of routes out of the countryside and into the cities, and restrictions on peasants' access to passports were eventually loosened in the 1970s.[34] But the assertion of bureaucratic control of movement and domicile helped codify different citizenship statuses for peasants and urban dwellers, relegating migrants from the countryside to the cities to a position little different than would-be migrants from one country to another.

CONSTRAINTS ON DEPARTURE IN THE UNITED STATES

Despite the growing importance of freedom of departure in the Euro-American societies of the Atlantic basin, that norm did not apply for all people even in those countries, many of which were populated by large numbers of African slaves and their descendants. The British announcement of a ban on the slave trade in 1808 signaled the wider shift to a freedom of movement, which, in turn, was connected to the spread of a burgeoning "free labor" ideology.[35] The prohibition of the trade in slaves was not the same, of course, as an end to slavery itself, which persisted for another half century in the United States and until the 1880s in Cuba and Brazil. Still, the early nineteenth-century ban on the importation into the United States of slaves from Africa, combined with relatively high rates of reproduction, meant that the proportion of African-born among southern slaves dwindled to insignificance well before "the peculiar institution" was abolished.[36]

As long as slavery persisted, it was synonymous with constraints on departure. Because of the overlap between servile status and color in the slave society of the American South, the restrictions on the movements of slaves were largely self-enforcing. Skin color alone suggested strongly that a black person moving about unaccompanied by his master was likely to be a runaway.[37] Yet there were of course a number of free blacks, especially in the North but also in southern cities such as Charleston, who had attained their freedom in one of a variety of ways, including by running away successfully, buying their freedom from their owners, or being emancipated by them. Similarly, southern black slaves with more humane masters might on occasion be permitted to "go abroad"—that is, to visit spouses, children, or relatives on other plantations. When they did so, possession of a pass document from their masters would have been essential as a safeguard against the suspicion that they were absconding from their proper place.

The existence of free and unfree blacks on American soil also opened up possibilities for the fraudulent use of papers in the interest of escape. In his attempt to gain freedom, for example, the famous orator and abolitionist Frederick Douglass "borrowed the identification papers of a free black sailor and took a train from Baltimore to Wilmington, Delaware, and then a boat to Philadelphia, all the time worrying that the considerable contrast between his friend's description and his own appearance would lead to his detection."[38] In a context in which most persons who looked like Douglass were slaves, identification papers were essential to establishing the individual's eligibility to move about on his own account.

The end of slavery brought in its wake the nominal legal elevation of blacks to the status of American citizens. Yet, as with the end of serfdom in Russia, the consequences of emancipation for the mobility of the southern black population were not as great as they might have been. To be sure, emancipation offered the prospect of movement unconstrained by the pass controls and slave patrols that permeated life under slavery. As a result, after the Civil War, freedpeople abandoned the countryside in substantial numbers, crowding into the towns and cities of the South in search of new opportunities or just to breathe the air of freedom.[39] Yet this newfound liberty would soon prove illusory for many blacks.

After the Civil War, whites—in response to the demise of the "Slave Power"—sought new modes of control over the black population, constraining the mobility of freedpeople in a variety of ways. Vagrancy laws, "the cornerstone of Black Codes passed by unrepentant Southern legislators," revived pass controls from the antebellum era by requiring that freedpeople be in a position to show proof that they were employed by whites. "[T]hese laws gave sheriffs and planters the authority to exert strict control over the goings and comings of local black workers."[40] Meanwhile, a system of sharecropping and debt peonage arose that was widely regarded as little better than slavery. Finally, where these mechanisms failed to restrict mobility within the bounds acceptable to the white population, extralegal violence offered recourse. This was the heyday of the Ku Klux Klan, which now shifted its focus from opposing popery to intimidating "uppity" blacks. Yet the Klan was only one of many vigilante groups that operated with impunity to terrorize, and thus to control the movements of, putatively free blacks. As a result of these various obstacles, there was considerable local movement of blacks within the South, but little emigration beyond its borders.

The sequestration of the vast majority of the American black population in the formerly Confederate states came to an end only after the beginning of the twentieth century, and especially from World War I on. With the labor demands of an industrial economy, the suspension of immigration from southern and eastern Europe following World War I, and the mechanization of cotton picking, some six million blacks left the South for the North between 1910 and 1970. Indeed, by 1970, "'urban' had become a euphemism for 'black,'"[41] reflecting a demographic transformation of stunning proportions. When blacks left the South in the "great black migration," they departed for "another country" in the sense that they were leaving behind the only territorial base the vast majority of them had ever known. In important respects they made a new country in the process—one that finally left behind the legal disfranchisement and the quasi-legal terrorization of its former slave population. By 1970, half of all African Americans lived outside the South. Yet the emigration of the American black population to the North did not lead to any rapid equalization of their economic status with the majority population. The shaky foothold in the industrial economy that blacks had gained by their large-scale departure from the South was short-lived, as the economy that had absorbed enormous quantities of relatively unskilled labor went into eclipse. In another form of restricted movement, blacks have thus been disproportionately consigned to ghettos and blighted urban spaces abandoned by the new, postindustrial economy.[42]

RESTRICTIONS ON DEPARTURE IN THE SOVIET UNION AND CHINA

The extraordinary physical and economic mobilization of the black population of the southern United States contrasts sharply with developments in the Communist world during roughly the same period. We have already noted that the Soviet regime in 1932 imposed internal passport controls in an effort primarily to lock down the peasantry, large numbers of whom were at least potentially inclined to abandon the countryside for the better-stocked cities. In the process, the regime defined certain areas—principally larger towns and cities—as subject to "passportization." These areas were further specified in a decree of April 28, 1933, and included twenty-five urban areas and a 100–kilometer zone along the west European frontier.[43]

In the 1960s and 1970s, the Soviet regime also developed a system of "closed cities," access to which was strictly (if not altogether successfully) regulated for outsiders. These urban enclaves were the capitals of national republics and all cities above 500,000 in population. Such restrictions sharply curtailed the access of non–city dwellers to the better economic, educational, and social opportunities typically available in the cities. The "closed cities" policy also led to the phenomenon of the *limitchiki,* rural-dwelling migrant workers with no permanent right to live and work in the cities. The *limitchiki* were recruited by enterprise managers, with special permission from the state, to fill out labor needs beyond the "limit" (quota) of those assigned to the enterprise by the state. But these workers' right to work in the enterprises that recruited them was restricted to a specified pe-riod, after which they were required to return to their homes (though they did not always do so, using various loopholes in the system in order to stay on). These migrant workers often lived temporarily in enterprise-owned housing and worked for very low wages, performing tasks that their more privileged brethren in the cities refused to do. They could sometimes hope for a permanent *propiska* (residency permit) in the closed city if they were able to remain in the city legally for a sufficient period. The *limitchiki* were, in short, a kind of internal "guest worker."[44] Although they had received official permission to leave their places of origin for the (state-defined) op-portunities available in the cities, their access to citizenship rights in the Marshallian sense was strictly limited, to the extent that these rights were available for Soviet citizens at all.

Likewise, there were severe restrictions on emigration abroad for Soviet citizens in general, and these measures were extended to the countries of the Soviet bloc after World War II. Authorization for such departures, which required a second, international passport in addition to the internal ver-sion, was normally accorded only to trusted functionaries—except during selected moments when the regimes in question decided to let off political (or ethnic) steam. The intermittent departures from the GDR of dissatisfied Germans, the emigration of Poles after the crackdown on Solidarity in the early 1980s, and the exit of Jews from the Soviet Union under strictly regu-lated circumstances are cases in point. Reflecting the modern norm that people should be free to go, the resurrection of constraints on departure in the Soviet sphere of influence was a major element of what one observer called "the contemporary assault on freedom of movement."[45]

The experience with documentary controls on departures in Communist China closely paralleled that of the Soviet Union, especially from the 1950s until at least the 1980s, and the system may well have been modeled on that of the USSR. Like the Bolsheviks and the French revolutionaries before them, the Chinese Communists criticized various identity card systems implemented under Kuomintang rule before the revolution, only to reintroduce and, when necessary, intensify their use after coming to power.[46] The major advance toward the passportization of Chinese Communist society came, as in the Soviet Union, with the collectivization of agriculture. The "Directive Concerning Establishment of a Permanent System of Household Registration" of June 22, 1955, marked a significant departure. In contrast to the earlier regulations, which had applied exclusively to the cities, the 1955 decree created a system embracing the entire country, both urban and rural. Detailed procedures were specified for individuals wishing to relocate from one place to another. These formalities included the requirement that such persons be in possession of a "migration certificate" from the appropriate authorities. In other words, official permission was required to move from one place to another, even within the same administrative jurisdiction. The rate of increase of the urban population fell considerably after the adoption of these measures.[47]

Again, as in the Soviet case, the household registration system was the central element of a wider effort to restrict population movements, especially the out-migration of peasants to the cities. In August 1955, the Chinese government announced measures that would make it more difficult for undocumented migrants to gain access to many foodstuffs, which were now to be rationed by the regime. Then, in November 1955, the regime promulgated "Regulations on the Criteria for Defining Urban and Rural Areas," which divided the country up into three types of zones: cities and towns; urban residential enclaves with significant numbers of state employees and their families; and villages. The designation of urban as opposed to rural areas was to be the major distinction, creating spatial hierarchies in Chinese society that reflected substantial differences in access to and quality of food, housing, schools, education, and much more.[48] The distinctions between urban and rural dwellers (as well as the partially overlapping one between state workers and collective farmers) would come to undergird a new caste-like system that sharply differentiated the life chances of the two groups. As a legal matter, Chinese peasants were bound to the land after the mid-1950s, both in the sense that they had no right to migrate freely and in the sense that they owed labor to the collective to which they belonged.[49]

Accordingly, to the Chinese villager, "the possession of the identification card of an urban resident is an important mark of status."[50]

With these various controls in place, the stage was set for China's effort to emulate the feverish pace of Soviet industrialization with the Great Leap Forward of 1958–60, Mao's maniacal attempt to squeeze greater capital accumulation out of reduced peasant consumption. An undertaking on the scale of the Great Leap, the Chinese leadership seemed to be aware, would require it to have a greater hold on the population than had existed theretofore. Accordingly, in early 1958, the Chinese Communist Party (CCP) adopted "Regulations on Household Registration (*hu kou*) in the People's Republic of China," which were still in effect in the 1990s. By extending the existing hu kou requirements to the Red Army, every Chinese citizen was included in the system. Now, in the absence of a certificate of urban employment or school admission, anyone wishing to switch residences needed a "moving-in certificate" issued by the police in the desired destination. This, in turn, was the prerequisite for obtaining a "moving-out certificate" from one's place of origin. The changes made it more difficult for peasants to move to the cities.[51]

The increasing administrative difficulties associated with rural-urban migration were nonetheless not enough to thwart all movement. Between 1957 and 1960, the urban population grew by more than thirty million. In response, the regime cracked down hard on migration from the countryside, laying off some twenty million state workers and returning them to rural areas. It also sharpened the distinction between peasants and urban workers, and made these statuses hereditary and hard to escape. Thereafter, it was possible to move down the hierarchy of place (from urban to rural) or status (worker to peasant), but upward movement became nearly impossible. At the heart of these social control measures, and of the massive forced repatriation to the countryside, was the hu kou of residential registration, which enabled the state to identify persons and subject them to its aims.[52] In the course of these developments, the heritable distinction between rural and urban personnel became "the most important social distinction in modern China,"[53] leading many Chinese to seek to replace their "peasant" status with the coveted title of "urban citizen" through such means as service in the armed forces, advancement through the ranks of the CCP, outstanding educational achievement or, for women, gaining collateral "worker" status by marrying a worker.[54]

In the mid-1980s, the Chinese government introduced new documentation measures that constituted, according to one observer of these matters, "the most significant change in personal documentation since the inauguration of the hu kou."[55] As a result of these new regulations, all Chinese over age sixteen were required to have an identity card resembling an American driver's license that included the bearer's name, address, date of birth, sex, and photograph. Unlike the previously existing hu kou, workbooks, and letters of introduction, only the identity card served as a universally acceptable form of legal certification of identity. The distribution of the new identity cards arose in the context of calls for changes in the hu kou system, in the face of a major upsurge of mobility in Chinese society since the reforms introduced by Deng Xiaoping.

In view of the fact that the hu kou system remains in place, the identity cards could be seen simply as a further extension of government control over movement. Yet compared with a situation in which peasants were subject to registration as part of the collective and had no automatic right to the documents necessary for moving about the country, it is possible that the new identity cards have contributed to greater freedom of movement for a large segment of the Chinese population. The identity cards help to free individual peasants from the constraints imposed by the impossibility of taking the old household registration document with them on their travels. Moreover, anecdotal evidence suggests that the Chinese find the identity cards a positive development.

Aside from the liberalization of movement represented by the new identity cards, the Chinese government appears to have temporarily abandoned enforcement of documentary controls on movement in the interest of creating a free market in labor. This slackening of enforcement has created a situation in which tens of millions of rural Chinese are making their way to the cities in search of work. The "floating population" of internal migrants, largely from the countryside to the city, is typically estimated to be at least one hundred million persons. The country's previous ability to avoid typically Third World patterns of urbanization may thus be superseded and the burgeoning cities swamped by waves of peasant migrants.[56] Recent reports indicate that the government plans to overhaul the hu kou system in response to continuing complaints about the functioning of the system and in order to achieve its own political and economic aims, including the more effective allocation of labor.[57]

As in China, systems of internal controls on movement and residence have been retained in a number of the member states of the former Soviet Union, in part because many people believe that "anarchy" would result if they were abolished.[58] The spatial hierarchies and distinctions in access to citizenship rights constructed by Communist regimes in the past have led to a curious revival of the notion prevalent in medieval Europe that "*Stadtluft macht frei*" ("[breathing] city air makes one free"). The recent relaxation of restrictions on emigration from the countryside both in post-Soviet regions and in China, and the resulting migration toward the cities in these areas, have made the distinction between urban "citizen" and rural quasi guest worker that much more apparent. Against the background of the norm of freedom of departure, the anomaly of nationals of a country who are less than full citizens—simply on the basis of where they come from within the country—becomes glaring.

CONCLUSION

The revolutionary French Constitution of September 1791 enshrined the notion that the freedom of departure should be available to all citizens. The claim was part of a broader assertion of the equality of citizens before the state. The promulgation of this norm, in combination with "free labor ideology," undermined restrictions on out-migration throughout Western Europe and the Americas. Plantation slavery and serfdom, which had previously immobilized huge rural populations in Europe and the Americas, did not survive the nineteenth century. Ironically, however, after these rural populations acquired the right, or at least the opportunity, to depart from much of Europe and from the American South, Communist regimes in the Soviet Union and its postwar satellites, as well as in China, rejuvenated or strengthened constraints on departure. In doing so, they invited criticism because they violated what had become one of the basic norms of modern citizenship—the right to leave without undue governmental interference or paperwork.

NOTES

1. See Jane Caplan and John Torpey, eds., *Documenting Individual Identity: The Development of State Practices in the Modern World* (Princeton, N.J.: Princeton University Press, 2001).

2. Aristide Zolberg, "International Migration Policies in a Changing World System," in *Human Migration: Patterns and Policies,* ed. William McNeill and Ruth Adams, 262–65 (Bloomington: Indiana University Press, 1978); see also Zolberg, chapter 2, in this volume.

3. See Daniel Nordman, "Sauf-conduits et passeports, en France, à la Renaissance," in *Voyager à la Renaissance: actes du colloque de Tours 30 juin-13 juillet*

1983, ed. Jean Céard and Jean-Claude Margolin, 4 (Paris: Maisonneuve et Larose, 1987); Vincenzo Grossi, "Emigrazione," in *Diritto amministrativo italiano*, ed. V. E. Orlando, 145 (Milan: Societá Editrice Libraria, 1905); and André Burguière and Jacques Revel, eds., *Histoire de la France*, vol. 1, *L'espace français* (Paris: Editions Seuil, 1989), 66.

4. See, for example, the *cahiers* of the parish of Neuilly-sur-Marne and of the bourg d'Ecouen in *Cahiers des états généraux*, vol. 4 (Paris: Librairie Administrative de Paul Dupont, 1868), 509 and 759. There were also those meeting in the estates-general who demanded more vigorous enforcement of the existing passport controls in the interest of greater public security; see, for example, the *cahiers* of the order of the *noblesse du bailliage* of Montargis (ibid., 21).

5. Donald Greer, *The Incidence of Emigration during the French Revolution* (Cambridge, Mass.: Harvard University Press, 1951), 26.

6. See "Décret qui ordonne d'arrêter toutes personnes quelconques sortant du royaume, et d'empêcher toute sortie d'effets, armes, munitions, ou espèces d'or et d'argent, etc." of June 21, 1791, in *Collection complète des lois, décrets, ordonnances, règlements, etc.*, ed. J. B. Duvergier, 3: 53 (Paris: A. Guyot, 1834 [hereafter: *Collection complète*]). The National Assembly's reaction to the announcement of the king's flight can be found in *Archives parlementaires de 1787 à 1860*, 1st series, vol. 27 (Paris: Société d'imprimerie et librairie administratives Paul Dupont, 1887 [hereafter *Archives*]), 358.

7. "Décret qui indique les formalités à observer pour sortir du royaume" of June 28, 1791, in *Collection complète*, 3:68–69.

8. Constitution française, *Collection complète*, 3:241.

9. *Archives*, 1st series, 30:621. The actual law of which Lafayette spoke was adopted on the following day (ibid., 632).

10. Echoes of this debate could be heard in the discussion about restrictions on civil liberties in the interest of enhancing security after the terrorist attacks of September 11 in the United States.

11. See Gérardin's remarks of January 27, 1792, in *Archives*, 1st series, 37:691–94. Italics added.

12. See James J. Sheehan, *German History, 1770–1866* (New York: Oxford University Press, 1989), 296–302; the quotation is from p. 301.

13. For the details of the law, see "Allgemeines Paßedikt für die Preussische Monarchie," June 22, 1817, in *Gesetzsammlung 1817*, 152–53. See also Andreas Fahrmeir, "Governments and Forgers: Passports in Nineteenth-Century Europe," in Caplan and Torpey, 219; see also Fahrmeir, chapter 8 in this volume.

14. Marcus Lee Hansen, *The Atlantic Migration, 1607–1860: A History of the Continuing Settlement of the United States*, ed. with a foreword by Arthur M. Schlesinger (1940; repr., New York: Harper and Row, 1961), 155–56.

15. See Van Eijl and Lucassen (chapter 7) and Feldman and Baldwin (chapter 6) in this volume.

16. Rogers Brubaker, *Citizenship and Nationhood in France and Germany* (Cambridge, Mass.: Harvard University Press, 1992), 65.

17. See Mack Walker, *Germany and the Emigration, 1816–1885* (Cambridge, Mass.: Harvard University Press, 1964), 95.

18. See Hansen, *Atlantic Migration,* 288–90, 304.

19. For a full account, see John Torpey, *The Invention of the Passport: Surveillance, Citizenship, and the State* (New York: Cambridge University Press, 2000), 81–92.

20. "Gesetz über die Freizügigkeit," November 1, 1867, *Bundes gesetzblatt des Norddeutschen Bundes, 1867* (Berlin, 1868), 55–58.

21. On this point, see Peter Kolchin, *Unfree Labor: American Slavery and Russian Serfdom* (Cambridge, Mass.: Belknap/Harvard University Press, 1987), chap. 1.

22. Mervyn Matthews, *The Passport Society: Controlling Movement in Russia and the USSR* (Boulder, Colo.: Westview Press, 1993), 1–2.

23. On this point, see Kolchin, *Unfree Labor,* 50, 362–64.

24. See John Torpey, "Coming and Going: On the State Monopolization of the Legitimate 'Means of Movement,'" *Sociological Theory* 16, no. 3 (November 1998): 239–59.

25. Matthews, *Passport Society,* 3–8.

26. Ibid., 10–12.

27. Walter Nugent, *Crossings: The Great Transatlantic Migrations, 1870–1914* (Bloomington: Indiana University Press, 1992), 90–94.

28. Theda Skocpol, *States and Social Revolutions: A Comparative Analysis of France, Russia, and China* (New York: Cambridge University Press, 1979), 216.

29. Matthews, *Passport Society,* 16–17.

30. For a recent account, see Nicolas Werth, "A State against Its People: Violence, Repression, and Terror in the Soviet Union," pt. 1 of *The Black Book of Communism: Crimes, Terror, Repression,* ed. Stéphane Courtois et al., trans. Jonathan Murphy and Mark Kramer (Cambridge, Mass.: Harvard University Press, 1999); see esp. chap. 8, "The Great Famine." See also Marc Garcelon, "Colonizing the Subject: The Genealogy and Legacy of the Soviet Internal Passport," in Caplan and Torpey, 94–96.

31. Matthews, *Passport Society,* 5.

32. Louise I. Shelley, *Policing Soviet Society: The Evolution of State Control* (New York: Routledge, 1996), xv.

33. Victor Zaslavski and Yuri Luryi, "The Passport System in the USSR and Changes in Soviet Society," *Soviet Union/Union Sovietique* 6, pt. 2 (1979), 139.

34. Sheila Fitzpatrick, *Stalin's Peasants: Resistance and Survival in the Russian Village After Collectivization* (New York: Oxford University Press, 1994), 95, 99–100.

35. The classic discussion in the United States context is Eric Foner, *Free Soil, Free Labor, Free Men: The Ideology of the Republican Party Before the Civil War* (New York: Oxford University Press, 1970). For a valuable discussion of the idea of free labor in its application to nineteenth-century Africa, see Fred Cooper, "Conditions Analogous to Slavery: Imperialism and Free Labor Ideology in Africa," in *Beyond*

Slavery: Explorations of Race, Labor, and Citizenship in Postemancipation Societies, ed. Frederick Cooper, Thomas C. Holt, and Rebecca J. Scott, 107–49 (Chapel Hill: University of North Carolina Press, 2000).

36. Kolchin, *Unfree Labor,* 235.

37. For recent studies of slave mobility and efforts to counter it, see John Hope Franklin and Loren Schweninger, *Runaway Slaves: Rebels on the Plantation* (New York: Oxford University Press, 1999); and Sally Hadden, *Slave Patrols: Law and Violence in Virginia and the Carolinas* (Cambridge, Mass.: Harvard University Press, 2001).

38. Peter Kolchin, *American Slavery, 1619–1877* (New York: Hill and Wang, 1993), 157–58.

39. See Eric Foner, *A Short History of Reconstruction* (New York: Harper and Row, 1990), 37.

40. Jacqueline Jones, *The Dispossessed: America's Underclasses from the Civil War to the Present* (New York: Basic Books, 1992), 25.

41. Nicholas Lemann, *The Promised Land: The Great Black Migration and How It Changed America* (New York: Knopf, 1991), 6.

42. This story is told well, using the example of Detroit, in Thomas J. Sugrue, *The Origins of the Urban Crisis: Race and Inequality in Postwar Detroit* (Princeton, N.J.: Princeton University Press, 1996). See also William Julius Wilson, *The Truly Disadvantaged: The Inner City, the Underclass, and Public Policy* (Chicago, Ill.: University of Chicago Press, 1987).

43. Matthews, *Passport Society,* 28–29.

44. Victor Zaslavsky, *The Neo-Stalinist State: Class, Ethnicity, and Consensus in Soviet Society* (Armonk, N.Y.: M. E. Sharpe, 1982), 139–55.

45. Alan Dowty, *Closed Borders: The Contemporary Assault on Freedom of Movement* (New Haven, Conn.: Yale University Press, 1987).

46. See Mervyn Matthews, "Residence Controls in Present-Day China," *Asian Affairs* (June 1989), 184. These various predecessors were directed toward identification and policing, though not the control of movement per se. I am grateful to Prof. Dorothy Solinger, Department of Political Science at the University of California–Irvine for clarification of this point.

47. Tiejun Cheng and Mark Selden, "The Origins and Social Consequences of China's *hukou* System," *China Quarterly* 139 (September 1994): 656.

48. See ibid., 657–59.

49. Mark Selden, *The Political Economy of Chinese Socialism* (Armonk, N.Y.: M. E. Sharpe, 1988), 184–85.

50. Sulamith Heins Potter and Jack M. Potter, *China's Peasants: The Anthropology of a Revolution* (New York: Cambridge University Press, 1990), 303.

51. Cheng and Selden, "Origins," 662–63.

52. Selden, *Political Economy,* 165–67.

53. Potter and Potter, *China's Peasants,* 297.

54. See ibid., 306–9.

55. Matthews, "Residence Controls," 189.

56. See Dorothy Solinger, *Contesting Citizenship in Urban China: Peasant Migrants, the State, and the Logic of the Market* (Berkeley: University of California Press, 1999).

57. Elisabeth Rosenthal, "China Eases Rules Binding People to Birth Regions," *New York Times*, West Coast edition, October 23, 2001, A6. Compare with the discussion of Chinese overseas emigration in Wang Gungwu, *The Chinese Overseas: From Earthbound China to the Quest for Autonomy* (Cambridge, Mass.: Harvard University Press, 2000); and Guerassimoff and Guerassimoff, chapter 12 in this volume.

58. See Matthews, *Passport Society*, 101–4; for a more critical view that regards the maintenance of Soviet-era controls on movement as a dangerous threat to democratization in Russia, see Marie Jego, "La liberté de mouvement est réduite dans la Russie 'démocrate'," *Le Monde* (January 26, 1996), 1.

2

THE EXIT REVOLUTION

Aristide R. Zolberg

High on the litany of grievances broadcast by the Americans in their Declaration of Independence is the king's egregious interference with their efforts to attract settlers: "He has endeavored to prevent the Population of these States; for that purpose obstructing the Laws for Naturalization of Foreigners, refusing to pass others to encourage their migration hither, and raising the conditions of new Appropriations of Lands." On the political agenda for several decades before 1776, these complaints represented merely the tip of the iceberg. The Americans' anger was further exacerbated by the British government's persistent attempts to discourage or even prohibit altogether the transatlantic migration of valuable *British* subjects, which suggested that His Majesty was in effect treating the colonies as if they had already turned into foreign states.[1]

In relation to the legal and political framework prevailing among the several European states as well as to the law of nations, the American complaint constituted a provocative proclamation of their right to appropriate manpower, which, at the time, represented the most valuable asset of any sovereign. The situation became even more threatening when, in the wake of their unexpected victory, the colonists enacted laws that fully accorded with their desires and arrogated to themselves the further right to transform the subjects of European monarchs into citizens of the new republic, thereby freeing them of allegiance and obligations to their "natural" rulers.

Overall, the irruption into the Atlantic world of an underpopulated republic that arrogated to itself an immense reserve of temperate lands—and determined to capitalize on this unique asset by marketing it to all comers—was a truly revolutionary event.[2] However, this did not suffice to transform established patterns of transnational migration in the Atlantic region, as the states of potential origin initially responded to the prospect of losing valuable population by erecting more effective barriers against exit. European states completed the transformation only when, in response to changing political and economic conditions, as well as a profound modification of population dynamics, they relinquished prevailing prohibitions against exit on behalf of a stance of "benign neglect" toward the push forces unleashed by the "Great Transformation."[3] The theoretical analysis of this signal policy shift presented here relates it to broader changes in transatlantic political and socioeconomic structures and outlooks, notably the European demographic revolution and the transition from mercantilism to laissez-faire.

THE MERCANTILIST BASELINE

The formation of modern states in Europe in the sixteenth and seventeenth centuries, together with the emergence and expansion of commercial capitalism, produced a profound transformation of human migration, in which the policies of the leading European states played a major role.[4] In the sixteenth century, there was much concern with overpopulation; but as European sovereigns engaged in state building and colonial expansion under conditions of slower demographic growth in the seventeenth century (when both economic production and warfare were still extremely labor-intensive), population came to be perceived as a scarce resource. Jean Bodin concisely summarized the doctrine that was to become an axiom until the early decades of the nineteenth century: "*Il n'est force ni richesse que d'hommes.*"[5] Accordingly, population policy was simultaneously protectionist and acquisitive.

Within the emergent system of states, the personal obligations of inhabitants to their landlords, which implied very limited geographic mobility, were transformed into those of monarchical subjects, and state authorities reinforced controls over the movements of goods and people. The principles of international law enunciated by Hugo Grotius and Samuel Pufendorf, on which law concerning exit, entry, and citizenship came to be founded, were devised in part for this very purpose. The sovereign also determined who was more useful at home and who in the colonies, coupled with concern for moral control as a foundation for allegiance.[6]

The basic objective of states was "primitive accumulation," maximizing the indigenous population by encouraging births and prohibiting departures, while acquiring a surplus from elsewhere by way of trade and conquest. Laws against expatriation singled out skilled workers for special attention.[7] (A major exception pertained to religious deviants. The economic irrationality of forced exile was well understood; reportedly, the Ottoman Sultan Bajazet exclaimed—when the Jews expelled by Spain in 1492 began to arrive—"What! Call ye this Ferdinand 'wise'—he who depopulates his own dominions in order to enrich mine?"[8]) The same principles governed movement to overseas colonies. Thickly populated tropical and subtropical regions were organized into a system of estate agriculture based on indentured labor, an arrangement that produced large-scale migrations within regions. For sparsely populated regions, massive involuntary migrations (for example, the importation of West Africans as slaves into the Americas) assured cheap labor. Plantations also stimulated a limited flow of Europeans, mostly voluntary and temporary, to provide supervisory personnel.

So long as governments believed that their populations exceeded home needs and that the surplus produced social and political disturbances, they encouraged colonial emigration (but preferred rotation for people of quality acting as supervisory personnel in the plantations and as imperial guards).[9] When overseas expansion itself produced economic growth at home, however, the surplus turned into a shortage, as was the case in Britain in the second half of the seventeenth century. It was now argued that the emigration of Englishmen to the colonies was warranted only if the colonies could be compelled to confine their trade to the mother country and if their activities provided labor for the homeland.[10]

The relocation of home dissenters in the colonies (including Ireland) constituted a combination of "voluntary exile" and "right of asylum" that eased religious and political dissent at home. Furthermore, in the early eighteenth century, Britain turned to non-English settlers as well.[11] Since emigration was nearly universally prohibited, these were almost necessarily refugees, whose loyalty to the asylum country could be counted upon, a policy also used by the Dutch in southern Africa. As the first capitalist powers, each of them independently recognized quite early the advantages of removing obstacles to population movements within and between their possessions.[12]

French policies provide an interesting contrast. Seaboard-dwelling Huguenots were very colonial minded, but when New France was restored in 1632, the king decreed that settlers must be Catholic.[13] However, the state failed to provide incentives for individuals to go. Consequently, there were only two thousand settlers in New France by 1660, and severe restrictions on the acquisition of individual property discouraged more massive departures. Furthermore, the small number of Huguenots who had gone to New France (as well as to the West Indies) in spite of the prohibition were expelled from all French colonies between 1683 and 1715, with little alternative but to relocate in neighboring English territories. As a result, by the eighteenth century the "English" outnumbered the French in America twenty to one. The growing numerical disparity in turn vastly facilitated the military expulsion of France from North America in the eighteenth century.

As Britain's gain was viewed as everyone else's loss, and improving conditions in the New World increased the transoceanic pull, concern with emigration to America rose throughout western and central Europe in the eighteenth century. Considerations were military as well as economic. Authorities opposed emigration by a combination of legal barriers and moral exhortation: "To emigrate was equivalent to desertion and meant forfeiture of all political and economic rights, with the penalty of imprisonment in case of return. The Bible was used to justify this position and government, fearing the loss of farmers and industrial workers, stressed the view that a person should remain in the land of his fathers. To depart was sinful, and the wage of sin was death."[14] Without New World colonies of their own, most German principalities, Swiss cantons, and the Austrian Empire imposed sanctions similar to those the French employed, prohibited propaganda by the promoters of emigration, issued their own counterpropaganda, and collaborated with each other to prevent their subjects from embarking. In particular, they made it extremely difficult to dispose of property in preparation for leaving, prevented the sending of financial aid to those who departed, and cut emigrants off from their inheritances by depriving them of their nationality. At the lower levels of society, serfdom and its sequels were still partly effective as a restriction on exit.

Nevertheless, departures did occur at all levels of society. The poor had little to lose, and states began to agree that the poor, the lame, and the marginal constituted no loss to them and no gain to others. However, "It was this attempt to dam the stream without paying attention to the headwaters that in the long run made all restrictive efforts a failure."[15] Moreover, there was a considerable hiatus between the restrictive intent of the state and the coercive apparatus available to enforce its will.

THE AMERICAN STRUGGLE FOR FREEDOM OF EXIT

For the newly independent Americans, the major referent remained Great Britain, shortly to become the United Kingdom of Great Britain and Ireland. Linked by way of established networks as the major components of a transatlantic migration system, the two states were at loggerheads. Britain's most urgent priorities were to stem the drain of valuable human capital to what was now an outright competitor, to rebuild an empire in North America, and to dispose of its accumulating human refuse.

Although emigration from Great Britain and Ireland ground to a halt during the American war for independence, the reopening of the Atlantic triggered a new wave of departures. In swift response, Parliament extended (to what was now a recognized foreign state) the general ban imposed in 1720 on the emigration of British seamen, artisans, and workers in key industries. Three years later, they extended the ban to cover Ireland as well. The prohibition, together with the breakdown of established financial links, undermined the transatlantic market in bound servants that had previously constituted the framework for much of the emigration to the American colonies. However, the prohibition was ineffective as a barrier to the exit of persons who paid their own way, and there were many holes in the fence: emigrants could, for example, make their way to America by sailing first to Canada, Nova Scotia, or New Brunswick.[16] The problem of the American drain thus remained on the British political agenda. As one writer complained in 1819, America had become "'*refugium pauperum et peccatorum*' [a refuge for paupers and sinners] in utter contempt of the British laws." How long, he wondered, "is this unjust and injurious practice to continue?"[17]

Mirroring the British position, the United States was determined to attract valuable human capital while deterring undesirables. From this perspective, the greatest problem was the British prohibition on emigration, which evoked considerable rancor. Although this did not prompt any official action by the United States, many Americans sought to persuade the British to change their ways, often by arguing that the policy was harmful for Britain itself. Benjamin Franklin did so shortly after the prohibition was imposed, in a letter to an English friend: "[Y]ou do wrong to discourage the Emigration of Englishmen to America," he explained, because (as demonstrated in his own writings on population) emigration "does not diminish but multiplies a Nation. You will not have fewer at home for those that go Abroad."[18]

In the same vein, James Madison also sought (seven years later) to demonstrate the benefits of emigration for countries "whose population is full."[19] Most astutely, he asserted not only that free movement would make everyone better off, but also that migration from the British Isles to America would promote the development of their distinctive political economies in harmonious complementarity. Freedom of movement benefits not only sending and receiving states, but it "is due to the general interests of humanity" and provides for a better distribution of people in relation to resources and opportunities. Madison cites the exorbitant cost of supporting the poor in England and France and argues that freedom of emigration also promotes morality, since crowding fosters promiscuity: "Provide an outlet for the surplus of population, and marriages will be increased in proportion."

In their initial moment of enthusiasm, the Americans even asserted the Lockean doctrine regarding the right of expatriation on behalf of their own people. (Later, however, the United States would be much less permissive regarding expatriation of Americans.[20]) In effect, American voluntarism challenged head on the common law doctrine of "perpetual allegiance"— that a subject was indissolubly linked to the sovereign—which constituted the foundation stone of the entire European state system.

EUROPEAN RESPONSES

From the European perspective, within the context of a protracted global war spanning an entire generation, the threat posed by the American magnet was exacerbated by the monstrous manpower requirements of the new mass armies and expanding navies. Prohibiting propaganda by the promoters of emigration, and issuing their own counterpropaganda in the form of pamphlets describing the horrors of American life, European seaboard states collaborated to prevent embarkation by pushing emigrants back at their borders.[21] The net effect was to reduce emigration among the population America most desired, the "middling classes" of society. Although the Treaty of Paris specifically authorized the departure of inhabitants from territory ceded by France (including most of present-day Belgium) for a period of six years, and the Treaty of Vienna, in establishing the German Confederation, provided for free emigration from any German state to any other, this required payment of a substantial tax.[22]

The United Kingdom was especially concerned with movement to the United States, not only on ordinary mercantilist grounds but also from the perspective of imperial security. This also dictated efforts to populate British North America as rapidly as possible. Observing the substantial influx of skilled British artisans into the United States despite the prohibitions on their exit, the British consul in Philadelphia, Phineas Bond, suggested in 1788 an alternative strategy that would "restrain for the present and finally annihilate" the traffic altogether: raise the standards of comfort on passenger ships to such a high level as to make the cost of the crossing prohibitive for the emigrants and simultaneously unprofitable for the shipper.[23]

The centerpiece of his proposal was a limitation on the number of passengers in relation to the tonnage of the vessel, a regulation that would have the immediate effect of raising the price of passage and of limiting total departures until additional ships could be built. In the same year, British abolitionists set forth the notion of such a regulatory mechanism as a way of "meliorating" the slave trade out of existence, a strategy adopted shortly thereafter by the Highland Society. Uprooted by a crisis of subsistence, Scottish Highlanders were being encouraged by the Colonial Office to emigrate as an "ethnic counterweight" to the French Canadians. However, a fraction of Scottish landlords, desperately seeking to stem the human drain, seized upon the "passengers per ton" strategy as a device for deterring Highland emigration as well, broadcasting information that Scots were subjected to even greater crowding and suffering than blacks.[24] The Society's concerns evoked a sympathetic response in Parliament, which in 1803 passed a Passenger Act limiting the number of passengers to *one per two tons* on British ships, as well as to an exorbitant ratio of *one per five tons* on foreign vessels.

Although the 1803 law has generated considerable interest as a historical turning point signaling the advent of "humanitarian" concerns in British public policy or even of a "collectivist" outlook anticipating the welfare state, what matters here is that the act was "cradled in mercantilism. . . . [I]f emigration was inevitable, British shipping and British North America, rather than American shipping and the United States" should gain whatever benefits it brought.[25] The preamble and final provisions of the act are quite explicit: the former refers to persons who "have been seduced to leave their native country under false representations," while the latter specifies that nothing in the present act repeals or alters any measures "for the restriction or regulation of artificers and others, from or in joining or passing from any part of the united kingdom to parts beyond the seas." Moreover, Lord Castlereagh, the British Foreign Minister, subsequently admitted in a letter to Secretary of State John Quincy Adams that the act's real purpose was to deter emigration to the United States.[26]

The measure was politically timely, as recent advances of the "right to leave" in France, as well as American criticism of the Crown's determination "to enslave its own people," made it difficult to continue denying freedom of movement to British subjects.[27] It also constituted a strikingly modern bureaucratic innovation, in that it is much more efficient to control the loading of a limited number of ships concentrated in ports than to control the movements of a large number of persons scattered throughout the country. In the short term, the Passenger Act's impact was made moot by the resumption of international conflict, and its subsequent effectiveness as a deterrent was somewhat mitigated by the fact that both emigrants and shippers quickly learned that it was possible to sail to a British North American port on a British ship, and then go on to an American destination by sea or by land. Nevertheless, after the Atlantic reopened, arrivals in the United States from Britain remained below the level of the 1790s, whereas those from the Continent substantially increased, and the law is generally credited with forestalling any attempts to revive the British servant trade.[28] It is noteworthy that although the act also covered Ireland, which had been incorporated into the United Kingdom two years before, it was hardly enforced in Irish ports; while this was perhaps attributable to the island's rudimentary governmental structures, it may also have reflected an emerging view of emigration as a solution to the "Irish Question," as we shall see.

Ironically, the British act not only emerged as the major target of American efforts to promote freedom of exit on behalf of desirable immigrants; it also provided a device that they themselves shortly adopted to restrict the *immigration* of paupers and other undesirables. Its centrality in American political perceptions is revealed by the vehement outpourings of the Baltimore-based publisher of the prominent *Niles' Weekly Register,* who reported that the Europeans reminded him of the fable of Saturn devouring his own children: "They had rather that their people should perish at home, than suffer them to emigrate, and possibly, strengthen the power and add to the resources of another country." England was not the only culprit: on the Continent, also, "measures have been taken to circumscribe emigration; but still it is powerful, and will increase." Niles was also highly critical of the British doctrine of "perpetual allegiance," which held that America's routinized and accessible naturalization law violated the law of nations. In the same vein, he criticized the imposition of alien laws in Britain and France that required travelers to obtain passports prior to departure and to register with the authorities upon arrival, contrasting this with open conditions in the United States.[29]

Yet in Washington, foreign policy considerations weighed toward the adoption of a more subdued stance, so as to allay European suspicions of American recruiters and to forestall even greater restrictions on exit. This attitude is evident in the response of Secretary of State John Quincy Adams to an emissary sent out by the German Diet in 1817: "It was explicitly stated to you, and your report has taken just notice of the statement, that the government of the United States has never adopted any measure to encourage or invite emigrants from any part of Europe. It has never held out any incitements to induce the subjects of any other sovereign to abandon their own country, to become inhabitants of this."[30] But Adams then added:

"Neither the general government of the union, nor those of the individual states, are ignorant or unobservant of the additional strength and wealth, which accrues to the nation, by the accession of a mass of healthy, industrious, and frugal laborers." The last phrase is a concise summary of the central economic objective of immigration policy as envisaged by one of the principal architects of the American system.[31]

TOWARD SELF-REMOVAL

In the early decades of the nineteenth century, the startling doctrine propounded by Thomas Malthus in 1798 appeared to be confirmed by the recently devised periodic census counts as well as by common experience. The population of England and Wales numbered 8.9 million in 1801, having probably grown by about half in the previous century. The next two decennial headcounts indicated it was now increasing at the huge annual rate of nearly 2 percent.[32] Concurrent movement from villages and towns enhanced perceptions of dramatic overall population growth, with dramatic growth in cities such as Birmingham, Manchester, and London.

Not only was population growing; the masses were also becoming more dangerous. As E. P. Thompson has noted, "The Wars ended amidst riots," prompting the codification and extension of repressive legislation, under which was launched "the most sustained campaign of prosecutions in the courts in British history," effectively putting an end to the "old Radicalism."[33] Repression was not the only possible response, however. As Albert Hirschman has demonstrated, when an organization believes that the increase of "voice" among its members is attributable to dissatisfactions arising from their growing number, it might seek to relieve internal pressure (should circumstances allow) by inducing some to avail themselves of "exit."[34] Britain had repeatedly resorted to "exit" by way of emigration to solve its problems, and this appeared even more appropriate as a remedy now that demographic expansion assured the country of a rapid replenishment of its labor pool and because Britain emerged from the Napoleonic Wars in possession of additional territories where settlers were needed.

Over the next decade, leading political and economic elites became "emigrationists," and legal obstacles to exit were swept away. By and large, the push-and-pull operating in the Atlantic sector came to be recognized as both politically beneficial and economically profitable; and the mercantilist outlook toward transnational population movement gave way to a liberal one, expressed in a policy of benign neglect.

The rapid surfacing of removal abroad as a panacea for Britain's social ills in the troubled postwar years is evident from William Cobbett's denunciation of the emigrationism of the upper classes as early as November 1816, in his famous "Address to the Journeymen and Labourers," the most influential protest writing since Paine's *Rights of Man:* "[Y]ou who help to maintain them by the taxes which you pay, have as good a right to remain in the country as they have!"[35] Cobbett's denunciation notwithstanding, there were undoubtedly already many in his working-class audience who viewed emigration as an opportunity rather than as a threat. Thus, on this issue as on no other, there was a degree of congruence between the interests of the upper and lower classes.

Emigration also helped solve some of the problems London confronted in its efforts to forge the culturally heterogeneous United Kingdom into a nation-state. Suffering and starvation in the peripheral kingdoms encouraged departures from the Scottish Highlands, the Hebrides, and the Lowlands, ultimately enhancing the relative weight of the English population. Ireland was in the grip of a "Malthusian crisis" long before its tragic climax in the Great Hunger of the 1840s. The island's population, estimated at two million in 1690, took off dramatically after the introduction of the potato allowed people to eke out subsistence from poor land. Reaching five million at the time of union with Great Britain in 1801, Ireland's population climbed to 6.8 million in 1821, one third of the United Kingdom's total. Large family size, a survival strategy developed by the southern Irish in response to the economic and political structures imposed on them after 1690, facilitated the formation of a household unit of production which combined subsistence agriculture on rented parcels with cash-producing activities such as home crafts and seasonal or perennial migration to Britain.[36] However, albeit rational in the short term and at the level of the individual household, this adaptation rendered Irish society as a whole more vulnerable to catastrophic economic events.

Britain had feared an invasion of Ireland by hostile foreign powers since the sixteenth century; "but the invasion, when it came, was of a different order; it was the invasion of England and Scotland by the Irish poor."[37] Successive enumerations revealed a differential between the British and Irish rates of natural reproduction that would result, over the long term, in an inexorable "Irishization" of the United Kingdom. The linking of the two islands by steamship starting in 1816 contributed to the further integration of the Irish into the British labor market. The social costs of the Irish migration exacerbated long-standing prejudices toward Ireland and its people within the British political class and came to be identified as one of the principal causes of increasing English pauperism, hence of the rising burden imposed on relief institutions under the Poor Law. For example, the Emigration Committee of 1827 warned that the influx threatened to "deluge Great Britain with poverty and wretchedness and gradually but certainly to equalize the state of the English and Irish peasantry."[38] Compounding the nightmare was the possibility that displacement would stimulate further *English* emigration, and thus further promote "Irishization." Participation by Irish workers in the social movements of the postwar era (as well as in Chartism later on) suggested moreover that they were as dangerous to the public order in Britain as they were at home. As one of the innumerable commissions appointed to deal with the Irish Question concluded, "The Irish . . . have practically decided, that emigrate they must—the only question for us to determine is whether it shall be to England or America."[39]

Increasingly desirable from a domestic point of view, emigration was also believed to serve imperial interests, so long as it flowed toward British possessions. Whereas the mercantilists abhorred settler colonies, Adam Smith suggested that the transfer of population to undeveloped lands would foster the development of a market for home industrial production while simultaneously meeting the problem of overpopulation in a positive instead of a negative way. The political realities of international trade made it further possible to argue the advantages of colonies even in a laissez-faire system. Colonial markets were safer and more predictable than those of foreign states; migration and colonization thus figured among the few exceptions to the rule against state interference.[40]

While theoretical obstacles to positive state intervention on behalf of colonial emigration had now been surmounted, there remained many difficulties in practice. Neither the distant Australian colonies nor the one recently taken from the Netherlands in southernmost Africa were yet suitable for mass emigration; in the absence of infrastructure and an established carrying trade, few wanted to go; and the creation of new settlements entailed considerable start-up costs, to be borne entirely by the metropolitan government. This left, for the time being, British North America as the main objective. However, most of those subject to the emigration push preferred the United States. Although it was possible to deflect their movement toward British North America by way of measures such as the Passenger Act of 1803, many who were driven there by cheaper fares subsequently moved on. It thus became evident that little progress would be made unless British North America itself were rendered more attractive; but this, in turn, could not be achieved without a fundamental restructuring of relationships between the *métropole* and its overseas possession.

Legislative enactments from 1815 to about 1860 can be viewed as a succession of attempts simultaneously to achieve the domestic and imperial objectives emigration was intended to serve. As soon as shipping resumed, the Passenger Act was amended to facilitate colonial emigration by establishing a fare differential in the ratio of about 3:1 between Quebec and New York.[41] The following year, a Select Committee on the Poor Laws recommended removing all remaining obstacles to the movement of labor to the colonies.[42] In the face of objections from the Colonial Office to the dumping of paupers in British North America, however, it was decided to limit assistance in favor of emigrants selected for their political and economic suitability. Candidates were recruited not only in Scotland, as before, but also in Northern Ireland, despite warnings from the lieutenant-governor, Robert Peel, that the departure of Protestant Ulstermen would reinforce Catholic power on the island. Following the disturbances occasioned by the "Catholic Rent" movement in Ireland, Peel urged that assistance be provided toward the relocation of Irish Catholics as well.[43] In 1819, a similar program was devised for the Cape Colony where, as in British North America, British subjects were needed to balance a settler population of foreign European stock.

By the mid-1820s, there was a consensus on the desirability of emigration, even with respect to England, but the state remained reluctant to subsidize it. In the days of sail, self-financed emigration was largely limited to the rural middle class, to whom were added urban artisans and skilled workers when legal obstacles were removed. The departure of the first waves of poor was rendered feasible when Poor Law boards throughout Britain discovered that their budget might be better expended on paying the poor to leave than on maintaining them at home. Although emigration of this kind was probably limited, "in some years it accounted for a not inconsiderable proportion of the departures from certain localities."[44] Ireland had no official system of poor relief of any kind; but, in the latter part of the decade, the opening of the British market to Irish grain as well as the disenfranchisement of freeholders gave landlords an incentive to clear their land by subsidizing the departure of subsistence farmers.

The shipping industry had a standing interest in emigration as well, as the Scots and Irish served as paying westbound ballast for the vessels plying the British North American timber trade from peripheral United Kingdom ports. Subsequently, the growing cotton trade gave them an incentive to make similar use of passengers on U.S. routes. Seeking to maximize income by filling ships to the limit at the lowest possible cost, they intervened repeatedly to reduce the space, food, and medical requirements imposed by passenger regulations. However, in 1819 the United States imposed passenger regulations of its own to deter undesirable "pauper" immigration, thereby in effect establishing a floor for transatlantic fares.

In 1824, Britain revoked the long-standing law prohibiting the emigration of skilled workers to foreign countries, "partly out of deference to free trade ideas, partly because of a feeling that it was unjust to discriminate against one class of the population, but mainly because it was apparent that the laws were not being and could not be enforced, and that their only effect was to discourage artificers who had gone abroad from returning home lest they be prosecuted."[45] Publicly subsidized emigration as a device for solving the problem of pauperism and for righting the ethnic balance at home and abroad moved to the forefront of official thinking in the mid-1820s under the leadership of R. J. Wilmot Horton, undersecretary for the Colonies who, as chairman of a Committee on Emigration, developed a comprehensive scheme for coupling assisted emigration, on a selective basis, with appropriate incentives in the colonies. Criticized in Parliament for its flagrant departures from laissez-faire, the proposal was returned to the Committee, which, in the chairman's absence, abruptly recommended the repeal of *all* existing passenger regulations. Acting with deliberate speed, Parliament approved the measure in April 1827, in time for the sailing season. Consequently, "emigration to British North America was regulated for the first time by market forces alone."[46] New regulations of 1828 confirmed the hegemony of laissez-faire, as the passenger ratio was established at three adults for every four tons, a level that "legalized crowding past belief, but kept fares at the lowest possible level."[47] The new regulations not only increased the total carrying capacity of British ships—thus facilitating the immediate expansion of emigration—and made travel more accessible to the poor, but such conditions gave the British shipping industry a considerable advantage over their American competitors.

It was becoming apparent, however, that if laissez-faire was serving Britain's domestic policy objectives, its impact on imperial policy was problematic. Around the time of the Reform Act, the recently appointed Emigration Commissioners concluded, on the basis of the statistical evidence at their disposal, that public intervention to stimulate overall departures would be superfluous, as they were increasing of their own accord. But as the number of emigrants rose, a higher proportion of them—nearly all the southern

Irish and many of the English and Welsh—ended up in the United States, with only the Scots more likely to remain in British North America.[48]

Of itself, the fact that the United Kingdom contributed to the expansion of the American population was no longer a source of concern, as the United States was emerging as the major market for British manufactured goods and as the preferred location for British overseas capital investment. That the southern Irish, voting with their feet, preferred the United States to the Empire, was surely not unwelcome either. However, little progress was being made toward populating the temperate imperial possessions. Seeking to resolve this problem, in 1829 Edward Gibbon Wakefield formulated a comprehensive plan for colonial development that entailed the rational organization of land sales and the use of resulting revenues to subsidize emigration, coupled with the grant of responsible government to the colonies so as to attract enterprising middle-class settlers. The scheme, which was mainly concerned with Canada and Australia—the latter "at first used only as a receptacle for those convicts who could no longer be transported to the American colonies"—established the terms of debate over colonial policy for the next thirty years.[49] It can be thought of as an attempt to foster the transformation of British overseas possessions along the lines of the United States, and of the empire as a whole into a confederation of liberal capitalist regimes ruled by a political class of British stock and culture.

Coming to power in an atmosphere of economic and political crisis, the reformist Whig administration responded with the Poor Law Amendment Act of 1834, a measure inspired by, among other things, "the current view, basically Malthusian, of the dangers of overpopulation or of a population uneconomically distributed because of restrictions on its free movement."[50] While most of the historical attention has focused on the institutionalization of the workhouse, emigration emerged as a major component of the new policy. It removed such restrictions to internal movement as remained by dissociating eligibility for assistance from residence in the parish of birth and enabled parishes to borrow money from the treasury for the purpose of sponsoring colonial emigration, thereby raising established local practice to the level of national policy. The Poor Law Commissioner further proposed in 1836 that emigration be centrally organized, with the expense borne equally by the government and the locality of origin; and that landowners who had assisted emigrants in the years immediately preceding passage of the act be repaid for half their expenses. A similar scheme was devised in 1838 for Ireland, with respect to which "the vision of relief by emigration was most persistent."[51]

Although these measures are highly significant indications of policy intent, their impact on the emigration process itself was probably limited. No more than fourteen thousand persons emigrated from England and Wales to British North America under the provisions of the Poor Law, of whom about five thousand did so in the first year of operation, 1835–36.[52] It has been suggested that the emigration clause fell by the wayside because it was overshadowed by the law itself, which left parish authorities with less incentive to organize emigration, since it lowered the cost of maintaining paupers in England. Nevertheless, the elimination of incentives to stay within one's native parish loosened a population for whom it was not much more difficult to relocate abroad than to a strange part of their own country.[53] Most important, as the choice Dickens attributes to Mr. Micawber in *David Copperfield* memorably highlights, the frightful prospect of incarceration held out by the new Poor Law provided a powerful incentive for the unfortunate to look upon self-removal, even to Australia, as a more desirable alternative.

As it was, laissez-faire generally continued to prevail in the Atlantic sector because public intervention to "shovel out paupers" was rendered impossible by the responses of intended or unintended receivers. In the United States, perception that the British government proposed to dump paupers propelled the issue of immigration, hitherto a matter of local concern, to the national level. Although the Poor Law authorities specified in 1836 that local finances could not be used to further emigration to a foreign state, Americans were certain that the English were in fact doing so surreptitiously and that, in any case, paupers landing in British North America would proceed southward, as so many emigrants had been doing all along. This perception prompted a round of more severely restrictive enactments.[54]

The situation was becoming urgent in British North America, which, as the population of the United States approached the ten million mark, barely reached 750,000, about half of whom were French-speaking and Roman Catholic *Canadiens*. Concern focused on Lower Canada, of whose 420,000 inhabitants, only 80,000 were of British origin, including relocated American loyalists. Although the *Canadiens* had shown little inclination to side with the strongly anti-Catholic American democracy or with a "godless" France in the war decades, their demographic weight afforded them the upper hand in the legislature, which they used with consummate skill as a platform from which to challenge the colonial executive. Powerless to restrict the entry of British immigrants, *Canadien* representatives sought to deter the flow indirectly by erecting obstacles to the emergence of a commercial market in land, and minimize the political effects of what immigration did take place by limiting the representation of new settlements in the legislature. An additional problem was that as immigration increased, it included a larger proportion of poor who required relief immediately upon landing. Although most of the Irish Catholics went on to the United States, those who remained in Lower Canada provided additional leadership and mass support for the French party, notwithstanding official efforts to appeal to them as "English" on the basis of linguistic affinity. Hence, as circumstances in the United Kingdom reinforced the shoveling out of paupers, British emigration policy emerged as a source of Canadian grievance, much as it had in the American colonies earlier.[55]

In response, the seaboard provinces of British North America imposed a head tax on immigrants for the purpose of creating a self-financed relief fund. It provided means for quarantine and hospital facilities when the cholera epidemic reached North America in the emigrants' wake. This tug-of-war contributed to the political crisis of 1836–38. "Alarmingly reminiscent of 1776," it moved imperial policy to the forefront of political concerns for the first time since the end of the Napoleonic Wars and also prompted the most concerted attempt in British history to organize colonial emigration and settlement on a comprehensive scale.[56] After suspending the Canadian constitution, London sent Lord Durham, a radically minded Whig politician, to investigate and make recommendations.

Durham was strongly influenced by the reformist ideas of Edward Gibbon Wakefield, who accompanied him as an unofficial adviser. His report was a major turning point not only in Canadian history but also in the history of the empire more generally. Among other things, it stipulated that defense and foreign affairs must remain under imperial control and that colonies could not interfere "with the immigration of British subjects and the disposal of its unoccupied lands, or the trade with Britain."[57] The British government implemented the "Irish solution" by way of the Canadian Union Act of 1840, which merged the two provinces into a single entity with a population of about one million, of whom already approximately 55 percent were English speaking. At the same time, a Colonial Land and Emigration Commission was established.

The creation of this body has been interpreted as a turning away from economic liberalism toward state intervention to protect individuals in response to welfare crises engendered by unforeseen circumstances.[58] It was that and much more. The commission functioned as the "economic bureau" of the Colonial Office, signaling acceptance of Edward Gibbon Wakefield's conception of the British Empire as an integral political and economic entity, within which land and labor could be centrally coordinated to equilibrate population surplus in one part of the empire and labor shortage elsewhere. In existence until 1878, the commission's activities reveal the emergence of a differentiation of the empire into two segments. With regard to the old plantation colonies and India, to which other tropical or semitropical possessions were added later, the commission acted as an international manpower agency, helping to organize the massive transfer of labor from one part of the empire to another. In relation to the settler colonies of the Pacific, the commission made it possible to limit settlement to the United Kingdom's ethnic groups, at little cost to the imperial treasury. Once self-government was achieved, this relatively homogeneous nucleus reproduced itself for the better part of a century by restricting immigration to related groups.[59]

With respect to the North Atlantic, however, laissez-faire prevailed. At no time was the commission allowed to impose regulations that might impair self-removal, even on humanitarian grounds. When the horrors induced by the sudden increase of departures after the onset of the Great Famine of the mid-1840s prompted the Commission to propose raising the space allotment as well as food and medical requirements, the colonial secretary insisted that "this was not the time to impose extra restrictions on emigrant ships" but merely to enforce existing regulations so as "to prevent public opinion both in this country and in the colonies from being directed against the system of emigration."[60] Nor were considerations of foreign policy allowed to interfere. For example, in 1864, when it was charged that "Irish emigrants were being enticed into the American army to be murdered," the British government, notwithstanding its leanings toward the Confederacy, replied unambiguously that "it was not for the Emigration Commissioners, or any Department of the Government, to undertake the paternal duty of persuading emigrants to go to one country rather than another."[61] Consequently, new settlement in Canada grew too slowly to fundamentally alter the ethnic balance.

COMPARATIVE PERSPECTIVES

Although nowhere in Europe was the Great Transformation as brutal, thorough, and concentrated in time as in the United Kingdom, by the middle decades of the nineteenth century, the nexus constituted by demographic expansion, the extension of the market system to land and labor, and the shift from agriculture and crafts to urban industry had surfaced throughout most of the western part of the continent. Accentuated by temporary conjunctures common to the entire international economy—rural distress on the morrow of the Napoleonic Wars, economic downturn in the late 1830s, and catastrophe a decade later—the phenomenon of "surplus population" became a permanent feature of the European landscape until the end of the century. Wherever it appeared, internal and external migration followed in its wake, not only because individuals wished to relocate in search of opportunity, but because their removal came to be viewed by the governing classes as an advantageous solution. As in the United Kingdom, the increasing "push" from parts of Europe came about not just because of an increasing expulsive force generated by the deteriorating economic plight of particular classes or areas, but by the loosening of former restraints that had inhibited the search for a solution by moving elsewhere.[62]

Germany's rural population had been emigrating eastward in search of land and peace ever since the dislocations wrought by the Thirty Years' War. In the first post-Napoleonic decade, Russia remained the most important destination. In southwestern Germany, governments were taken aback when the famine of 1816–17 drove people out toward North America as well. Although their outlook was still mercantilist—or, in this case, "cameralist"—circumstances undermined the prevailing doctrine: "[A]s local officials vigorously pointed out, a large body of indigent subjects constituted a social danger and a serious burden on meager public funds; better to let them go." Consequently, "Noncoercive, vaguely anti-emigrationist state policies were . . . in large part frustrated . . . by local officials and civic leaders." Much as in Britain, emigrationists such as Hans von Gagern pointed out further that freedom to emigrate was also "one of the best ways to remove the roots of Jacobinism, conspiracy, and revolution."[63] Compounded by rising food prices, the cholera epidemic, and the progress of economic liberalism (which swept away traditional protections of trades and crafts), in the 1830s the "emigration fever" was directed almost entirely toward the United States.[64]

Changing international arrangements facilitated movement as well. The Treaty of Vienna provided freedom of emigration in territories that changed masters, as was the case in western Germany. The constitution of the German Confederation, which insured free travel from one state to another, facilitated access to ports of embarkation. The enlargement of the economic area by way of the *Zollverein* (customs union) contributed to mobility as well, and Malthusian legislation designed to reduce population growth by raising the legal age of marriage provided further incentives to seek personal freedom abroad. Neighboring countries such as Belgium, the Netherlands, and France lowered transit costs to encourage the use of their ports; by mid-century, Hamburg and Bremen also began to view the emigrant trade as an important source of revenue.[65]

Much as in the United Kingdom, as cheaper transportation became available, emigration extended from the middling classes toward the poor. Here also, many communities discovered in the 1840s that it was cheaper to subsidize their departure than to maintain them at home. In the absence of German colonies, Brazil appeared to provide the best opportunity for officially organized "shoveling out" programs. Some of the poor "were merely sent to ports where they obtained help from agents of Brazilian governments."[66] However, adverse publicity concerning the slavery-like conditions to which Germans were subjected in the receiving country, as well as its perennial political upheavals, repeatedly interfered with such schemes. This left the United States, whose negative reactions to openly conducted pauper removal fostered surreptitious arrangements to the same effect.[67]

In the spirit of liberalism, the Frankfurt Parliament resolved, "Freedom of emigration may not be restricted in the interests of the state."[68] Although liberalism itself was short lived, the restoration regimes became emigrationist for reasons of their own: "Hopeful that emigration might prevent renewed outbreaks of disorder, they jettisoned the multitude of regulations which had hitherto hindered departure. Legal formalities were simplified, and although the obligation to perform military service remained, it became increasingly easy to evade."[69] By this time, sponsorship was superfluous as the process of self-removal was well established.

With minor differences in timing, similar emigration stances emerged in Belgium, the Netherlands, the Swiss Confederation, and Scandinavia.[70] In 1840, Sweden repealed its 1768 law restricting emigration "mainly because of the need to meet the growing problem of pauperism"; and the last serious obstacle to departure was removed twenty years later.[71] Spain and Portugal followed suit as well, and in the 1840s, mass emigration from the Iberian Peninsula to Central and South America resumed for the first time since the late seventeenth century.

The outstanding exception to the general European pattern is France. Although in the Constitution of 1791 it became the first state to specifically include freedom of exit among basic citizenship rights, subsequent regimes returned to a restrictive posture. Under Article 17 of the Napoleonic Code, Frenchmen lost their citizenship if they established themselves abroad with no intention of returning. Additional administrative restrictions were imposed by the restored monarchy (1814–1830), and during the Second Empire (1852–1870) border controls were strengthened and the activities of foreign recruitment agencies severely curtailed. This policy stance was maintained under the Third Republic as well. Article 17 was finally revoked in 1889, but restrictive administrative practices were maintained until World War I.

Overall, the French state consistently shunned the emigrationist posture of its neighbors except for the specific purpose of colonizing Algeria. Even Jean-Baptiste Say, the most prominent French follower of the British political economists in the early nineteenth century, opposed emigration: "The departure of 100,000 emigrants per year is equivalent to the loss of 100,000 men who, year in year out, were to drown with arms and baggage while crossing the border."[72] It is also the case that France not only had the lowest rate of emigration in relation to population for the century as a whole, but (from the 1850s on) it also gained more people than it lost. Estimated at an average annual level of 2,500 during 1821–30, the outflow rose to 14,000 in the next decade and climbed to an annual average of 26,000 during 1841–50. Although emigration to the United States alone reached a high of 20,040 in 1847 (France ranking as the third largest source of U.S. immigration), the French contribution (amounting to only 8.5 percent of the incoming total) fell well below that of the United Kingdom and Germany.[73]

Since we know from other European cases that even draconian prohibitions on emigration were largely ineffective, it is unlikely that French emigration policy provides a sufficient explanation for this outcome. Moreover, there is evidence within France itself that local authorities were not eager to enforce the regulations, probably for the same reasons as in Germany.[74]

The French exceptionalism of small emigration was attributed to the French people's love of their land; for example, one French author wrote in 1860: "[I]t must be recognized that the French rarely emigrate. The fact is that among the various races of Europe there is none with a greater regard for his native land than the French, with a more instinctive, more inviolable affection for his home, his village, and his country. . . . Only religious or political persecution have led in France to emigration on a scale of any importance."[75] However, the key to the difference is to be found within the distinctive French pattern of economic development in the long nineteenth century, the major feature of which was the survival of a large agrarian sector. On the eve of the French Revolution, the productivity of workers employed in British agriculture was already well above that of the French; in familiar fashion, the more favorable British land-to-labor ratios fostered more capital-intensive agriculture, producing a surplus for urban investment, which in turn increased rural out-migration. But in France, the revolution "gave the peasantry what they had long wanted—full rights of ownership and freedom from the burden of feudal exactions from all kinds."[76] Although French agricultural output remained consistently below that of the British, the landless peasantry formed a far smaller proportion of the rural population. The characteristics of the agrarian sector in turn conditioned the pace and pattern of industrial development along different lines. Compared with Britain, the workshop sector in France survived much longer, and industry used much less unskilled labor. Most significant for the present purpose, the rural exodus was long delayed. The French could afford to love their land, so long as they kept their families small.[77]

In short, France made the transition from agriculture to industry and from rural to urban life without experiencing the shock of the Great Transformation. Not only did fewer of the French leave France, but fewer also moved to great urban centers, because the push on rural localities was much weaker than elsewhere. If "migration begets migration," the reverse is true as well: the absence of emigration in the early period of transition makes it less likely that, should a "push" subsequently arise, emigration will follow. Concomitantly, in the absence of surplus population, the state had no reason to turn emigrationist. Although the precocious limitation of fertility in the middle decades of the nineteenth century was rational from the economic perspective of the rural population, it was problematic in other respects. Hence, uniquely in Europe, from the middle of the century onward, the French state became decidedly immigrationist.

CONCLUSION

The demographic revolution, which originated in western Europe around the middle of the eighteenth century and rapidly spread to most of the region, had a fundamentally deflationary effect on the value of population from the perspective of elites concerned with economic production and military power. Attributable mostly to the lowering of infant and adult mortality—thanks to improved nutrition and, somewhat later, the containment of deadly epidemics—the change fostered an enlargement of average family size. This in turn allowed the tenant peasantry to adopt a distinctive strategy for economic survival under the new circumstances, whereby female adult family members and children remained to work the land while males became cash-generating migrant workers. The pattern's viability depended on the maintenance of an authority structure that insured that the progeny continued its economic contribution to the parental household well into adulthood. Arising precociously in Ireland, it emerged also in parts of continental Europe (notably Flanders) where similar conditions prevailed.[78] The development of the Irish movement to Britain and of British responses to it thus strikingly foreshadows the dynamics of intra- or transnational labor migrations from peripheries to developing centers in the industrial epoch more generally.

The Irish migration to Britain was a prominent empirical referent for Marx's analysis of how capitalism created "surplus population," and of the role of such population as a "disposable industrial army" necessary for the functioning of the capitalist mode of production. While the "necessity" of this process may be exaggerated, there is no gainsaying that the inflow enhances the elasticity of the receiving economy's labor supply (and thereby lowers wages), while the costs of maintaining the reserve when not needed are borne largely by the society of origin. Habituation to a lower standard of living and participation in a household economy in the manner indicated enables the migrants to sell their labor below the level required by natives to ensure subsistence in the more developed segment, or conventionally established there as the acceptable minimum. Employers often prefer migrants to natives because they are considered more docile; they stand to benefit as well from the divisive consequences of labor competition.[79] Although some contemporary economists have suggested that the wage-depressing effects of labor importation are compensated for by lower prices in the receiving economy, from which wage earners benefit as consumers, they generally acknowledge that the income effects are mostly negative at the lowermost levels, where migrants not only depress wages, but often displace natives altogether.[80] It therefore stands to reason that workers in the receiving society are generally hostile to immigrants.

In retrospect, it is evident that we would achieve a much better historical understanding of the dynamics involved in this process if we overcame the conventional distinction between "internal" and "international" migrations. Once mobile, populations are prone to engage in more extensive migrations, some of which become permanent and some of which are international; whether they are internal or international depends largely on opportunities. However wrenching these experiences were, the choice of exit benefits most of those who avail themselves of it, and "surplus" populations largely financed their own self-removal. Furthermore, long-distance movement within and between countries was vastly facilitated by the transportation revolution, which began with steamships plying the Irish Sea, then was amplified by the railroad, and culminated in the building of iron steamships capable of transatlantic crossings.

By the time of the constitutional revolution of the 1830s, the British political class had become thoroughly emigrationist, with the exception of some radical Tories who argued that the poor were a part of the nation and who therefore had the right to live in England even if they required charity and relief.[81] Consequently, for about half a century, within the Atlantic economy constituted by the United Kingdom, Canada, and the United States, the only governmental intervention regarding human movement was by way of the immigration policies of the receivers, whose effect in relation to population transfers originating in the United Kingdom was marginal. Hence transatlantic movement from the British Isles was governed by the complex interplay of economic conjuncture in the diverse regions of origin and the countries of destination, whose respective contributions to "push" and "pull" are difficult to sort out.[82]

The United States, from the outset, was both "immigrationist" and "restrictionist." It wanted immigrants, and hence objected to constraints on departure imposed by European states; but it also wanted to exercise selectiveness, and thus objected to what was perceived as "dumping" of undesirables.[83] Already in the colonial era, some of the colonies precociously insisted on exercising control over the flow, and this became a more prominent concern after independence, especially in the wake of the Napoleonic Wars, when emigration spread to the lower classes and encompassed groups that many Americans doubted were assimilable, notably the Irish. By the mid-nineteenth century, the burden of control shifted largely to the receivers. However, the tug-of-war re-emerges perennially, as poorer states seek to retain valuable populations while welcoming opportunities to "shovel out" the surplus, and while richer ones are equally intent upon acquiring valuable populations while deterring the entry of undesirables.

NOTES

1. Although the colonists were also inflamed by Britain's obstruction of the negative side of their immigration policy (notably, enactments to deter the dumping of convicts), I shall not discuss this aspect of the situation here. For a full treatment of the origins of American immigration policy, see my book *A Nation by Design* (Cambridge, Mass.: Harvard University Press and the Russell Sage Foundation, 2006).

2. Robert H. Wiebe, *The Segmented Society: An Introduction to the Meaning of America* (New York: Oxford University Press, 1975), 130.

3. Karl Polanyi, *The Great Transformation: The Political and Economic Origins of Our Time* (1944; repr., Boston: Beacon Press, 1957).

4. For an elaboration, see Aristide R. Zolberg, "The Patterning of International Migration Policies in a Changing World System," in *Human Migration: Patterns and Policies,* ed. William H. McNeill and Ruth S. Adams, 241–86 (Bloomington: Indiana University Press, 1978).

5. "Without men, there is neither strength nor wealth." Cited in Roger Mols, S.J., "Population in Europe 1500–1700," in *The Fontana Economic History of Europe,* vol. 2, ed. Carlo M. Cipolla, 32 (London: Collins, 1973).

6. My overall approach parallels Michael Mann's in *The Sources of Social Power,* vol 1. (Cambridge: Cambridge University Press, 1986). See also Richard Plender, *International Migration Law* (Leiden: A. W. Sythoff, 1972), 41; and, on the general relationship between physical and moral control, Michel Foucault, *Surveiller et punir: Naissance de la prison* (Paris: Gallimard, 1975).

7. Walter Minchinton, "Patterns and Structure of Demand, 1500–1750," in Cipolla, *Fontana,* 2:153. Examples cited are drawn from, D. V. Glass, *Population: Policies and Movements in Europe* (1940; repr., London: Frank Cass, 1967), 91–96; John Duncan Brite, "The Attitude of European States toward Emigration to the American Colonies and the United States, 1607–1820" (PhD diss., Department of History, University of Chicago, 1937), 194–200.

8. Cecil Roth, *History of the Jews* (New York: Shocken, 1961), 252.

9. Julius Isaac, *Economics of Migration* (London: K. Paul, Trench, Trubner, 1947), 15.

10. Christopher Hill, "Caliban's Gift," review of *The First Images of America: The Impact of the New World on the Old,* ed. by Fredi Chiappelli, *New York Review of Books* 23, no. 19 (November 25, 1976), 43; H. J. M. Johnston, *British Emigration Policy 1815–30: "Shovelling Out Paupers"* (Oxford: Clarendon Press, 1972), 13.

11. Marcus Lee Hansen, *The Atlantic Migration, 1607–1850* (1940; repr., New York: Harper Torchbooks, 1961), 45.

12. Ibid., 6–7. The distinctive orientation of Britain and the Netherlands accords well with the distinction between commercial and agrarian societies put forth by Edward W. Fox in *History in Geographic Perspective: The Other France* (New York: W. W. Norton, 1971).

13. Brite, "Attitude of European States," 200.

14. Ibid., 195, 270; see also Hansen, *Atlantic Migration,* 5–8.

15. Brite, "Attitudes of European States," 198.

16. Campbell Gibson, "The Contribution of Immigration to the Growth and Ethnic Diversity of the American Population," *Proceedings of the American Philosophical Society* 136, no. 2 (June 1992), 157–75; Hans-Jurgen Grabbe, "European Immigration to the United States in the Early National Period, 1783–1820," *Proceedings of the American Philosophical Society* 133, no. 2 (June 1989): 190–214; Maldwyn A. Jones, "The Background to Emigration from Great Britain in the Nineteenth Century," *Perspectives in American History* 7 (1973): 12. The act is 25 Geo. III, c. 67.

17. Reprinted in *Niles' Weekly Register* [hereafter *NWR*], Nov. 27, 1819.

18. Benjamin Franklin, *Writings,* ed. J. A. Leo Lemay (New York: The Library of America, 1987), 1098–1102 (letter dated August 12, 1784).

19. Drew McCoy, *The Elusive Republic: Political Economy in Jeffersonian America* (Chapel Hill: University of North Carolina Press, 1980), 155–56.

20. Rogers M. Smith, *Civic Ideals: Conflicting Visions of Citizenship in U.S. History* (New Haven, Conn.: Yale University Press, 1997), 155–59, 169–70, 192–94.

21. Brite, "Attitude of European States"; Thomas W. Page, "The Transportation of Immigrants and Reception Arrangements in the Nineteenth Century," *Journal of Political Economy* 19 (January-December 1911): 732.

22. Max J. Kohler, *Immigration and Aliens in the United States: Studies of American Immigration Laws and the Legal Status of Aliens in the United States* (New York: Bloch Publishing Co., 1936), 301, 303.

23. Herbert Heaton, "The Industrial Immigrant in the United States, 1783–1812," *American Philosophical Society: Proceedings* 95 (1951): 522–23.

24. This account is based on Katherine A. Walpole's "The Humanitarian Movement of the Early Nineteenth Century to Remedy Abuses on Emigrant Vessels to America," *Transactions of the Royal Historical Society* Fourth Series, XIV (1931): 197–224; and Oliver MacDonagh, *A Pattern of Government Growth, the Passenger Acts and Their Enforcement* (London: MacGibbon and Kee, 1961).

25. MacDonagh, *Pattern,* 64. For the text of the 1803 law, see Great Britain, *Statutes at Large,* 43 Geo. III 1803 (44), 189–97.

26. Jones, "Background to Immigration," 9–10.

27. The French Declaration of the Rights of Man guaranteed "free sojourn and free circulation," and the Constitution of 1791 provided "freedom to move about, to remain, and to leave." However, article 17 of the civil code subsequently deprived Frenchmen of their citizenship if they established themselves abroad with no intention of returning; Louis Chevalier, "Émigration française au XIXe siècle," *Études d'histoire moderne et contemporaine* 1 (1947): 127–71.

28. David W. Galenson, "The Rise and Fall of Indentured Servitude in the Americas: An Economic Analysis," *Journal of Economic History* 46 (1984): 13.

29. *NWR,* June 21, 1817; August 23, 1817; September 27, 1817; May 4 and 11, 1816; November 9, 1816; December 14, 1816; March 22, 1817.

30. Cited in *NWR,* April 29, 1820, 157–58. The original text, "The republic, he said, invites none to come; it will not keep out those who have the courage to cross the Atlantic," is more sharply worded than the paraphrase presented by Hansen in *Atlantic Migration,* 97.

31. Daniel Walker Howe, *The Political Culture of the American Whigs* (Chicago: University of Chicago Press, 1979), 43–68.

32. B. R. Mitchell, *European Historical Statistics* (New York: Columbia University Press, 1976), 24.

33. Edward P. Thompson, *The Making of the English Working Class* (New York: Vintage, 1963), 603, 700, 705.

34. Albert O. Hirschman, *Exit, Voice and Loyalty* (Cambridge, Mass.: Harvard University Press, 1970), 102–3.

35. Thompson, *English Working Class,* 621.

36. J. C. Beckett, *The Making of Modern Ireland, 1603–1923* (New York: Alfred A. Knopf, 1973), 173, 244, 272; Mitchell, *European Historical Statistics,* 21; Barbara Kerr, "Irish Seasonal Migration to Great Britain 1800–1838," *Irish Historical Studies* 3 (1942–43): 365–80; J. H. Clapham, "Irish Immigration into Great Britain in the Nineteenth Century," *Bulletin of the International Committee of Historical Sciences,* vol. 5 (1933): 596–604; Eric J. Hobsbawm, *Industry and Empire* (Baltimore: Penguin, 1969), 309–12.

37. Thompson, *English Working Class,* 430.

38. Jones, "Background to Immigration," 11.

39. Johnston, *British Emigration Policy,* 143.

40. Brinley Thomas, *Migration and Economic Growth: A Study of Great Britain and the Atlantic Economy* (1954; repr. London: Cambridge University Press, 1973), 3.

41. Walpole, "Humanitarian Movement," 202–3; Johnston, *British Emigration Policy,* 119–20.

42. Johnston, *British Emigration Policy,* 14; Hobsbawm, *Industry and Empire,* 105; Mark Blaug, "The Myth of the Old Poor Law and the Making of the New," *Journal of Economic History* 23, no. 2 (June 1963): 180–81.

43. Johnston, *British Emigration Policy,* 14–16, 32, 122; Walpole, "Humanitarian Movement," 204.

44. Edwin C. Guillet, *The Great Migration: The Atlantic Crossing by Sailing Ship Since 1770* (Toronto: Thomas Nelson and Sons, 1937), 24; Jones, "Background to Immigration," 40. See also Charlotte Erickson, ed., *Emigration from Europe, 1815–1914: Select Documents* (London: A. and C. Black 1987), 137; and J. C. Beckett, *The Making of Modern Ireland, 1603–1923* (New York: Alfred A. Knopf, 1973), 319.

45. Jones, "Background to Immigration," 11.

46. Johnston, *British Emigration Policy,* 122, 123; Walpole, "Humanitarian Movement," 204.

47. Walpole, "Humanitarian Movement," 206.

48. Since statistical information pertaining to transatlantic movement in the first half of the nineteenth century is notoriously unreliable and practically nonexistent with respect to movement between British North America and the United States, the estimates cited are used here as indicators of general trends *as they appeared to decision makers at the time.* They are based on the study of available statistics from British official sources compiled by N. H. Carrier and J. R. Jeffrey, *External Migration: A Study of Available Statistics 1815–1910* (London: General Registry Office, 1951), 17–30, and by the U.S. Bureau of the Census, *Historical Statistics of the United States,*

Colonial Times to 1970 (Washington, D.C.: Government Printing Office, 1975), 57, with additional gleanings from Jones, "Background to Immigration," 26–32.

49. Fred H. Hitchins, *The Colonial Land and Emigration Commission* (Philadelphia: University of Pennsylvania Press, 1931), 2, 7; R. K. Webb, *Modern England: From the 18th Century to the Present* (New York: Dodd, Mead, 1972), 214–17.

50. Webb, *Modern England*, 243.

51. Beckett, *Making of Modern Ireland*, 320.

52. Erickson, *Emigration from Europe*, 127; Great Britain, *External Migration*, 30.

53. J. D. Gould, "European Inter-Continental Emigration: The Role of 'Diffusion' and 'Feedback,'" *Journal of European Economic History* 9 (1980): 267–315.

54. Abbott, *Historical Aspects*, 86.

55. Jacques Henripin, "From Acceptance of Nature to Control: The Demography of the French Canadians Since the Seventeenth Century," in *French-Canadian Society*, ed. Marcel Rioux and Yves Martin (Toronto: McClelland and Stewart, 1964), 1:207–9; Helen Taft Manning, *The Revolt of French Canada, 1800–1835: A Chapter in the History of the British Commonwealth* (London: Macmillan, 1962), esp. 16, 203, 205–6.

56. Webb, *Modern England*, 216; Norman Macdonald, *Canada 1763–1841: Immigration and Settlement; The Administration of Imperial Land Regulation* (London: Longmans, Green and Co., 1939), 24; *Canadian Yearbook* (Toronto: Albert Hewett, 1957–58), 165; Hitchins, *Colonial Land*, 193; Erickson, *Emigration from Europe*, 160–65.

57. Hitchins, *Colonial Land*, 33n85; Mason Wade, *The French Canadians 1760–1967*, rev. ed. (Toronto: Macmillan, 1968), 195–99.

58. MacDonagh, *Pattern*, 144.

59. Hitchins, *Colonial Land*; Erickson, *Emigration from Europe*, 122.

60. Erickson, 132.

61. Hitchins, *Colonial Land*, 300.

62. Gould, "European Inter-Continental Emigration," 616.

63. Mack Walker, *Germany and the Emigration, 1816–1885* (Cambridge, Mass.: Harvard University Press, 1964), 16, 20, 25.

64. Maldwyn Jones, *American Immigration* (Chicago: University of Chicago Press, 1960), 100–101.

65. Camille Maire, *En route pour l'Amérique, L'odyssée des émigrants en France au XIXe siècle* (Nancy: Presses Universitaires de Nancy, 1993). See also, in this volume, Weil (chapter 5) and Van Eijl and Lucassen (chapter 7).

66. Erickson, *Emigration from Europe*, 128.

67. Walker, *Germany*, 75, 169, 171, 173; Erickson, *Emigration from Europe*, 175.

68. Walker, *Germany*, 75.

69. Jones, *American Immigration*, 102.

70. See Abbott, *Historical Aspects*, 152–55.

71. Jones, *American Immigration,* 103; Franklin D. Scott, "Sweden's Constructive Opposition to Emigration," *Journal of Modern History* 37 (September 1965): 307.

72. Cited in Chevalier, "Émigration française," 166.

73. Erickson, *Emigration from Europe,* 29; Chevalier, "Émigration française," 136, 132; André Armengaud, *La population française au XXe siècle* (Paris: Presses Universitaires de France, 1973), 85–93; U.S. Bureau of the Census, *Historical Statistics,* 57.

74. Chevalier, "Émigration française," 134. See esp. Weil, chapter 5 in this volume.

75. Abbott, *Historical Aspects,* 150.

76. Patrick O'Brien and Caglar Keyder, *Economic Growth in Britain and France 1780–1914: Two Paths to the Twentieth Century* (London: Allen and Unwin, 1978), 189–90.

77. Ibid., 194.

78. This analysis is elaborated in Aristide R. Zolberg's "The Making of Flemings and Walloons, 1830–1914," *Journal of Interdisciplinary History* 5, no. 2 (Fall 1974): 212–67. See also Zolberg, "Wanted but Not Welcome: Alien Labor in Western Development," in *Population in an Interacting World,* ed. William Alonso, 36–74 (Cambridge, Mass.: Harvard University Press, 1987).

79. Thompson, *English Working Class,* 429–44. See also Marx's analysis of the political effects of Irish migration on the British working class, as cited in Michael Hechter, *Internal Colonialism: The Celtic Fringe in British National Development, 1536–1966* (Berkeley: University of California Press, 1975), 15.

80. This is a major argument in George J. Borjas's "The Economics of Immigration," *Journal of Economic Literature* 3, no. 2 (December 1994), 1667–1717.

81. Johnston, *British Emigration Policy,* 132.

82. Thomas, *Migration and Economic Growth;* Jones, "Background to Immigration"; J. D. Gould, "European Inter-Continental Emigration 1815–1914: Patterns and Causes," *Journal of European Economic History* 8, no. 3 (1979): 628–70.

83. See Schneider, chapter 9 in this volume.

PART II

NATION BUILDING AND THE ADMINISTRATIVE FRAMEWORK

3

EMIGRATION AND NATION BUILDING
DURING THE MASS MIGRATIONS FROM EUROPE

Donna R. Gabaccia, Dirk Hoerder,
and Adam Walaszek

Is it possible for a country to imagine itself a "nation of emigrants" in the same way the United States has proclaimed itself a "nation of immigrants"? With as many as fifty-five million persons (a fifth of Europe's population in 1800) leaving for North America (thirty-five million), South America (eight million), and other parts of the world between 1815 and 1939, and with a larger number moving about within Europe, mobility was a demographic fact of life during Europe's great age of nationalism.[1] It was especially common in those newer nations that formed after the first national states—Spain, Portugal, Britain, France—emerged out of the empire-building, imperial wars, and revolutions of the first era of European expansion.[2] Surrounded by demographic change, builders of newer nations could easily have defined themselves as "nations of emigrants" had they so chosen. But did they?

It seems an unlikely choice. Emigration's negative demographic impact made it too easy to cast emigrants in the role of traitors, draining rather than building national strength. But humans regularly espouse improbable ideas, and historian Emilio Franzina has proposed a positive relationship between emigration and nation building that is worth exploring, whether or not any country ultimately imagined itself as a "nation of emigrants."[3]

Migration and the concept of the nation are closely entwined. The phenomenon scholars now call "emigration" exists in a Janus-like relationship with "immigration." "Emigrants" are simultaneously also "immigrants"; distinguishing the two makes sense only in a world organized as a system of states that accept each other's "embrace"[4] of particular populations as subjects (or citizens) and that recognize international borders as significant dividers between national territories. It is the point of view of the national state that transforms an emigrant (exiting from one national territory) into an immigrant (entering a second national territory). By focusing on policy and terminology toward the mobile, we inevitably discover national self-understandings.

This chapter seeks to identify constitutive elements of the relationship of migration and nation building in three newer European nations known for their especially sizeable contributions to the mass "emigrations" of the long nineteenth century. Germany, Italy, and Poland each had a distinctive national history that must be treated as unique in many respects. In the case of Italy, "emigration" (from northern regions to transalpine Europe and to the Plata River area of South America) began prior to its unification as a country of about twenty-six million in 1861; national debates arose only with the enormous exodus of fourteen million (from all corners of the new country) that followed between 1876 and 1914, and continued from 1915 to 1945 with a significant movement of four million more.[5] By contrast, the formation of the second German Reich in 1871 occurred toward the end of a mass migration that lasted for more than a century—first from the southwestern provinces in the late 1700s and early 1800s and then again from 1846 to 1857, and later from the center and northeast, from 1864 to 1873 and 1879 to 1893. As many as five million left the territory of what became the German Reich (a country of about 49.5 million in 1890) between the 1760s and the early 1890s. Thereafter, with rapid industrialization, emigration dwindled while foreigners began seeking work in Germany.[6] Nation building also overlapped with mass emigration from Poland in the nineteenth century. Partitioned for 123 years between the Hapsburg and Romanov dynasties and first Hohenzollern and then German empires, territories of the formerly independent republic of Poland and Lithuania of the eighteenth century attained nationhood only after World War I; by then ten million Poles—of a total population of about thirty million in 1920—had left, often temporarily, for Germany, France, Austria-Hungary, and the Americas.[7] Another two million departed the second Polish republic in the interwar years.

Despite differences in the timing of migration and nation building, nationalists in all three cases demanded that the nation "protect" its mobile members. No matter how negatively it viewed emigration, each national state also "embraced" those who left it. Debates about migration and the terminology affixed to mobile persons by laws, statistical records, and state agencies evolved in tandem with changing national concepts. All three countries reserved the term "emigration" for those who left home permanently. All generated one or more discourses that portrayed emigration as a vital contribution to national strength. After the 1890s, nationalists in all three places dreamed that emigration would spread their cultures to less developed areas of the world, increasing their international influence. With World War I, as the world itself moved into a half century of international warfare, and new world countries imposed sharp limits on immigration, the national states of Poland, Germany, and Italy all sought to bind their citizens abroad—whether imagined as *Polonia, italiani nel mondo,* or *Auslandsdeutsche*—more closely to their national homelands.

GERMANY

Germany provides a striking early example of the difficulties of nation building in a mobile, multiethnic world. Cultural nationalists of the early nineteenth century were quite aware that Europe's German speakers lived widely scattered in linguistically, religiously, and culturally diverse areas. Linguistic variation among German speakers was itself notorious. Even those living under German rulers were, in 1815, divided among small principalities, free cities, and the multilingual and multiethnic Hohenzollern empire (with its large populations of Jews, Poles, and Sorbs). Large German-speaking populations lived in the cantons of republican and multilingual Switzerland, in the culturally diverse Hapsburg empire (and later dual monarchy), and, farther east in Russia, under the rule of a Romanov dynasty that repeatedly invited Germans to settle its agricultural frontiers and to send craftsmen, skilled workers, and professionals to its cities. Germans had traveled to British North America since the 1700s; by 1870, they were found in the cities as well as in the vast, internal farming districts of the United States, Canada, Argentina, Brazil, and Mexico.[8]

Discussions of *Auswanderung* (the permanent movement of persons out of and away from the territory that became modern Germany in 1871) began in regional debates in a "Germany" that did not yet exist. These typically pitted followers of eighteenth-century mercantilist (cameralist) ideas—"that emigration of subjects is detrimental for the respective state" (1824)—against those who claimed that loss of a population impoverished by insufficient local resources instead provided a politically useful safety valve.[9] Since they portrayed migrants as helping their state by leaving, proponents of emigration wanted rulers to support and protect them; the German port of Bremen, hoping to improve the reputation and competitive position of its shippers, passed regulations to protect emigrants in 1832.[10] Supporters of migration, especially cultural nationalists, saw migrants carrying German culture and spreading national influence, while some noted that paupers and prisoners improved their circumstances by migrating.

Terminology for migration evolved within these regional debates. German speakers in the eighteenth century borrowed from French, transforming *émigrés* into *Emigranten,* for example, when they discussed the German migrants fleeing to the Americas to avoid religious persecution. By the 1820s and 1830s, debates over migrations to North America referred to the mobile almost exclusively as *Auswanderer* (one who has departed from a place). A national viewpoint was also obvious in discussions of those traveling in groups to farm in frontier agricultural regions. These *Ansiedler* (settlers) formed a community that, whether in Texas, Iowa, or Russia, was termed a *Colonie* rather than merely a *Siedlung* (settlement). Concerns for the nation motivated the formation of colonization societies whether by states and their rulers or by middle-class Germans encouraging migration of the poor—persons who could make no claims to either *Wirtschaftsbürgertum* (economic citizenry) or *Bildungsbürgertum* (educated or cultured citizenry) at home.

Between the 1848 revolutions and the formation of the German empire in 1871, migrations from Germany again increased sharply, debates over migration became national, and discussions of migration now used the terms *Auswanderung* and *Auswanderer* (with their assumptions about a national territory) almost exclusively. In the Revolution of 1848, a Committee on the National Economy of the National Assembly called for protective legislation,[11] and to this old demand added a new one: recognition of the right to emigrate. In 1866–67 the constitution of the North German Federation made emigration a federal and (after 1871) a national responsibility. But emigration was so massive in the 1850s that the government of the German federation refused to introduce a law regulating it for fear that mere mention of the topic would raise the volume of departures.

With the formation of the second empire in 1871, Germany "embraced" as citizens all those born on its national territories (jus soli), regardless of culture or language; this, for example, gave German citizenship to the ethnic Poles in the eastern region of Prussia.[12] German emigrants did not lose their citizenship by leaving but only by serving in foreign armies or renouncing loyalties to their German rulers. Cultural nationalists continued to express pride in German presence around the world, although emigration was relatively low in the 1870s (a period of economic depression in the United States). Nationalists' awareness of demands (notably in the United States) for the assimilation and naturalization of immigrants encouraged fears that emigrants from Germany would not long retain their German language, customs, or "racial" characteristics. Demands for state-financed emigrant colonies produced little action. Instead, after 1871 a *Reichskommissar für das Auswanderungswesen* (Imperial Commissioner for the Conditions of Emigration) merely assumed responsibility for inspecting emigration ships and assuring adherence to regulations governing safety and sanitation.[13] Most counseling of and services for emigrants remained in the hands of the churches and their missions, even when emigration resumed vigorously again in the 1880s.

Thereafter, fears of emigration's negative impact on the nation increased, and the concept of the German nation changed. When a committee of the National Diet suggested a liberal emigration law in the 1880s, representatives of the large eastern landowners protested, fearing higher labor costs. Issues of class conflict shaped debates: Germany's 1878 antisocialist law induced politically motivated emigration for several decades. The kaiser questioned social democratic workers' national loyalties, whether they intended to emigrate or not, and summarily labeled them *vaterlandslose Gesellen* (workers without a fatherland). Germany's growing labor and Social Democratic movements demanded both political representation for workers and the economic reforms that would allow their members to recognize that "your America is here."[14] In this way, awareness of emigration opportunities made countries in the Americas points of reference for domestic debates about the political and economic reform of Germany.

By the time Germany passed its first emigration law in 1897, emigration to the Americas and elsewhere was waning and the concept of the German nation was becoming racialized. Henceforth, Germany's emigration policy aimed to strengthen its emerging colonial empire. The 1897 law extended protective regulations, prohibited the recruitment of emigrants, and punished those who solicited women emigrants to work as prostitutes. But it also made the licensing of agents and entrepreneurs running emigration-related businesses the responsibility of top political institutions, and it bypassed existing church emigrant aid societies in order to create an emigrant information bureau within the German Colonial Association. The state hoped thereby to channel emigrants toward Germany's colonies in Africa or to destinations where they might retain their language and culture (as they believed was possible in South America).[15] This hope was not fulfilled; imperial policies mobilized few migrants.

Besides attention to *Erhalt des Deutschtums* (retention of Germanness, often understood as a racial inheritance) and colonial expansion, discus-

sions of emigration after 1890 focused on the "threat of over-foreigniza-
tion" (*Überfremdungsgefahr*) as large numbers of foreigners began to enter
Germany, either to work or to travel to its emigration ports. Despite a half
century of debates over *Auswanderung*, Germans did not view those arriving as an *Einwanderung* (immigration) of *Einwanderer* (immigrants)
but rather as an *Ausländerzufuhr* (import of foreigners) of *Fremdarbeiter*
(alien workers). Many demanded a national *Abwehrpolitik* (defense policy)
to be conducted at the borders of Germany's national territories. The goal
was to limit the racial threat to the German nation from a growing population of foreigners. Debates quickened once it was recognized that foreigners were almost 2 percent of Germany's population at the time of the
1910 census. However, Germans also still drew sharp distinctions between
Inlandspolen (ethnic Poles who were German citizens) and labor migrants
from Polish-speaking Austria and Russia; the latter were required to leave
after each harvest.[16]

Modern Germany had, since its creation in 1871, been a "small Germany,"
leaving the Hapsburg's Austrian German speakers outside of the Hohenzollern's Reich. A century of mass migration left an even smaller proportion
of both central Europe's and the worldwide diaspora of Germans living in
the Reich's multiethnic territory (which included not only large numbers
of Poles but Masurians and Alsatians as well; Jews—who spoke German—
were still considered Germans).[17] Rising numbers of non-German workers
in Germany set the stage for a hot debate over a new citizenship law in 1913.
When the Reich was formed in 1871, citizenship had not received much attention; in fact, the "citizens" of Germany were still "subjects" of the state's
rulers. In the new, increasingly chauvinist context of the early twentieth century, the new citizenship law attempted to extend the reach of the German
nation far beyond its national territories. Working-class Social Democrats
and liberals seemed to lose in their defense of jus soli principles: the new law
made descent or "blood" (jus sanguinis) the basis of German citizenship,
thus binding those outside Germany more closely to their national homeland.[18] The new law did not, however, as is usually assumed, totally eliminate jus soli grounds for citizenship: for one thing, too many "non-Germans" already lived in Germany as citizens.[19] Natives of German colonies
and the children born in Germany of alien workers could, in fact, natural-
ize.[20] Nevertheless, the law's intention was unmistakable, for it declared jus
soli "incompatible with the purity of our race and the original peculiarities
of our people."[21] In an imperialist move, the new law also extended citizenship to the considerable population of descendants of German parents liv-

ing abroad, expanding the potential "embrace" of its national state into the Americas and central and eastern Europe.[22]

Only a few years later, Germany's territorial and population losses in World War I intensified the fears evident in these debates about citizenship. Demand for foreign labor dropped during the postwar economic crisis, but government documents, including the census, now distinguished between the German-speaking and *fremdsprachige* (foreign-language-speaking) portions of the German population. The German nation itself was no longer the *Volk* (people) imagined by early nineteenth-century cultural nationalists but a blood or descent group. While Weimar Republic educators insisted on the hegemony of German culture, they replaced the older term *Deutschtum* (Germanness) with *Deutsches Volkstum* (German peopleness);[23] non-Germans in Germany increasingly organized as *nationale Minderheiten* (national or ethnic minorities). Although Germany had in fact lost about 6.5 million of its "non-Germans" in 1918, new census categories revealed for the first time how numerous the national minorities were: 1.1 million Polish people; 174,000 Masurians; 29,500 Czech people; 20,000 Lithuanians; and 14,000 Danes. In each group, between 92 and 98 percent were monolingual.[24]

A new law protecting emigrants passed in 1924, but otherwise the Weimar Republic did little to change Germany's citizenship or migration policies. Anticipating German "return migrants" (*deutsche Rückwanderer*) from its lost colonies, government offices for "return migration, emigration, and immigration" were established mainly to discourage emigration or to direct emigrants to places (such as South America) where *Deutsches Volkstum* supposedly flourished.[25] At the same time, and building on the long tradition of viewing emigration as a way to spread German culture's influence abroad, new research institutes and publications on the *Grenzdeutsche* (Germans living outside of Germany but close to the new borders in Alsace, Lorraine, or Poland) and *Auslandsdeutsche* farther away (in the Soviet Union and the United States) took on new urgency. Later National Socialist efforts to bring other European Germans *heim ins Reich* (home into the empire) and to have the support of the *Auslandsdeutsche* for new empire building built on this foundation.

ITALY: EMIGRATI, COLONI, AND ITALIANI ALL'ESTERO

Despite an inauspicious beginning, Italy's national state ultimately transformed many of its recent emigrants into supporters of their national homeland. Yet some scholars have viewed Italy in 1861 as a "state without a nation."[26] At the time, the loyalties of Italy's huge population of poor peasants and workers were uncertain. In fact, Italy's early cultural nationalists—concerned with Italy's "civilizing mission" and the nation's role in the creation of European culture—had argued there was no place for them in the nation at all. Observers after 1861 noted that "sentiments of *italianità* [Italianness] among our peasants are not very lively."[27] Italy's elite faced the task of building a nation ("making Italians," one called it) on a foundation that was already shaky before emigration attained substantial proportions.

Emigration was at first a peripheral concern of Italy's new government. During the 1860s, the survival and boundaries of Italy were still in question. Revolts in southern regions sparked a debate about the "problem of the Mezzogiorno [the south of Italy]," whose inhabitants were soon stigmatized as racially inferior. Incorporating Rome and Venice into national territory while failing to wrest other Italian speakers from Austrian rule seemed more important measures of national strength.

But mobility was never absent from the minds of state builders. A census taken immediately after unification in 1861—"almost before the smoke had cleared from the battlefields"—was the Italian state's first act of possession of its citizens, and it counted all born in Italy, whether they lived there or not.[28] The 1861 census reported a *popolazione fuori di regno* (population outside the realm) that numbered 400,000 citizens.[29] An 1865 civil code then "embraced" as citizens all born on Italian national soil, according to the principles of jus soli.[30] In 1871, census takers counted a million Italians "not present"—three-quarters had been absent for more than six months.[31] Shortly thereafter, Italy's newly appointed consuls provided additional information about a half million *italiani residente all'estero* (Italians abroad).[32] Clearly, the poor of Italy had become citizens. Among their few civil rights was the liberty—regarded by Italian republicans as "incontestable"—to emigrate.[33]

From an early date, nationalists also linked *italiani all'estero* to empire building.[34] Even before unification, Italy's cultural nationalists had associated *colonizzazione* (colonization) with emigration.[35] And even while distracted by war and state building, nationalist writers like Cristoforo Negri (founder of the Italian Geographical Society) argued that Italians living outside Italy promised an expansive, larger (*più grande*) Italian nation.[36] But while writers in the 1860s expounded on *colonizzazione* and celebrated the formation of migrant Italian *colonie* (colonies, usually called "Little Italys" in English), they rarely called migrants *coloni* (a term for both settlers and agriculturalists).[37] In his book *Delle colonie e dell'emigrazione d'italiani all'estero*, Leone Carpi referred to Italians outside Italy as "our *connazionali* (co-nationals)" and portrayed them as attached to their homeland (*madrepatria,* or motherland birthplace) through blood and descent, trade, and commerce.[38] For Carpi, inhabitants of Italy's "colonies" were more than citizens. Thus, Carpi counted among the *italiani all'estero* those Italian speakers in the eastern Mediterranean who were descendants of Venetian or Genoese traders; indeed, he saw Venice and Genoa as models for empire building.

In the late 1870s and 1880s, as migration rose, so did controversies over it.[39] Discussions of *italiani all'estero* almost disappeared as more negative portrayals of emigration seized national attention. Italy began statistically enumerating emigration in 1876, albeit in somewhat peculiar fashion. Rather than count persons as they passed through ports or border roads and rail stations, the Ministry of Agriculture, Industry, and Commerce (publisher of *Statistica della emigrazione italiana*) required local officials to report the numbers applying for a *nulla osta*—a certificate of good conduct required of those leaving their *patria* (birthplace or hometown).[40] Of course, such counts measured little more than intentions to depart. Discussions of these *espatriati* (expatriates) were almost as common as discussions of *emigrati*. The large numbers of returning migrants (probably more than 50 percent) went unrecorded.

Shortly after the government began counting the mobile, a nationwide inquest into life and work in Italy's impoverished rural districts intensified debates. The inquest's investigators argued that some migrations drained the strength of the nation while others built it. Temporary and seasonal migrations leaving mountain areas for well-known transalpine European destinations were described as "well organized" and a "normal part of life" that contributed vitally important infusions of foreign currency to national wealth.[41] By contrast, "unorganized" or "artificial" migrations of peasants (from Venice and the south) were provoked by steamship representatives and recruiters; these were dangerous.[42] Because they were long-distance moves and supposedly permanent, transoceanic emigrations especially endangered the nation.[43] (Until 1904, the *Statistica* routinely, and incorrectly, reported all migrants destined for the Americas as permanent departures, and all traveling to Europe as temporary sojourners.)[44]

Permanent, "unorganized" emigrations endangered citizens too. Investigators insisted that peasants boarding ships in Genoa and Naples did not even know their destinations. They argued that a government should do more than guarantee a citizen's right to leave; it should protect (but also "discipline") transatlantic emigrations undertaken by ignorant citizens with "an exaggerated sense of individual liberty."[45] Calls for governmental action had limited effect, however. Italy's first emigration law, passed in 1888, was generally acknowledged as ineffective even in regulating ticket agents, labor contractors, and transatlantic sea vessels; it completely ignored transalpine migrations. As in Germany, protective work was left entirely to the consuls and to private secular and church "missions" to emigrants.

By then, too, the *Statistica della emigrazione* had established that migrants from Sicily, Calabria, Basilicata, Puglie, and Abruzzi-Molise—Italy's southernmost provinces—emigrated mainly to America. More Northern Italians, by contrast, went to other European countries. Thus, nation-threatening "emigrations" emerged from the rebellious, southern districts that positivist scientists and military generals had already portrayed as backward, racially inferior, and criminal. By declaring emigration a southern phenomenon, contemporaries reinforced their view of the *mezzogiorno* as an ungovernable danger to national strength. (Tellingly, a second parliamentary inquest on Italian peasant life, published in 1909, scrutinized life only in the south and Sicily; it assessed emigration's impact negatively, noting how it inflated costs for land and labor, spread tuberculosis, and encouraged moral depravity and over-work among women.)[46] Contemporary debates of emigration thus rendered invisible the majority of impoverished migrants who actually left from Italy's center and north.[47] Even today, many Italians believe emigration was an exclusively southern movement.

Debate continued with increases in emigration after 1893, but a changing international context also again linked emigration more positively to Italy's empire-building aspirations. In 1891, Brazil's new constitution declared all foreigners who had been in the country already in 1889 to be citizens. Yet under Italy's 1865 Civil Code, a person who became a citizen of a foreign country automatically lost his Italian citizenship. Together with Portugal, Spain, and Austria-Hungary, Italy denounced Brazil's "predatory naturalization" as a denial of individual freedom.[48] Brazil's act raised troubling questions about how effectively migrants could in fact carry Italian national influence into the wider world.

Events in 1896 and 1898 also revealed competing understandings of the state's role in coordinating migration and colonial expansion. Outspoken imperialists in the 1880s had imagined empire building on a Roman model, with the Italian state pursuing colonies in Africa. There, Italy gained Somalia (as a protectorate) in 1889 and claimed Eritrea as a colony shortly thereafter. The country's subsequent defeat to Ethiopian troops at Adowa in 1896 smashed advocates' (such as Prime Minister and Sicilian Francesco Crispi's) hopes that African colonies could absorb southern emigrants otherwise "lost" to America. But in 1898, as the result of a Turin commercial exhibition that devoted a special section of its space to the economic activities of *italiani all'estero*, economist Luigi Einaudi, along with other liberals, revived the older vision of "voluntary" or "free" colonization, championed earlier by Leone Carpi. Einaudi's book *Il principe mercante* focused attention on the entrepreneurial Italians living in the Plata region of South America.[49] Einaudi asserted that these businessmen were like the Venetian and Genoese merchants of the Middle Ages. Without any state intervention, the Italian flag would follow businessmen, ships, and Italian consumers, thus "Italianizing" Argentina in the same way the British had shaped North America. With remittances from emigrants pouring into Italy, the benefits to the nation of "free colonization" seemed self-evident.[50]

The first decade of the century was the peak of Italy's mass migrations. The Italian state's belated decision to regulate and protect emigration more effectively in 1901, when it created a General Emigration Commission, scarcely changed Italy's awkward methods for enumerating migration. The result was inflated estimates of Italian emigration that produced occasionally panicky assessments of emigration as a hemorrhage draining the blood of the national "body." But Italy did assert its power to protect citizens, temporarily suspending migration to both Brazil and Argentina. Terminology for migrants changed little in the process. "Emigration" still referred mainly to transoceanic movements. The commission's *Bollettino dell' emigrazione* (Bulletin of Emigration) spoke of *emigrati* almost exclusively when discussing ports or the protection of migrants prior to embarkation or on board ships to America, as well as in "warnings to emigrants" about disease, unemployment, and strikes abroad. Elsewhere it called migrants *italiani all'estero, espatriati, lavoratori* (workers), or even *immigrati*.

Demands for state recognition and support for the *italiani all'estero* mounted after 1900 as a new generation of Italian nationalists, including Enrico Corradini, Gabriele D'Annunzio, and (after 1910) the Italian Nationalist Association, again called on the Italian state to take up the mantel of the Roman Empire and provide outlets for Italy's "proletarian nation."[51] New voices demanding political representation for Italians abroad and a meeting of those living abroad came mainly from within Italy, however.[52] Held in October 1908 and again in June 1911 under the auspices of the newly founded Italian Colonial Institute (and without significant representation of emigrants from abroad), the first and second congresses of *italiani all'estero* considered a wide variety of issues related to nationality and citizenship, from military service to political representation.[53] Working through Catholic missionary channels, an independent initiative created a new organization for *italiani all'estero* called Italica Gens.[54]

Demands for a new citizenship law predictably followed, intensified by Italy's 1911 war with Turkey over Libya. Already in 1903, the Emigration Commission had addressed questions about the nationality of Italian migrants in Europe. Critics insisted that Italy's citizenship law was "out of step" with other modern states.[55] Much as in Germany, a new law passed in 1912 now based migrants' citizenship on jus sanguinis: nationality could be revoked only by a willful act of a mature citizen; their children born abroad (who acquired citizenship by birth in American nations) could revoke their Italian nationality only when they achieved the age of majority. In addition, even those who revoked their citizenship while abroad could easily reclaim it if they returned to live in Italy for two years.

When World War I finally delivered to Italy the Austrian territories it had long sought, increasing Italy's population and territory, more than nine million migrants from Italy still lived abroad. Along with their children, they increased Italy's population of citizens by 25 percent; they also now possessed a juridically "strong" Italian nationality that could not easily be discarded. Much like their counterparts in Germany, Italy's liberal legislators had quietly constructed an important cornerstone for the imperialist and racist policies that would follow under Mussolini's fascist dictatorship. After coming to power in 1922, Mussolini at first did little about either his proclaimed opposition to emigration or nationalists' hopes that the fascist state could "valorize" migration by making it advantageous to nation and emigrant alike. In 1926, however, Mussolini abolished the Emigration Commission, replacing it with a Directorship for Italians Abroad, with its activities overseen by the Colonial Office. Passports were soon out of reach to most employed Italians. For the next decade, Mussolini aimed at having the support of the *italiani all'estero* for his policies; and in more than one country—most notably in the United States during Italy's 1935 invasion of Ethiopia—his plea that the *italiani all'estero* protect and support their homeland did not go unheeded.

POLAND AND POLONIA

Polish nationalists too were concerned with the protection of emigrants; at least from the 1890s onward, they also devoted considerable attention to migrants' role in nation building. In rather sharp contrast to Italy (where homeland elites invented the *italiani all'estero*), the term *Polonia* (which we would today translate as "Polish diaspora") was used first in the United States in 1875. Already in 1863, emigrants in the United States had reacted to the Polish revolt in Russia by organizing a Central Polish Committee; other nationalist organizations followed, and Juliusz Andrzejkowicz, a founder of the Polish National Alliance, even believed that the foundations for an independent Poland were being created in the United States. Only twenty years later did the Reverend Jan Ciemieniewski introduce the term Polonia to central Europe.[56] By then, Polish nationalists were paying close attention to migration and debating its impact.[57]

Unsurprisingly, it was the democratic Polish nationalists who in the 1890s first showed strong interest in the migrations of thousands of plebeian Polish-speakers. For Jan Ludwik Popławski, one of the founders and principle ideologues of this group, migrations among the three imperial portions of formerly Polish territory were of little concern; these were temporary, had no effect on the country's "national substance," and (on the contrary) revealed that, although divided, Poland continued to form a "natural unit," one "living economic system, one big labor market." Nationalists wrote of "emigration" only when Poles departed for regions inhabited by other peoples. Thus, what Germans deemed an internal migration (in other words, of Poles who were German subjects going from Posen to the Rheinland), Polish nationalists called *emigracja* (emigration). Like Italians and Germans, Polish speakers also identified overseas migrations—to the United States, Argentina, and Brazil—as "*wychodźstwo stałe*" (permanent emigration). Popławski at first distinguished permanent emigration from "*wychodźstwo zarobkowe*" (labor migration) and considered the former a threat.[58]

Why? It seemed at first obvious that any nationalist movement, to succeed, needed a strong, growing, and supportive population. Thus, a prominent Socialist in Austria called emigration "Galicia's gravest social sickness."[59] The Peasants' Party, formed in Galicia in 1895, agreed.[60] Such negative assessments did not extend to the migration of local Russyns, Ruthenians, or Jews, however, since these emigrations were believed to help "Polonize" the local populations.[61] As late as World War I, nationalists occasionally referred to the emigration of Polish speakers as "bloodletting."[62] Educated and urban nationalists sometimes claimed that emigrants were in any case illiterate people, with no great love of the Polish nation or sense of national community, who still adhered mainly to their villages, towns, or "private homelands."[63] From abroad came grim reports of emigrants' lack of national sentiments. In Canada and the United States, emigrants were reported to "depolonize." If there was to be a Polonia, this suggested, nationalists in Europe had much work to do.[64]

But not all among the nationalists viewed even permanent emigration so negatively, and many observed that emigrants discovered their national loyalties and promptly forgot their regional differences once confronted with persons of radically different cultures.[65] Already in 1879, Agaton Giller, an exile living at the time in Switzerland, had reported that "every Polish peasant, from whatever Polish province he comes . . . when transferred to a strange soil among foreigners develops a Polish sentiment and consciousness of his national character."[66] By the early twentieth century, most agreed that even the peasant who went abroad "learns from other nationalities how to respect what he has and how to love his homeland."[67] The development of an almost spiritual national consciousness among emigrants was as common in Budapest, where Poles lived among Magyars, Germans, Italians, Croats, Slovaks, and Czechs, as it was in the equally multiethnic immigrant cities of the United States. Even Popławski had to admit, "It is not a negative element of our life," and the democratic nationalists' journal on migration and diaspora life, *Przegląd Wszechpolski,* concurred.[68]

It may seem odd that nationalists who sought to escape colonial status under Germany, Austria, and Russia would then link their more positive evaluation of emigration to the "colonial potential" they saw in the Polish nation.[69] Polish nationalists proved as concerned with cultural retention and international influence as their Italian or German counterparts, and like them, they saw South America as holding particularly good prospects for emigrants to succeed economically while preserving their Polishness. Like their counterparts, they pinned hopes on the formation of "homogeneous agricultural colonies" of Polish emigrants, especially in Parana in Brazil, where Józef Siemiradzki insisted a "New Poland" was emerging, and where, he predicted, Poles, Italians, and Germans would soon divide south Brazil among them.[70]

By the onset of World War I, then, nationalists' images of Polish migrants and their nation had changed considerably. Few hesitated in calling emigrants to the Americas anything other than "Poles." Views of Polonia as an expression of a national culture were now racialized by a vision expressed by Wacław Kruszka, the first historian of Poles in North America, who declared, "Poland is not just land along the Vistula River but a collection of people with a common origin and lineage. Wherever a Pole settles, there a piece of Poland is born. Origin forms a nation, not soil, soil molds fellow citizens, not countrymen."[71] Without a national territory, nationalists could more easily view American Polonia as "the fourth district of Poland" (the other three were in the three European empires). Brazilian Polonia, in turn, became "the fifth district." Not long after the italiani all'estero met for the first time in Rome, the first meeting of worldwide Polonia (the Polish National Congress) was held in Washington, D.C.[72]

Polish nationalists achieved their dream of an independent Polish national state in 1918. While still in formation during the war, the government focused attention on the possibility of a large return of Poles who had either fled during the course of the war or been prohibited by Germany from returning; in 1917, the Ministry of Internal Affairs of the semi-autonomous Regency Council (established under German occupation of formerly Russian Poland) tried to help migrating Poles through a Re-emigration Department. By 1918, the Ministry of Public Health, Labor, and Social Welfare also had an emigration section,[73] and shortly thereafter a State Office for the Problems of Returning Prisoners, Refugees, and Workers (JUR) was created; it continued its work until the end of 1920. With immigration under intense scrutiny in the United States, and with the passage of draconian U.S. restrictions on European immigration between 1917 and 1924, Poland's new rulers also debated the impact of returnees from America. Already, during the war some had predicted mass unemployment for them while others hoped that returnees would help "Polonize" the multiethnic country and contribute to building the national economy through trade and commerce. Debates continued after the war, but since no massive return followed (and those who did return generally re-emigrated again to the United States), fears quickly abated.[74]

Concerns about migration were not foremost in defining Polish citizenship either. Instead, Poland's citizenship law, passed in 1920, reflected the international treaties that regulated it. The law seemed to honor jus soli at a time when Germany and Italy had instead moved toward jus sanguinis: former bearers of German, Austrian, Hungarian, and Russian citizenship assumed Polish citizenship if they lived on Polish territory on January 10, 1920. But Polish citizenship, too, could "travel" with its emigrants under the law, which also "embraced" through blood and kinship ties those Poles abroad who had parents permanently living in Polish territory. Dual citizenship, however, was forbidden: if a Pole naturalized, adopting the citizenship of the United States or France, he lost his Polish citizenship.[75]

As in Italy, Poland's new rulers in the 1920s saw emigration as "an evil necessity"—but also as a "politically delicate issue"[76] that was an element of the nation's foreign policy. Already in 1919, the government signed a treaty agreeing to provide Polish workers for France and heard opposition from Polish workers and peasants' groups that preferred the government to oppose emigrants' "depolonization" and help returnees.[77] Established in 1920, the new country's Emigration Office, which replaced the JUR, nevertheless became part of the Ministry of Labor; its main responsibilities were to prepare legislation, oversee the contracts of Polish workers traveling abroad, and prepare migration statistics. A 1927 regulation revealed the association of emigration with work when it defined the emigrant as "the Polish citizen who is leaving, or who has left, the territory of the Polish Republic in search of labor, or in order to work, or to join his spouse, relatives or kin who had emigrated previously."[78] Efforts to protect emigrants also soon followed. In 1924 the Polish Colonization Society renamed itself the Polish Emigration Society while its weekly journal, *Wychodźca* (The Emigrant), debated how Poland might best help its many emigrants.

This does not mean that nationalists' earlier linkage of emigration and colonization was forgotten with independence, however. Beginning in 1925, with a joint meeting of parliamentary and foreign affairs specialists on emigration, Poland's government considered ways to accommodate the necessity of emigration while directing emigrants toward countries where they could retain their Polishness and spread national influence.[79] Most attention focused on Brazil, although experts also discussed founding Polish settlements in southern France, European Turkey, Germany, the United States, Canada, Argentina, Uruguay, Peru, Chile, Brazil, Angola, Algeria, Morocco, Madagascar, and the Dutch Indies. Polish plans for colonization of Brazil resulted in exploration and the formation of settlement societies for Peruvian Montania and Brazilian Parana. No matter how unrealistic, this persistent dream of Polish colonies in South America continued well into the 1930s. As late as 1937, Poland signed an emigration convention with Bolivia allowing Polish settlements, but the onset of World War II prevented its ratification.[80]

While attempting to discourage or to direct the emigration of Poles toward South America, some Polish nationalists by the 1930s also argued for forced migrations for Ukrainian and Jewish citizens of Poland; using terminology little different from Germany's, they called them Poland's "national minorities."[81] The government took no action on these proposals but looked with sympathy on the spread of Zionist propaganda. And in 1936, the Ministry of Foreign Affairs actually began to develop an assisted emigration plan for Byelorussians and Ukrainians, and for Jews (mainly to Palestine).[82]

As in Italy, Poland's government in the 1920s and 1930s also attempted to "valorize" emigration by encouraging closer ties between Polonia, the new national homeland, and its new national state. Emigrants were seen and believed to be the "nation's power and wealth."[83] Polish excursions from the United States (commonly called "pilgrimages") received a warm welcome. In fact, apart from the many governmental agencies, at least twenty-five social organizations aimed to bring together Polonia and the new Poland in the 1920s, thus maintaining national and patriotic feelings among emigrants living abroad.[84]

After a May 1926 coup d'état by Jozef Pilsudski, Polish diplomats extended and politicized their activities in Polonia creating an "ideological transmission belt." In 1927 Polish officials began to prepare for the first Congress of Poles from Abroad. The meeting, held in Warsaw in July 1929, resulted in the creation of the Rada Organizacyjna Polaków z Zagranicy (Organizational Council of Poles from Abroad), with delegates from around the world. After 1932, when the government transferred oversight of emigration to the Ministry of Foreign Affairs, governmental efforts concentrated almost exclusively on guaranteeing Polonia's support of Pilsudski and his dictatorship.[85] A second Congress was held in 1934, and a World Alliance of Poles from Abroad (Światowy Związek Polaków z Zagranicy [Światpol]) formed: its motto was "Poland is for Poles but Poles are for Poland, and Poland exists wherever Poles are."[86] High expectations of political loyalty and support for an increasingly undemocratic government disturbed emigrants in many areas of Polonia. The Polish National Alliance stressed how different Polish-Americans had become from Poles in the homeland.[87] In France and the United States, Polish emigrants were especially hostile to *Światpol*'s efforts to create a politicized "transmission belt," while in Germany, Denmark, and South America, Polish emigrants more resembled their Italian counterparts who supported Mussolini's expansionist and racist foreign policy.[88]

CONCLUSION

Although the new countries of Germany, Italy, and Poland all lost millions of "their" nationals to emigration, none ultimately imagined itself as a "nation of emigrants." Terminology for migrants evolved with nationalist movements seeking to create independent states for the nations they imagined; they also reflected debates about nation, race, and citizenship within the broader Atlantic world. In Germany, the language for discussing human mobility became more national in the 1820s and 1830s as earlier references to *émigrés* and *Emigranten* gave way to discussions of *Auswanderer*; the existence of a discourse about *Auswanderung* did not, however, facilitate recognition of workers entering Germany to work after 1893 as *Einwanderer*. (When Germans used the term *Einwanderung*, they referred exclusively to Germans settling in the United States.) In Italy, debates referred interchangeably to the mobile as *emigrati* and *immigrati* into the twentieth century, suggesting a far less comprehensive "nationalization" of terminology. In all three countries, fears of the negative national consequences of emigration became affixed almost exclusively to overseas, America-bound, and purportedly permanent migrations; these were the most likely to be called "emigration" and to be distinguished from intra-European migrations, understood more often to be seasonal and no great threat to the nation. In all three countries, too, positive evaluations of emigration focused on the notion that the mobile "carried their culture" along with them. After the 1890s, nationalists in Germany, Poland, and Italy all sought to promote cultural retention among emigrants.

From an early date in all three nationalist movements, positive evaluations of emigration linked the "traveling cultures" of emigrants to dreams of national expansion that were usually called, quite explicitly in all three countries, "colonization." Colonization meant many different things of course; for example, in Italy, liberal supporters of free colonization on the model of Genoa or Venice disagreed sharply with those supporting state-funded imperialism in Africa on a Roman model. In Germany, state efforts beginning in the 1890s to direct emigrants toward its African colonies would be replicated in Italy in the 1920s. Most surprising, of course, was Polish nationalists' development of a positive evaluation of emigration as colonization. They began discussing the Polish potential for colonial expansion even while still colonized and divided by three European empires. Tellingly, too, visions of demographic colonization through emigration focused on parts of the world perceived as culturally or racially inferior to Europe. Schemes for the colonization of South America and Africa figured prominently in all three countries, although perhaps the greatest attention focused on emigrants to Brazil and (in the Italian case) Argentina—countries where large numbers of emigrants from Poland, Germany, and Italy lived in the countryside, rather than in cities. The fact that German, Polish, and Italian nationalists all imagined Latin America as a place where emigrants could retain and spread their own cultures is striking, especially when contrasted to their fears that emigrants in the United States retained their culture only with great difficulty. In fact, it was Brazil, not the United

States, that "predatorily" naturalized emigrants in the 1890s; over the long run, it was in the United States—not in Latin America—where hyphenated identities developed and where support for the homeland, at least in the form of Mussolini's antidemocratic regime, seemed strongest among Italian-Americans in the 1930s.

Discussions of how emigrants spread Polish, Italian, and German influence internationally also revealed a transition that we might characterize as a shift from predominantly cultural or romantic to increasingly racial or biological understandings of the three nations. The transition began in the 1880s in Germany, in the 1890s in Poland and Italy, and culminated in the years bracketing World War I in all three countries. During this transition, discussions of Polonia, Auslandsdeutsche, and italiani all'estero became relatively more important than the regulation or protection of emigration. Discussions of cultural reproduction and state support for cultural programs so that emigrants could retain their culture gave way to a new concern with biological reproduction, best expressed in new laws governing nationality or citizenship. The citizenship laws of Italy, Germany, and Poland—passed in 1912, 1913, and 1920, respectively—all created "stronger" national forms in which citizenship was not only carried abroad by emigrants but which, in the case of Poles, passed automatically to their emigrant children or, in the case of Germans and Italians, could be passed on, through biological reproduction, even to emigrants' children born abroad. "Diaspora" organizations of co-nationals living outside of their European homelands developed among Italians (prior to World War I and again during the 1920s) and Poles (in the 1920s and 1930s). Initiatives for organizing the italiani all'estero, and for binding them to Italy through visits, fundraising, political representation, and consular and clerical services came mainly from the homeland; in the case of Polonia, emigrants themselves played a considerable role. In both cases, however, these diaspora organizations were sponsored and encouraged by their respective national states. States saw them as potential "transmission belts" to encourage support for the changing foreign policies of the homeland. In the case of Italy's diaspora, the strongest support for the homeland came not from the temporary migrants living in nearby France or in Latin America, where emigrants supposedly had the greatest freedom to retain their national loyalties, but rather from the United States. In the case of Poland's diaspora, however, it was the Poles of Germany and South America who proved most receptive to political overtures from Pilsudski's government.

By focusing on policies, polemics, and terminology for migration from

Poland, Germany, and Italy this chapter has, of course, also privileged the viewpoints of their elites, and particularly their nationalist elites. We have considerable evidence from the emigration statistics so carefully collected by all three states that potential emigrants viewed the world rather differently. German, Italian, and Polish migrants rarely responded with any enthusiasm to state-directed colonial schemes. On the contrary, they generally "voted with their feet" by rejecting the destinations in Brazil or Africa so fervently advocated by their rulers. By the 1930s, the number of Italians living in all of Italy's African colonies did not equal the number in New York City or Buenos Aires alone. Germans in the 1920s mockingly referred to the central office offering help and advice to potential migrants (while, of course attempting to direct them to destinations favored by the nationalist elites) as the *"Amt der verlorenen Wörter"* ("The Office of Lost [or Empty] Words"). In both Italy and Poland, where return from other European countries and from the United States was quite common, the governing classes welcomed returnees as symbols of emigrants' attachment to their national homeland. Italian and Polish peasants, by contrast, called the returnees *"americani"* and *"Amerykanie"* (Americans) or *"tedeschi"* and *"Niemcy"* (Germans), thus emphasizing the degree to which they differed from their fellow villagers who had remained at home. Here we see hints—surely worthy of further study—of what we might call "emigration discourses from below." These not only paralleled but (in all three cases) rejected nationalist "discourses from above." While the "nationalization" of the mobile people of nineteenth-century Europe surely accelerated with nation building—as the numbers of deaths in World War I and World War II document—migration continued to complicate each nation's "embrace" of its subjects and citizens well into the twentieth century.

NOTES

1. Perhaps seven million of this number returned again to Europe; see Dirk Hoerder, *Cultures in Contact: World Migrations in the Second Millenium* (Durham, N.C.: Duke University Press, 2002), chapter 14.

2. Ernest Gellner, *Nations and Nationalism* (Oxford, Eng.: Blackwell, 1983); Miroslav Hroch, *Social Preconditions of National Revival in Europe* (Cambridge, Eng.: Cambridge University Press, 1985); Hagen Schulze, *Staat und Nation in der europäischen Geschichte* (Munich: Beck, 1999).

3. See Emilio Franzina's plausible suggestion that emigrants were themselves nation builders, in *Gli italiani al nuovo mondo* (Milan: Arnoldo Mondadori Editore, 1995), 15.

4. We borrow this term from John Torpey, *The Invention of the Passport: Surveillance, Citizenship, and the State* (Cambridge, Eng.: Cambridge University Press, 2000).

5. For the numbers, see Gianfausto Rosoli, ed., *Un secolo di emigrazione italiana, 1876–1976* (Rome: Centro Studi Emigrazione, 1976). Repeated temporary migrations diminished emigration's overall demographic impact, of course. See Donna R. Gabaccia, *Italy's Many Diasporas* (London: University College of London Press, 2000).

6. Peter Marschalck, *Bevölkerungsgeschichte Deutschlands im 19. und 20. Jahrhundert* (Frankfurt/Main: Suhrkamp, 1984), 151.

7. Only about 3.6 million left permanently. Edward Kołodziej, "Emigracja z ziem polskich od końca XIX w. do czasów współczesnych i tworzenie się skupisk polonijnych," in *Emigracja z ziem polskich w XX wieku. Drogi awansu emigrantów* (Pułtusk, 1998), ed. Adam Koseski, 17–19.

8. For the beginnings of a multicultural history of Europe, see Dirk Hoerder with Christiane Harzig and Adrian Shubert, eds., *Diversity in History: Transcultural Interaction from the Early Modern Mediterranean World to the 20th century Postcolonial World* (New York: Berghahn, 2003); Peter Marschalck, *Deutsche Überseewanderung im 19. Jahrhundert: Ein Beitrag zur soziologischen Theorie der Bevölkerung* (Stuttgart: Klett, 1973); Klaus J. Bade, ed., *Deutsche im Ausland, Fremde in Deutschland: Migration in Geshichte und Gegenwart* (Munich: Beck, 1992); Dirk Hoerder, "The German-Language Diasporas: A Survey, Critique, and Interpretation," *Diaspora* (2003), 7–44.

9. Georg Smolka, *Die Auswanderung als politisches Problem in der Ära des Deutschen Bundes (1815–1866)* (Speyer: Forschungsstelle für öffentliche Verwaltung, 1993), 199–273.

10. Hamburg followed suit in 1837 but was less dependent on the emigrant trade. See Dirk Hoerder, "The Traffic of Emigration via Bremen/Bremerhaven: Merchants' Interests, Protective Legislation, and Migrants' Experiences," *Journal of American Ethnic History* 13 (1993): 68–101.

11. *Gesetz betreffend den Schutz und die Fürsorge des Reichs für die deutsche Auswanderung* (Law concerning the protection of emigration and the responsibility of the Reich).

12. Here, it borrowed from the Prussian *Gesetz über die Erwerbung und den Verlust der Eigenschaft als preußischer Untertan sowie über den Eintritt in fremde Staatsdienste,* December 31, 1812. Matthias Lichter, *Die Staatsangehörigkeit nach deutschem und ausländischem Recht,* 2nd ed. (Berlin: Heymann, 1955), 519–24, 528–30.

13. The office was disbanded only in 1939, with the onset of World War II.

14. Emigrants, in the United States in particular, joined the debate both on the nationalist and internationalist side. See Elliott Shore, Ken Fones-Wolf, and James P. Danky, eds., *The German American Radical Press: The Shaping of a Left Political Culture, 1850–1940* (Urbana: University of Illinois Press, 1991); Dirk Hoerder,

"Labour Migrants' Views of 'America,'" *Renaissance and Modern Studies* 35 (1992): 1–17.

15. Felix Stoerk, *Das Reichsgesetz über das Auswanderungswesen vom 9. Juni 1897 nebst Ausführungsverordnungen und Anlagen* (Berlin: J. Guttentag, 1899).

16. In 1910, about 1.26 million foreigners were counted in the Reich as 1.95 percent of the total population, but the statistics were taken on December 1, at a wintertime low, since some four hundred thousand to five hundred thousand Polish seasonal workers in agriculture were required to leave after the harvests: Kaiserliches Statistisches Amt, *Die Volkszählung im Deutschen Reiche am 1. Dezember 1910*: Statistik des Deutschen Reiches, vol. 240 (Berlin: Kaiserliches Statistiches Amt, 1915); Ulrich Herbert, *A History of Foreign Labor in Germany, 1880–1980: Seasonal Workers, Forced Laborers, Guest Workers,* trans. William Templer (Ann Arbor: University of Michigan Press, 1990; orig. published in Germany in 1986), 34–40; Lothar Elsner and Joachim Lehmann, *Ausländische Arbeiter unter dem deutschen Imperialismus, 1900–1985* (Berlin: Dietz[-Ost], 1988).

17. The western section of the Hapsburg empire included the mixed Czech-German Sudeten borderlands (which would be annexed after the re-establishment of a third, Nazi empire) and "Great Germany," combining Germany and Austria in 1938.

18. "*Reichs- und Staatsangehörigkeitsgesetz,*" 22. Juli 1913, repr. in Lichter, *Staatsangehörigkeit,* 50–167; Rolf Grawert, *Staat und Staatsangehörigkeit: Verfassungsrechtliche Untersuchung zur Entstehung der Staatsangehörigkeit* (Berlin: Duncker Humblot, 1973), 164–212.

19. The 1910 census distinguished only between citizens and foreigners. It has been estimated that approximately 2.5 million Poles (3.9 percent of the population), a small minority of Sorbs (of whom about 83 percent spoke only Wendish), a sizeable group of Jews ("Germans of Mosaic faith"), and French-speaking Alsatians, in addition to the approximately 1.26 million foreigners (1.95 percent of the population), lived in Germany at that time.

20. See paragraphs 2, 3 (nos. 2–4), 4, 8, 12, 14–16, and 33 of the "*Reichs- und Staatsangehörigkeitsgesetz.*" Any woman marrying a German man, under the 1913 law, became a German citizen without a right to refuse naturalization. A foreigner living within the German states could be naturalized if he was *unbeschränkt geschäftsfähig* (an adult not mentally impaired for work); of *unbescholtenem Lebenswandel* (not convicted for criminal or civil offenses); the owner of an apartment, house, or accommodation; and, finally, if capable of providing for any relatives in Germany. The latter two provisions were derived from early modern poor-law provisions. The 1913 law did not include a minimum period of residence for naturalization. Other provisions for citizenship acquisition included any foreign man who had served in the German army or navy for one year or more "like a German." Any foreign man who had been accepted into employment as a civil servant of the Reich, a federal state, a municipality, as a teacher in the public school, or as an employee of a rec-

ognized religious creed, was naturalized automatically unless the contract specified otherwise. See Lichter, *Staatsangehörigkeit*, 70, 79.

21. *"Mit der Reinerhaltung der Rasse und der Eigenart unseres Volkes unverträglich,"* quoted in Lichter, *Staatsangehörigkeit*, 55–56.

22. To put these debates in long-term perspective, see Harold James, *Deutsche Identität, 1770–1990* (Frankfurt/Main: Campus, 1991); Otto W. Johnston, *Der deutsche Nationalmythos: Ursprung eines politischen Programms* (Stuttgart: Metzler, 1990)

23. Ferdinande Knabe, "'Im Geiste des deutschen Volkstums': Bemerkungen zur Erlaß- und Gesetzeslage des Minderheitenschulwesens in der Weimarer Republik," in *Das nationale Selbstverständnis der Bildung*, ed. Ingrid Gogolin, 103–14 (Münster: Waxmann, 1994). See also Marianne Krüger-Potratz, "Der verlängerte Arm nationalstaatlicher Bildungspolitik: Elemente völkischer Bildungspolitik in der Weimarer Republik," Gogolin, 81–102; Dirk Jasper, "'Das Deutsche Reich ist demnach ein sprachlich sehr einheitlicher Staat': Zur Instrumentalisierung der Muttersprachenstatistik in der Weimarer Republik," Gogolin, 115–30; Helmut Pieper, *Die Minderheitenfrage und das Deutsche Reich 1919–1933/34* (Frankfurt/Main: Metzner, 1974).

24. *Statistik des Deutschen Reichs*, vol. 401 (Berlin: Hobbing, 1930), 412–23, 491–92, 623–40.

25. Karl C. Thalheim, *Das deutsche Auswanderungsproblem der Nachkriegszeit* [post–World War I] (Crimmitschau: Rohland Berthold Verlag, 1926; Quellen und Studien zur Kunde des Grenz- und Auslandsdeutschtums, Bd. 1). See also Klaus J. Bade, "'Amt der verlorenen Worte'—das Reichswanderungamt 1918–1924," *Zeitschrift für Kulturaustausch* 39, no. 3 (1989): 312–25; *Vom Reichskommissar für das Auswanderungswesen zum Bundesverwaltungamt. Staatlicher Schutz für Auswanderer seit 120 Jahren* (exhibition catalog) (Köln: Bundesverwaltungsamt, 1989).

26. Zeffiro Ciuffoletti, "Stato senza nazione," in *La costruzione dello stato in Italia e Germania* (Manduria: Lacaita, 1993), 57–68.

27. *Atti della Giunta parlamentare per l'inchiesta agraria* (Rome: Forzani, 1881–86), vol. 11, pt. 2, 606.

28. Silvana Patriarca, *Numbers and Nationhood: Writing Statistics in Nineteenth-Century Italy* (Cambridge, Eng.: Cambridge University Press, 1996), 177; quote from Carl Ipsen, *Dictating Demography: The Problem of Population in Fascist Italy* (Cambridge, Eng.: Cambridge University Press, 1996), 38.

29. Ministero d'Agricoltura, Industria e Commercio, *Statistica del Regno d'Italia: Popolazione, Censimento Generale (31 Dic. 1861)* (Turin: Tip. Letteraria, 1865), lxiii; see also Direzione della Statistica Generale del Regno, *Statistica d'Italia, Popolazione, Parte 1, Censimento Generale (31 Dic. 1861)* (Florence: Tip. Di G. Barbera, 1867), 4, 151, 152.

30. Ferruccio Pastore, "Nationality Law and International Migration: The Italian Case," in *Towards a European Nationality: Citizenship, Immigration and Nationality Law in the EU*, ed. Randall Hansen and Patrick Weil, 96 (New York: Palgrave, 2001).

31. Direzione generale della statistica, *Popolazione, Censimento 31 dicembre, 1871* (Rome: Stamperia Reale, 1874–1876), vol. 1, 306.

32. Leone Carpi, *Delle colonie e dell'emigrazione d'italiani all'estero sotto l'aspetto dell'industria commercio, agricoltura* (Milan: Tip. Editrice Lombarda, già D. Salvi, 1874).

33. *Inchiesta agraria*, vol. 8, tome 1, fasc. 2, 746, 754.

34. Mark Choate, "Emigration and Colonialism in 'Greater Italy,' 1880–1914," PhD diss., Yale University, 2001.

35. Cristoforo Negri, *Della potenza proporzionale degli stati Europei, sui mari e sulle colonie memoria* (Milan: Coi tipi di L. di G. Pirola, 1840).

36. Cristoforo Negri, *La grandezza dell'Italia* (Turin: Tipografia Paravia e Comp., 1864); G. Scavia, *Delle migrazioni e colonie* (Turin, 1869), cited in Fernando Manzotti, *La polemica sull'emigrazione nell'Italia unità (fino alla prima guerra mondiale)* (Milan: Società Editrice Dante Alghieri, 1962), 7.

37. In ancient Rome, *coloni* settled and then cultivated empty or frontier lands. In nineteenth century censuses, tenant farmers in Italy were called *coloni*, and demands for small-scale rural colonization projects within Italy persisted until the 1920s, when fascist policy actually built several new model rural settlements for *coloni*.

38. Carpi, *Delle colonie*, vol. 1.

39. Manzotti, *La polemica*.

40. *Statistica della emigrazione italiana* (Rome: 1878–79, 1881–). Issuance of a *nulla osta* indicated that the potential migrant had no unpaid taxes, unfulfilled military service, or outstanding criminal charges.

41. *Inchiesta agraria*, vol. 6, fasc. 1, 44–45, 165.

42. Marchese Di Cosentino, *Delle perdite morali e materiali cagionate al'Italia dall'emigrazione artificiale* (Rome, 1874).

43. *Inchiesta agraria*, vol. 12, fasc. 1, 485.

44. Direzione Generale della Statistica, *Annuario Statistico, 1905–1907* (Rome: Tip. Nazionale di G. Bertero, 1908), 151–52. Although rates of return among transalpine migrants were undoubtedly higher, scholars now estimate return rates from the United States and Argentina at about 50 percent. See Samuel L. Baily, *Immigrants in the Lands of Promise: Italians in Buenos Aires and New York City, 1870–1914* (Ithaca, N.Y.: Cornell University Press, 1999), 24, table 2.

45. *Inchiesta agraria*, vol. 15, 84–85, 88–89.

46. See, for example, Cesare Jarach, *Abruzzi e Molise*, vol. 2 of *Inchiesta parlamentare sulle condizioni dei contadini nelle provincie meridionali e nella Sicilia* (Rome: Tip. Nazionale di Giovanni Bertero, 1909), 154–57, 159, 203, 254–55, 258, and table 5.

47. Gabaccia, *Italy's Many Diasporas*, tables I.1 and I.2.

48. Pastore, "Nationality Law," 97.

49. On the exhibit see G. Lerda, "Gli Italiani all'estero," *Rivista Italiana di Sociologia*, vol. 3 (1899): 619–31; Luigi Einaudi, *Un principe mercante; Studio sulla espansione coloniale italiana* (Turin: Fratelli Bocca, 1900).

50. Dino Cinel, *The National Integration of Italian Return Migration, 1870–1929* (New York: Cambridge University Press, 1991).

51. See Enrico Corradini, *Scritti e discorsi, 1901–1914*, ed. Lucia Strappini (Turin: Einaudi, 1980).

52. C. Ferrua, "Gli Italiani all'estero, La rappresentanza parlamentare degli italiani all'estero," *Nuova Antologia* 81, 4 (1907): 135–38.

53. Istituto Coloniale Italiano, *Atti del Primo Congresso degli italiani all'estero* (Rome: Cooperativa Tipografia Manuzio, 1910); Istituto Coloniale Italiano, *Atti del Primo Congresso degli italiani all'estero* (Rome: Tipografia Editrice Nationale, n.d.). See also Giuseppe Fumagalli, *La stampa periodica italiana all'estero* (Milan: Presso il Comitato ordinatore, 1909).

54. Silvano M. Tomasi, "Fede e patria: The 'Italica Gens' in the United States and Canada, 1908–1936," *Studi Emigrazione* 103 (September 1991): 319–41.

55. Cesare Festa, *L'emigrazione nella legislazione comparata* (Castrocaro: Tipografia Moderna, 1904), 419–21.

56. Adam Walaszek, ed., *Polska diaspora* (Cracow: Wydawnictwo Literackie, 2001); Krzysztof Groniowski, "'Czwarta dzielnica'. Zadania Polonii amerykańskiej wobec kraju (do 1918 r.)," *Przegląd Zachodni* 39, no. 1 (1983), 27–28; Ewa Morawska, "Changing Images of the Old Country in the Development of Ethnic Identity among East European Immigrants, 1880s–1930s: A Comparison of Jewish and Slavic Representations," *YIVO Annual of the Social Sciences* 29 (1994), 283–85; Andrzej Brożek, *Polish Americans 1854–1939*, trans. W. Worsztynowicz (Warsaw: Interpress, 1985), 175–76. Portions of this section have been published in A. Walaczek, "Wychodzcy, Emigrants or Poles? Fears and Hopes about Emigration in Poland, 1870–1939," *AEMI Journal* 1 (2003): 78–93.

57. On the consequences of migrations see Adam Walaszek, "Preserving or Transforming Role? Migrants and Polish Territories in the Era of Mass Migrations," in *People in Transit; German Migrations in Comparative Perspective*, ed. Dirk Hoerder and Jörg Nagler, (Cambridge. Eng.: Cambridge University Press, 1995); Ewa Morawska, "Labor Migrations of Poles in the Atlantic World Economy, 1880–1914," *Comparative Studies in Society and History* 31, 2 (1989): 237–72.

58. J. L. Popławski, *Pisma polityczne*, vol. 2 (Cracow-Warsaw: Gebethner i Wolff, 1910), 188. See also Józef Okołowicz, *Wychodźstwo i osadnictwo polskie przed wojną s'wiatową* (Warsaw: Nakladem Urzedu Emigracyjnego, 1920), 10–11.

59. *Naprzód* (Cracow edition), vol. 119 (May 28, 1913), 3.

60. "Pierwszy program stronnictwa ludowego," *Przyjaciel Ludu*, 18 (1895) in *Galicja w dobie autonomicznej 1850–1914*, ed. Stefan Kieniewicz, 268–70 (Wrocław: Ossolineum, 1952).

61. Popławski, *Pisma polityczne*, 201. Austrian authorities tried to stop the migration of Ruthenians, although most of this migration to Canada came from Galicia; see Andrzej A. Zięba, *Ukraińcy w Kanadzie wobec Polaków i Polski (1914–1939)* (Cracow: Księgarnia Akademicka, 1998), 16–18.

62. Mieczysław Szawleski, *Kwestia emigracji w Polsce* (Warsaw: Polskie Towarzystwo Emigracyjne, 1927), 25, 49–50, 59–60.

63. Leopold Caro and Karol English, *Emigracja i polityka emigracyjna ze szczególnem uwzględnieniem stosunków polskich* (Posen: Księgarnia św. Wojciecha, 1914), 23; Benjamin Murdzek, *Emigration in Polish Social-Political Thought, 1870–1914* (New York: Columbia University Press, 1977), 174, 135–36; L. Caro, "Nasi wychodźcy zamorscy," *Przegląd Powszechny* 8, no. 296 (1908): 157–58; Krystyna Murzynowska, "Związki polskiego wychodźstwa zarobkowego w Zagłbiu Ruhry z krajem w latach 1870–1918," in *Polska klasa robotnicza: Studia historyczne*, ed. Elżbieta Kaczyńska, 102 (Warsaw: Książka i Wiedza, 1983); the phrase "private homelands" is from Stanisław Ossowski, "Analiza socjologiczna pojęcia ojczyzny," in his *Z zagadnień psychologii społecznej* (Warsaw: PWN, 1967).

64. Florian Znaniecki, "Widoki dla wychodźców polskich w Kanadzie," *Wychodźca Polski* 11–12 (1912): 7–13; "IV Zjazd prawników i ekonomistów polskich: Obrady sekcji ekonomicznej," *Czasopismo prawnicze i ekonomiczne* 8 (1907), 189, 219; Roman Dmowski, "Wychodźcy galicyjscy w Kanadzie," *Słowo Polskie* (Lwów), May 9, 1904, 1; "Ze zjazdu prawników i ekonomistów (Dokończenie)," *Słowo Polskie* 457 (Oct. 9, 1906), 3; also Florian Znaniecki, "Wstrzymywanie kolonizacji brazylijskiej," *Wychodźca Polski* 10–11, no. 1–2 (1911): 1–3.

65. Jan Molenda, *Chłopi, naród, niepodległość: Kształtowanie się postaw narodowych i obywatelskich chłopów w Galicji i Królestwie Polskim w przededniu odrodzenia Polski* (Warsaw: Neriton, 1999), 39–40; Tomasz Kizwalter, *O nowoczesności narodu. Przypadek polski* (Warsaw: Semper, 1999).

66. Quoted in Frank Renkiewicz, *Poles in America 1608–1972. A Chronology and Fact Book* (Dobbs Ferry, N.Y.: Oceana, 1973), 64.

67. *Zaranie* 38 (Sept. 18, 1913); Murdzek, *Emigration in Polish Thought*, 161–62.

68. Murdzek, *Emigration in Polish Thought*, 161; Popławski, *Pisma polityczne*, 199, 207; *Przegląd Wszechpolski* 1 (Jan. 1, 1895), 3.

69. "Skupienie wychodźstwa polskiego w Paranie," *Dziennik Polski* 26 (January 26, 1897), 1.

70. Popławski, *Pisma polityczne*, 207–12. During the Fourth Conference of Polish Economists and Jurists in 1906, its Emigration Section supported this idea as well. Similarly, the Polish Commercial-Geographical Association of Galicia (which had organized to help migrants in various ways) advertised for permanent settlers for Parana in Brazil. "IV Zjazd Prawników," 8 (1907), 191; "Zjazd prawników," *Słowo Polskie*, (Lwów) 450 (October 5, 1906); Kula, *Polonia brazylijska* (Warsaw: LSW, 1980), 102–5; Caro and English, *Emigracja i polityka emigracyjna*, 369.

71. Wacław Kruszka, *A History of the Poles in America to 1908*, pt. 1, ed. James P. Pula, trans. Krystyna Jankowski (Washington, D.C.: The Catholic University of America Press, 1993), 13.

72. Groniowski, "Czwarta dzielnica," 30–39; "Piąta prowincja," *Zgoda* 25 (June 18, 1896), 1; Brożek, *Polish Americans*, 80.

73. Szawleski, *Kwestia emigracji w Polsce,* 83. Piotr Kraszewski, *Polska emigracja zarobkowa w latach 1870–1939: Praktyka i refleksja* (Posen: Polska Akademia Nauk, 1995), 145.

74. Adam Walaszek, "How Could It All Appear So Rosy? Re-emigrants from the United States in Poland, 1919–1924," *Polish American Studies* 49, no. 2 (1992): 43–60; Walaszek, *Reemigracja ze StanówZjednoczonych do Polski po I wojnie światowej, 1919–1924* (Cracow: PWN, 1984).

75. Franciszek Ryszka, ed., *Historia państwa i prawa Polski 1918–1939,* pt. I (Warsaw: PWN, 1962), 63–66.

76. Kraszewski, *Polska emigracja zarobkowa w latach,* 167–68; Halina Janowska, *Emigracja zarobkowa z Polski 1918–1939* (Warsaw: PWN, 1981), 126–29; Piotr Kraszewski, "Polsko-francuska konwencja emigracyjna z 3 września 1919 roku," *Przegląd Polonijny* 1, no. 2 (1975): 103–10.

77. Stanislaw Lato, *Programy stronnictw ludowych: Zbiór dokumentów* (Warsaw: Panstwowe Wydawnictwo Naukowe, 1969), 27, 189.

78. Kraszewski, *Polska emigracja zarobkowa w latach,* 150–51, 178.

79. Piotr Kraszewski, "Problem sezonowego wychodźstwa polskich robotników rolnych do Niemiec w latach 1919–1932," *Przegląd Zachodni,* 1985, no. 4, 31; Kraszewski, *Polska emigracja zarobkowa w latach,* 180–81; Kraszewski, "Ostatni etap polsko-niemieckich rokowań o Układ w sprawie robotników sezonowych (styczeń-listopad 1927)," *Przegląd Zachodni* 5/6 (1984), 48; Szawleski, *Kwestia emigracji,* 95; Kraszewski, *Polska emigracja zarobkowa w latach,* 157, 174, 176, 180–81.

80. Piotr Kraszewski, "Problem osadnictwa polskiego w Peru w okresie międzywojennym," *Studia Historyczne* 4 (1979), 588; Maria T. Koreywo-Rybczyńska, "Polityka Polski wobec emigracji w Ameryce Łacińskiej," in *Dzieje Polonii w Ameryce Łacińskiej,* ed. Marcin Kula (Wroclaw: Ossolineum, 1983), 467; Kraszewski, *Polska,* 186–87; Piotr Kraszewski, "Polsko-boliwijska umowa emigracyjna z 21 XII 1937 r.," *Kwartalnik Historyczny,* no. 2 (1977): 264–66.

81. Szyja Bronsztejn, *Ludność żydowska w Polsce w okresie międzywojennym* (Wroclaw: Ossolineum, 1963), 106–07; Janowska, *Polska emigracja,* 143–46.

82. Janowska, *Polska emigracja,* 143–45; Jerzy Tomaszewski, "Niepodleg a Rzeczpospolita," in *Najnowsze dzieje Żydów w Polsce (do 1950 r.),* ed. Jerzy Tomaszewski (Warsaw: PWN, 1993), 162–67; Edward Kołodziej, *Wychodźstwo zarobkowe z Polski 1918–1939: Studia nad polityką emigracyjną II Rzeczypospolitej* (Warsaw: Książka i Wiedza, 1982), 202–4.

83. Adam Jarzyna, *Polityka emigracyjna* (Lwów: Dom Ksiazki Polskiej, 1933); Biblioteka Polskiego Towarzystwa Emigracyjnego, vol. 3, 125–77.

84. Wojciech Wrzesiński, "Polacy za granicą w polityce II Rzeczpospolitej (1918–1939)," in *Problemy dziejów Polonii,* ed. Marian M. Drozdowski (Warsaw: PWN, 1979), 31.

85. Cezary Lusiński, *II Rzeczpospolita a Polonia 1922–1939. Geneza i działalność Rady Organizacyjnej Polaków z Zagranicy i Światowego Związku Polaków z Zagranicy*

(Warsaw: Instytut Historii PAN, 1998). The group declared itself open to "Poles from abroad, linked with the motherland by indissoluble ties of blood, culture, and history." See *Pięć lat pracy dla Polonii zagranicznej. Sprawozdanie z działalności Rady Organizacyjnej Polaków z Zagranicy za okres od lipca 1929 do lipca 1934* (Warsaw: n.p., 1934), 20; Wrzesiński, "Polacy za granicą," 42.

86. T. Kowalski, "Służba narodowa młodzieży," *Polacy Za Granicą* vol. 6 (1938): 2.

87. "Cenzor Świetlik o stosunku naszym do Polski," *Zgoda* (Chicago edition), no. 26, June 27, 1935: 1; Brożek, *Polish-Americans,* 188–89.

88. Lusiński, *II Rzeczpospolita,* 101–8.

4

THE LIBERAL ITALIAN STATE AND MASS EMIGRATION, 1860–1914

Caroline Douki

Translated from the French by Amy Jacobs

When emigration from the Italian peninsula became massive, an image of crowds of emigrants, abandoned to face the adversity and dangers of exile, began to appear in print, ranging from novels to polemic debates. The new liberal state was accused of grossly neglecting its migrant nationals. Whether humanist or nationalist, these writings revealed the disarray of migrants struggling to cope with the material difficulties of the trip and subjected, once abroad, to multiple forms of economic exploitation, xenophobia, and social rejection. The texts were perhaps, above all, expressions of the elites' concern at seeing the departure of an ever-increasing number of workers.

Some historiographic studies of the phenomenon subscribe to this general image, offering various explanations for the regime's inaction: the state was cut off from the masses, disengaged and inattentive from the outset to the impoverished part of the population; the state was attached to its liberal principals, and out of either pragmatism or cynicism allowed emigration to function as a safety valve and necessary evil; the state was ineffective, hamstrung by a congenital lack of administrative and financial means. More recently, rediscovery of the specific legislation with which the Italian state tried to surround emigration in the early twentieth century has led to the idea of a utilitarian state acting with regard to emigrants as if they were a kind of "export merchandise."[1]

These varying interpretations raise a crucial question for historians of European states at the turn of the nineteenth and twentieth centuries: what ways of apprehending and handling major social problems are available to a liberal state? And if such a state implements a policy for action, namely with regard to migration, should that policy necessarily be interpreted as a means of taking control or instrumentalizing the phenomenon?

To begin to answer these questions for the case at hand, it seems necessary to set discourse aside and examine the state's real practices. For though in the first decades following unification emigrants were not much mentioned in political speeches, administrative practices indicate concern at a completely different level. Also, chronological breaks should be noted; the era of the liberal state in Italy was not continuous. Though in its first actions the Italian state was feeling its way, uncertain as to both principles and means, it would be mistaken to call it disinterested. The state's will to know, and its concern to assert its sovereignty over migrant nationals, are clear. Moreover, the first decade of the twentieth century marked the beginning of a period in which the state displayed a true concern to intervene and protect. It was in this period that clear policy aims were developed, along with institutional tools for effecting them—indications of a full-fledged emigration policy.

DEFINING THE PLACE OF EMIGRANTS IN THE NATION-STATE

In the years immediately following Italian unification, at precisely the moment the new state was working to assert its control over its nationals and the territory as a whole, the departure of an increasing number of persons constituted a real challenge. Recent historiography has underlined the extent to which strong scholarly and administrative efforts at the time aimed to produce a coherent, all-encompassing image of the Italian nation.[2] The purpose was first and foremost practical. Consistent with the positivist convictions of the liberal ruling class, the idea was to obtain better knowledge of the geographical, social, and economic realities of the national territory and thereby provide the government with means to practice effective and modern administration.[3] But the issue was also symbolic. To describe the nation—present its geographical, social, demographic, and economic substance, establish clearly how far it extended, be able to reduce it to maps and statistics—was to make it exist as a legitimate representation, validated by state science.

These views implied forging an overall, organic image of the Italian population, and it very soon became clear that emigrants had to be included, for three reasons. First, if the government wanted to acquire knowledge of the country's demographic and socioeconomic realities, it had no choice but to assess migration flows. Second, in the interests of civic pedagogy, it was important to give all Italians, both migrants and not, an image of themselves as a unit, a representation susceptible of developing their consciousness of belonging to the same nation. Third, the Italian state, intending to assert its weight on the international scene, wanted to make clear that people from the peninsula, dispersed either temporarily or for the long term throughout the world, nonetheless came under its sovereign power.

The new unitary state was thus moved to include emigrants in the overall picture of "scattered members" of the nation that it was working to compose with the help of administrative surveys and statistics.[4] The issue was indeed one of sovereignty, as reflected through the 1870s in important actions and symbols. But affirming that the scattered emigrant population was a full-fledged component of the Italian population involved not so much explicit notification in political discourse as administrative and learned means of the sort that were being used everywhere at the time to establish the legitimate administrative competence of the state. The first major effort was to make the counting of the emigrant population and of departures the exclusive domain of state science, which, as we know, is not only a neutral instrument for acquiring knowledge but also a means of asserting sovereignty and the legitimate competence of the state in such matters.[5] In 1871, in addition to the population census being conducted on the peninsula, Italians abroad were counted for the first time, with the help of the consulates.[6] Then, in 1876, Italy decided to institute an official, annual statistical report on Italian emigration, to be focused on departure counts.

Some authors have stressed that the state only set up statistical accounting fifteen years after unification, after private actors had begun to organize and publish statistical accounts and commentary on the results. It is true that in its first years of existence, the government took little notice of the population statistics that had been collected in the mid-nineteenth century by the preunification Italian states. It began to focus seriously on the rise in emigration only after parts of the economic, intellectual, and religious elites, as well as certain local milieus, had already become worried by it.[7] Can this inattention be blamed on the central state's guilty lack of interest in the emigrant population? It should be noted that emigration was increasing at an irregular pace at the time and that different regions were quite diversely affected by it. Some, though touched quite early by the exodus—the Veneto, for instance[8]—did not themselves become integrated into the nation until 1866. The delay in government concern can also be explained by the difficult situation of the entire administrative apparatus, then engaged in a long-term effort to reorganize its central and peripheral structures.[9] In fact, the new state did not correspond to a clearly defined territory until the 1870s. It was only after Rome was taken that the last stage of organizing the state apparatus could occur: the definitive establishment of all central services in the new capital. The delay in state action must thus be relativized.

After a period of procrastination, the central state began waging what appears to have been an all-out battle to establish a monopoly over migration statistics, against initiatives by Italian private interests and also foreign states, which had begun to produce their own counts of immigrants in their territories. The person responsible for this initiative for many years was Luigi Bodio, director of the Direzione Generale della Statistica (DGS) from 1872 to 1880. From this position he set about imposing his conception of centralized, professionalized state statistical reports, to be recognized as the only official, competent source of a reliable, legitimate, scientific reading of the social world.[10] Logically, the emigrant population (which continually increased, raising ever more questions about the nation's demographic and economic wealth and the extension of state sovereignty) was quickly identified as an "object" to be studied exclusively by Bodio's administration, whose game plan involved two complementary actions.[11] First, he set about ensuring that counting was not done by private interests or on the initiative of local actors, all of whom were likely either to underestimate or exaggerate, depending on whether they were for or against emigration.[12] Second, he worked to constitute truly national, centralized departure statistics, using peripheral administrative services (town halls and prefectures) to collect information (but imposing homogeneous norms for collection), and reserving to the central services the work of processing the data, calculating and formalizing the results, and commenting on them.

This undertaking led to the instituting in 1876 of the "annual Italian emigration statistics" report, produced and published under the sole, centralized authority of the DGS.[13] The significance of this was crucial, given that the Italian state was seeking to show the relationship that existed between the state and the emigrant population, and to convey that it did not consider this group secondary or lost to the country of origin; it intended to find out whether migrants were lost to the nation or not. This explains the DGS's continual effort to find a classificatory and technical approach that would enable it to distinguish temporary distancing from definitive departure.[14] The institution also affirmed that emigration statistics should be a matter of Italian administrative knowledge, not an object for private interests or one that could be shared by official statistics bureaus in destination states. Making the practice of closely following emigrant movements and census counts of Italians abroad an ordinary, regular component of national statistical reporting amounted to asserting continuity over space and time in the Italian state's oversight of its migrant nationals. In this perspective, such statistics had more than a symbolic function; they were also a government tool. For decades, the state worked incessantly with this instrument to understand emigration—to identify, ever more precisely, the regional, demographic, and socio-occupational characteristics of migrants. It was with this aim that Luigi Bodio required the new statistical accounts of emigration to follow much stricter methodological and technical rules than those used in earlier initiatives.[15]

The complexity of migratory movements no doubt thwarted the DGS's taxonomical efforts, and the figures it produced were far from reliable. But the continuity of its efforts deserves to be stressed. Moreover, alongside official emigration statistics, other practices show that there was concern to integrate emigrants into official representations of the national population. With the exception of the minority of persons who had not reappeared on the peninsula for a long time or had declared their intention to settle definitively abroad, emigrants continued to be included in all counts of the Italian population. In decennial censuses, they were included in the "legal population" and categorized as part of the "resident," as opposed to "present" population. Likewise, the names of those who had not indicated definitive settlement abroad were maintained in the registers of the *populazione stabile* for their town or city. Even though these principles were applied with varying degrees of consistency from one census to the next and by different towns or villages, the results they produced attested that migrants remained part of the very substance of the nation.

This official interest in migrants was nonetheless marked by two types of ambivalence. First, what dominated in the state's early awareness of emigration was its will to affirm sovereignty and uphold state legitimacy. Migrants were passive objects of administrative understanding; like any other segment of the population in Italy during the same period, they were not so much citizen nationals as an administered population. Second, all efforts made to integrate them into a coherent picture of the national population ultimately led the state to regard them with suspicion.

THE ADMINISTRATIVE CONSTRUCTION OF A SINGULAR, PROBLEMATIC GROUP

The increased efforts to apprehend and delimit the phenomenon of migrant mobility had a paradoxical result: in describing the mobile population and continually seeking to delineate its contours, the administration ended up constituting it as a specific group distinct from the rest of the population. Statistical identification and categorization thus had reifying and stigmatizing effects,[16] artificially hardening the separation between leavers and nonleavers, whereas in reality, socioeconomic practices in the regions from which people were migrating meant the two groups were thoroughly intertwined. Migrants and nonmigrants were part of the same families: they often shared the same revenues, and local Italian economies were irrigated by capital and know-how brought in from abroad.[17]

Two dynamics worked toward this end. First, in casting about for statistical categories and developing practical counting techniques, the official statisticians multiplied ways of conceptually carving up a highly complex social reality, as is always the case with a fluctuating population. At the formal level, the incessant readjustments were aimed at finding the best observation point. Which authorities were best situated and most competent to do the observing? At first the task went to mayors of towns, villages, or other administrative units; in 1904, it became the work of the police. There was also the question of the best information source. At first it was passport requests, then passports actually delivered; later, two information sources were combined: counts in Italy before departure and consulate information after migrants' arrival. Throughout this process, those chosen to observe emigration were increasingly likely to be guardians of law and order and the usual censors of deviation from the norm. The move from mayors to the police was one from mediators close to migrant societies to an observation force external to those societies. Increasingly, there was a tendency to apply legal-administrative categories and a legal-administrative reading key to practices that, for the migrants, were primarily socioeconomic. It is worth noting the incessant efforts deployed by the state's central services to impose this normative logic more deeply on society: the task was taken away from the mayors because they were judged not to be performing it with sufficient zeal. Indeed, mayors often did not have a very administrative view of residents' mobility and were reluctant to count as emigrants those citizens who left to work abroad for a few months without a passport. Such temporary departures were well known and quite common in their towns; they claimed it was not "proper emigration" and often did not record or count such movements, considering them an entirely natural part of local reality.[18]

In the 1880s, one of the main concerns of the central administration (the DGS assisted by Agriculture and Interior Ministry services) was to inculcate in representatives stationed in rural areas a new conception of emigration as a specific category to be reported regardless of the form it took, old or new (temporary or not, with or without passport or papers). The work of acculturating agents to the official reading of the phenomenon, with its segmentation of the social world in legal terms, was done with energy; all possible bureaucratic and pedagogical means were mobilized (explanatory circulars from the DGS or Agriculture or Interior ministries, use of prefectures for transmitting injunctions, instruction details, strong reminders). By instituting an official count and continually perfecting methodology, the Italian authorities via the peripheral administrations presented a particular definition of the emigration phenomenon to the country as a whole, and by fixing a statistical category, it gave shape to a group now identified as particular: "emigrants."

The way in which emigrants' movements were described and they themselves were indexed produced a theoretical dividing line between emigrants and their country. All counting and categorizing focused on the act of leaving: town or village of departure; month of leaving; age and occupation of person departing, and so forth. Up until the early twentieth century, only "leavers" were counted in official Italian statistics, even though elites and observers at the central and local levels were fully aware that mobility consisted not only in leaving but also in returning, and in movement back and forth. It was not until 1902 that official statistics began registering returns, and then only for Italians returning from overseas, not persons who had been working in neighboring European countries (though they were by far the more numerous).[19] The problem was surely due to material constraints: it was easier for the Italian services to count departures, which increasingly required an administrative act—requesting a passport—than returns, which required no declaration. But the reason was not exclusively practical: it also concerned the political underpinnings of the statistical operation. The important point was to count and identify leavers, to chart flows *out* of Italy. This meant that official emigration statistics were much more than a descriptive classifying scheme. They isolated leavers and "absents" within a reality that, on the contrary, was made up of numerous to-and-fro movements and that, before the outbreak of World War I, much more closely resembled a vast turnover than a continuous outflow of Italians into foreign lands.

Be that as it may, and despite the fact that some statistical commentaries indicated that the official counts did not reflect the complexity of mobility, these statistics and graphs were published, disseminated, used by the whole of the state apparatus and political elites, and occasionally cited in debates on emigration. Increasingly, migrants were represented as leavers or people who had moved away—"absent" persons.

This meant that the Italian state often identified them as a problem group. For despite the scholarly and administrative efforts to classify them, they continued to represent a challenge to state control. They were a problem for administrative control first of all, as their incessant movement from one country to another, involving complex changes in life surroundings and activities, meant that they were still difficult to identify and classify in social or occupational terms. This is of course the hiatus discernible in most states in the nineteenth century: confronted with the increasing mobility of their populations, states continued for a long time to manage their societies primarily in territorial terms, those of an administrative netting anchored in space and covering districts that the state was seeking to make as stable and homogeneous as possible. Certain changes in the administrative and police structures of European states at the end of the nineteenth century would in fact be aimed at controlling mobility by means of newly invented, more dynamic networks of information.[20]

But before this shift had fully occurred, and until the end of the nineteenth century, the Italian state was considerably discommoded by emigration, especially since migrants were also a challenge for public order. They seemed too easily able to escape the eye of the new national and local authorities, and their moving far away or toward the major cities aroused or intensified suspicions about their political and moral behavior. Up against this problematic reality, the Italian state multiplied its investigations and surveys. All ministries concerned for one reason or another by mobility (Foreign Affairs; the Interior, worried about public order; Agriculture, Industry, and Commerce, all concerned about correctly balancing the country's economic activities and its manual workforce) multiplied their questionnaires. Reports by mayors, prefects, and consular officers, which were printed in official state publications and then taken up by the newspapers and in university circles, had their own ways of tracing the contours of the phenomenon, and they provided material for a whole range of literature that, while sharing the view that emigration was a problem, presented or examined it from extremely diverse angles—economic, moral, demographic, etc. In this way, the group known as "migrants" came to be associated with the major tensions running through Italian society: the agrarian crisis, the issue of the Mezzogiorno, child labor, public health, Italy's stature and cultural prestige in the world, and so forth.[21]

Gradual elaboration of specific legislation consolidated the process of categorizing migrants as a problematic group. The first major set of measures, passed in 1888, has features of a policing law of the sort that, in identifying emigration as first and foremost a border-crossing movement motivated by poverty,[22] ended up defining migrants as a part of the population detached from the rest by spatial distance and social difficulties.

LONG-INADEQUATE HANDLING OF MIGRATION AND MIGRANTS

The myriad difficulties inherent in migrant "representation" help explain the discrepancy between incessant state efforts to *know* about emigration and its actual handling of the phenomenon, which remained quite limited until the end of the century, despite the law of 1888. The state's actual intervention was rather fragmentary, motivated primarily by a concern for public order, or by geopolitical aims that went far beyond concern about the migrants themselves.

Until the 1890s, emigration was handled primarily by policing the borders and controlling and monitoring exits from the national territory through passport issuance. It is important not to overestimate the intentions and effects of these practices by interpreting them as an indication that the state was taking firm control of emigration. This was simply the ordinary way of practicing sovereignty for a nation-state in the liberal period; there was no particular plan to coerce or thwart would-be migrants. The aim of controlling exits was primarily to obtain obedience to a few rules of national life such as compulsory military service (young men likely to be called up for duty were not issued passports, for example). And the state could only exercise a certain degree of control in any case since it did not have the means to prevent departures. Regulation through passport issuance was highly theoretical in a world where, until the late nineteenth century, it was easy to move around without a passport. Other types of papers, certificates, or declarations could be used and closely watched destinations avoided. Moreover, the local offices of the national administration, whose work was to authorize passports, were not particularly zealous in applying official directives to limit issuance, when such directives existed.[23]

This is related to a completely different phenomenon, which quickly reduced any impulse to limit departures. The socioeconomic situation in the Italian countryside was such that, starting in the 1880s, the state perceived emigration as an indispensable safety valve and even a relatively easy solution to the problems of Italian society.[24] From then on, emigrants were freely allowed to flow out of the country, and indeed no coercive policy was exercised with regard to migration. It would seem, on the contrary, that after 1880, the more closely the Italian state administered emigration flows, the more it actually facilitated emigration. State regulatory actions at this time were clearly aimed at facilitating the departure of "undesirables," namely, unoccupied peasants, subversive elements, even convicts (to whom, at the end of the century, passports were readily granted after completion of prison sentence).

Consistent with its liberal character, the Italian government limited its intervention into the doings of emigrants until the end of the century, even though the need for guidance, supervision, and assistance increased with the swelling flow. For many years, migrants (either in the process of leaving or already abroad) could count only on their families, village connections, or private aid organizations.[25] In fact, the state only intervened when international respect for Italian power was at issue. But this concern came to have wider-ranging effects at the end of the century, consistent with the general tendency for nation-states at the time to affirm their sovereignty over nationals abroad more concretely—namely, by defending them more effectively.[26] In this the Italian authorities were particularly forthright—especially Crispi (1887–1896), who used emigration in diplomatic relations between his country and migrant-receiving countries as a playing card in his larger game plan of making Italy a world power.[27] The diplomatic protection thereby made available to emigrants won recognition for them as nationals, and this was a major development that moved migrants to value the potential advantages of membership in their nation-state of origin.[28] Still, the nation-state hardly responded adequately to the most urgent needs of the mobile population, especially socioeconomic protection. The major turning point came in the first decade of the twentieth century, when this now-specific group finally became the object of a thoroughgoing policy that took into account its socioeconomic reality.

THE BEGINNINGS OF A PUBLIC POLICY FOR EMIGRATION

After 1900, when departures from all regions of the peninsula began to multiply rapidly (placing the issue of emigration at the core of Italian society), a part of the state as well as some of the intellectual and economic elites began to disengage the phenomenon from policing, political, or diplomatic concerns—the only ones that had been relevant until then. This went together with a much clearer perception of the social problems linked to emigration, as well as of the positive economic effects it could have on the country. The changes fairly quickly led to a policy of social supervision and assistance that was both thoroughgoing and pragmatic. It is important to take the full measure of the new awareness and action, so as not to reduce the attitude of political officials and economic elites in the early twentieth century to a nationalist discourse denouncing emigration in noisy, alarmist tones as a loss of vitality for Italy.[29] Indeed, at the beginning of the century there were two types of discourse on emigration, distinct but not necessarily contradictory on basic matters. Emigrants were perceived by all as a source of wealth for the nation,[30] and alongside the thundering, ideological discourse of the nationalists lamenting the "loss" of this wealth was a much more pragmatic perception, dictating that this human component of the national wealth should be effectively supervised and protected precisely because emigration was inevitable and emigrants indispensable to the country. In the Giolitti period, the state's determined intervention resulted from a concern for social justice combined with a managerial approach to the general emigration question.

This new phase of relations between state power and the migration phenomenon should be resituated within the general framework of the Giolitti period, characterized by an all-encompassing policy for integrating the masses into the frameworks of national life and the liberal state. The attempt to integrate extended to all the specific groups who for various reasons had developed on the margins of the political or social system: Catholics, socialists, workers, and emigrants. The policy combined procedures for extending political citizenship (broadening of suffrage in 1912, for example) and socioeconomic measures that represented the embryo of a social welfare state.

The measures directed toward emigrants show that the new policy was indeed concerned with citizenship of the masses and integration of citizens through recognition of social welfare rights.

The legislation instituted by the first major organic law on emigration, the law of January 31, 1901 (to which several additions and modifications were made from 1901 to 1913), laid the foundations for what was meant as a thorough and consistent policy. The new definition of emigration in this law reflects a full-fledged, new understanding of the characteristics of the phenomenon, an understanding that had in turn evolved and been sharpened through the first genuine national debate on the matter. Parliament, academics, and emigration administrators actively collaborated in defining emigration for the draft legislation, and they continued to collaborate throughout the Giolitti period to improve legislative, regulatory, and administrative measures.[31]

For the new legislation, emigration was no longer defined as a border-crossing movement but referred explicitly to the mobility of workers. The emigrant was no longer a poor wretch forced to take emergency measures to flee poverty or a person caressing vain illusions of acquiring wealth in distant lands but rather someone who went abroad to work.[32] Emigrants were thus no longer perceived uniquely in terms of departure or distancing but as nationals, citizens among citizens, who simply went to work outside their country, in most cases bringing the fruits of their labor back into it. This was a fundamental change. Emigration was no longer seen as a purely demographic phenomenon, an issue of public order, or an irrepressible outward flow, but more as a work–income exchange occurring beyond borders.

This new understanding was accompanied by a modification in the framework and procedures for statistical data collecting. While efforts were still made to perfect departure counts,[33] the administration now showed great interest in knowing about returns, back-and-forth movements, in understanding all the dimensions of what was now perceived much more clearly as circulation on a grand scale of a labor force and revenues. The initial, vain attempt to distinguish distancing from definitive emigration was soon abandoned, and investigations for measuring real returns multiplied. Returns from America began to be counted in 1902; in 1908, local population registers were used for the first time in an attempt to grasp the relative volumes of temporary and definitive absences by counting emigrants who had left long ago or been born abroad and had themselves reregistered, or registered on their return.[34] The Commissariato Generale dell'Emigrazione increased the number of surveys and calculations to arrive at an estimate of the average length of transatlantic stays.[35] Simultaneously, then, a new definition of emigration emerged and the overall, statistically formalized image of emigration was changing, with equal emphasis now on circulation and departure.[36] The new data enabled the economist Francesco Coletti to highlight the turnover phenomenon in his 1911 table, realized for the fiftieth anniversary of the creation of the nation-state.[37]

Because emigration was now considered not in exclusively legal-administrative terms but rather as a specific mode of work, it came to be read in two new ways: as one of several types of economic behavior—a legitimate one, the exercise of which was guaranteed by the law of 1901; and a social issue. This fueled a two-part public policy for accompanying and supervising emigration. The first part reflected a concern for social welfare; the second was clearly focused on the economic and financial aspects of the phenomenon.

The law of 1901 went beyond the classic diplomatic protection a state owes its nationals and established full-fledged oversight of emigration. The aim was to help emigrants get their bearings in the international labor market, guarantee them assistance, and combat the abusive confidence schemes and swindling they were often victims to, both in Italy and abroad. Efforts were made to inform would-be emigrants about employment prospects and reception conditions abroad, and associations and organizations were created specifically to guide and assist them, and, if necessary, provide legal protection. This arrangement was in theory meant to accompany and assist emigrants at all stages of their trip.[38]

The pivotal role in policy implementation went to the Commissariato Generale dell'Emigrazione (CGE), which took its orders from the Ministry of Foreign Affairs. The program was to set up town committees in departure areas in order to provide free assistance to emigrants and monitor the dealings of recruiting agents. The committees were made up of representatives of the local authority and members of civil society. In the major embarkation ports, an inspector checked that departures proceeded by the rules, and during the voyage itinerant inspectors and doctors surveyed safety and hygiene conditions. In destination ports, newcomers were met and assisted by inspectors and representatives of private patronage companies subsidized by the CGE.

In this way, the Italian state worked to offer genuine protection to nationals in transit. The nationals in turn were increasingly willing to put themselves in the hands of the arbitrating institutions made available to them. Migrants who considered themselves legally wronged by dishonest navigation companies or intermediaries now had recourse to emigration officials in the main embarkation ports and, as of 1910, in Milan for emigration within Europe. Provincial arbitration commissions were also set up in the main regions of departure.

It is true that protective legislation and specialized institutions came on the scene late, only after a generation of massive emigration. And the official organizations functioned inadequately (until they were reformed in 1910): funding was irregular, there were long delays in getting provincial commissions going, and destination port inspectors, the most effective legal representatives, were overwhelmed with appeals for help.[39] Furthermore, the administrative setup left a considerable portion of assistance up to the secular or religious associations it subsidized. And finally, the state's greatest efforts were reserved for transatlantic emigration, which meant that problems raised by temporary emigration within Europe, particularly issues relating to emigration of women and children, were not appropriately handled until the second decade of the nineteenth century.

Despite these reservations, the positive effects of the new overall arrangement cannot be underestimated. As well, regular improvements were made after 1901, making it possible to handle migrants' most recurrent material problems, and in general coordinating action as a whole, gradually giving it a more national character. Though the measures arrived late, they did benefit the people who made up the great numbers of emigrant waves departing Italy between 1900 and 1913 and thereby made them particularly conscious that the nation-state could be a useful protective resource and guarantor of certain basic rights.

In the social supervision component of the policy, emigrant rights were taken seriously for the first time: civic citizenship rights first of all, in that the policy was aimed at helping emigrants determine and choose how to behave by making information available to them, encouraging them to appeal to the state in case of problems, and facilitating access to legal help. Concern for social citizenship rights is also discernible in the policy: recognition of the formal right to emigrate and work abroad went together with measures enabling emigrants to exercise that right without the fruit of their labor being amputated by intermediaries—recruiting agents, navigation and insurance companies, and the like, whose trade was flourishing on the emigration market. Most important, these measures were part of the larger process deliberately pursued during the Giolitti period of establishing institutions for handling social phenomena in general and labor relations in particular.[40] The Italian state may be seen asserting itself through these measures, working to be more of an arbiter and protector. While it had always been concerned with social order, it was now also concerned with social cohesion and with integrating the most fragile segment of the population into the nation. It had begun to lay the foundations for a social welfare state.

Emigrants, then, were one of the first social groups to benefit from the beginnings of an Italian welfare state. There are several explanations for this. To begin with, their need was most urgent. The volume of emigration skyrocketed between 1900 and 1913, and the phenomenon intersected with most social issues in Italy: underdevelopment in the rural south, crisis of rural industry in the north and center, unemployment of skilled laborers due to the economic situation, sanitation problems, illiteracy.[41] Second, because emigrants had been considered a problem (because they had been tirelessly scrutinized through statistical reports and surveys), they constituted the working population best known to the public authorities at the beginning of the century. Last, emigrants were the group that the public authorities could reach and affect most easily, because they necessarily went through readily identifiable circulation or assembly points (ports, borders, and railroad stations of major cities such as Milan, whence they departed the country). Paradoxically, then, despite the fact that migrants were highly mobile, they constituted the segment of the working population the least able to escape the administration. They were also the least reluctant to use the institutions. Because of their frequent contact for over a generation with the peripheral services of the Italian state, they were quicker than other parts of the population to become accustomed, or acculturated—by constraint as much as interest—to being administered.[42]

EFFORTS TO IMPROVE ECONOMIC INTEGRATION

Once emigration began to be perceived more as a modern work relation, it came to be thought of in various sectors of the state and certain political and economic milieus as a general economic fact, a work-for-capital exchange occurring beyond borders. From the early twentieth century, increasing attempts were made by the administration and all variety of economists to assess the value of revenues sent home by emigrants.[43] The results, though partial and difficult to systematize because there were so many formal and informal channels for sending wealth back, were sufficiently conclusive to make a convincing case not only that the amount was high, but also that those resources were indispensable to certain regions. From then on, the state sought means to tighten and even institutionalize ties between the Italian economy (then undergoing major changes) and emigrants abroad. This was hardly a vision of emigration as lost wealth. Indeed, the second aim of the public policy initiated in 1901 seems clearly to have been economic and even managerial. The aim was to make the profit emigration produced available to a national economy worthy of the name, especially since the accelerated industrialization of the country required hitherto unheard of amounts of capital.[44]

There were several components to the state's economic action. First, the idea was to ensure that the maximum amount of emigrant revenues from all sources, highest to lowest incomes, did indeed get sent back to Italy. To prevent emigrant savings being dispersed or invested abroad, it was necessary to facilitate money transfer operations. The second aim was to channel such transfers into modernized Italian banking and finance networks (to avoid all loss and protect emigrants against unreliable intermediaries) and above all to concentrate the funds and thereby make them more rapidly and directly available to service the country's financial needs. Two provisions arranged for this, both decided by the state. In 1901, the Banco di Napoli became the official, state-guaranteed intermediary for insuring transfers from emigrants settled across the Atlantic. This concerned emigrants from the Mezzogiorno in particular, whose labor channels and networks with America were strong.[45] Simultaneously, the rural postal network, whose offices served as savings deposit banks, was extended to the most out-of-the-way locales (and thereby to regions where emigration was strong) and its services made directly available to Italians settled abroad.

A number of contemporary writers perceived the economic aspect of the state's emigration policy as an effective, deliberate exploitation of the migration process. For them, the state that implemented it considered emigrants "export merchandise."[46] I would argue that there are three points that counter this negative judgment. First, the economic portion of the migration policy cannot be interpreted independently of the social one. The policy as a whole was conceived as a new task for a state now concerned to protect and arbitrate. Second, the authorities' financial preoccupations dovetailed with the migrants' economic interests and their demand, expressed since the turn of the century, for banking institutions and wealth-transferring channels adapted to their needs.[47] Third, this policy, which aimed to attract the migrant manna and make it multiply, and which led to an increasingly large place being made for such wealth in the relevant national statistics, also promoted recognition that, symbolically at least, emigrants played an economically active part within and in the service of the nation.

The public policy intentions that gave rise to the legislative measures and practical provisions of the Giolitti period were thus fairly ambitious, even if they were not devoid of ambivalence. While founded on a real concern to integrate and valorize emigration in the life of the nation, the policy also proposed both treating emigrants as a mass—or pawn—in a process that the state wanted to manage the best it could, and considering them citizen-actors in the economic development and modernization of Italian society.

THE NATIONALIST COUNTER-CHALLENGE

As emigrants were further integrated into the social, economic, and even civic life of the nation, a nationalist discourse was being developed in which emigration was denounced for weakening the nation.

Relations became tense within the internal political context during the first decade of the century as nationalism progressed in Italian society. Emigration remained the focal point of contradictory political visions. In the nationalist interpretation, it was railed against as an injury inflicted by an unfair international order, emptying Italy of its substance, depriving it of its human wealth and labor power. In this view, emigration was not the circulation of manual labor and revenues but rather the tangible manifestation, both means and symbol, of Italy's subjection to an unfair exchange arrangement; it was not foremost a necessary evil but a quantity of suffering imposed by wealthy countries on "the proletarian nation"; it was not the movement of persons going to work beyond the nation's borders, but a scandalous exile in which a mass of valiant manual workers were exploited and humiliated.[48]

From 1905 to 1911, this negative vision of emigration spread among the Italian elites, partially in the form of a virulent political polemic aimed at denouncing the liberal state altogether for its ineffectiveness, slogging bureaucracy, and pusillanimous foreign policy. The fate of emigrants, decidedly hard (since the work relation often did mean economic exploitation and xenophobic stigmatization), seems nonetheless in many cases to have been instrumentalized by Italian nationalist discourse, which could be both plaintive and aggressive. But the nationalist representation of emigration also spread throughout the Italian state, where nationalist and imperialist themes and approaches were rapidly gaining ground, and it gradually became superimposed on the more positive conception and pragmatic approach presented above.

There is a striking paradox in the coexistence of a policy for integrating and valorizing emigration as an ineluctable fact (which the state knows to be indispensable, facilitates, and even uses) and a discourse that, by vehemently refusing to accept the fait accompli, ultimately conveyed an image of emigrants not as active citizen-workers but victims of exploitation. In fact, within the state, emigration was considered both a source of wealth (and treated as such) and a loss and abnormality.

How can we account for this paradox? It must be remembered first of all, as recent historiography has repeatedly underlined, that the state is never a compact block.[49] The apparently contradictory representations of emigration were not present within the same sectors of the Italian state. While those sectors operated in a shared social and political space, each approached the realities and issues of emigration from its own perspective and, because of its specific function, produced distinct images of the phenomenon. The administrative structures designed to manage emigration socially and economically (the CGE[50] and its peripheral relay offices, and the statistics bureaus that assessed returning wealth) treated and presented it as an inevitable and ultimately profitable fact. In Italian diplomatic circles, meanwhile, where the focus was on Italy's "greatness," the discourse both received and produced was one of concern and alarm. The second type of representation informed all consular reports purporting to describe the concrete realities of "colonies" of Italians working or settled abroad.[51] These reports, though a mine of factual information, are also highly selective, "constructed" representations of Italian communities abroad. The refrain taken up in most of them about the danger of Italians becoming denationalized abroad focused attention on populations long established ·outside the country, forgetting that the majority of migrants stayed away only temporarily and pretending to ignore the fact that emigrants did not feel any less Italian than the peninsula's rural masses. The political designs of such discourse, set as it was against a background of international rivalry, are obvious: emigrant colonies were to be maintained firmly within the orbit of the motherland so they could function as bridgeheads for a policy of Italian presence, prestige, and power in the world at large.

Up against the highly composite reality of Italian emigration—a mixture of exploitation in the workplace, difficult socioeconomic integration, but also genuine social successes and non-negligible financial returns—Italian elites and the Italian state could indeed proffer an ambiguous, context-dependent, two-edged discourse characterized in turn by pride, a sense of victimization, and realpolitik. These representations, while often distinct, were in the final analysis linked together because they proceeded out of one and the same inferiority complex: that of a weak national power. Whether emigration was used politically (as a figure of endangered national dignity that had to be defended) or evaluated economically (as a major source of revenue), it was ultimately envisaged in terms of national power. And it was always with the aim of attaining greater power that the Italian elites integrated emigration into a strategy of economic development or transformed it into a foreign policy issue with intransigent speeches about protecting nationals—a discourse that was increasingly used to justify demands for a right to colonize so as to offer emigrants a haven of work and respect.

The two sides of a single policy for increasing national power, an aim in relation to which emigration was an increasingly important issue, reveal that emigrants were indeed at the core of questions about the identity and future of the nation. In 1912, new provisions were drawn up on the nationality of emigrants abroad, whereby persons who had acquired the nationality of the country they resided in automatically kept their Italian citizenship unless they made an explicit request not to. This is particularly revealing of the new manner of considering emigrants both as a means to realize a program for increasing national power and as nationals whose protection and rights continue to be guaranteed by the state of origin.

Shifting the focus of historical analysis from political discourse to the concrete practices of the state enables us to discern the real breadth of the emigration policy that was gradually developed by the liberal Italian state, even though that policy had very little time to show its potential effects before the outbreak of World War I. Some neighboring Mediterranean states, confronted during the same period with the identical challenge of mass emigration, saw Italian migration policy as a highly useful model for the changing times, and they were not mistaken. From 1901–1911, Greece, for example, repeatedly sent high-level functionaries to study the workings of the Italian emigration services.[52]

NOTES

1. Géraldine Rieucau, *Emigrants et salariés: Deux catégories nouvelles en Italie et en Espagne (1861–1975)* (Paris: La Documentation française, 1997).

2. Simonetta Soldani and Gabriele Turi, eds., *Fare gli Italiani: Scuola e cultura nell'Italia contemporanea*, vol. 1, *La nascità dello Stato nazionale* (Bologna: Il Mulino, 1993); Raffaele Romanelli, ed., *Storia dello stato italiano dall'Unità a oggi* (Rome: Donzelli, 1995); Ilaria Porciani, *La festa della nazione: Rappresentazione dello Stato e spazi sociali nell'Italia unita* (Bologna: Il Mulino, 1997); Silvana Patriarca, *Numbers and Nationhood: Writing Statistics in Nineteenth-Century Italy* (Cambridge, Eng.: Cambridge University Press, 1996); Dora Marucco, *L'amministrazione della statistica italiana dall'Unità al fascismo* (Turin: Pluriverso, 1992); Gilles Pécout, *Naissance de l'Italie contemporaine (1770–1922)* (Paris: Nathan, 1997), 170–78.

3. Carlo Pazzagli, "Statistica 'investigatrice' e scienze 'positive' nell'Italia dei primi decenni unitari," *Quaderni storici* 15 (1980): 779–822.

4. Patriarca, *Numbers and Nationhood*, chap.7.

5. "Science de l'Etat," *Actes de la Recherche en Sciences Sociales* 133 (June 2000).

6. The results were presented by the director of the central Italian statistical bureau: Luigi Bodio, *L'Italia economica* (Rome: Giunta Centrale di Statistica, 1873).

7. Fernando Manzotti, *La polemica sull'emigrazione nell'Italia unita* (Città di Castello: Società editrice Dante Alighieri, 1969).

8. Emilio Franzina, *La grande emigrazione: L'esodo dei rurali dal Veneto durante il secolo XIX* (Venice: Marsilio, 1976).

9. Romanelli, *Storia dello stato italiano.*

10. Marucco, *L'amministrazione della statistica;* Franco Bonelli, "Luigi Bodio," *Dizionario Biografico degli Italiani,* vol. 13 (Instituto della Enciclopedia italiana: Rome, 1971), 103–7.

11. See Emilio Franzina, "Il 'biometro delle nazioni'. Primi rilevamenti sull'emigrazione," *Quaderni storici* 15 (1980): 966–1005.

12. Manzotti, *La polemica sull'emigrazione.*

13. The statistics were collected annually and published every two years: Ministero di Agricoltura, Industria e Commercio (hereinafter MAIC), Direzione Generale della Statistica, *Statistica della emigrazione italiana all'estero,* 1876–1925, 29 vols. (Rome: 1876–1925).

14. The difficulties were at times insurmountable, since the emigration dynamic is never simply a matter of counting departures. However, the veritable classifying obsession undertaken in this domain shows how important the issue was considered.

15. He sketched a methodology for the study of emigration in his talk at the "Commissione per l'emigrazione: Seduta del 26 marzo 1877," MAIC, *Annali* (Rome: 1878), 192–200.

16. The bibliography concerning the performative effects of statistics is abundant: for Italy, see Patriarca, *Numbers and Nationhood;* for comparison, see Michel Volle, ed., *Pour une histoire de la statistique,* 2 vols. (Paris: Economica, 1977–1987); Alain Desrosières, *La politique des grands nombres: Histoire de la raison statistique* (Paris: La Découverte, 1993). On the ways in which administrative categories stigmatize immigrants, see Gérard Noiriel, *La tyrannie du national: Le droit d'asile en Europe, 1793–1993* (Paris: Calmann-Lévy, 1991); or Noiriel, *Etat, nation et immigration: Vers une histoire du pouvoir* (Paris: Belin, 2001).

17. See, for example, Valerio Castronovo, ed., *Biellesi nel mondo,* 4 vols. (Milan: Fondazione Sella-Electa, 1986–1990); C. Douki, "Le territoire économique d'une région d'émigration: Campagnes et montagnes lucquoises du milieu du XIXe siècle à 1914," *Revue d'histoire moderne et contemporaine* 48, 2/3 (April-September 2001): 192–244.

18. For a description of the way in which local administrators assembled statistics concerning departures and proposed their own view of the emigratory phenomenon, see C. Douki, "Les maires de l'Italie libérale à l'épreuve de l'émigration," *Mélanges de l'Ecole française de Rome-Italie et Méditerranée* 1 (1994): 333–64.

19. CGE, *Annuario statistico della emigrazione italiana dal 1876 al 1925,* xviii–xix.

20. Marie-Claude Blanc-Chaléard, Caroline Douki, Nicole Dyonnet, and Vincent Milliot, ed., *Police et migrants en France, 1667–1939* (Rennes: Presses Universitaires de Rennes, 2001).

21. Franzina, "Il biometro," 982–83.

22. Carlo Furno, *L'evoluzione sociale delle leggi italiane sull'emigrazione* (Varese: 1958); Rieucau, *Emigrants et salariés.*

23. Whereas from 1873 to 1875 the Italian government officially adopted a policy

of limiting departures (the Lanza decree), it was never applied. Manzotti, *La polemica*, 11–53; on the very relative implementation of this policy and that of issuing the *nulla osta* necessary prior to obtaining a passport, see C. Douki, "Les maires," 345–48.

24. Daniel Grange, *L'Italie et la Méditerranée (1896–1911): Les fondements d'une politique étrangère* (Rome: Ecole française de Rome, 1994), 2:941.

25. See, for example, Paola Corti, *Paesi d'emigranti: Mestieri, itinerari, identità collettive* (Milan: Angeli, 1990); Donna Gabaccia, *From Sicily to Elizabeth Street: Housing and Social Change among Italian Immigrants, 1880–1930* (Albany: State University of New York Press, 1983).

26. Noiriel, *La tyrannie.*

27. Fabio Grassi, "Il primo governo Crispi e l'emigrazione come fattore di una politica di potenza," in *Gli Italiani fuori d'Italia*, Bruno Bezza, ed., 45–100 (Milan: F. Angeli, 1983).

28. See, for example, the formal diplomatic protests and the concrete aid proffered by the Italian state in 1893 when Italian workers were attacked during the riots of Aigues-Mortes in southern France. Archivio storico del ministero degli affair esteri (ASMAE), serie Z-contenzioso, pos. 105: Fatti di Aigues-Mortes, agosto 1893, b.128–145; Pierre Milza, *Français et Italiens à la fin du XIXe siècle: Aux origines du rapprochement franco-italien de 1900–1902* (Rome: École française de Rome, 1981), 101–4 and 274–84.

29. Grange, *L'Italie et la Méditerranée*, 944–1033.

30. Patricia Salvetti, *Immagine nazionale ed emigrazione nella Società Dante Alighieri* (Rome: Bonacci, 1995).

31. Manzotti, *La polemica sull'emigrazione*, 105–24.

32. On this new definition, which explicitly linked emigration to the search for work, see C. Furno, *L'evoluzione sociale delle leggi*, 35–43; Manzotti, *La polemica sull'emigrazione*; Rieucau, *Emigrants et salariés*, 41–49.

33. From 1904 on, the estimates were based on the number of passports effectively delivered as well as the requests made by the Italian consular services on behalf of emigrants, who, once abroad, decided to ask for proper papers. Thus, a non-negligible part of the so-called clandestine departures ended up being taken into account in the official estimates. MAIC, DGS, *Statistica della emigrazione italiana per l'estero negli anni 1904 e 1905*, v–vi.

34. CGE, *Annuario statistico della emigrazione italiana dal 1876 al 1925* (Rome: 1926), xviii–xix.

35. The average stay in the United States was estimated to be five years, and between two and five years for Latin America.

36. These transformations should also be understood in connection with the general evolution of the culture of statistical inquiry. As Italian statistics became more autonomous, they were also increasingly sophisticated technically, including the use of new mathematical methods of formalization. See Jean-Guy Prévost, "Ge-

nèse particulière d'une science des nombres: L'autonomisation de la statistique en Italie entre 1900 et 1914," *Actes de la Recherche en Sciences Sociales* 141–42 (March 2002): 98–109.

37. Francesco Coletti, *Dell'emigrazione italiana: Cinquant'anni di storia italianna 1860–1910*, vol. 3 (Milan: Hoepli, 1911), 71–79.

38. For the exact wording of the law, see Furno, *L'evoluzione sociale,* 26–42. For details on the organization of aid, see Francesca Grispo, ed., *La struttura e il funzionamento degli organi preposti all'emigrazione (1901–1919),* series "Fonti per la storia dell'emigrazione" (Rome: Ministero degli affari esteri, 1986), 1:1–18.

39. Grispo, *La struttura;* Maria Rosaria Ostuni, "Momenti della contrasta vita del Commissariato Generale dell'Emigrazione, 1901–1927," in Bezza, *Gli Italiani,* 101–18.

40. Alain Dewerpe, "Quelques remarques à propos de l'institutionnalisation du marché du travail industriel dans l'Italie unifiée (1860–1914)," *Revue du Nord,* 307 (October-December 1994), 789–800.

41. A. Dewerpe, "Verso l'Italia industriale," in *Storia dell'economia italiana,* vol. 3: *L'età contemporanea: un paese nuovo,* 5–58 (Turin: Einaudi, 1991).

42. On this mixture of constraint and interest when migrants approached local administrative offices, see Douki, "Les maires"; Douki, "Lucquois au travail ou émigrés italiens? Les identités à l'épreuve de la mobilité transnationale, 1850–1914," *Le Mouvement social* 188 (July-September 1999), 17–41.

43. C. Douki, "Les retombées financières de l'émigration et le développement régional en Italie entre XIXe et XXe siècle," in *Crise espagnole et nouveau siècle en Méditerranée: Politiques publiques et mutations structurelles des économies dans l'Europe méditerranéenne (fin XIXe-début XXe siècle),* ed. Gérard Chastagnaret, 131–45 (Madrid-Aix-en-Provence: Casa de Velazquez-Publications de l'Université de Provence, 2000).

44. On the importance of remittances during this phase of increased industrial development, see Lucio Cafagna, *Dualismo e sviluppo nella storia d'Italia* (Venice: Marsilio, 1989); F. Bonelli, "Il capitalismo italiano: Linee generali di interpretazione," in *Storia d'Italia. Annali,* vol. 1 (Turin: Einaudi, 1978), 1195–1255; Luigi Mittone, "Le rimesse degli emigrati sino al 1914," *Affari sociali internazionali* 4 (1984): 125–60; Luigi De Rosa, *Emigranti, capitali, banche 1896–1906* (Naples: Ed. del Banco di Napoli, 1980).

45. Francesco Balletta, *Il Banco di Napoli e le rimesse degli emigranti (1914–1925)* (Naples: Ed. del Banco di Napoli, 1972).

46. This interpretation is suggested by Rieucau, *Emigrants et salariés,* 39.

47. For a precise description of this encounter between the emigrants' interests and the official position in a region of strong out-migration, see C. Douki, "Le territoire économique."

48. On the theme of emigration in nationalist discourse and its growing importance between 1905 and 1912, see Franco Gaeta, *Il nazionalismo italiano* (Rome-Bari:

Laterza, 1981); Silvio Lanaro, *Nazione e lavoro: Saggio sulla cultura borghese in Italia, 1870–1925* (Venice: Marsilio, 1979); Grange, *L'Italie et la Méditerranée*, 2:977–1034.

49. Among others: Robert Descimon, Jean-Frédéric Schaub, and Bernard Vincent eds., *Les figures de l'administrateur: Institutions, réseaux, pouvoirs en Espagne, en France et au Portugal, XVIe-XIXe siècle* (Paris: Editions de l'EHESS, 1997); Philippe Minard, "Faire l'histoire sociale des institutions: Démarches et enjeux," *Bulletin de la Société d'Histoire Moderne et Contemporaine*, no. 3–4 (2000): 119–23; Marc-Olivier Baruch and Vincent Duclert, eds., *Serviteurs de l'Etat: Une histoire politique de l'administration française, 1875–1945* (Paris: La Découverte, 2000).

50. The CGE had a globally positive attitude, even if it was placed, for practical reasons, within the Ministry of Foreign Affairs, where indeed it was poorly located and found itself in competition for resources with the diplomatic services. Ostuni, "Momenti della contrasta."

51. Ministero degli Affari Esteri, *Emigrazione e colonie. Raccolta di rapporti degli Agenti diplomatici e consolari*, 3 vols. (Rome, 1903).

52. I would like to thank Nicolas Manitakis for this information; he found elements of the Italian law in the archives of the Greek Ministry of Foreign Affairs. A draft law of 1909 was inspired by the Italian legislation, and an investigative study was effected in Italy in March-April 1911 by a high-ranking Greek official who visited the CGE in Rome and emigration inspection offices in Naples, Genoa, and Palermo.

5

THE FRENCH STATE AND

TRANSOCEANIC EMIGRATION

François Weil

In the fall of 1835, the French minister of the interior heard for the first time of an emigration movement from the border *département* of Basses-Pyrénées to Uruguay. He was alerted almost simultaneously by the French consul in Montevideo and the local prefect in Pau, Leroy, that "a society had been formed in order to establish a French colony in Montevideo and its agents were recruiting peasants and various kinds of artisans in [Pau]."[1] This set the state machine in motion. The interior minister immediately wrote back to demand more detailed information from the prefect, who forwarded the order to his deputy in Bayonne. Through the Foreign Ministry, the minister of the interior also requested more specific information from the French consul in Montevideo. Prefect Leroy repeatedly wrote the minister in Paris to ask for instructions and to report on the situation.

Local newspapers began to discuss the issue. Bayonne's *Phare* and *Sentinelle des Pyrénées* supported emigration; Pau's *Mémorial des Pyrénées* criticized the movement. The person responsible for organizing these departures was Alfred-Auguste Bellemare, who acted as agent for Lafone, Wilson, and Company of Montevideo; Lafone, Robinson and Company of Buenos Aires; and George Barker and Company of Liverpool. Bellemare regularly wrote to the prefect and his deputy, published several pamphlets on the subject, and published several articles in the local newspapers. By the spring of 1836, Prefect Leroy deemed the situation serious enough to send a printed circular letter to the deputies and the mayors of his département. He acknowledged the existence of "rather lively polemical debates" in the local newspapers and officially deplored the emigration movement. The emigration question remained a matter of public discussion throughout 1836 in the Basses-Pyrénées, but by 1837 it disappeared from public notice and official reports.[2]

This incident is of interest because of how little we know about the actual process of emigration from France. For reasons I have investigated elsewhere, historians often neglect or underestimate the importance of French migration overseas between the 1820s and the 1920s. Yet, hundreds of thousands of men and women elected to leave their home in France and emigrate to Argentina, the United States, or Canada. Recent works have only begun to explore and reintegrate their history into French history, migration history, or the history of their host countries.[3] However, much remains to be done. One important aspect of this larger story that requires analysis is the attitude of the French state toward emigration. That such a theme remains poorly understood is hardly surprising given historians' scant knowledge about the French state's actual modus operandi. As Pierre Rosanvallon rightly notes, "It seems as though it is considered that the state has no true history, that its development is only a pure reproduction, ever enlarged, of an image created at the beginning."[4] In a sense, then, I also hope to use the lens of emigration to contribute to the much-needed investigation of the process of national and administrative construction at work in nineteenth-century France.

I want to argue here that, contrary to conventional wisdom, emigration from France was a matter of public debate and public policy in the nineteenth century. Scholarly interpretations of this subject are few. The earliest was the work of Gustave Chandèze, a civil servant at the Ministry of Commerce in the late 1880s and a major figure in the organization in Paris of an international conference devoted to public intervention with regard to emigration and immigration. The conference took place during the 1889 Paris World Exhibition, with Chandèze as its general secretary. He gave a paper on emigration agencies, which he published the following year, and embarked upon the preparation of a law thesis that he defended and published in 1898. In this book, he offered a broad comparative view of public intervention in emigration in various European countries, concluding that public authorities were incapable of either forbidding or developing emigration, and could only attempt to redirect the flow toward their colonies.[5]

According to Chandèze, emigration policy throughout Europe experienced three successive stages. Before the nineteenth century, European states tightly controlled emigration and granted emigration privileges only to certain individuals or companies. By the early nineteenth century, emigrants were allowed to leave as they wished, provided they fulfilled certain administrative obligations. Around 1850, Chandèze argued, things changed. Various European countries adopted laws "regulating emigration in a very special way".[6] They had come to the conclusion that in order to protect emigrants from various types of abuse, "the state's direct intervention either in the choice of those individuals who want to become emigration agents or in the prescription of various measures to prevent abuse . . . was the best way to protect emigrants efficiently."[7] Although by the 1880s the number of emigrants was much higher than three decades earlier, Chandèze pointed out that this trend did not create "an important opinion movement in favor of a less liberal type of public intervention."[8]

Very little has been written about this topic since Gustave Chandèze. The only significant contribution is that of Nicole Fouché and Camille Maire, based on their analyses of Alsace and Lorraine, respectively. Fouché and Maire are convinced that "French political and administrative authorities [were] viscerally opposed to emigration" and attempted to prevent it using different strategies, such as denying passports to potential emigrants, using persuasion, publishing inaccurate descriptions of the host countries, etc.[9]

In a sense, the apparent contradiction between Chandèze's analysis on the one hand and Fouché and Maire's perspective on the other one is a consequence of the very different sources these authors use. Chandèze focuses on legal sources at the national or international level, while Fouché and Maire's description of the situation in Alsace and Lorraine is based on their exploration in local archives. In contrast, I start from a different premise and explore two interrelated topics in order to account for the web of complex decisions and attitudes that became France's public policy toward emigration, describing first how French authorities developed new ways of conceptualizing the phenomenon in the nineteenth century and then analyzing how they created an administrative apparatus in order to deal with it.

DISCOVERING EMIGRATION

It took three decades for emigration to emerge fully as a matter of debate, policy, and administration. Until the late 1830s, French officials were not much interested in the subject, except when it meant delivering passports. They did not discuss emigration publicly. Throughout the 1820s and 1830s, however, prefects from various parts of France repeatedly broached the subject with their superiors at the Ministry of Interior, as they reported the existence of various voluntary or induced departures for Latin or North America, and ministers requested notes on the subject from their collaborators. In late 1825 and early 1826, for instance, the Baron de Damas (minister of interior), the Comte de Corbière (foreign minister), the prefects of the départements of Gironde, Hautes-Pyrénées, Basses-Pyrénées, Haute-

Garonne, Ariège, Bouches-du-Rhône, Charente-Inférieure, and Dordogne, as well as the Paris police and the mayor of Toulouse, all closely monitored the activities of an emigration agent, Varaigne, who attempted to encourage departures of French artisans and workers for Buenos Aires.[10] On several occasions the prefects provided information and requested instructions, sometimes crudely revealing their ignorance of the legal and political context of emigration. "I do not know whether or not the mission of the Buenos Ayres emigration agents is legal," the deputy prefect of Dordogne wrote his prefect from Bergerac in May 1826, "and whether or not it meets with the government's approval." The prefect hardly knew better, and wrote the minister of the interior that he was "uncertain of the conduct [he was to] follow." This mixture of uncertainty and administrative concern for emigration well describes the attitude of many French officials during the 1820s and 1830s.[11]

During this period, many emigrants came from Alsace and Lorraine, the regions used by Nicole Fouché and Camille Maire to argue that French authorities clearly opposed emigration.[12] There is no doubt that emigration was an administrative concern there throughout this period: in 1838, for instance, the prefect of Bas-Rhin instructed his subordinates to provide him with a list of emigrants who had left the département since 1828. The lists that were established (extraordinarily detailed, by French administrative standards) testify to the administrative importance given to the issue.[13] Concern is not synonymous with systematic opposition, however. A more nuanced appreciation of the French official attitude toward emigration might come from the notion that until the 1850s, French civil servants made strong distinctions between various types of emigrants. They fought departures based on contract labor (*embauchage*), because this practice was specifically forbidden by article 417 of the penal code in order to prevent recruiting agents (*embaucheurs*) from hiring out artisans and laborers. Thus, when the prefect of Doubs, Milon de Mesne, reported to the minister of the interior in April 1828 that Italian emigration agents were trying to recruit French metalworkers for transalpine factories, the Interior Minister Martignac answered that this was "a kind of contract labor" (*une espèce d'embauchage*) and ordered the prefect "to keep a close watch on those individuals, foreigners or not, who would form these schemes against French industry," and to examine "whether they should be presented" to judicial authorities in application "of article 417 of the Penal Code."[14]

Prefects and other governmental officials were no less hostile to emigration when they encountered fraudulent emigration projects that misled and potentially endangered emigrants, forcing French authorities to act to protect them. One such emigration scam mobilized French authorities' attention for almost ten years. In 1823, a Scottish adventurer, Sir Gregor MacGregor, sold his claimed rights to certain lands in the Central American region of Cape Gracias a Dios (in today's Nicaragua) to a certain Lehuby, who created an emigration society, the *Compagnie de Nouvelle-Neustrie*. By 1825, the French police were continuously watching Lehuby, whom they unsuccessfully attempted to arrest in August and September 1825. Lehuby was finally arrested in the Netherlands in April 1826, then extradited to France, tried, and sentenced to thirteen months in jail. The project disappeared from public view for three years and resurfaced in late 1829, as the French ship *Glaneuse* sailed from Le Havre for Cape Gracias a Dios with more than sixty passengers. By June 1830, the Foreign Ministry reported that disaster had struck as the would-be colonists had found no settlement on the Cape, where they had been coldly received by the local Indians. Some went to Jamaica, others to Belize or Cuba, before they were repatriated to France at the expense of the government.[15] The impact of such disasters on French official attitude toward emigration should not be underestimated. The memory of the Cape Gracias a Dios incident and others remained alive in administrative circles long after the unfortunate colonists had returned home. In 1838, for instance, the Interior Minister Montalivet was reminded by the Foreign Ministry that diplomats had often warned of "the sad result of the schemes undertaken in France to colonize America," with little result since "the publicity that was given to these disasters unfortunately did not suffice to prevent their recurrence." To illustrate the point, the letter mentioned the Lehuby incident among others in Mexico and Venezuela and concluded that "France's dignity suffered and its interests were compromised" because of these incidents.[16]

For all other emigrants French authorities usually showed little sympathy, as historians Fouché and Maire correctly argue. But their attitudes varied considerably over time or place. Much depended on the personality of the prefect, minister, or civil servant in charge of the matter. Confidential instructions from the ministers of the interior to the prefects often reminded these local officials of their obligation to abide by the law, whatever their personal feelings may have been vis-à-vis emigration. In 1828, for instance, D'Allouin, the prefect of Meurthe, wrote from Nancy to inquire whether he could deliver a passport for the United States to a young man before the conscription drawing for his military class had taken place. In the prefect's view, the question was important "on the one hand, in the interest of individual freedom, on the other in the interest, no less precious, of the army and of the population." The emigration "of young men around the time of the drawing" will "lead to a smaller number of men carrying a load that should naturally be shared among a larger number."[17] The minister's answer, however, was quite clear. Had the young man been hired by a recruiting agent? If so, both should be prosecuted for "*embauchage*." If the prefect found this not to be the case, he should attempt to persuade the young man and other potential emigrants to abandon their project. Should they persist, they should receive the passports they requested. As for potential soldiers, the minister reminded the prefect, "[I]t is not possible, in the current state of legislation, to refuse to deliver them passports. Since they are not soldiers until they become so, they may enjoy the rights that belong to all Frenchmen, and there is no disposition that would enable us to keep them in the kingdom." Should these men be drawn for the army, and not answer the call, they would be prosecuted as deserters, but the prefects could not prevent potential soldiers from emigrating.[18] Moreover, although some prefects, like D'Allouin, were resolute opponents of emigration, others were much more moderate. Whatever their personal feelings, however, these senior civil servants always respected the instructions they received from Paris.

By the late 1830s, three key elements changed the political and ideological context of emigration: ten times more emigrants left France every year than in the 1820s; after the conquest of Algeria, colonization had become an issue once again; and a Malthusian vision of French demography gave way to populationism. As a result, emigration entered public debates, from administrative offices in Paris and the provinces to political circles, numerous books, newspapers, and official reports.

The Bellemare incident described in the introduction of this chapter, for instance, stirred a local public debate that lasted from 1835 to 1837 among political and administrative officials, businessmen, journalists, and publicists. All took sides, as did the General Council of the Basses-Pyrénées a few years later, when emigration to La Plata experienced important growth.[19] Debates of this type were not continuous, but they never disappeared for good. In the case of the Basses-Pyrénées, for instance, emigration was widely debated in 1835–37, in the early 1840s, in the mid-1850s, in the mid-1860s, and almost without interruption from the 1870s to World War I.[20]

Everywhere, opponents of emigration argued that it accelerated depopulation and weakened the country. Partisans of emigration disagreed, suggesting that emigration signaled a healthy demography and that it helped spread throughout the world what they considered to be France's civilizing mission.[21] However, they did serve to pave the way for the French state's collective elaboration of a policy toward emigration. Particularly important in this regard was a group of civil servants who were professionally interested in emigration because it could have an impact on French demographic evolution. These statistician-demographers, as they are sometimes called, were few in number but their action was decisive.[22]

Alfred Legoyt is a case in point. Legoyt (1812–1885) began his career in the 1830s as a clerk in the Ministry of the Interior. By 1839, he was deputy chief of the ministry's Bureau of Statistics. In the 1850s, he was transferred to the Ministry of Commerce where he headed the statistics bureau and later the division of statistics (the Statistique générale de la France, or SGF) until the fall of the Second Empire in 1870. As such, Legoyt was France's most important official statistician during those decades, representing his country in international conferences on statistics in the 1850s and organizing France's census of 1856, 1861, and 1866. He was also one of the founders and the permanent general secretary of the powerful Paris Statistical Society. Legoyt wrote extensively on migration, particularly in an 1861 essay on *L'émigration européenne, son importance, ses causes, ses effets* [*European Emigration: Its Importance, Its Causes, Its Effects*]. He did not think that emigration threatened French demography, and he publicized his views in official circles. Likewise, Legoyt's colleagues Charles Lavollée and Charles Desmaze, who both later headed the Ministry of Interior's Bureau of Emigration, were quite clear that emigration was demographically harmless but commercially important for France.[23]

One of the clearest positive visions of emigration was that of Jules Duval, the author in 1862 of an important *Histoire de l'émigration européenne, asiatique et africaine au XIXe siècle: Ses causes, ses caractères, ses effets* [*History of European, Asian, and African Emigration in the Nineteenth Century: Its Causes, Its Characters, Its Effects*]. Born in Aveyron in 1813, Duval moved to Algeria, where he became a journalist and the secretary of the General Council of the Province of Oran in the late 1850s. In 1860, the Paris-based Academy of Moral and Political Sciences offered a prize for the best book addressing emigration. Duval won, suggesting in his work that not only was emigration an opportunity for a country, but that the lack thereof denoted "an exhaustion of vital sap," "a symptom of disease and decline." Duval argued: "Like stagnant waters, stagnant populations rot."[24]

Perhaps because of this animated and undecided debate between proponents and opponents of emigration, the French government's first elaboration of a policy toward emigration carefully avoided any value judgment on the subject. In the summer of 1854, the Minister of Agriculture, Magne, appointed an ad hoc commission to investigate claims by Le Havre businessmen that Hamburg and Bremen's capacity to attract German America-bound emigrants could endanger the French port's economy. The commission included the mayors of Le Havre and Strasbourg, and ten senior civil servants, including the director-general of public security, the director of colonization, and various officials in charge of customs, foreign affairs, commerce, and railroads. A few months later, the commission's head, Nicolas Heurtier, a senior civil servant who was at the time the ministry's director-general of agriculture and commerce, submitted a 390–page report to Napoleon III. Heurtier's report contained over 330 pages of statistics, legal briefs, and data on French and European migration movements, as well as the commission's conclusions and propositions.[25]

Acknowledging the new importance of international migrations, commission members focused mostly on foreign nationals transiting through France, but their conclusions applied as well to French emigrants. Quite explicitly, they proposed to "substitute the government's paternal intervention" to the previous "regime of *laissez-faire* and *laissez-passer*," in order to achieve some control over emigration. By control, they did not mean an interdiction but rather a means to protect emigrants from unscrupulous emigration agents or ship captains. Emigrants were "worthy of special protection" and commission members easily recognized that there was more to it than "humanitarian reasons." France's commerce could not afford to lose the "benefits of the important transit" of German emigrants bound to America. Since this governmental intervention was already a "flagrant violation" of free trade principles, commission members suggested regulation should be minimal. The government should limit its action to controlling emigration agencies and protecting emigrants on French soil and ships.[26]

Within a few months, the commission's suggestions became law and framed the contours of the State's intervention vis-à-vis emigration. On January 15, 1855, an imperial decree emphasized moderate interventionism aimed at protecting emigrants and business interests. It defined the rules that emigration agencies had to respect in order to operate. Emigration agents were to apply for and receive an authorization that could be taken away from them in case of abuse; they were to put down a monetary guarantee that would assure their commitment to their operations; their various obligations vis-à-vis emigrants were detailed. Like the Heurtier report, the 1855 decree was clearly aimed primarily at foreign nationals transiting through France, while at the same time it applied to French emigrants. It neither prohibited nor encouraged emigration, although potential French emigrants were openly encouraged to choose to settle in the French colonies rather than go to the Americas. As Gustave Chandèze later noted, France's policy toward emigration was not very different from Great Britain's, and certainly less hostile to emigration than Spain's or Italy's.[27]

The 1855 imperial decree (modified in content but not in spirit by the law of July 18, 1860, and decrees of 1861, 1868, and 1874) defined France's *official* and *theoretical* attitude toward emigration. In practice, however, things were quite different. Controlling emigration and protecting emigrants could mean very different things, depending on the period, the place, and the civil servants involved. Emigration control first meant delivering and stamping passports and overseeing the activities of private emigration agencies. Prefects regularly reported to the Ministry of Interior on emigration-related subjects, and in return, they frequently received instructions or warnings from the ministry. In 1889, for instance, the ministry alerted all French prefects about the unusual size of emigration to Argentina. The obvious lack of sympathy the ministry's official circulars often displayed toward emigration and emigration agencies bordered, at times, on straightforward hostility. In 1886, a circular encouraged French prefects to convince the mayors to take "useful action" against emigration agencies. In 1912, another circular, stamped "highly confidential," encouraged all prefects to prevent emigration to Argentina. In order to avoid a diplomatic crisis with Buenos Aires, however, prefects were to pass on confidential instructions to their deputies and only verbal instructions to the mayors.[28] The ministry based this type of administrative regulation on its own paternalistic definition of what was good or bad for the state and for emigrants.

Protecting emigrants, indeed, was a difficult task. Government authorities never betrayed the letter of the law by forbidding emigration. As in the past, official circulars were always careful to remind prefects that French men and women could emigrate if they wished. Civil servants even provided information to would-be emigrants: when Louis Bouisset, a cartwright in the Vaucluse town of Valréas, wrote to the Ministry of the Interior in late 1888 to request the address of an emigration agency for Buenos Aires close to his residence, the ministry asked the prefect of Vaucluse to forward him the names of four emigration agents in Marseilles.[29] More often, however, French officials attempted to discourage, and therefore protect, potential emigrants by making public negative information on the various host countries. What they often had in mind, of course, was to redirect emigrants toward French colonies. The task, however, was difficult. In 1857, a senior civil servant at the Ministry of the Interior commented on the difficulties prospective colonials found in Algeria and made clear his hopes that "Algeria offer as soon as possible interesting possibilities of settlement," because "it will be the best way to capture the emigration flow that attracts too many of our nationals towards Southern American countries."[30] For most emigrants, however, the North American and Latin American magnet always remained stronger than its colonial, Algerian counterpart.

More successfully, French authorities created several levels of administrative controls in order to protect emigrants, be they French nationals or foreigners transiting through France, against unscrupulous emigration agencies. Prompted by several incidents in the 1840s and 1850s, these types of administrative measures also aimed at regulating attempts to encourage European immigration made by Argentina, Canada, Chile, and even the United States during the Civil War. Government protection also extended to French emigrants abroad. They could seek the assistance of consular services and in some cases have the state pay for their repatriation. Local French archives contain traces of many such incidents. In September 1875, for instance, a Madame Estève, of Sérignan, Vaucluse, wrote to the foreign minister about her husband and her son, both of whom were in Montevideo, apparently wanting to return to France but with no money to pay for the trip. Madame Estève's petition was transmitted to the Ministry of the Interior, then to the prefect of the Vaucluse, the deputy prefect, and finally to Serignan's mayor, who testified that the Estève family was honorable and deserved "an act of benevolence from the government."[31] It is not known whether Madame Estève's request was satisfied in the end, but the example was typical of the protection some emigrants and emigrant families expected from the state.

EMIGRATION AND ADMINISTRATIVE SPECIALIZATION WITHIN THE STATE

In order to fulfill these various tasks, French authorities built a multilayered administrative structure. This took time, since they had to assess the magnitude and nature of, and define proper administrative answers to, emigration. During the Restoration, the government considered emigration to be a simple matter of general policing. As such, it came under the purview of the Interior Ministry, which was, at the time, in charge of all police, administrative, agricultural, and commercial matters. What mattered most to

Interior officials was passport control. When they left their place of residence, French citizens needed a passport to travel within France (*passeport à l'intérieur*) or to leave the country (*passeport à l'étranger,* or *à l'extérieur*). Until 1828, potential emigrants submitted passport applications to their town's mayor. Applications then began a lengthy and hierarchical administrative journey from the mayor's office to the deputy prefect, the prefect, and finally the Ministry of the Interior in Paris. Once a decision was made, it was sent back down this hierarchy until it reached the applicant.[32]

By 1828, this highly centralized system had become impracticable, and each prefect received the authority to deliver passports in his own département. The 1830s and 1840s saw little change at the Ministry of Interior, which lost its supervisory role on commerce and public works but remained solidly in charge of all police matters, including population movements. However, the state displayed a relatively new concern for statistics, as the creation of the Statistique générale de la France (SGF) demonstrated in 1840. The SGF was the heir to the Bureau of Statistics that had existed under the Consulate and First Empire before the Restoration regime had transferred its duties to the department of general administration in the Ministry of the Interior. The SGF's creation testified to the growing importance of the relatively new Ministry of Commerce and Public Works, a July Monarchy byproduct that included a statistical section, the Second Bureau of the Superior Council of Commerce. This section became the SGF in 1840. Moreau de Jonnès, long-standing chief of the bureau, became SGF's first head, with authority over population statistics. At the same time, however, the Ministry of the Interior developed its own bureau of statistics, headed by Alfred Legoyt. With the creation of these bureaus and the statistical tools they developed, civil servants began to view emigration not only as a police matter, but also as a question linked to larger issues of demography and economics.[33]

Not surprisingly, major administrative and political changes in France's management of emigration took place during the Second Empire. Administratively, emigration remained largely a police matter under the supervision of the Ministry of the Interior and its civil servants (prefects, deputy prefects, and police commissioners) in Paris and the various départements and towns, but at the Ministry's headquarters it came under the purview of the Third Bureau of the General Direction of Public Security. This bureau centralized all the information the ministry received from the provinces and began extending its activity and publishing annual statistics of emigration beginning in 1855. Moreover, the ministry appointed special police commissioners to deal specifically with immigration matters in several border and port cities, as well as in Paris.

In contrast with the first half of the nineteenth century, emigration became a matter of special, not general, police surveillance, and as such it involved other administrative actors along with civil servants from the Ministry of the Interior. What "special police" actually meant, Charles Desmaze, head of the ministry's emigration bureau in the late 1850s, explained quite clearly in his 1857 report to the minister of the interior. The administration was in a "delicate situation," since at the same time it had to protect emigrants, avoid raising transportation costs by overregulating emigration agencies, and make it easy for foreign nationals to leave from France rather than Antwerp, Bremen, or Hamburg. He concluded that because emigration was "a major commercial and industrial interest that had to be protected," its regulation involved the Ministry of Commerce and not only the Ministry of the Interior. "This is what gives a special character to the emigration police, and essentially distinguishes it from the ordinary police force. It would be dangerous for our commercial interests to confuse the two, either from a theoretical or a practical point of view."[34]

Since emigration was no "ordinary" police matter, it also received "special" administrative treatment involving the Ministries of the Interior, Commerce, and Foreign Affairs. The Ministry of the Interior's ad hoc office regularly requested information from the prefects and prepared confidential circulars for the minister's signature. On October 1, 1875, for instance, a circular requested that all prefects provide within two months all their available statistics on emigration from 1864 to 1875, since the ministry's archives had been destroyed in 1871 during the Paris Commune. Statistics by sex, occupation, age, nationality, military situation, and country of emigration were thus duly provided by each *arrondissement*. In the following years similarly detailed reports on emigration were compiled and published by the Ministry of the Interior, either on its own or as a section of the *Annuaire statistique de la France*.[35]

As Desmaze suggests, the Ministries of Commerce and Foreign Affairs were also systematically consulted on emigration matters. Commerce was also home to the SGF, which was reorganized in 1852 under Legoyt and became a division in 1861. The SGF remained in charge of measuring internal and outward population movements, and of preparing the national census. Beyond its demographic interest in emigration, the Ministry of Commerce defended its vested interest in the economic benefits of emigration. As for the Foreign Ministry, not only did it display considerable interest toward French emigrants through its embassies and consular services, but it also had the responsibility of managing diplomatic incidents with foreign governments in relation to emigration or the repatriation of emigrants.

CONCLUSION

By the end of the Second Empire, French authorities had created a three-tiered, specialized system of administrative management of emigration based on the cooperation of the Ministries of Interior, Commerce, and Foreign Affairs. This system did not experience any important change until World War I, although the names of the various administrative departments involved could vary, as in the case of the General Direction of Public Security, which became the Direction of General Security. The type and content of regulation, however, remained largely the same. It was based on a compromise between laissez-faire and intervention, freedom and protection, the interest of the state and the interest of the emigrants. Unwilling and unable either to prevent or to encourage emigration, French authorities chose to regulate it. Writing the entry on emigration in Léon Say and Joseph Chailley's 1891 *Nouveau dictionnaire d'économie politique,* the statistician Victor Turquan, head of the SGF from 1887 to 1896, summarized France's official attitude toward emigration. "In principle," he argued, state intervention to encourage or discourage emigration was "dangerous" and inconsistent with the laws of laissez-faire. However, states had obligations vis-à-vis their citizens. "If emigration is free, it is the duty of the authorities to oversee it and require serious guarantees of emigration agents." On the other hand, if the state is given the right to interfere with the recruitment of emigrants, "it cannot be refused the right to favor one type of emigration over another." In the last analysis, Turquan concluded, "one cannot prevent public authorities from intervening in emigration matters, but they must act only in the interest of the emigrants of society."[36] In order to achieve their goal, French authorities created specialized legal, administrative, and statistical tools, which they used to measure, police, and protect emigration and emigrants. By the late nineteenth century, as elsewhere in Europe, the French state had learned to deal with emigrants, just as emigrants had learned to deal with the state's attitude toward their decision to leave.

1. Foreign minister to the minister of the interior, November 4, 1835; minister of the interior to the prefect of Basses-Pyrénées, November 6, 1835; prefect of Basses-Pyrénées to the minister, November 10 and 12, 1835, folder "Amérique du Sud: Emigration pour la République de l'Uruguay; Etablissement d'une colonie française à Montévidéo," Archives nationals Paris [hereafter AN] F7 9335.

2. Minister of the interior to the prefect of Basses-Pyrénées, November, 20, December 24 and 25, 1835; May 16, June 12, December 18, 1836; prefect of Basses-Pyrénées to the minister of the interior, December 9 and 18, 1835; May 19 and 26, June 25, 1836; January 19, 1837, AN F7 9335; A.-A. Bellemare, *Notice sur la république orientale de l'Uruguay, suivie d'un recueil de pièces officielles relatives aux encouragements qu'y trouvent l'agriculture, l'industrie et le commerce* (Bayonne: Imprimerie de Lamaignére, 1835); Bellemare, *Rapport adressé à M. le Préfet des Basses-Pyrénées, sur les expéditions de passagers basques et béarnais, qui ont lieu à Bayonne pour Montévidéo* (Bayonne: Imprimerie de Lamaignère, 1835); Bellemare to the deputy prefect of Bayonne, November 30, 1835; *Phare de Bayonne*, December 15, 1835; Bellemare to Leroy, March 27, 1836; *Sentinelle des Pyrénées*, March 22 and 31, 1836; *Mémorial des Pyrénées*, March 26, April 7, May 21, 1836; "Emigration pour Montévidéo," circular letter, May 26, 1836, *Recueil des actes administratifs du département des Basses-Pyrénées* 14 (1836): 165–67; Bellemare to the minister, November 27, 1836; foreign minister to the minister of the interior, March 31 and December 13, 1836; all in "Amérique du Sud," AN F7 9335.

3. François Weil, "French Migration to the Americas in the 19th and 20th Centuries as a Historical Problem," *Studi Emigrazione: Etudes migrations* 33 (1996): 443–60; Weil, "Les migrants français aux Amériques (19e-20e siècles), nouvel objet d'histoire," *Annales de démographie historique* (2000): 5–10. For an example, see Annick Foucrier, *Le rêve californien: Migrants français sur la côte Pacifique (XVIIIe-XXe siècles)* (Paris: Belin, 1999). For a European-wide perspective, see Leslie Page Moch, *Moving Europeans: Migration in Western Europe since 1650* (Bloomington: Indiana University Press, 1992).

4. Pierre Rosanvallon, *L'État en France de 1789 à nos jours* (Paris: Editions du Seuil, 1990), 10. Since 1990 the work of various scholars, such as Gérard Noiriel and others, have contributed to our better understanding of the process of state building in nineteenth-century France.

5. Gustave Chandèze, *Surveillance des agents d'émigration: Législation comparée des pays d'Europe* (Paris: Bibliothèque des *Annales économiques*, Société d'éditions scientifiques, 1890); Chandèze, *L'émigration: Intervention des pouvoirs publics au XIXe siècle* (Paris: Imprimerie Paul Dupont, 1898), 359–60. On the 1889 International Conference on Emigration and Immigration, see Nancy L. Green, "'Filling the Void': Immigration to France Before World War I," in *Labor Migration in the Atlantic Economies: The European and North American Working Classes during the*

Period of Industrialization, ed. Dirk Hoerder, 143–61 (Wesport, Conn.: Greenwood, 1985); *Congrès international de l'intervention des pouvoirs publics dans l'émigration et l'immigration, tenu à Paris, les 12, 13 et 14 août 1889* (Paris: Bibliothèque des *Annales économiques,* Société d'éditions scientifiques, 1890); Prince de Cassano, *Procès-verbaux sommaires du Congrès international de l'intervention des pouvoirs publics dans l'émigration et l'immigration, tenu à Paris du 12 au 14 août 1889: Exposition universelle internationale de 1889* (Paris: Imprimerie nationale, 1890).

6. Chandèze, *L'émigration,* 9.

7. Chandèze, *Surveillance,* 3.

8. Ibid., 24.

9. Nicole Fouché and Camille Maire. "L'émigration, un 'droit' contesté en Alsace et en Lorraine," in *Les Français des Etats-Unis d'hier à aujourd'hui,* ed. Ronald Creagh with John P. Clark, 239 (Montpellier: Université Paul Valéry and Editions Espaces, 1994).

10. Paris police prefect to the minister of the interior, August 19 and 30, September 13, October 11, 1825; minister of the interior to the Paris police prefect, August 24, September 4, 1825; Baron de Damas, foreign minister, to the Count de Corbière, minister of the interior, September 21, 1825; prefect of Gironde to the minister of the interior, September 27 and November 25, 1825; prefect of Hautes-Pyrénées to the minister, December 16, 1825, February 4, 1826; prefect of Basses-Pyrénées to the minister, December 20, 1825; prefect of Haute-Garonne to the minister, December 21, 1825, March 13, April 28, 1826; prefect of Ariège to the minister, December 21, 1825; prefect of Bouches-du-Rhône to the minister, January 9, 1826; Baron de Montbel, mayor of Toulouse to the minister, March 9, 1826; prefect of Charente-Inférieure to the minister, April 10, 1826; deputy prefect of Dordogne to the prefect, May 13, 1826; prefect of Dordogne to the minister, May 13, 1826; minister of the interior to the prefect of Gironde, October 9 and December 6, 1825; Haute-Garonne, December 26, 1825 and March 22, 1826; Basses-Pyrénées, December 27, 1825; Ariège, December 28, 1825; Dordogne, May 25, 1826; and to the mayor of Toulouse, March 17, 1826, "Emigration à Buenos-Ayres," AN F7 9334.

11. Underprefect of Dordogne to the prefect, May 13, 1826; prefect of Dordogne to the minister, May 13, 1826, AN F7 9334.

12. Fouché and Maire, "L'émigration."

13. Archives départementales du Bas-Rhin, 3 M 703. On these lists, see Nicole Fouché, *Émigration alsacienne aux Etats-Unis, 1815–1870* (Paris: Publications de la Sorbonne, 1992), 50–57; Jean-Pierre Kintz, "Une enquête administrative sur l'émigration en Amérique sous la monarchie de Juillet: Le cas des Alsaciens," in *Mesurer et comprendre: Mélanges offerts à Jacques Dupâquier,* ed. Jean-Pierre Bardet, François Lebrun, and René Le Mée, 265–75 (Paris: Presses universitaires de France, 1993). A similar investigation was undertaken in the Basses-Pyrénées in 1841–1842; see prefect of Basses-Pyrénées to the minister of the interior, December 17, 1841 and October 5, 1842, "Amérique du Sud," AN F7 9335.

14. Prefect of Doubs to the minister of the interior, April 17, 1828; minister to the prefect, May 2, 1828, "Emigration des sujets bavarois, badois, et wurtembergeois," AN F7 9334.

15. Paris police prefect to the minister of the interior, August 24, September 19, 1825; minister of the interior to the prefects of Nord, Aisne, Oise, Seine-et-Oise, April 24, 1826; Paris police prefect to the minister of the interior, November 29, 1826; minister of navy and the colonies to the minister of the interior, February 22, 1830; foreign minister to minister of the interior, June 12, July 3 and 8, November 15, December 27, 1830, "Nouvelle Neustrie," AN F7 9334.

16. Foreign Ministry (Direction commerciale et du contentieux), to the minister of the interior, August 4, 1838, "Amérique du Sud, terres à coloniser au Mexique, Goazacoalcos, Jicaltepec, Mosquitos, 1831–1838," AN F7 9334.

17. Prefect of Meurthe to the minister of the interior, May 6, 1828, "Emigration pour l'Amérique du Nord", AN F7 9334.

18. Minister of the interior to the prefect of Meurthe, May 13, 1828, "Emigration pour l'Amérique du Nord", AN F7 9334.

19. Département des Basses-Pyrénées, *Procès-verbaux et délibérations du Conseil général: Session de 1841* (Pau: Imprimerie et lithographie de E. Vignancour, 1841), 12; ibid., *Session de 1842* (1842), 35–36, 117.

20. François Brie, *Considérations sur l'émigration basque à Montévidéo, suivies d'une appréciation justificative des démêlés que l'auteur a eus avec le tribunal de Bayonne, au sujet de cette émigration* (Bayonne: Imprimerie de Lamaignère, 1841); P. O'Quin, *Du décroissement de la population dans le département des Basses-Pyrénées* (Pau: Imprimerie Vignancour, 1856); Elisée Reclus, "Les Basques: Un peuple qui s'en va," *Revue des Deux Mondes* (March 15, 1867): 313–40; M. Planté, *Rapport sur l'émigration (présenté au Conseil général des Basses-Pyrénées)* (Pau, 1873); Dr. Fuster, "Des progrès de l'émigration dans les Basses-Pyrénées," *Congrès scientifique de France, 39e session, Pau, 1873* (Pau, 1873); Pierre Barberen, *L'émigration basco-béarnaise* (Pau: Imprimerie Vignancour, 1886); Louis Etcheverry, "Les Basques et leur émigration en Amérique," *La Réforme sociale* 11 (1886): 491–515; Louis Etcheverry, "L'émigration dans les Basses-Pyrénées pendant soixante ans," *Association française pour l'avancement des sciences* 2 (1892): 1092–1104 (reprinted in *Revue des Pyrénées* [1893]: 509–20); Adrien Planté, *Rapport sur l'émigration: L'émigration à la ville. L'émigration à l'étranger* (Bayonne: Lasserre, 1911).

21. On these debates, see Weil, "French Migration to the Americas."

22. On the statistician-demographers, see in particular Zheng Kang, "Lieu de savoir social: La Société de statistique de Paris au 19e siècle (1860–1910)," PhD diss., Ecole des Hautes Etudes en Sciences Sociales, Paris, 1989.

23. Alfred Legoyt, *L'émigration européenne, son importance, ses causes, ses effets, avec un appendice sur l'émigration africaine, hindoue et chinoise* (Paris: Guillaumin, 1861); Charles Lavollée, "L'émigration européenne dans le Nouveau-Monde," *Revue des Deux Mondes* 16 (October 1, 1852): 92–129; [Charles Desmaze], *Rapports*

à Son Excellence le Ministre de l'Intérieur sur l'émigration: Années 1857 et 1858 (Paris: Imprimerie impériale, 1859), 8, 16.

24. Jules Duval, *Histoire de l'émigration européenne, asiatique et africaine au XIXe siècle: ses causes, ses caractères, ses effets* (Paris: Librairie Guillaumin Cie, 1862), vii. On Duval, see Jacques Valette, "Socialisme utopique et idée coloniale: Jules Duval (1813–1870)," PhD diss. (*thèse d'Etat*), University of Paris I, 1975.

25. Nicolas Jean Jacques François Heurtier, *Rapport à Son Excellence le Ministre de l'Agriculture, du Commerce et des Travaux Publics fait au nom de la Commission chargée d'étudier les différentes questions qui se rattachent à l'émigration européenne* (Paris: Imprimerie impériale, 1854). On the Heurtier Commission, see Fouché, *Emigration*, 68–90; Camille Maire, *En route pour l'Amérique. L'odyssée des émigrants en France au XIXe siècle* (Nancy: Presses universitaires de Nancy, 1993), 79–94.

26. Heurtier, *Rapport*, 11, 15, 25.

27. Chandèze, *L'émigration*, chap. 1–3. Chandèze made a distinction between countries that attempted to prevent emigration (Spain, Portugal, Austria, Italy), countries that tolerated emigration and attempted to protect emigrants (Switzerland, Belgium, Holland, and the Scandinavian countries), and countries that attempted to protect emigrants and redirect emigration to their colonies (England, France, Germany, Russia).

28. Circular letter of the minister of the interior to the prefects, January 16, 1886, April 18, 1889, June 6, 1912, Archives départementales du Finistère, 6 M 881 and 6 M 882.

29. Direction de la Sûreté générale (3e Bureau, Emigration) to the prefect of Vaucluse, January 24, 1889, "Dossiers d'émigrants, 1875–1901," Archives départementales du Vaucluse, 6 M 330.

30. [Desmaze], *Rapports*, 10.

31. Madame Estève to the foreign minister, September 2, 1875; mayor of Sérignan to the deputy prefect of the Vaucluse, September 20, 1875, "Dossiers d'émigrés, 1875–1901," Archives départementales du Vaucluse, 6 M 330.

32. On the history of the passport in France, see the older works by Adrien Sée, *Le passeport en France* (Chartres, 1907) and Maurice d'Hartoy, *Histoire du passeport français depuis l'Antiquité jusqu'à nos jours* (Paris, 1937), and the more recent ones by Gérard Noiriel, "Contribution à l'histoire du passeport en France de la Ire à la IIIe République," *Genèses* 30 (March 1998): 77–100; John Torpey, *The Invention of the Passport: Surveillance, Citizenship, and the State* (Cambridge, Eng.: Cambridge University Press, 2000), esp. chap. 2. See also Jane Caplan and John Torpey, eds. *Documenting Individual Identity: The Development of State Practices in the Modern World* (Princeton, N.J.: Princeton University Press, 2001); and Andreas Fahrmeir, Olivier Faron, and Patrick Weil, eds. *Migration Control in the North Atlantic World: The Evolution of State Practices in Europe and the United States from the French Revolution to the Inter-War Period* (New York: Berghahn, 2002).

33. On the SGF, see in particular Jacques Dupâquier and Renè Le Mée, "La con-

naissance des faits démographiques, de 1789 à 1914," in *Histoire de la population française. 3. De 1789 à 1914,* ed. Jacques Dupâquier, 15–62 (Paris: Presses universitaires de France, 1988). We still lack a modern history of the ministry of the interior. See H. Terson, *Origines et évolution du ministère de l'Intérieur* (Montpellier, 1913) and Association du corps préfectoral et des hauts fonctionnaires du ministère de l'Intérieur, *Histoire du ministère de l'Intérieur de 1790 à nos jours* (Paris: La Documentation française, 1993).

34. Desmaze, *Rapports,* 16.

35. Circular letter of the minister of the interior (Direction générale de la sûreté publique, 3e Bureau, Emigration) to the prefects, October 1, 1875, Archives départementales du Finistère, 6 M 881, and Archives départementales du Vaucluse, 6 M 329; Ministère de l'Intérieur, *Mouvement de l'émigration en France, Années 1875 à 1877: Rapport à M. le Ministre de l'Intérieur* (Paris: Imprimerie nationale, 1879); Ministère de l'Intérieur, *Mouvement de l'émigration en France, Années 1878 à 1881* (1883).

36. Victor Turquan, "Émigration," in *Nouveau dictionnaire d'économie politique,* ed. Léon Say and Joseph Chailley, 1:802–3 (Paris: Guillaumin, 1891).

PART III

THE COSTS
OF EMIGRATION

6

EMIGRATION AND THE BRITISH STATE,
CA. 1815–1925

David Feldman and M. Page Baldwin

Between the conclusion of one world war in 1815 and the start of another in 1914, approximately sixteen million people emigrated from the United Kingdom. During this extended period more migrants were recorded leaving the British Isles than any other European country.[1] The greatest part of this emigrant stream was destined for the United States; in other words, the majority of emigrants not only left the country but also settled outside the British Empire. In the 1880s and 1890s, for instance, fewer than one-third of emigrants left for destinations within the empire. Toward the end of our period, however, this emphasis was first checked and then reversed: in the first half of the twentieth century the proportion of emigrants traveling to the Dominions rose to one-half, and in the 1920s it reached 65 percent.[2]

It was not only the flow of emigrants but also government policy on emigration that underwent a striking shift in the early twentieth century. For more than a hundred years following the Napoleonic Wars, British governments resisted successive schemes brought forward by politicians and philanthropists, radicals and conservatives that aimed to involve the state in large-scale financial support for schemes of assisted emigration and colonization. In 1919 and, more decisively, in 1922 the British government reversed this policy. In 1922 the Empire Settlement Act authorized expenditure of up to £3 million per year for fifteen years to encourage migration to the Dominions. This chapter sets out to explain and characterize government policy toward emigration in the century following the Napoleonic Wars and to account for the abrupt change of direction after 1918.

THE FISCAL LIMITS TO POLICY

At the beginning of the nineteenth century, British governments did not encourage emigration. The manpower needs of the war against France, as well as the view that emigration was a drain on population—the very basis of national wealth—made the idea unattractive. Moreover, the experience of the American War of Independence suggested that no good would come from the creation of large imperial colonies; empire was intended to promote commerce without sizeable settlement. New South Wales, for instance, founded in 1788, was broadly disregarded by British governments except as a repository for convicts.[3]

Attitudes began to shift with the onset of peace. For more than three decades after 1815, the British governing class believed it lived in the shadow of a Malthusian crisis. Population growth threatened to outstrip the demand for labor and, in doing so, cause widespread immiseration, agitation, and revolt. In the case of Ireland the predicament was chronic. In Britain, in urban and industrial districts, the crisis was intermittent but certain to recur whenever the trade cycle dipped. In the agrarian south and east the crisis was persistent, giving rise to social disruption, violence, and soaring levels of poor relief, which had to be supported by the local property tax. Expenditure on poor relief in England and Wales rose rapidly from £2 million in 1783–85 to a peak of £7.9 million in 1818, remaining around £6–7 million per year for the next sixteen years.[4]

For many people, emigration appeared to be a palliative or even a solution to these problems.[5] This point of view was expounded at length in the 1826 report of the House of Commons Select Committee on Emigration. The chairman and driving force behind this committee was the leading political advocate of state-sponsored emigration at this time, Robert Wilmot-Horton. The committee reported that there were extensive districts in Ireland and also parts of England in which the supply of labor greatly exceeded employment. This imbalance gave rise to destitution, misery, and a general deterioration of wages below the level necessary to secure a healthy and satisfactory condition for the community. As a result, in England (where there was statutory poor relief), local taxation absorbed ever-greater portions of wealth, and in Ireland (where there was no poor law until 1838), growing numbers depended on charity or petty theft.[6] Moreover, the depth of the Malthusian crisis in Ireland also threatened the rest of the United Kingdom. The problems of Ireland, it was widely believed, were bound, literally, to migrate to England, Scotland, and Wales and so reduce those countries to the condition of their neighbor to the west. "Your Committee cannot too strongly impress upon the House, that between countries so intimately connected as Great Britain and Ireland, two different rates of wages, and two different conditions of the labouring population, cannot permanently co-exist. One of two results appears inevitable—the Irish population must be raised towards the standard of the English, or the English depressed towards that of the Irish. The question whether an extensive plan of Emigration shall be adopted, appears to your Committee to resolve itself into this simple point, Whether the wheat-fed population of Great Britain shall or shall not be supplanted by the potato-fed population of Ireland; whether Great Britain shall or shall not progressively become what Ireland is at the present moment."[7]

Whereas as the British Isles appeared overpopulated, colonies in North America, the Cape of Good Hope, and Australia contained large tracts of unappropriated, fertile land. They were in a position to receive and support "the redundant population of this country," who would thereby be transformed from a collective danger to a source of wealth.[8] For Wilmot-Horton and his colleagues, this happy transformation was predicated on the complete political and economic identity of the colonies and the mother country: "The unemployed labourer at home necessarily consumes more than he produces, and the national wealth is diminished in that proportion. When transferred to new countries where soil of the first quality is unappropriated, and where the rate of wages is consequently high, it will be found that he produces infinitely more than he consumes, and the national wealth will be increased by the change, if the Colonies are to be considered as integral parts of the nation at large."[9]

In the decade preceding the report of Wilmot-Horton's committee, the British government had supported a small number of emigration experiments, both in Canada and the Cape of Good Hope. In 1823 and 1825, for example, the government financed the emigration of twenty-five hundred people from Ireland to Canada at a cost of £56,000. The report of the select committee, however, led to the formulation of a more ambitious plan. It recommended a loan of £1.14 million to finance the removal of ninety-five thousand people over three years. As an initial step, Lieutenant Colonel Cockburn was instructed to survey some three hundred thousand acres in Nova Scotia, New Brunswick, and Prince Edward Island, and to prepare for the settlement there of ten thousand emigrants.[10] In fact, both the grand scheme and Cockburn's particular project were abandoned. Similarly, the select committee's recommendation that the government create a board of emigration, under the control of a department of state, was not acted upon.

This record of nonachievement requires explanation—all the more so in view of the dire fears provoked by population growth in Britain and Ireland and the general support for emigration as a partial solution to the problem.

To a degree, failure can be explained by a history of political maneuvering in which, repeatedly, the advocates of state-sponsored emigration lost out. Wilmot-Horton, for instance, aligned himself with the wrong faction in the late 1820s and was ousted. No longer a minister, he became a privileged sort of state-sponsored emigrant when, in 1831, he was appointed governor-general of Ceylon.[11] Similarly, in 1848, Lord John Russell, the Liberal prime minister, proposed state-sponsored emigration as one response to the Irish famine, but found he could not win the support of key ministers. Russell's most modest suggestion was that in the cases of indigent emigrants, the British government should pay the head tax levied by the authorities in British North America, but even this was overruled.[12]

These consistent outcomes suggest the need for a structural as well as contingent explanations for failure. From the late 1820s, on all occasions the fundamental objection to state-sponsored emigration was cost. Thus Sir Robert Peel, the Conservative home secretary (and future prime minister) objected to Wilmot-Horton's plan in 1828, arguing that for a great outlay of funds, it would remove only a fraction of the distressed population. He concluded, "He could not consent to the policy of laying out large sums of public money to encourage emigration."[13] Russell's proposal that the land tax or income tax should be extended to Ireland to finance emigration was similarly defeated by the fervent advocates of cheap government.[14]

Policy on emigration, therefore, should be viewed in the context of British fiscal policy and, specifically, the policy of fiscal containment that rapidly developed in the years following the Napoleonic Wars. At the wars' end, total state expenditure amounted to £672 million annually; 94 percent of this sum was taken up by defense expenditure and by debt service. In the postwar years there was a shift to a policy of retrenchment and tax remission. Public expenditure was reduced by 25 percent in the two decades after Waterloo. This decline was caused primarily, of course, by a cut in military expenditure. However, it is also important to note that public expenditure was not reallocated to spending on civil purposes; it was only in the 1840s that per capita spending on civil government began to rise. But even in this context, total government expenditure fell from 23 percent of gross domestic product in 1810 to 11 percent in 1840, and it remained at roughly this level until the outbreak of war in 1914.[15]

Retrenchment, therefore, expressed a long-term strategy; it was more than a temporary adjustment to peacetime conditions. Cheap government was a policy designed to protect the legitimacy of the state by pursuing policies that appeared to place government at one remove from, and above, the direct interests of particular groups of property holders. It was a response to the widespread radical critique of government during and after the French wars that the apparatus of the state had become a reservoir of funds, robbed from the productive classes by heavy taxation, and then distributed among contractors and sinecurists, as well as speculators who invested in the national debt. In the postwar decades, ministers reoriented policy to isolate radicals and to prevent their alliance with rural landowners who objected to the high level of wartime taxation and soaring poor rates. In doing so they presented themselves as diligent, disinterested public servants, dedicated to a policy of honesty and frugality.[16]

From this perspective, we can see that proponents of state-sponsored emigration were advocating a cure that to many others appeared worse than the disease itself. If the relationship between population and employment threatened political stability, the answer did not lie in higher taxes and the activity of the state replacing voluntary initiatives. For the governments of the period, schemes for state-sponsored emigration threatened to burden the state with additional and avoidable expenditure when all inessential public spending appeared to endanger political stability.

Moreover, state-sponsored emigration appeared to offer dangerous confirmation of the radical view that the state apparatus was a conspiracy against the poor. Opponents construed state-sponsored emigration as a taxpayers' subsidy to British and Irish landowners to rid them of the need to improve their lands, to bring wastes into cultivation, and to attend to the comfort and happiness of their (the landowners') tenancy—a declaration that the government cared so little for the nation's poor that they were content to export them to the furthest reaches of the empire. In the eighteenth century this policy had been reserved for undesirables and foreigners in transit. Opponents saw its continuation in the proposals of the emigration lobby: in 1831, the National Union of the Working Classes called not only for annual parliaments, universal suffrage, and the secret ballot, but also for an end to "Transportation Laws." This last referred to schemes for compulsory emigration, which the petition characterized as "unjust, wicked and unconstitutional."[17] In 1835, the handloom weavers petitioned parliament to intervene in order to halt the decline of wages in their trade. When the economist George Poulett Scrope advised them that they would be better off asking the government for state-assisted emigration to the colonies, Jeremiah Dewhirst, the leader of the West Yorkshire handloom weavers, treated him to the following riposte: "WE WILL NOT GO—we'll die here, where we were born. . . . So find another scheme. We have found one already. Our request is reasonable. If you *will* TAX labour, then give direct REPRESENTATION to Labour and let each *Householder* have a vote and the [secret] Ballot to protect it .... We ask but for fair play—we are willing to work, to live in peace, and obey the laws—but not to starve and not to 'Shove off.'"[18] For members of the governing elite concerned for the legitimacy of their rule, state-sponsored emigration appeared a policy fraught with danger. At this time, emigration did raise issues surrounding the concept of citizenship. But the citizenship in question did not concern the status of emigrants; instead, it pertained to the relationship of government to both taxpayers and to the domestic laboring poor.

PROMOTING EMIGRATION

The unwillingness of successive governments in nineteenth-century Britain to commit treasury funds to support emigration does not mean they were hostile or indifferent to the movement overseas of millions of subjects. The old practice of discouragement was overturned decisively in 1824, when the ineffective prohibition on the emigration of artisans was repealed.[19] But official policy went beyond the removal of futile laws. "The proper duty of government," Lord Stanley, the colonial secretary, asserted in 1843, "is not to force and compel emigration, but to assist, guide and protect its course."[20]

This policy can be traced to the beginning of the 1830s. In 1831, the Colonial Secretary, Viscount Goderich, launched two experimental schemes to promote emigration to Australia, one to encourage female emigration, the other to promote the emigration of mechanics. The former operated by offering assisted passages, the latter by offering a loan of £20. Significantly, in each case the funds for the scheme were taken from land sales in Australia and not from the domestic exchequer.[21] In the 1830s, however, emigration policy remained experimental. This was expressed in the hesitancy with which the Colonial Office took responsibility for assisted emigration. Between 1832 and 1836, for instance, the administration of assisted emigration was delegated to a voluntary charity, the London Emigration Committee. In 1836, this arrangement came to an end. A civil servant, Thomas Frederick Elliot, was appointed agent-general for emigration, responsible for the selection of emigrants, their care and discipline on board ship, and for provisioning vessels. He reported directly to a government minister, the secretary of state for the colonies, and, through him, to parliament. But these arrangements were still regarded by Lord Glenelg, the colonial secretary, "as in great measure experimental."[22] In 1839, the new office was established on a permanent basis, and in 1840 it was absorbed within the Colonial Land and Emigration Commission (CLEC), with Elliot installed as one of three commissioners.[23] It was only at the end of the decade, therefore, that policy moved decisively beyond tentative beginnings and its administration was vested in a stable bureaucracy charged to oversee and promote emigration.

The CLEC issued circulars, pamphlets, placards, and notices providing prospective emigrants with vital information. Through the work of the CLEC, the British state acted in partnership with colonial authorities, voluntary charities, local authorities and private individuals. Most fundamentally, the CLEC used a portion of the revenues from colonial land sales to assist emigration.[24] In this way the government found a way of giving emigrants financial support without drawing on the proceeds of domestic taxation, extending the national debt, or laying itself open to the charge of promoting compulsory emigration.

The idea that land sales should be used to finance emigration was stimulated by the ideas of Edward Wakefield and promoted by the National Colonisation Society, formed in 1830. Wakefield maintained that the basis of successful colonization depended on maintaining a proper ratio between the amount of alienated land in any colony and the supply of labor. If lands were given away too freely, there would be a labor shortage, as few people would toil for wages if they could easily become landowners. Wakefield believed that by selling land at auction, at a guaranteed minimum price, a labor supply could be assured. This was the case, he argued, first, because aspirant landowners would have to work for wages while they accumulated money to purchase land and, second, because the proceeds from sales could be used to assist further emigration.[25] By passing the cost of emigration on to the colonies, Wakefield rendered state-support for emigration compatible with what British political leaders, both Liberals and Conservatives, perceived to be the fiscal foundations of domestic stability.

Between 1840 and 1856, the CLEC was responsible for the sale of land in the Australian colonies.[26] In 1842, the Australian Wastes Act fixed a minimum price for the sale of all Australian land and required that one-half of the money raised was to be used to promote immigration. The commission was responsible for selecting those emigrants who would receive free passages, for chartering and fitting out ships, appointing a surgeon for the voyage, and drawing up the requirements for diet, ventilation, and discipline onboard.[27] From 1856, responsibility for this activity gradually passed to the Australian colonies as more of them received constitutions granting them self-government and responsibility for their own waste lands. By 1869, the

CLEC's emigration work had been superseded by colonial bodies; before this happened, however, it had been directly responsible for the passage of nearly four hundred thousand emigrants.[28]

But even the most favored emigrants to Australia were left to provide a portion of the cost of their voyage: £3–6 per adult and a proportionate cost for children.[29] Inevitably, most of these emigrants depended on state aid being supplemented by money from local authorities, charities, or familial sources. For example, section 62 of the 1834 Poor Law Amendment Act allowed parishes in England and Wales to subsidize emigration. In 1838, this was extended to the new poor law authority in Ireland. Poor Law emigration amounted to only a small fraction of all those who left the country to start a new life overseas. Between 1834 and 1860, just twenty-six thousand people, mostly agricultural workers and their families, were helped to emigrate from England and Wales in this way. Although the number of emigrants was small, the scheme itself is further testimony of the preparedness of the British government to encourage emigration, as long as its cost could be passed elsewhere—in this case, to local authorities.[30]

Policies on emigration were the outcome of competing and, at times, contradictory imperatives. So far we have dwelt on the need felt by governments to steer a course between the rival demands arising from fiscal virtue on one side, and Malthusian pessimism on the other. But these were not the only influences. Public opinion and colonial governments in Australasia and British North America were torn between their appetite for development (and, therefore, for immigrants) and their countervailing concern that they were being sent paupers without the necessary physical or moral qualifications for success as settlers.[31] Another set of conflicts arose from, on one side, governments' desire to promote emigration by relaxing regulations and so allow fares to fall, and, on the other, humanitarian concern at the overcrowded, disease-ridden, and ill-provisioned ships that ferried human cargo. The wretched condition in which emigrants arrived in British North America, in particular, aroused humanitarians in the Colonial Office. It also confirmed the worst fears of colonial governments over the sorts of migrants they were receiving.[32]

In 1827, the government's enthusiasm for voluntary emigration led it to repeal all legislation regulating the traffic in emigrants. The resulting disorderly shipboard conditions provoked an outbreak of typhus at Quebec that spread rapidly from ships to the surrounding population. The resulting pressure from British North America contributed to new legislation—the Passenger Act of 1828,[33] which limited the number of people to be carried to three for every four tons of burden; and there was a minimum height between decks of 5 feet 6 inches, and passenger ships were now required to carry fifty gallons of water and fifty pounds of breadstuff per person on board. However, the task of enforcement was charged to customs officers who did not greatly concern themselves with the law regarding conditions on board ships. Neither the terms of the act nor its administration could prevent the Atlantic passage of cholera in 1832.[34]

From 1833, the government appointed naval officers to superintend emigration from the main ports of departure and charged them with enforcing the Passenger Act.[35] This was a further part of the policy experiment of these years that aimed to promote emigration and protect emigrants. Until 1842, however, the officers lacked legal authority and depended on the force of their personalities, the prestige of their uniforms, and support from the local magistracy. Change was stimulated by more complaints about the emigrant trade, particularly from the Canadian authorities. A new Passenger Act of 1842 not only invested emigration agents with legal authority to enforce its provisions, but it also greatly extended the minimum amounts of space and food to be provided for emigrants and instituted a mechanism that required ship owners, charterers, and masters to perform their legal obligations.[36] Inevitably, new legislation and the activity of emigration officers challenged profits and placed an upward pressure on transatlantic fares. It carried the possibility that it would reduce the number able to make the voyage. Governments wanted to promote emigration but, at the same time, fiscal, humanitarian, and political costs marked the limits to this policy.

EMIGRATION AND NATIONALITY

Emigration policy developed within constraints, but inside these the British state created a framework in which it became easier for individuals to choose to emigrate. Changes in British nationality law were sympathetic to this broad policy toward emigration; in 1870, the law was changed to allow for expatriation and thus acknowledged the fact that most emigrants settled in the United States, beyond the boundaries of the empire.

British nationality was built on the feudal concept of personal allegiance. At the start of the nineteenth century, it remained untouched by concepts of citizenship and nationality that emerged from the American and French revolutions. In the present context, two features of the legal doctrine of allegiance are significant. First, British subjects throughout the empire enjoyed a uniform national status based on their personal allegiance to the Crown. Being born in a territory governed by the monarch created allegiance. A subject of the monarch in one of the Crown's territories was a subject in another. Second, allegiance was understood to be a law made in nature and given by God, and not a legal system devised by human hands. Based on the laws of nature, allegiance was unalterable.[37]

In the eighteenth century, while British emigration remained almost entirely within the confines of the empire, the doctrine of allegiance was highly convenient. Emigrants carried their nationality with them as they traveled to the colonies, even as they developed their own administrative and legal systems. In the nineteenth century, as emigrants increasingly traveled beyond the boundaries of the British Empire, the doctrine of allegiance gave rise to difficulties. Circumstances arose that mocked the British government's claim to offer protection to and receive obedience from British subjects living in other states.

During the Napoleonic Wars, the government called on all British subjects to assist the country in its war and, in 1807, issued a proclamation recalling seamen employed on foreign vessels. It made clear that the terms of the proclamation extended to British subjects who had certificates of naturalization.[38] The Anglo-American war in 1812, caused by border disputes and by the neutral stance the United States had adopted during Britain's war with France, was further aggravated by the affront caused to American citizenship and pride by Britain's refusal to relinquish its subjects. In 1813, the prince regent reiterated his belief in the inalienable nature of allegiance: "There is no right more clearly established than the right which a Sovereign has to the allegiance of his subjects, more especially in time of war. Their allegiance is no optional duty, which they can decline and resume at pleasure. It is a call which they are bound to obey: it began with their birth and can only terminate with their existence."[39] In practice, in the middle decades of the century, British governments significantly modified this uncompromising doctrine. From 1842, the Foreign Office made clear that dual nationality did not entitle British subjects to protection from the country of their birth. Similarly, in 1851, it issued a circular that exempted naturalized Britons from protection outside British territory.[40]

The American Civil War made the issue of allegiance once again a matter of urgent and practical significance. As state militias began conscription in order to meet federal troop quotas, some British subjects approached consulates to claim exemption from military service. Following the policy that had been in force since the 1840s, the Foreign Office held that people with dual American and British nationality—either sons born of British fathers in America or sons of Americans born in British territory—were not entitled to claim British protection to escape military service.[41]

In addition, the rights of British subjects were now also heavily qualified by the concept of domicile or a person's permanent home. The British government held that subjects living abroad acquired rights and incurred obligations in their country of residence. Specifically, it agreed that British subjects whose permanent home was in America could be liable to serve in the militia, national guard, or local police for the maintenance of internal peace and order or even, to a limited extent, defense of the territory from foreign invasion—these being "obligations ordinarily incident to such foreign domicile."[42]

In the course of their war, both the Confederate states and the Union government tried to enlist British residents. In each case the British government insisted that British subjects who agreed to leave America should not be forced to enlist but, at the same time, it did not object to the enlistment of subjects who refused this option.[43] In cases where British subjects had exercised the vote in the United States, the British government did not stand in the way of their conscription.[44]

In 1868, the government initiated a decisive review of naturalization law. This was stimulated by the ill feeling between Britain and the United States that arose as a result of attacks in Britain by Fenians in 1866–67, among them many Irish-born, naturalized Americans. The British government suspended habeas corpus and detained suspected conspirators, among them naturalized Americans, who were not allowed access to the American consul. Lord Clarendon declared that no British-born subject could renounce his allegiance under any circumstances. Seward, the American secretary of state, asserted the contrary doctrine, that "the process of naturalization in this country absolves the person complying with it from foreign allegiance."[45] The controversy gave rise to the Royal Commission on the Laws of Nationality and Allegiance, appointed in May 1868. It reported a year later, and its proposals formed the basis of the 1870 Nationality Act. The new legislation amended the concept of allegiance so that Britons who naturalized abroad automatically lost their British nationality. Dealing with dual nationality, the act allowed British subjects to make a declaration of alienage and thereby cease to be British subjects.[46]

The act, especially those sections that dealt with expatriation, passed amid little controversy. William Harcourt, a future Liberal chancellor of the exchequer and, at this time, a member of the Royal Commission on

Nationality and Allegiance, asked in *The Times*, "Why should we confer the privileges and impose the obligations of citizenship to those who did not desire the one and deserve the other?"[47] At the 1868 Social Science Association meeting on international law reform, Robert Marsden Pankhurst argued that the right to expatriation should become a doctrine of international law. Allegiance, he suggested, should "rest in principle upon deliberate choice."[48] The new doctrine of allegiance not only came to terms with the facts of emigration, it also reflected the decisive step taken in Britain in 1867 toward a more democratic polity.[49] The bonds of allegiance did not now follow God-given laws of nature but required a degree of explicit or implicit consent. Emigration was now recognized as one way in which consent could be withdrawn.

POLICY TRANSFORMED

The relative prosperity of the mid-Victorian decades meant that emigration retreated from the mid-1850s until the 1870s, both as a demographic phenomenon and as a subject for public debate. Between 1847 and 1854, the average annual emigration from the United Kingdom was over three hundred thousand. In 1855, the number of emigrants fell by roughly half this number and continued to decline to a low point in 1861, when just sixty-five thousand emigrated. It was only in the 1870s, driven by agricultural depression, and in the 1880s, driven by an urban crisis, that emigration both resumed its former high level and also regained its place in public debate.[50]

By the 1870s, the institutional context for emigration had altered significantly. The power of land sales had been passed to the self-governing institutions in Australia as well as in Canada. This radical reduction in the responsibilities of the CLEC signaled the end of direct assistance for immigrants channeled through the imperial government. In these decades, in light of Britain's dominant position in world markets, the government's role was to maintain the conditions of free trade—in goods, capital, and people—that secured prosperity. In this respect, it is relevant to note that the empire accounted for less than half of all trade and overseas investment.[51] Emigration continued apace without government intervention and, given the wide distribution of British capital, there was no compelling economic argument to direct emigration to imperial destinations.

The government continued to superintend the passenger trade, but since this had passed entirely from sail to steam ships, many of the problems that the Passenger Acts had been intended to regulate had by now been reduced.

The CLEC had finally been dissolved in 1878. In 1886, the Emigrants' Information Office was established to publicize opportunities for emigration. Significantly, however, it offered information on destinations both within and beyond the empire.[52]

In these years, the British government took only a very limited direct involvement in emigration. Between 1880 and 1913, the emigration clause of the Poor Law was used to send 16,108 people, mostly children, to Canada; the Home Office sent other children under the Reformatory and Industrial Schools Act of 1891. Adult emigrants received assistance from passage of the Unemployed Workmen's Act of 1905; 27,465 received aid to leave the country from 1906–14.[53] But the total number affected by these initiatives remained small, and the policy seemed to return to the ideas of the 1820s and earlier when emigration presented a solution for paupers, law-breakers, and other misfits.

Once again, this did not mean that governments opposed emigration. In 1883, reflecting on urban poverty, the colonial secretary, Lord Derby, made the following statement to the House of Lords: "Emigration is the only real remedy for the distress which exists in what we may call the congested districts. All the other plans for the relief of the distress are in comparison very imperfect and temporary expedients. I may go further and say, on behalf of my colleagues, as well as myself, that we have been and are anxious to promote emigration . . . by all reasonable and practicable means."[54]

The crucial point, however, came in the final caveat: what was "reasonable and practicable" did not amount to very much. For more than a century after 1815, British governments encouraged emigration, but their commitment to this policy was qualified mightily by their still greater commitment to cheap administration. Yet following the First World War there was a significant turnaround in government policy, when the state not only gave financial assistance to emigrants but also directed them to imperial destinations.

As late as 1918, the predominant theme of government policy was to discourage emigration. As they contemplated postwar reconstruction, ministers feared there would be a labor shortage and that the emigration of men, following the losses of the war, would exacerbate the numerical imbalance between the sexes.[55] Following the general election of 1918, the wartime coalition of Conservatives and Liberals led by Lloyd George remained in power with a massive parliamentary majority. But despite this basic continuity, there were also changes in personnel. Among these were the appointment of Lord Milner as colonial secretary and Leo Amery as undersecretary for the colonies. Both men were imperial enthusiasts with a concern for social reform. Milner was an established proponent of imperial unity, while Amery provided the impetus behind the empire settlement policy.

At the heart of Amery's political and economic vision was the idea that Britain and the Dominions had a single identity and interest. He told the House of Commons in 1918, "I shall be glad if the word 'emigration' with its implied suggestion of expatriation of the individual and of loss on the part of community which he leaves, could be habitually confined to migration to foreign countries. Change of residence to another part of the empire is . . . more appropriately described by some such term as 'oversea settlement.'"[56] Amery's thinking in this respect was characteristic of other imperial visionaries. For example, General William Booth, the founder of the Salvation Army and another enthusiast for imperial emigration, described the empire as "simply pieces of Britain distributed about the world enabling the Britisher to have access to the richest parts of the earth."[57] Amery pictured the empire as central to Britain's postwar economy. He expounded upon this theme in a memorandum for the War Cabinet in 1919. "The development of the population and wealth of the whole British Empire is the key to the problem of post-war reconstruction. The heavy burden of war debt upon every part of the Empire makes this development an immediate and urgent necessity. The growth of population in the Dominions, in so far as it adds directly to their strength and prosperity, and consequently to the strength and prosperity of the whole, and in so far as it increases the number of our own best customers and purveyors of essential foodstuffs and raw materials, is so obviously desirable . . . that emigration should so far as possible, be *directed* to countries within the confines of the British empire."[58]

In the early months of 1919, Amery developed a policy of free passages to the Dominions for ex-servicemen and women and their dependents. This was agreed by the cabinet at the end of March and announced to parliament in April. The scheme lasted until the end of 1922. Over the three years of its existence, it cost £2.7 million and was used to emigrate by 82,196 people.[59] Originally, the ex-servicemen's scheme was intended to last only until the end of 1921, but in October of that year Milner persuaded the Cabinet to extend the scheme for another twelve months, pointing out that it would relieve some of the effects of postwar unemployment and reduce the housing problem.[60]

The emigration assistance offered to ex-servicemen and their families introduced in 1919 was, by definition, a transitional and limited measure—an immediate response to the end of hostilities, targeted at a particular group, not a strategic reversal of a century-long policy. By contrast, the Empire Settlement Act of 1922 did decisively liberate emigration policy from the fiscal constraints of the previous hundred years. The Act initiated a broad scheme of subsidized emigration. The British government would now contribute to emigration and imperial settlement by cooperating with Dominion governments and with public or private organizations in the United Kingdom. Crucially, it would contribute up to 50 percent of the total cost of each particular scheme. To this end, the Act allowed grants of up to £3 million per year for fifteen years to assist emigration "to any part of His Majesty's Overseas Dominions."[61]

How can we account for this transformation of emigration policy? Of course, we must take into account the initiatives of key political actors. Most notably, Amery was a tireless advocate of state-sponsored emigration to the Dominions. Imperial politics also played a part; it certainly assisted Amery inasmuch that in November 1921, the Australian government added its support to the emigration scheme.[62] Yet in the same way as high politics reveals the narrative but not the structure of emigration policy in the nineteenth century, so too when we consider the reversal of that policy, we have to look beyond a blow-by-blow account of particular decisions.

The economic crisis and social dislocation of the postwar years provides the context in which Amery was able successfully to persuade the government to subsidize emigration. From 1920 to 1921, unemployment grew from below 4 percent of the insured workforce to 17 percent.[63] In December 1921, in a paper presented to the cabinet, Winston Churchill, Milner's successor as colonial secretary, presented state-sponsored emigration as a significant response to this problem. "The problem of unemployment is essentially a problem of the right distribution of population. . . . The key to the employment situation is the shifting of British population . . . to the Dominions. Such a policy . . . would secure a real and lasting improvement at far less cost than the present system of relief and doles. . . . The whole of this great expenditure affords a purely temporary relief. It effects no permanent cure."[64] But Amery's victory signified both more and less than the political triumph of social reform in the face of economic depression. Social reform was high on the political agenda between 1918 and 1920 without any advantage to the proponents of state-sponsored emigration. Instead, the welfare program of 1918–20 had focused on the extension of unemployment insurance, on more generous old-age pensions and, above all, on an ambitious program of state-subsidized housing—"homes fit for heroes." The depression decimated many of these plans as the treasury demanded reductions in expenditure on welfare. According to the Treasury, higher state expenditure would only worsen unemployment. In August 1921 the government appointed a committee, under the chairmanship of Sir Patrick Geddes, whose task was to present a program of determined retrenchment.[65]

Paradoxically, it was at this moment, when expenditure on extensive social reform came under attack, that Amery was able to assemble a coalition of support for his plans. Sir Alfred Mond—who was not only the minister of health appointed to oversee the strangulation of the housing program but also chairman of the Cabinet Unemployment Committee—now called for "liberal assistance from public funds for emigration." He could see no permanent solution for unemployment, he told the Cabinet, without a vigorous policy of emigration. This line was also supported by the Ministry of Labour and the Board of Trade.[66] Although the depression radically changed the fiscal and political context for welfare, it could not eradicate social reform. The housing program was reduced substantially, but the basis of social support for the working class—unemployment insurance—was, in its fundamentals, left untouched and, indeed, extended.[67] In fact, the Geddes committee offered a green light to cautious spending on migration to the Dominions.[68] Amery's victory and the program of state-sponsored emigration is further testimony to the government's belief that it could not abandon the poor to local and voluntary agencies.

It is in this political sense that we can find the greatest significance of the Empire Settlement Act. In other respects, the act was a disappointment. Between 1922 and 1927, the Colonial Office helped 249,000 people, 55 percent of all migrants who left Britain. But more had been expected. Indeed, the response from potential emigrants was too low for the Colonial Office to spend its £3 million annual budget for assisted emigration. By 1926, emigration to the Dominions began to fall away. In that year Australia received 31,260 assisted migrants. Four years later, the figure was just 2,683.[69] In a period of falling agricultural prices, the plan to connect emigration to an extension of agricultural production for markets in which farmers were already suffering was fundamentally misconceived. By the end of the 1920s, the Dominions were reducing their own schemes for assisted emigration and, indeed, had introduced restrictions on entry. The victory enjoyed in 1922 by the advocates of state-sponsored emigration was due, in many respects, to the economic depression that followed the Great War. But it was the global longevity of this same depression that meant that the hopes invested in the Empire Settlement Act ended in disappointment.

If we compare government policy on state-sponsored emigration in the aftermath of both the Napoleonic War and World War I, we find, at one level, a significant contrast. Whereas (formerly) governments had been content to set the framework within which emigrants, charities, shipping companies, and migration agents operated, now it actively sponsored and subsidized "oversea settlement." A mix of fear (provided by industrial unrest and the shadow thrown by the Bolshevik revolution) and compassion for ex-servicemen drove the new policy after 1918. In the postwar climate of working-class militancy and of alarmism on the part of the government, a policy of concession was seen to be vital, as the Prime Minister Lloyd George stated in 1921: "No government could hope to face the opprobrium which would fall upon it if extreme measures had to be taken against starving men who had fought for their country and were driven to violent courses by the desperation of their position."[70]

The contrast between the 1820s and 1920s, however, should not mask what was, perhaps, a more profound continuity. Both outcomes, inaction and action, expressed a politics of concession, a politics intended to avoid confrontation and contain dissent, and which ostentatiously presented the state as independent of the interests of any single social class. In the 1820s, it was not the working classes who carried the greatest threat. Policy on emigration was framed, as we have seen, by a fiscal strategy designed to reassure the gentry and assuage the urban middle classes. In the 1920s, a constructive emigration policy was underpinned by a disinclination to abandon the working class to the tides of economic depression and to the appeal of communism. In this light, the turnaround in policy that the Empire Settlement Act represents might also indicate a significant continuity in the political culture of the British governing class.

NOTES

1. S. Constantine, "Introduction: Empire Migration and Imperial Harmony" in *Emigrants and Empire: British settlement in the Dominions Between the War*, ed. S. Constantine, 1 (Manchester, Eng.: Manchester University Press, 1990); D. Baines, *Emigration from Europe, 1815–1930* (Cambridge, Eng.: Cambridge University Press, 1995), 3–4. But the incidence of emigration was not uniform. Its impact was most marked in Ireland (Baines, *Emigration*, 4). But even if we take the case of Britain alone, there were ten million emigrants—about 20 percent of all European emigration—in the period of extensive emigration before the First World War. See D. Baines, *Migration in a Mature Economy* (Cambridge, Eng.: Cambridge University Press, 1985), 45.

2. Constantine, *Emigrants and Empire,* "Introduction," 2.

3. P. J. Marshall, "Britain without America: A Second Empire," in *The Oxford History of the British Empire: The Eighteenth Century,* ed. P. J. Marshall, 588–89 (Oxford, Eng.: Oxford University Press, 2001); R. B. Madgwick, *Immigration into Eastern Australia, 1788–1851* (London: Longmans, 1937), 1–6.

4. B. R. Mitchell, *British Historical Statistics* (Cambridge, Eng.: Cambridge University Press, 1985), 605.

5. See R. D. C. Black, *Economic Thought and the Irish Question* (Cambridge, Eng.: Cambridge University Press, 1960); D. Winch, *Classical Political Economy and the Colonies* (London: G. Bell and Sons, 1965); H. J. M. Johnston, *British Emigration Policy 1815–30: "Shovelling Out Paupers"* (Oxford, Eng.: Clarendon Press, 1972).

6. Parliamentary Papers 1826 IV, *First Report from the Select Committee on Emigration,* 3.

7. Parliamentary Papers 1826 IV, *Third Report from the Select Committee on Emigration,* 229.

8. Parliamentary Papers 1826 IV, *First Report,* 3.

9. Ibid., 4.

10. S. C. Johnson, *A History of Emigration from the United Kingdom to North America, 1763–1912* (London: Routledge, 1913), 18–19.

11. Black, *Economic Thought,* 216.

12. S. Walpole, *Lord John Russell,* vol. 2 (London: Longmans, 1889), 78–81.

13. Black, *Economic Thought,* 215.

14. Ibid., 232–34.

15. P. Harling and P. Mandler, "From the 'Fiscal-Military State' to the 'Laissez-Faire State,' 1760–1850," *Journal of British Studies* (January 1993): 47–57; R. Middleton, *Government versus the Market: The Growth of the Public Sector, Economic Management and British Economic Performance, c. 1890–1979* (Cheltenham, Eng.: Edward Elgar, 1996), 90–91; M. Daunton, *Trusting Leviathan: The Politics of Taxation in Britain 1799–1914* (Cambridge, Eng.: Cambridge University Press, 2001), 65.

16. Daunton, 52–66.

17. A. Redford, *Labour Migration in England, 1800–1850,* 2nd ed. (Manchester, Eng.: Manchester University Press, 1964), 174–75.

18. *Political Economy versus the Handloom Weavers* (Bradford, Eng.: H. Warman, 1835), 16.

19. D. J. Jeffrey, "Damming the Flood: British Government Efforts to Check the Outflow of Technicians and Machinery, 1780–1845," *Business History Review* (Spring 1977): 18.

20. *Parliamentary Debates,* 1843, lxviii, col. 548–49.

21. Madgwick, *Immigration into Eastern Australia,* 92–93.

22. Ibid., 125; F. H. Hitchins, *The Colonial Land and Emigration Commission* (Philadelphia: University of Pennsylvania Press, 1931), 14, 21–22.

23. Hitchins, *Colonial Land,* 27–59.

24. Ibid., ch. 8. In general, the CLEC had no power over land sales in British North America, where these powers were vested in local authorities. Ibid., 50.

25. E. G. Wakefield, *A Letter from Sydney* (London: Joseph Cross, 1829).

26. Hitchins, *Colonial Land,* 203. In British North America, the sale of land was the responsibility of the colonial authorities. Ibid., 50.

27. Ibid., ch. 8.

28. Ibid., 207–12.

29. In the mid-nineteenth century, the cost of an adult passage to Australia was roughly £17. This sum was beyond the means of laboring families in Britain and Ireland, and roughly one-half of all British and Irish emigrants were helped by the colony to which they traveled. R. Haines, "'The Idle and the Drunken Won't Do There': Poverty, the New Poor Law and Nineteenth-Century Government-Assisted Emigration to Australia from the United Kingdom," *Australian Historical Studies* (April 1997): 7–8.

30. On this scheme and its operation, see A. Redford, *Labour Migration in England, 1800–50* (Manchester: Manchester University Press, 1964), 99–100; R. Haines, *Emigration and the Labouring Poor: Australian Recruitment in Britain and Ireland, 1831–60* (Basingstoke, Eng.: Macmillan, 1997), ch. 4.

31. Madgwick, *Immigration into Eastern Australia,* 146–47.

32. O. Macdonagh, "Emigration and the State," *Transactions of the Royal Historical Society,* 5th series (1955): 133–59; O. Macdonagh, *A Pattern of Government Growth, 1800–60* (London: Macgibbon and Kee, 1961); P. Dunkley, "Emigration and the State, 1803–42: The Nineteenth-Century Revolution in Government Reconsidered," *Historical Journal* (June 1980): 353–80.

33. Dunkley, "Emigration and the State," 356.

34. Macdonagh, "Emigration and the State," 135.

35. Ibid., 135–43. We can recognize the divergent imperatives driving government policy when we also notice that these same officers were also asked to provide information to clergy, parish officers, and landowners who wanted to assist emigration.

36. Dunkley, "Emigration and the State," 372. Despite these advances, the emigration agents enjoyed only a brief period of effective action. By 1847, they were overwhelmed by the greater numbers as a result of the Irish famine. This reached a climax in 1851, when more than a quarter-million Irish emigrated. As the large numbers traveling created a chasm between the letter of the Passenger Act and its enforcement, the officials, philanthropists, and parliament called for new, stricter, and more extensive laws regulating the emigration trade. Six new Passenger Acts were passed between 1847 and 1855. The number of emigration agents, however, did not grow alongside the new demands being made upon them. In 1851, four men were expected to control the annual emigration of two hundred thousand people from the port of Liverpool. Macdonagh, "The State and Emigration," 156.

37. *Calvin's Case* (7 Co Reb 12b) in *English Reports: King's Bench,* vol. 77 (London, 1907); David Martin Jones, "Sir Edward Coke and the Interpretation of Lawful Alle-

giance in Seventeenth Century England," *History of Political Thought* 7, no. 2 (1986): 321–40.

38. Parliamentary Papers 1869 XXV, *Report of the Royal Commissioners on the Laws of Naturalization and Allegiance,* 33.

39. Ibid., 35.

40. Ibid., 60–61, 67, 96; *British Digest of International Law,* vol. 5, ed. Clive Parry (London: Steven and Sons, 1965), 320, 350–52.

41. Parliamentary Papers 1869 XXV, *Laws of Naturalization and Allegiance,* 41–42.

42. Ibid., 42.

43. Ibid., 44–45; *British Digest of International Law,* vol. VI, 381–84.

44. Parliamentary Papers 1869 XXV, *Laws of Naturalization and Allegiance,* 43.

45. Cited in C. C. Tansill, *America and the Fight for Irish Freedom* (New York: Devin-Adair Co., 1935), 35.

46. *1870 Naturalization Act,* 33 and 34 Vict., c. 14. The sections on expatriation covered both British subjects by descent who were considered to be nationals by the country of their birth, and those who were British subjects and foreign nationals by virtue of their parentage.

47. *The Times,* December 11, 1867.

48. *Transactions of the National Association for the Promotion of Social Science, 1868* (1869): 164.

49. C. Hall, K. McClelland, and J. Rendall, *Defining the Victorian Nation: Class, Race, Gender and the Reform Act of 1867* (Cambridge, Eng.: Cambridge University Press, 2000).

50. Mitchell, *British Historical Statistics,* 81; Baines, *Migration,* chap. 7; H. Malchow, *Population Pressures: Emigration and Government in Late-Nineteenth-Century Britain* (Palo Alto, Calif.: Society for the Promotion of Science and Scholarship, 1979).

51. François Crouzet, "Trade and Empire: The British Experience from the Establishment of Free Trade until the First World War," in *Great Britain and Her World, 1850–1914: Essays in Honour of W.O. Henderson,* ed. B. M. Ratcliffe, 214, 222 (Manchester, Eng: Manchester University Press, 1975).

52. K. Williams, "'A Way Out of Our Troubles': The Politics of Empire Settlement, 1900–22," in Constantine, *Emigrants and Empire,* 24.

53. Constantine, "Empire," in Constantine, *Emigrants and Empire,* 72.

54. Cited in H. Malchow, *Population,* 162.

55. I. M. Drummond, *Imperial Economic Policy, 1917–1939* (London, 1974), 44–54.

56. Cited in Williams, "Way Out," 25.

57. Constantine, "Empire," 76.

58. Quoted in Drummond, *Imperial,* 60–61.

59. I. M. Drummond, *British Economic Policy and the Empire* (London: Allen and Unwin, 1972), 74.

60. Ibid., 75. On the scheme more generally, see K. Fedorowich, *Unfit for Heroes: Reconstruction and Soldier Settlement in the Empire Between the Wars* (Manchester, Eng.: Manchester University Press, 1995), ch.2.

61. Drummond, *British Economic Policy*, 82.

62. M. Roe, *Australia, Britain and Migration, 1915–40* (Cambridge, Eng.: Cambridge University Press, 1995).

63. W. R. Garside, *British Unemployment 1919–1939: A Study in Public Policy* (Cambridge, Eng.: Cambridge University Press, 1990), 4.

64. CAB 24/131 CP3582, Overseas Settlement. Memorandum from the Chairman of the Overseas Settlement Committee.

65. K. O. Morgan, *Consensus and Disunity: The Lloyd George Coalition Government, 1918–22* (Oxford, Eng: Clarendon Press, 1977).

66. Drummond, *Imperial*, 78–79.

67. B. B. Gilbert, *British Social Policy 1914–39* (London: B. T. Batsford, 1970), 61–86.

68. In fact, Geddes had a longstanding enthusiasm for emigration as a strategic policy. See J. Barnes and D. Nicholson, eds., *The Leo Amery Diaries*, (London: Hutchison, 1980), vol. 1, 256–57.

69. Drummond, *Imperial*, 118.

70. A. Deacon, "Concession or Coercion: The Politics of Unemployment Insurance in the 1920s," in *Essays in Labour History 1918–1939*, ed. A. Briggs and J. Saville, 11 (London: Croom Helm, 1977).

7

HOLLAND BEYOND THE BORDERS:
EMIGRATION AND THE DUTCH STATE,
1850–1940

Corrie van Eijl and Leo Lucassen

Emigration is largely considered a definitive departure of people to another state, especially to transatlantic immigration countries like the United States, Canada, Argentina, and Australia. Although we know that in reality many people only stayed temporarily,[1] the implicit assumption is that emigrants left "far away and forever" the sphere of influence of their former fatherland and would, in time, lose their original nationality. From this perspective it is hardly surprising that the relation between sending states and their emigrants has not received much attention.[2] Instead, migration historians have focused on the reception of emigrants, and thus on the immigration policy in the countries of destination. The few studies that deal with the relations between the state and its emigrants concentrate on state policies aimed at either obstructing or stimulating emigration, and studies that focus on political discourse.[3]

This leaves us with little knowledge about the actual relations between sending states and their emigrants, and with the notion that, apart from political or cultural matters, states were not interested in their subjects once they had crossed the border. As we will argue here, the involvement of the Dutch state with its subjects abroad was not so much framed in terms of political discourse, but it did have important social and economic dimensions. Moreover, emigration created some interesting dilemmas for states and their citizens abroad, especially when emigrants did not wish to give up their citizenship or when descendants of former citizens claimed the membership of the country of their forefathers. In many of these cases the issue turned on which state was financially responsible for poor migrants.

These points are made clearer by looking at Dutch migrants in Germany, Switzerland, and Russia. Although many Dutch stayed permanently in Germany, the majority of the migrants returned after a number of years. Consequently, this emigration to bordering countries was not seen as a final move. In this sense, these migrants differed from transatlantic emigrants, who were assumed to have left once and for all and were no longer considered real subjects; they also differed from migrants who went to the colonies overseas but never left the empire or the sphere of influence of the national state. Emigrants in neighboring countries were on the edge of the nation state: they lived abroad but remained to some extent within the reach of their home country. They were neither proper citizens nor real aliens, which raises interesting questions about the relationship between states and their subjects and about the content of citizenship. Why and to what extent did the Dutch state remain connected to these (former) citizens in neighboring countries? How does an analysis of social and economic relations between nations and subjects abroad contribute to our understanding of the meaning of nationality and citizenship? Before we follow the Dutch into Germany and Switzerland, a short overview of emigration and emigration policies from the Netherlands from 1840 onward is in order.

DUTCH EMIGRATION AND EMIGRATION POLICY, 1840–1940

When, in the course of the eighteenth century, the economic power of the republic gradually diminished and the Netherlands stopped being a major magnet for immigrants, emigration of Dutch citizens gradually increased, especially from the 1840s onward. Nevertheless, the number of emigrants hardly ever rose to more than 5 percent of the population and was very small in number compared with the mass emigration from Germany or Ireland. As in most countries, the attention of historians has been drawn to this transatlantic Dutch emigration, especially to North America, but until the 1920s most people emigrated to European destinations. Emigration from the Netherlands to countries outside of Europe only became predominant after World War II (table 7.1).[4]

Although estimates of the total number of Dutch emigrants vary, it is clear that many migrated to Germany and Belgium; the number of Dutch migrants in other European countries has always been limited. Initially, Belgium was the most important target country, but after 1870 the booming German Ruhr area heavily influenced Dutch migration.[5] At the outbreak of World War I, an estimated 140,000 Dutch citizens lived in Germany, far more than in any other country. During the war and the following economic depression, this migration to Germany decreased significantly.

Through 1960, the number of Dutch citizens abroad exceeded the number of immigrants living in the Netherlands (table 7.2). Despite this negative migration balance, there was hardly any political or public debate on emigration, and the Dutch government sought neither to stimulate nor to constrain it. The only legislation concerning emigration had to do with the regulation of recruitment, transportation, and the treatment of emigrants to the United States.

In the public debate on poverty around 1850, however, emigration received some attention, possibly stimulated by the upsurge in emigration to the United States between 1847 and 1857. Poverty and unemployment were considered to be the main reasons for leaving the country. Commentators regretted that the most enterprising of the working class turned their backs on their country; they pleaded for other solutions to fight poverty and unemployment—either land reclamation and stimulation of other employment in the Netherlands, or emigration to the Dutch colonies.[6] But this debate soon faded away, and a new upswing in emigration to the United States after 1865 did not coincide with similar discussions on poverty.

Interest in emigration increased again after 1900, influenced by relatively strong population growth and rising unemployment figures in 1907 and 1908. From 1850 to 1900, the Dutch population had increased by 64 percent, compared to only 39 percent in the rest of northwestern Europe. In the next fifty years, growth in the Netherlands would be 95 percent, compared with 27 percent for other countries in the region.[7] The prospect of overpopulation and unemployment created concerns among politicians and policymakers, whose focus on emigration was inextricably linked to the growing intervention of the state in socioeconomic matters.

Several social laws at the turn of the century and the creation of the State Commission for Unemployment (1909) marked the beginning of the modern welfare state. Due to its involvement with unemployment benefits, the state became more active in regulating the labor market. In 1916, a state bureau was established within the Ministry of Labour to coordinate measures aimed at reducing unemployment. Interestingly, this influential bureau combined policies for both immigration and emigration: from 1918, measures were taken to restrict and monitor immigrants in the Dutch labor market, whereas at the same time emigration, viewed primarily as a means to export unemployment, was encouraged.[8] Accordingly, the government financed the Dutch Emigration Foundation (*Nederlandse Vereniging Landverhuizing*), established in 1913, and supplied interest-free loans for emigrants who went to Canada from 1923 on.[9] These small-scale initiatives were not very successful (not in the least because of the poor economic prospects and immigration restrictions in most overseas countries), but the foundation was thus laid for a more intensive state emigration policy after 1945.[10]

Although state policy with regard to emigration in general was limited before World War II, Dutch officials became increasingly involved in the (temporary) stay of Dutch citizens in other European countries—mainly Germany and Belgium, home to the majority of Dutch sojourners abroad. To analyze this complex and interactive configuration, we will focus on Germany, which was more important as a destination than the United States or any other country between 1880 and 1940.

THE DUTCH IN GERMANY

The border between Germany and the Netherlands stretches three hundred kilometers. Labor migration and cross-border work are old traditions in the region, so this border has long been only an artificial boundary in a common labor market. However, "trespassing" became more complicated with immigration restrictions in the interwar period.

For most of the nineteenth century, migration went primarily from Germany to the Netherlands, but after 1870 this drift toward the North Sea was reversed.[11] More and more unskilled and semiskilled (mainly male) Dutch migrants went to Germany as farm workers, construction workers, or as miners in the industrial areas of western Germany. This migration reached its peak just before World War I, when some 140,000 Dutch people lived in Germany. After the war, many Dutch repatriated, changing the direction of migration once again. In the next fifteen years, the number of German migrants in the Netherlands rose steeply, due primarily to the large number of German domestic servants (table 7.3).[12]

Convinced of the benefits of free trade, the Dutch government tried to stimulate the crossing of frontiers without hindrance and barely intervened in the migration process in the nineteenth century. At the same time, however, states that experienced large-scale immigration, such as Germany, France, and Switzerland, began to draw the line more firmly between their own citizens and aliens, especially because they did not want to be burdened with costs for poor relief of noncitizens. The attitude of the German authorities toward Dutch labor migrants and the response it evoked from the Dutch government illustrate this point. Arguments arose most often between the Netherlands and Prussia, which was not only the most powerful state in Germany but also the state that accommodated the overwhelming majority of Dutch migrants.

In the 1860s, passport controls were abolished in most European countries, and crossing borders was fairly easy.[13] Nevertheless, many Dutch migrants still used some sort of document, including passports, to state their (national) identity.[14] However, Prussia, afraid of being burdened by too many poor, foreign migrants whose nationality was unclear and who therefore would be difficult to expel, engaged in a good deal of diplomatic consultation with the Netherlands (among other nations) on the crucial question of whether or not a poor migrant was still a Dutch citizen.

According to the 1850 Dutch nationality law, citizens who stayed abroad for more than five years with the "unmistakable intention not to return" could lose their Dutch nationality.[15] In the new nationality law of 1892, the loss of nationality was confined to citizens who resided abroad for more than ten years, unless a notification was given to the mayor or the consul that they wanted to remain Dutch citizens. In practice, the "unmistakable intention" in the 1850 law was hard to prove, and it is not likely that many citizens did lose their nationality. Usually, the minister of justice opposed nullifying citizenship if there were no clear proof of a citizen's intention not to return. In this respect, there seemed to be little difference between the 1850 jus soli nationality law and the 1892 jus sanguinis law, further illustrated by the following examples.

In 1868, a former Prussian citizen, Mrs. Klop, and her five children were expelled from Prussia because her late husband was believed to be Dutch. The Dutch Home Department, liable for poor relief in cases like this, assumed that the man had left the Netherlands "with the clear intention not to return" and was no longer Dutch. The minister of justice, however, did not agree because there was not enough evidence of Mr. Klop's intention not to return. So Mr. Klop was Dutch at the time of his marriage, and since his wife was (therefore) Dutch, she could not be refused re-entry.[16]

In contrast, the minister objected in 1895 to the intended expulsion of Mrs. Nelissen, also a widow and a former Prussian citizen. According to the Prussian administration, she had acquired the Dutch nationality of her late husband. On closer examination, the Dutch minister concluded that her husband had left the Netherlands in 1864 and clearly intended not to return. At the moment of his marriage (1875), he was therefore no longer Dutch, nor was his widow.[17]

Although in practice Dutch citizens did not easily lose their citizenship, the legal provisions in the Dutch nationality law meant that the Prussian administration was never sure whether Dutch citizens were still accepted as such. When passports were no longer compulsory, the need for clarity on nationality increased. Prussia therefore insisted in the 1870s on some proof that the Dutch state still recognized their citizens living in Prussia. The risk of poverty (and relief) was not the only reason for this demand: Prussia complained that Dutch residents, often married to Prussian women, could profit from social services but had few obligations to their new country. The fact that these Dutch residents and their Dutch sons were not liable to military service in Prussia, nor in the Netherlands, met with increasing opposition, a fact which meant the Dutch could therefore easily compete in the labor market and be favored over their Prussian neighbors and cousins.[18]

The Prussian government tried to end this inequality. In 1874, Dutch citizens who had lived in Prussia for five years or longer were given notice that they had to apply for Prussian nationality or else return to the Netherlands. The Dutch government, wanting to prevent their expulsion, entered into negotiations and agreed to provide Dutch citizens who resided in or went to Prussia (and other parts of Germany) with a certificate similar to the German *Heimatschein*. This certificate of nationality, previously unknown in the Netherlands, stated that someone was a Dutch citizen and would be accepted in the Netherlands whenever he or she wanted to return (or was no longer welcome abroad). Applicants had to declare whether they had fulfilled their military duties in the Netherlands and if they had the intention to return there. In Germany, the fulfillment of military duties was required for a *Heimatschein,* but it was not required for the Dutch certificate. The question on the intention to return was probably introduced to facilitate investigations concerning nationality. If emigrants intended to return, they remained Dutch citizens, but if they stated that they had no plans to leave their new foreign residence, then they lost their Dutch nationality after five years. Therefore, it is not likely that many people answered this question affirmatively.

The certificate initially had to be renewed each year, but in 1901 this renewal requirement was dropped. However, after the Dutch-German immigration treaty of 1906, the certificate's validity was restricted to five years. Between 1900 and 1914, some four hundred thousand certificates were issued. These figures (see table 7.4) are an indication of the emigration trend but are not very accurate. Not everyone who went to Germany applied for a certificate, and some of the applicants changed their minds and did not leave at all.

The certificate of nationality did not end the disagreement on military duties with Prussia. Occasionally, there were rumors of Dutch citizens in Prussia who, under pressure, applied for naturalization and were subsequently drafted into the German army.[19] When negotiations for an immigration treaty between Germany and the Netherlands started at the end of the 1890s, disagreements over military duties constituted a major obstacle. Germany was very reluctant to accept foreign residents who had not fulfilled their military duties in their home countries. In the interest of Dutch citizens in Germany, the Dutch government agreed to revise Dutch military law. As of 1901, Dutch citizens in Germany (and Belgium) were liable for military duty in the Netherlands. Although military service in the Netherlands was not as long and severe as in Germany, with this modification the Dutch government met the German demands.

Thus, unintentionally, German policy strengthened the relationship between the Dutch state and its citizens abroad. With the certificate of nationality (and the frequent renewals), the government of the Netherlands acknowledged its responsibility for its citizens beyond its borders, even if they lived in Germany for a very long period. The amendment of the military law was significant to the meaning of citizenship for nationals living abroad. Until 1901, citizenship had implied only *rights,* but thenceforth male citizens living in Germany and Belgium were subject to the responsibility of military service in the Netherlands.

JOBS

As we have seen, labor migration from the Netherlands to Germany was a long-lasting tradition, and the Dutch state did little either to stimulate or constrain such movement. This changed gradually, however, after 1900, influenced by periods of high unemployment in the Netherlands. The initiative to exploit the healthier German labor market was at first taken up by private and local organizations. Then, the local employment bureau in The Hague tried to reduce unemployment (and relief) by finding employment in German coal mines and construction work.[20] High unemployment also led to the formation of the Amsterdam Emigration Society in 1907, whose aim it was to advise and support those willing to emigrate to Germany. With the society's help, some fifteen- to sixteen hundred emigrants moved to Germany between 1908 and 1911. In the same period, there were local initiatives in Haarlem and Arnhem; Catholics and Protestants also founded associations to support their Dutch counterparts in Germany.[21]

In 1908, the Dutch government established a special Department of Employment Exchange in Oberhausen, Germany. This organization worked mainly for the benefit of Dutch citizens who wanted to work in the new industrial areas in Germany. In the next twenty-five years, this department placed some eleven thousand Dutch unemployed abroad (table 7.5). After World War I, the main thrust of their activity shifted to finding employment in the Netherlands for Dutch repatriates as well as for Germans, who were mainly miners and domestics.

Government interest in emigration during this period is further apparent in the reports of the Government Committee on Unemployment, established in 1909. This committee examined at length the extent of emigration and the possibilities of emigration and employment abroad. The report emphasized the importance of more extensive and accurate statistics on Dutch emigrants in order to better estimate the opportunities available in various parts of the world. The committee recommended the creation of a central bureau of emigration to collect information and advise the public.

With the development of the welfare state and the addition of unemployment insurance in 1916, the government had an even greater interest in keeping unemployment as low as possible. Intervention with respect to emigration grew especially intense in the 1930s, as the economic situation in Germany became much more favorable than that in the Netherlands. Government pressure on the unemployed to accept jobs in Germany increased. Under the penalty of losing their benefits, Dutch unemployed were forced to work in Germany, which increasingly led to complaints after the Nazis came into power.[22]

As before, the Dutch government focused primarily on open borders, not only to reduce temporary unemployment but also with an eye to the future. Policymakers expected that, in the long run, the Dutch economy would not be able to provide enough employment and that the Netherlands would have to depend on access to foreign labor markets to keep the continually increasing population at work. This open-border policy also influenced Dutch immigration policy in the 1930s. The Dutch government was very reluctant to take measures to restrict immigration, in spite of complaints by unions and members of parliament that foreigners were freely admitted to the Dutch labor market while other countries increasingly excluded Dutch workers. Eventually, the government agreed on restrictions for foreign workers (in 1934) and for some groups of foreign self-employed (1937).

These regulations, which were established primarily to meet ever-increasing complaints, only marginally contributed to the decrease of unemployment. However, policymakers secretly hoped for some other results. In

1938, the head of the employment department of the Ministry of Social Affairs explicitly stated that these immigration restrictions were also meant as a tool to enforce open borders in other countries and thus to enhance employment for Dutch citizens in neighboring countries.[23] With laws hindering the entrance of German and Belgian workers into the Netherlands, the Dutch government had a much stronger bargaining position. Subsequent to voting these immigration restrictions, the Dutch government was able to negotiate with Germany and Belgium for better treatment and employment of Dutch citizens. This resulted in bilateral agreements that decreased employment restrictions for Dutch citizens in those countries.

POOR RELIEF

Despite bilateral treaties and other agreements, Dutch citizens in Germany suffered from unemployment, especially during the economic depression after the First World War. According to the 1906 immigration treaty between Germany and the Netherlands, Dutch citizens who were without means of existence were entitled to poor relief in Germany, but after a few months the German government had the right to expel them. Frequently, those citizens had left the Netherlands many years before, were married to a German wife or had friends and relatives in Germany, and had no wish to repatriate. Besides, the Dutch government was not so keen on repatriating poor, unemployed people who had severed all connections with their country of origin. Therefore, the Dutch government and Germany mutually agreed in 1908 that their citizens would not be expelled if the home country wished to cover the costs of poor relief.

There is little evidence that Germany supported many German citizens in the Netherlands. The Dutch government, on the other hand, made frequent use of the agreement. Initially there were only a few scattered instances, but when the situation of Dutch citizens deteriorated during World War I, financial support increased, although many people were still repatriated. This policy changed in the 1920s when unemployment increased considerably. Duisburg, for instance, had some eighteen hundred Dutch citizens unemployed in 1920, accounting for 18 percent of the city's total unemployment.[24]

In 1920, the Dutch home secretary argued for an increase of poor relief to Dutch citizens living in Germany, not only because those citizens themselves preferred to stay in Germany and had a better chance of finding employment there, but also because of the housing shortage in the

Netherlands.[25] In the years following, the miserable conditions of Dutch citizens in Germany also received a lot of attention in the Dutch press and in parliament, which resulted in the creation of several committees aimed at supporting poor Dutch citizens in Germany or Dutch children abroad. Members of parliament requested more financial support and a generous attitude toward the unemployed.

Occasionally, individuals wrote from Germany to the minister or to the queen. In those letters, written half in German and half in Dutch, they explain their miserable conditions and plead for support. Sometimes they explicitly refer to their patriotism, like the Dutchmen in Rheinhausen who complained to the Home Secretary that they hardly received any relief: "Although we live in Germany, we are still good Dutchmen. Thousands of Dutch people in Duisburg, including the undersigned, participated in the big demonstration on the occasion of the Queen's jubilee. . . . We did not forget our fatherland in good times, and we hope that your Excellency will come to our rescue in these bad times, because we are destitute."[26]

Before the First World War, the yearly expenditure for poor relief to Dutch citizens abroad probably amounted to no more than 10–20,000 guilders. At the end of 1923 and again in 1931, the total expenditure on poor relief increased steeply (table 7.6). Although these amounts refer to all Dutch citizens abroad, the major portion was spent on poor relief in Germany.[27] In 1932, a special Government Office for needy Dutchmen abroad was set up to help them find employment and to decrease poor relief. There is little indication that this office served these purposes and people frequently complained about the uncompromising attitude of these officials. The reduction of the number of people receiving poor relief after 1934 had little to do with the activities of the government office but was related to the growing economy and increasing employment opportunities in Germany.

In 1918 at least twelve hundred Dutch people were allowed to stay in Germany with Dutch financial support; the number rose to well over forty-five hundred in 1923 and almost seventy-five hundred in 1933 (table 7.7).[28] Some of them were more or less continually supported; others only received poor relief for a short period. The situation strengthened the ties between the Dutch state and its many thousands of citizens in Germany, and it might even have caused or revived patriotic feelings among Dutch citizens abroad. But that was not the issue. Poor relief from the Dutch government was meant to prevent the repatriation of thousands of Dutch citizens from Germany to the Netherlands, and that was precisely what it did.

Relations between the Dutch state and its subjects in Germany were probably different from those in other countries, in light of the fact that the Dutch government was very keen on good relations with Germany and free access to the German labor market. But what about the situation of Dutch citizens in Switzerland, a European country that was not very important for Dutch migration? Were there similar requests and claims from citizens on the basis of their Dutch nationality, and how did the Dutch government react to those appeals?

THE DUTCH IN SWITZERLAND

Compared with the number of Dutch migrants in Germany, the number in Switzerland was very small, probably no more than one thousand at any time.[29] Yet there were some interesting disagreements among Dutch authorities concerning people residing in Switzerland who claimed Dutch nationality. These disputes arose mainly after 1874, when a new Swiss law obliged resident foreigners to carry a passport. This regulation was probably meant to prevent foreigners from being no longer recognized by their home country, which would result in their being immune from expulsion in the event of poverty. This quest for identification papers created problems for the Dutch consul general in Switzerland and illustrates the dilemma of states whose citizens migrated abroad. When was the claim for citizenship justified, and how long could such individuals be considered as subjects?

After the 1874 law, more and more people applied to the Dutch consuls in the Swiss cantons for a passport. Those requests were forwarded to the consul general, who resided both in Lausanne and Bern. Although Aristide Zolberg has correctly characterized the role of the consulates as a form of "remote control" on emigrants, in this case the situation was more ambiguous.[30] The correspondence with the Dutch Foreign Ministry in The Hague illustrates that the consul did not so much act as a gatekeeper of Dutch nationality as much as he attempted to resolve the problems of the people who turned to him. People who called on the Dutch consul general often had only a birth certificate, a declaration of marriage, or an old and expired passport, and in some cases even this documentation was lacking. Yet the consul general, who found it tiresome to consult his Dutch superiors for approval every time, issued passports to people without proof that they were still Dutch citizens, sometimes on the sole grounds that "they looked decent and spoke Dutch, whereupon I felt it my duty to settle their impossible position in this country."[31]

The consul general was faced with the problem that some applicants for passports had no proof of their nationality. Some of these were clearly Dutch (they had old records, could speak the language) but could have lost their Dutch nationality by simply having been gone too long. And there were others for whom it was highly doubtful that they ever possessed Dutch nationality. For the first category he was generally quite lenient. This course of action was also encouraged by the fact that the consul lacked the means to prove that they were not still Dutch citizens. According to the law, they would have lost their Dutch nationality if they had left their fatherland with the intention not to return (*animus non redeundi*).[32] As the consul general made clear, this was almost impossible to determine.

The minister of foreign affairs was not very happy with this loose policy of the consul general in Switzerland. The fact that people spoke Dutch was irrelevant; what counted were the formal criteria and proof. However, when confronted with specific requests from the consul general, the Dutch authorities were less adamant. A good example is the case of the Hernass family. This family got into trouble because the Swiss police threatened to withdraw their *permis de séjour* (residence permit) unless they handed over a valid (Dutch) passport. The head of the family appeared to be a sailor born in the Prussian town of Pillau. He had once lived in Rotterdam and had been given equal rights to Dutch citizenship on the basis of his long-term residence there (at least six years). Yet he was never formally naturalized and this equivalent status was nullified when he left the Netherlands. Therefore the Foreign Affairs office advised the consul general not to issue him a Dutch passport. Hernass, in the meantime, put in a complaint. He insisted that he had never realized that leaving the Netherlands would have such far-reaching consequences: he would lose his shop and means of existence if his passport were refused. Furthermore, it appeared that Hernass and his Swiss wife had chosen domicile at the address of a Rotterdam firm. In the end, the Foreign Affairs office gave in and allowed the consul general to issue him a passport.[33]

This example, and many others, illustrate that Dutch officials were not very strict when it came to issuing passports. Even people like the Prussian-born Hernass and his Swiss wife, neither of whom had ever been Dutch and had already lived for many years in Switzerland, were given the benefit of the doubt. This lenient policy is all the more remarkable when we realize that most of the people who applied for a Dutch passport without proof of their Dutch nationality were, in the eyes of their contemporaries, not exactly the *fine fleur* of the Dutch nation. In general, these were highly mobile people who often practiced itinerant trades, moving around with their family.[34]

Marcus Cohen, born in the Dutch town of Leeuwarden in 1833, for example, was at one time a high-wire walker, later a peddler. He must have left the Netherlands in his early twenties, as all of his six children were born abroad (Belgium, France, and Switzerland). A clear case of *animus non redeundi,* one would say, but the consul general nevertheless issued him a passport in 1875 without even asking permission of the Ministry of Foreign Affairs.[35]

This rather lenient attitude seems to be linked to the Nationality Act of 1850. During the parliamentary debates concerning this act, several deputies were very critical about the proposal that Dutch nationals would lose their nationality when they stayed abroad for more than five years. One of them declared, "The state, the fatherland is towards its subjects, as a father towards his children he cannot renounce them. I think that the fatherland should act as the father of a lost son. . . . The fatherland should not abandon its children."[36] Many agreed with this point of view, and the government was forced to accept an amendment that implied that Dutch citizens who stayed abroad for more than five years would lose their nationality only if the state could demonstrate that they had no intention to return. In the correspondence between the consul general in Bern and the Dutch Foreign Office, however, these kinds of ideological arguments were rarely uttered. Human concerns and practical arguments seemed to prevail. Thus, even the home secretary, who was responsible for poor relief, stated in 1878 that the request for a Dutch passport proved that the applicant had no *animus non redeundi:* "Even when an applicant resides abroad for years, he should be given a passport. Everyone is free to keep or renounce his nationality, and it is unjust that one would force him, by refusing a document that is needed to prove his Dutch nationality, to give up his nationality or to return to his fatherland."[37] Interestingly, he added that the Dutch state would in fact benefit if such citizens stayed abroad. In accordance with the 1870 Poor Law, poor Dutch could only get relief if they returned to the Netherlands. A passport would both give people the opportunity to stay abroad and relieve the Dutch state from paying for poor relief. Paradoxically then, the issuance of Dutch passports to people who had left the Netherlands and would probably never return was a means to assure that they would *not* come back.

Nevertheless, the authorities were not always so tolerant with migrants whose Dutch roots were questionable. Karl Trautwein, for instance, presented himself to the consul general in Bern in 1878. The only documentation he provided was an old extract from the Amsterdam population register (showing that he had once been a resident) and a document that stated he had fulfilled his military obligations. Moreover, his parents appeared to be living in Amsterdam. The consultation of various authorities in the Netherlands made clear that Trautwein was born in Germany and that his parents were not Dutch, nor Dutch residents, at the moment of his birth. He had therefore never possessed Dutch nationality, and his request for a Dutch passport had to be turned down.[38] This example shows that in this period the policy was far from uniform and often quite arbitrary. In everyday bureaucratic practice, ideas and conceptions about who was a "real" Dutch national remained ambiguous and, depending on an individual's legal knowledge *and* interpretation, could result in opposite outcomes for more or less similar cases.

The Nationality Acts of 1850 and especially 1892, in which the jus sanguinis principle was deeply rooted, stressed the tight bond between the national state and its subjects. Yet descendants of Dutch emigrants were not always received with open arms. It might seem that those emigrants for whom it was clear that they had once possessed Dutch nationality, especially by birth, were treated with leniency, whereas persons like Trautwein, whose claim to Dutch nationality was much weaker, had a much harder time convincing Dutch officials. Yet, one last example—that of the policy toward the Dutch and their offspring in Russia—shows that this conclusion is too general, and it highlights how other factors also came into play. After 1870, the Russian authorities put more pressure on foreigners to prove their nationality, mainly because they suspected people were trying to avoid Russian military service.[39] In this case, Dutch authorities were very hesitant to acknowledge any national responsibility toward former citizens and their children who had emigrated to Russia. Both the Dutch chargé d'affaires in Saint Petersburg and the Ministry of Foreign Affairs in The Hague deemed it undesirable to extend Dutch nationality to the children (or grandchildren) of Dutch emigrants who had left the country long ago. Thus Thomas Bartelink, whose grandfather settled in Russia and had never returned, was denied a Dutch passport, notwithstanding the fact that the Russian state considered him to be (still) Dutch.[40] The much harsher attitude of the Dutch state toward their former citizens in Russia shows, in a contrasting way, the importance of the poor-relief factor. In contrast to Switzerland (and other surrounding countries), Dutch authorities probably assumed that the chance that long-settled Dutch emigrants, and especially their offspring, would ever come back from Russia was very slim, and therefore the probability that they would burden Dutch poor relief funds was negligible.

We have argued that emigrants do not always shut the door behind them when they leave home and cross borders. However, migration studies hardly ever focus on relations between emigrants and their home countries: both the influence of the sending state on emigrants and the influence of emigrants on the meaning of citizenship are neglected areas of research. Studies of transnationalism and international politics have stimulated the attention to emigration, but they are generally restricted to the political domain.

The study of Dutch migrants in Germany underlines the importance of taking a wider view. First, it illustrates that, even in the heyday of nationalism, citizenship of foreigners within state borders and of subjects abroad was not simply a question of principle but was mainly relevant when it came to financial and judicial consequences. Germany and the Netherlands negotiated on questions like poor relief and military service, and although they were framed in national terms, jus soli or jus sanguinis arguments played only a minor role. The Dutch state was not so much interested in keeping contact with its subjects or in furthering patriotic feelings among its citizens in Germany as it was driven by social and economic considerations.

The widely held conviction among politicians and policymakers that the Netherlands needed the German labor market to solve its own problems of unemployment and overpopulation heavily influenced the extraterritorial policy. It was deemed of utmost importance that the German labor market remain open for Dutch migrants. This implied that the Dutch state had to meet German demands for nationality documents and for its own revision of the Dutch military service law, and had to support its unemployed citizens abroad; this was accepted as inevitable.

The Swiss case is different because Switzerland was irrelevant for such an extended labor market policy. It is similar, however, with regard to the importance of social and economic considerations. Dutch citizens, and even those whose claims to Dutch nationality were dubious, were accepted as such and issued passports because as long as they were able to extend their stay outside the country, they were not entitled to poor relief at home. Although at first glance all this involvement of the Dutch state with its citizens abroad seems to have strengthened the ties between Dutch emigrants and their country of origin, in reality the opposite was intended and achieved: papers and poor relief abroad prevented the emigrants from being expelled and at least postponed their return to the Netherlands.

Table 7.1. Geographical distribution of Dutch Emigrants, 1849–1960

	Germany (%)	Belgium (%)	Elsewhere in Europe (%)	Outside of Europe (%)	Total number of Dutch emigrants (excl. Dutch colonies)	Dutch colonies
1849	16	50	8	27	64,000	9,200
1859	15	37	9	39	90,000	13,000
1869	24	28	9	39	125,000	15,400
1879	25	28	7	40	148,000	20,300
1889	26	23	7	43	201,000	20,200
1899	34	20	6	39	263,000	23,000
1909	41	18	4	37	352,000	n.a.
1920	29	16	5	50	287,000	n.a.
1960	12	12	5	72	567,000	n.a.

Sources: 1849–99: C. A. Oomens, De loop der bevolking van Nederland in de negentiende eeuw (Graven-hage: SDU, 1989); 1909–60: P. R. D. Stokvis, "Nederland en de internationale migratie, 1815–1960," in De Nederlandse samenleving sinds 1815. Wording en samenhang, ed. F. L. Holthoon (Assen: Van Gorcum, 1985): 72–73. These are rough estimates, and Oomens and Stokvis disagree on the number of emigrants.

Table 7.2. Number of emigrants and immigrants in the Netherlands, as percentage of the total Dutch population, 1849–1960

	Born in the Netherlands	Foreign nationality, living in the Netherlands
1849	2.2	n.a.
1869	3.1	n.a.
1889	4.0	1.1
1909	6.0	1.2
1930	4.3	2.2
1960	4.9	1.0

Sources: P. R. D. Stokvis, "Nederland en de internationale migratie, 1815–1960." in De Nederlandse samenleving sinds 1815. Wording en samenhang, ed. F.L. Holthoon (Assen: Van Gorcum, 1985) 72–73; Dutch censuses.

Table 7.3. Dutch in Germany, Germans in the Netherlands, 1889–1933

Dutch (German) census	Dutch in Germany	Germans in the Netherlands
1889 (1890)	37,000	28,800
1899 (1900)	88,100	31,900
1909 (1910)	144,200	37,500
1920	n.a.	56,400
1925	82,300	*
1930	n.a.	102,000
1933 (Prussia)	n.a.	74,300

* not a census year

Sources: Dutch censuses; Jochen Oltmer, Migration als Gefahr. Transnationale Migration und Wanderungspolitik in der Weimarer Republik (Habilitationsschrift, Osnabrück 2001), 300, 401; 1933: ARA, FA, 2.5.21, file 950, 22-12-1934.

Table 7.4. Number of nationality certificates issued in the Netherlands, 1901–14

Years	Total number of certificates	Average per year
1901–6	135,087	22,515
1907–14	250,765	31,346
Total	385,852	27,561

Source: *Maandschriften van het Centraal Bureau voor de Statistiek,* 1905–18.

Table 7.5. Number of Dutch people placed in Germany by the Employment Exchange in Oberhausen, 1908–32

Years	Number	Yearly average
1908–14	4,154	593
1915–18	4,227	1,057
1919–32	2,702	193
Total	11,083	443

Source: Th. van Lier, "Arbeidsbemiddeling tussen Nederland en Duitschland," *Tijdschrift van den Nederlandschen Werkloosheids-Raad,* 16 (1933): 109–23.

Table 7. 6. Estimated yearly expenditure (in guilders) for poor relief of Dutch citizens abroad, 1920–38

1920–21	50,000	1933	4,000,000
1923	550,000	1934	3,100,000
1924	2,000,000	1935	2,500,000
1925–30	1,000,000	1936	1,700,000
1931	1,200,000	1937	1,400,000
1932	2,100,000	1938	1,000,000

Sources: National Budget, Home Department, *Parliamentary Protocols* II (1920–38). Included is the cost of the Government Office for relief of needy Dutchmen abroad (since 1932, about 150,000 guilders annually). Up until 1929 the figures are rough estimates, because the national budgets of the Home Department are not detailed enough.

Table 7.7. Number of Dutch who received poor relief in Germany, 1933–36

December 31, 1933	7,463
December 31, 1934	6,300
December 31, 1935	5,102
December 31, 1936	3,732
December 31, 1937	2,980

Source: Report from the Home Secretary, 13-6-1938, ARA, FA, 2.05.21, file 951.

1. Return migration was important, even in typical immigration countries like the United States. See Walter Nugent, *Crossings: The Great Atlantic Migrations, 1870–1914* (Bloomington: Indiana University Press, 1992); Mark Wyman, *Round-Trip to America: The Immigrants Return to Europe, 1880–1930* (Ithaca, N.Y.: Cornell University Press, 1993); and Donna Gabaccia, *Italy's Many Diasporas* (London: UCL Press, 2000).

2. Lately this has changed somewhat. See, for example, Gabaccia, *Italy's Many Diasporas*, 136–41.

3. Especially in German states: Axel Lubinski, *Entlassen aus dem Untertanenverband: Die Amerika-Auswanderung aus Mecklenburg-Strelitz im 19. Jahrhundert* (Osnabrück: Rasch, 1997); Georg Fertig, *Lokales Leben, atlantische Welt: Die Entscheidung zur Auswanderung vom Rhein nach Nordamerika im 18. Jahrhundert* (Osnabrück: Rasch, 2000).

4. Jan Lucassen, *Dutch Long-Distance Migration: A Concise History, 1600–1900* (Amsterdam: IISH Research Papers, 1994); for emigration to the United States, see R. P. Swierenga, ed., *The Dutch in America: Immigration, Settlement, and Cultural Change* (New Brunswick, N.J.: Rutgers University Press, 1985); Annemieke Galema, *Frisians to America 1880–1914: With the Baggage of the Fatherland* (Groningen: Regio Projekt Uitgevers, 1996).

5. A smaller part worked as unskilled and semiskilled workers in agriculture and infrastructure in northern Germany; see, for example, Michael Kösters-Kraft, *Grossbaustelle und Arbeitswanderung: Niederländer beim Bau des Dortmund-Ems-Kanals 1892–1900* (Osnabrück: Rasch, 2000).

6. "Geschriften over de landverhuizing," *Algemeen Letterlievend Maandschrift*, 32 (1848): 166–98.

7. William Petersen, *Some Factors Influencing Postwar Emigration from the Netherlands* (The Hague: Martinus Nijhoff, 1952), 1–13.

8. Leo Lucassen, "The Great War and the Origins of Migration Control in Western Europe and the United States (1880–1920)," in *Regulation of Migration: International Experiences*, ed. Anita Böcker et al., 45–72 (Amsterdam: Het Spinhuis Publishers, 1998).

9. J. A. A. Hartland, *De geschiedenis van de Nederlandse emigratie tot de Tweede Wereldoorlog* (The Hague: Nederlandse Emigratiedienst, 1959), 46–48, 62.

10. Marijke van Faassen, "Min of meer misbaar: Naoorlogse emigratie vanuit Nederland; Achtergronden en organisatie, particuliere motieven en overheidsprikkels, 1946–1967," in *Van hot naar her. Nederlandse migratie vroeger, nu en morgen*, ed. Saskia Poldervaart et al., 50–67 (Amsterdam: Stichting Beheer IISG, 2001).

11. Jan Lucassen, *Migrant Labour in Europe 1600–1900: The Drift to the North Sea* (London: Croom Helm, 1987).

12. Leo Lucassen, "Bringing Structure Back In: Economic and Political Determi-

nants of Immigration in Dutch Cities (1920–1940)," *Social Science History* 26, no. 3 (Fall 2002): 503–29.

13. John Torpey, *The Invention of the Passport: Surveillance, Citizenship and the State* (Cambridge, Eng.: Cambridge University Press, 2000); Leslie Page Moch, *Moving Europeans: Migration in Western Europe since 1650* (Bloomington: Indiana University Press, 1992).

14. Leo Lucassen, "A Many-Headed Monster: The Evolution of the Passport System in the Netherlands and Germany in the Long Nineteenth Century," in *Documenting Individual Identity: The Development of State Practices in the Modern World*, ed. John Torpey and Jane Caplan, 235–55 (Princeton, N.J.: Princeton University Press, 2001).

15. Fahrmeir wrongly assumes that only citizens of German states could lose their citizenship upon emigration. Andreas K. Fahrmeir, "Nineteenth-Century German Citizenships: A Reconstruction," *The Historical Journal*, 40 (1997): 721–52.

16. National Archive, The Hague (hereinafter NA), Justice Department (JD), 2.09.01, file 5188, October 3, 1868.

17. NA, Foreign Affairs (FA), 2.05.03, file 424, 28–3–1895.

18. NA, FA, 2.05.03, file 53, complaint by the Prussian home secretary, October 31, 1874.

19. *Parliamentary Protocols* II (1896–1897) 325, 330.

20. *Deutsche Wochenzeitung in den Niederlanden*, July 12, 1908, 5–6.

21. *Verslagen van de Staatscommissie over de werkloosheid* (The Hague: Algemene Landsdrukkerij, 1913–14), *Deel IX Eindverslag:* 554–56.

22. B. A. Sijes, *De arbeidsinzet: De gedwongen arbeid van Nederlanders in Duitsland, 1940–1945* (The Hague: Martinus Nijhoff, 1966); Ulrich Herbert, *A History of Foreign Labour in Germany, 1880–1980: Seasonal Workers/Forced Laborers/Guest Workers* (Ann Arbor: University of Michigan Press, 1990).

23. NA, Social Affairs (SA), 2.15.13, file 24, meeting of the Dutch Unemployment Council, November 16, 1938.

24. NA, Home Department (HD), 2.04.55, file 468, October 24, 1924. See also (for Duisburg) James H. Jackson, *Migration and Urbanization in the Ruhr Valley, 1821–1914* (Atlantic Highlands, N.J.: Humanities Press, 1997): 228. Thus, in 1910, the Dutch population in this town was almost twelve thousand people.

25. NA, HD, 2.04.55, file 947, 27–8–1920.

26. NA, HD, 2.04.55, file 464, 30–10–1933.

27. NA, HD, 2.04.55, file 477. In 1931 there were about 300 Dutch families with poor relief in Belgium, rising to almost 700 in 1933; it decreased to 350 in 1938.

28. NA, HD, 2.04.55, file 462.

29. In 1870, about two hundred; around 1900, about nine hundred. See C. A. Oomens, *De loop der bevolking: van Nederland in de negentiende eeuw* (The Hague: SDU), 33.

30. Aristide Zolberg, "The Great Wall against China: Responses to the First Im-

migration Crisis, 1885–1925," in *Migration, Migration History, History: Old Paradigms and New Perspectives*, ed. Jan Lucassen and Leo Lucassen, 291–316, esp. 308 (Bern: Peter Lang, 1997).

31. NA, FA, 2.05.03, file 332, consul general in Bern to the Ministry of Foreign Affairs, February 22, 1875.

32. The principle derived from the French Code Civil: "Établissement dans un pays étranger sans esprit de retour." This principle was formulated by the French lawyer Robert Joseph Pothier (1699–1772) in his *Traités des personnes et des choses, du domaine de propriété, de la possession, de la prescription, de l'hypothèque, des fiefs, des cens, des champarts*. It was laid down in the Nationality Act of 1850 as explained by Eric Heijs, *Van vreemdeling tot Nederlander: De verlening van het Nederlanderschap aan vreemdelingen 1813–1992* (Amsterdam: Het Spinhuis, 1995): 33–34.

33. NA, FA 2.05.03, file 332, letter of the consul general to Foreign Affairs, April 24, 1875.

34. On the attitude toward travelers, see Leo Lucassen, Wim Willems, and Annemarie Cottaar, *Gypsies and Other Travellers: A Socio-Historical Approach* (Houndmills: Macmillan and New York: St. Martin's Press, 1998).

35. NA, FA, 2.05.03, file 332, letter of the consul general to Foreign Affairs, August 5, 1875.

36. Donker Curtius, cited by Heijs, *Van vreemdeling*, 33.

37. NA, FA, 2.05.03, file 332, Home Department to Foreign Affairs, January 14, 1878.

38. NA, FA. 2.05.03, file 332, mayor of Amsterdam to the provincial authorities of North-Holland, September 12, 1878.

39. NA, FA, 2.05.03, file 332, minister of foreign affairs to his colleague of justice, October 11, 1877.

40. NA, FA, 2.05.03, file 332, Foreign Affairs to the chargé d'affaires in St. Petersburg, August 7, 1878.

8

FROM ECONOMICS TO ETHNICITY AND BACK: REFLECTIONS ON EMIGRATION CONTROL IN GERMANY, 1800–2000

Andreas Fahrmeir

In the modern industrialized world of today, it has become difficult to imagine emigration control as a major political topic. As all industrial societies face pressing problems of unemployment in almost all professions, preventing people from going elsewhere is hardly an issue. What is an issue is how to decide who gets admission to the world's few islands of prosperity, security, and stability. Admittedly, there are a few regions of the industrialized world where significant out-migration, particularly of the relatively young and relatively qualified, is an economic and demographic problem, Germany's no longer quite-so-new eastern *Länder* being one of them. However, given the fact that most of the out-migrants remain within the same country, not even this development can spark a national emigration debate.

There is also a deeper reason for the absence of emigration debates. The hands of modern liberal states are tied when it comes to regulating emigration through anything other than direct economic incentives, while their powers to regulate immigration are substantial. And economic incentives are difficult to initiate, given the significant reduction of state expenditure advocated almost everywhere. Hence the typical reaction of countries facing labor shortages in certain regions or certain sectors is to put targeted immigration programs in place, even if one of the causes of the shortage is emigration to countries where salaries are higher or living conditions are better.

One reason for the focus on immigration control and the lack of focus on emigration control is that the right to emigrate ranks high in the canon of fundamental liberties. Except in wartime or for prisoners, the right to move away is a basic human right. In German states, the right to emigrate was already generally recognized as basic by the nineteenth century,[1] a statement which, on its face, should end the debate: if the liberty to emigrate were an untouchable fundamental human right, then the state could do nothing to influence emigration. In fact, the consequences were less absolute. It is important to note that the recognition of a right to depart severely restricted the regulation of emigration and complicated the political discourse on emigration control. Nevertheless, the recognition of this right did not prevent emigration restrictions altogether.

This meant that states' desire to hinder emigration could not be expressed directly, not least because this would have evoked echoes of feudal serfdom. Direct restrictions on emigration would also have contradicted constitutions that protected the right to emigrate from the early 1800s.[2] Governments keen on emigration restrictions were thus forced to introduce them through the back door—through inheritance and tax laws, for instance, or through passport and registration laws, the laws regarding military conscription, or the regulation of passenger shipping. But the status of the right to emigrate makes it difficult to identify those measures that were mainly emigration oriented (and not motivated primarily by fiscal, military, or safety concerns). It also made public or even semipublic debates on emigration policy difficult to conduct, because such debates could only lead to one conclusion: that the right to emigrate could not be abrogated.

Furthermore, the decision to emigrate is a personal one. It is not necessarily made when would-be emigrants leave the country, and it is certainly not possible to ascertain each time people cross a border whether they intend to leave for a fixed period or to emigrate—they themselves may not yet know. The decision may be made in stages, for instance after a few weeks or months into what was conceived as a temporary migration. A planned emigration may fail and end in return migration, amounting to no more than temporary absence. Regular seasonal migration can culminate in permanent migration: a temporary laborer from Poland may find regular seasonal employment in the Ruhr region and ultimately decide to stay there for good; a merchant from Hamburg may identify business opportunities in Lyon, decide to open a branch office of his firm there (where he visits frequently), and ultimately shift his main office and permanent residence to France. The key point is that there are many instances in which the decision to move from temporary absence to permanent emigration is made outside the country of origin.

In this case, the country of emigration is in a very different position from the country of immigration. The officials of the country of emigration have no direct access to the emigrants. If the country of immigration does not approve of someone's decision to stay, it can coerce or force the immigrant to leave; if the country of emigration does not approve of a person's decision to remain abroad, it can hardly instruct its officials to compel the emigrant to return. Prosecutions relating to violations of passport regulations or other laws are possible, but they can never achieve more than the confiscation of property left in the native state and/or the threat of a prison sentence if and when emigrants return to their native country. In order to be effective, any emigration policy thus requires an early-warning system that identifies the emigrants among the many travelers crossing borders.

This chapter looks at some of the problems this involves, using examples from Germany, a country that presents an interesting case of the development of emigration policy. One reason is that the states'—and then the state's—attitudes toward emigrants underwent a series of drastic revisions in the course of the nineteenth and twentieth centuries. Another reason is that German states, the German empire in its various incarnations, and finally the Federal Republic, practiced relatively extreme policies, first by completely repudiating all ties to emigrants, then by maintaining extremely strong legal ties to at least some of the emigrants and their descendants. Germany is also interesting because of the shift in its motives behind official emigration policy. Whereas the potential cost of emigrants was the dominant consideration in the nineteenth century, the importance of linking all people of ethnic German descent grew in the minds of officials and political agitators in the German empire. In some ways, the National Socialist regime represented the climax of those developments, but with a precise geographical focus on eastern Europe. Being forced to deal with the legacy of the "Third Reich," the Federal Republic retained a focus on ethnic Germans in eastern Europe, but in the Federal Republic, ethnic considerations were always in competition with economic ones, which appeared to gain the upper hand again.

NINETEENTH-CENTURY CONTRADICTIONS

In the first half of the nineteenth century, most German states experienced a rapid shift of attitudes toward population policy. Previously, mercantilist ideas had encouraged states to increase the number of their inhabitants through, for instance, systematic population transfer to less densely settled areas, such as the eastern parts of the Hapsburg empire and Prussia. After 1815, the goal was precisely the reverse. The introduction of marriage restrictions (designed to slow population growth)[3] and restrictions on the admission of new citizens arose out of fear that poverty resulted from an uncontrolled population increase—described with the catchword "pauperism." Immigrants had to prove—to the locality where they wished to reside and to the government of the state that was to accept them as either long-term residents or citizens (the two concepts not being clearly distinguished)—that they were able to provide for themselves. In theory, this ought to have encouraged a liberal stance toward emigration. In practice, the situation was more complex.

It is one of the many peculiarities of official attitudes toward emigration that both states involved in any population flow tend to be of the opinion that they receive a bad deal. The countries where emigrants move often suspect that the places they come from are, in one way or another, "shoveling out" paupers and/or criminals. By contrast, the countries of origin frequently fear losing their more dynamic citizens to more attractive competitors in a global battle for wealth and talent. In German states, there was also considerable concern that unsuccessful emigration attempts could cause people who had so far been able to support themselves to end up destitute, which would thus place an additional burden on poor relief systems. Such fears were not entirely unrealistic. Craftsmen or farmers who wished to emigrate had to turn their assets into cash, and if they lost that cash due to fraud, or if the amount was insufficient to cover the expenses of the entire journey, they would return with nothing and "fall into a much more lamentable state than the one which they thought to have escaped forever."[4]

Finally, the bureaucracy of the German states distrusted movement in general. The ideal subject was someone who had a fixed abode and left it infrequently. Anyone who was to be found on the roads was suspected of having a sinister purpose, unless he was obviously involved in legitimate trade. This attitude—expressed in such formulations as "concerning strangers and suspicious native persons"[5]—was at first limited to the lower social orders, where the boundaries between vagrancy and legitimate peddling, journeymen's tours and begging, may indeed not have always been easy to pinpoint. With the growing political upheavals of the 1830s and 1840s, however, the "higher estates," people who had previously been all but exempt from police surveillance during their travels, were subjected to closer supervision as well. Even in the 1850s, one of the police officers at Minden, a main-entry checkpoint for travelers entering Prussia from the kingdom of Hanover, still considered mere presence at the station to be proof of membership in the revolutionary party. It was only by the 1860s that this attitude began to soften, and it took much longer for it to transform itself into the positive evaluation of travel as a sign of dynamism we are more inclined toward today.[6]

The result of the aims pursued by governments and localities—population stabilization or reduction, the limitation and control of travel, and the attraction and retention of wealth and talent—was a system of migration regulation in which different levels of the administration pursued different emigration policies. No German state prohibited emigration as such. However, throughout the nineteenth century and into the interwar period, German governments sought to keep emigration in check. The first means of doing so was limiting access to information. The criminal offence of "enticing natives to leave" was not removed from the statute books before World War I. The offence was aggravated if the information given to would-be emigrants was incorrect, but even factually correct information could be judged illegal if it was considered too enticing.[7]

A second method of persuading emigrants to think twice was the erection of bureaucratic obstacles that did not amount to a prohibition but required the expenditure of a considerable sum of money (roughly 12 *Gulden*) and quite a lot of time on the obligatory emigration permit—a sort of cooling-off period before the critical decision became irrevocable, combined with a test of means. In addition almost twenty supporting certificates and published notifications of departure were required.[8]

The emigration permit procedure had two aims. One was to ensure that the emigration plan was feasible; that emigrants actually had tickets; that these tickets had been issued by a respectable and trustworthy company; that the emigrants' food supply was guaranteed by the shipping agent; and that the emigrants would not be mistreated at their destination (if, for instance, they had subscribed to labor contracts amounting to personal servitude for a fixed or indefinite period). The second purpose was less paternalistic: it was to ensure that the state did not suffer any financial loss through the departure of the emigrant, because once the emigrants were gone, they could no longer be called to account. Emigrants had to prove that their dependents were provided for; all their taxes had been paid; no civil or criminal lawsuits were pending against them; any military service had been completed (or that they were not leaving mainly or exclusively in order to avoid it); the state had received reimbursement for the cost of any education they had received free or with the aid of scholarships, and so on.

Clearly, this procedure erected considerable obstacles against emigration. It could not be avoided if the would-be emigrants possessed real estate and desired to keep it in their possession after they moved abroad, or if selling it might attract the particular notice of local officials. But in all other cases, it was possible to circumvent the constraints. For residents of Bavaria or Baden, one possibility was to slip away over the French or Swiss frontier, where officials did not care about the regulations of German states, only whether travelers had sufficient funds.[9] At least in the 1850s, travelers seem to have been viewed as potential emigrants only if they had considerable amounts of luggage with them; if they had sent their bags ahead, they could sometimes even travel without a passport, and certainly without an emigration permit.[10] Another way to bypass emigration restrictions was to disguise emigration as a normal business or pleasure trip in official papers by applying for a regular passport, not for an emigration permit. There is a substantial amount of evidence that local authorities encouraged this by providing the required certificates.[11]

Unless emigrants had circumvented conscription laws (and could therefore be charged with desertion), the prohibition of "illegal" emigration was extremely difficult to enforce and unlikely to be detected if an emigrant, in spite of once having "the intention never to return," changed his or her mind and returned, having remained legally resident in his or her locality during a "temporary" absence. Leaving one's status open not only had the advantage of avoiding the application for an emigration permit, but in case one did wish to return, it saved the bother of applying for readmission to residence and citizenship.

The way in which bureaucratic requirements were met or avoided mattered little for the politics of expatriation. German governments were very clear on two points: they did not encourage emigration, but as soon as citizens were actually gone, they wanted to ensure that all links between the emigrants and their country of origin were severed immediately, completely, and irrevocably. This minimized the risk of having to deal with impoverished return migrants claiming readmission, residence rights, and poor relief.

The legal position was therefore quite clear: emigrants ceased to be citizens as soon as they crossed the border of their native state "with the intention never to return"—regardless of whether the required formalities had been duly attended to or not.[12] The difficulty lay in ascertaining the intention "never to return" if it was not explicitly stated. In most cases, the test of time was thought to serve the purpose well enough: a continued absence of more than ten years definitely meant loss of citizenship. In practice, there were endless problems, the most contentious issue being military service, because "illegal emigrants" who returned to German states after a number of years could still be prosecuted for "desertion" for failing to meet the demands of conscription laws, even if they had not only officially ceased to be citizens—but had also adopted the citizenship of another country.[13]

The official attitude to emigrants was therefore determined by indifference, and official policy saw to it that the links with former citizens were severed as soon as possible. But in this respect, too, there were problems. Non-German states were not likely to accept the quick denationalization of immigrants who would have to wait between five and ten years for naturalization in their new state of residence, and they insisted that German states take back emigrants who were deported. Nevertheless, the consulates of German states usually stood firm and denied financial assistance to emigrants, even if they were shipwrecked in the course of the journey to their destination. But this strict official policy coexisted with semiofficial contributions German state governments made to private societies with the aim of assisting foreigners in distress, or to hospitals for German visitors and emigrants.[14]

The policy of German states toward emigrants in the nineteenth century reflected a number of prevalent preconceptions about citizenship and the economic effects of migration. One was that citizenship was linked to residence and changed with the permanent place of residence. The Bancroft Treaty between the United States and German states of 1868, for instance, assumed that naturalization in either the United States or a German state was void if its beneficiaries returned to the country of their birth for more than two years.[15] As German states were eager to rid themselves of obligations to former citizens, it was understandable that they desired the change of citizenship to occur as soon as possible. This point was uncontroversial. But when it came to laying down guidelines for emigration policy, several aims came into conflict. Assisted emigration was sometimes perceived as a means of easing social problems, particularly by villages or towns that saw it as a quick and safe way of reducing poor relief.[16]

But there was one major obstacle to using emigration policy as a means of solving social and financial problems. The states of destination, not least the United States, objected to accepting paupers or criminals and had no qualms about returning them on the next ship. This forced German state governments to ensure that only those who were likely to be successful overseas were permitted to leave, and this left them with a dilemma. Encouraging "promising" emigrants to depart was the only realistic emigration policy, but it meant that those people who represented the least problem and greatest asset were lost to the state. As a result, the hands of the governments of most European states were tied. (The only exception was Britain, where a significant proportion of emigrants were likely to remain within the British Empire.) Assisted emigration on a large scale was not acceptable to the major countries of destination. Limiting emigration by setting high financial and bureaucratic hurdles was of course feasible, but it interfered with generally accepted fundamental rights, and it risked increasing the outflow of talent and money. By the mid-nineteenth century, another objection arose. Increasingly vocal groups were unhappy with the abandonment of emigrants by German states. German policies were contrasted unfavorably with those of countries whose emigrants peopled colonies; such policies were considered a leading cause for the failure of Germany to become a colonial power on a par with Britain or France, in line with its military and economic standing in Europe.

In spite of the increasing agitation of nationalist pressure groups after the unification of German states in 1871, official attitudes to emigration and emigrants hardly changed in the empire. Emigration policy still steered an uncertain course between paternalistic advice and bureaucratic hindrance, while the number of emigrants reached new heights. Some attempts were undertaken to provide closer links between emigrants and Germany, for instance, by permitting emigrants to retain their citizenship abroad for more than ten years and by making it easier to resume German citizenship after returning. This did not, however, make emigrants immune from prosecution for leaving the country clandestinely, and it did not absolve them from going through the bureaucratic procedure and expense of reapplying for their original citizenship after their return.[17]

SHIFTING ATTITUDES

Permitting emigrants to remain citizens was not only a result of a new view of emigration. Attempts to do away with various inconsistencies of citizenship laws in Europe and North America can be observed throughout the nineteenth century, and their pace increased from the late 1860s onward.[18] One major aim was to make laws about the loss and acquisition of citizenship compatible in order to prevent people from being claimed as citizens by more than one country. Jus soli, jus domicilii, or jus sanguinis were modified to something approaching an international standard, either by law or by judicial and administrative interpretation. For instance, British officials accepted that the law of the land, which considered the children of British subjects born abroad to be British, could not take precedence over a jus soli applied by the country of birth; Britain abandoned the doctrine of inalienable allegiance, which prevented a full change of citizenship by naturalization, just as Germany eased the rule of automatic denationalization upon emigration. In many of these cases, the United States was the driving force because it had a clear interest in securing a well-defined status for its citizens, many of whom were American by naturalization, when they returned to Europe on business or for official purposes.[19]

The trend toward removing conflicting attributions of citizenship as much as possible was a consequence of the increasing importance of citizenship as such. In addition to conferring rights of residence, and duties such as military service, citizenship now also determined, for instance, the type and range of claims that could be made on national insurance schemes against accidents, illness, or unemployment.[20] Until the 1870s, domicile had a significant impact (if not necessarily on the acquisition of citizenship itself) on the transmission of citizenship in many countries. It was clear that the transmission of citizenship to the next generation was difficult if one was no longer resident in the country of one's citizenship. In German states and the German empire, this was ensured by the loss of citizenship through emigration; in the United Kingdom, it was recognized that the children of a British father had a claim to British citizenship even if they were born abroad, but this claim could only be activated when and if they left the country of their birth; while they were there, it was invalid. Such mechanisms were not abolished immediately, but it did gradually become easier to remain a citizen of one's country of birth after moving permanently to another one. The connection between emigration and a change of citizenship thus became less direct.

This general European trend had an additional twist in Germany. Other western and central European countries experienced emigration either to their own colonies or to the territories of actual or political allies. By contrast, by moving to the British Empire or the United States, German emigrants departed for territories of (potential) political rivals. The stronger links between emigrants and their mother country thus also had a political implication. The German political right hoped that tying emigrants more closely to their country of birth would strengthen their political links to that country and thus strengthen Germany's influence in the world by establishing "little Germanys" with political clout overseas. This logic was never particularly convincing, especially insofar as emigrants who maintained their German citizenship could not participate in elections in their state of residence, which meant that they could never become a political factor to be reckoned with there. Nevertheless, thinking along such lines influenced a reform of German citizenship law in 1913 that made it possible to retain and pass on German citizenship overseas indefinitely.[21] The effects of this law could never really be tested, because World War I led to the internment and eventual repatriation of those German immigrants who had not been naturalized in almost all belligerent countries.[22] This experience fundamentally changed the framework for emigrants in the interwar period, because it made clear that emigrating without being prepared to change one's citizenship was extremely risky and could lead to long-term internment, as well as to the loss and destruction of one's economic position, at least as long as the international political climate remained highly volatile.

The restrictions on travel brought about by World War I had interrupted emigration movements from Europe. For the first years after the end of the war, potential German emigrants were also barred from migrating to the former enemy countries. But emigration was allowed to resume relatively quickly. By the early 1920s, emigration to the United States, Canada, and other countries was once again an option for German citizens, an option many Germans hoping to escape their country's dire political and economic situation were keen to pursue.[23] In the face of what threatened to be a rising tide of emigrants, the German government attempted to pull the gates shut again to prevent the departure of workers and potential soldiers. The German government's position was made easier by the travel restrictions imposed by the war, which were not dismantled afterwards. Between the 1860s and 1914, passport controls had been lifted in western Europe. Travelers needed to possess official identification of one sort or another, but there were no frontier checkpoints and no visa requirements. The war had once again turned international travel into a tightly regulated anomaly. Emigrants now required, at the very least, a passport valid *to* the destination, and the destination would be apparent to officials checking the document on exit because it had to contain a visa for the destination. The visa might also contain a statement of the purpose of the trip. It was thus difficult to avoid emigration controls after 1919.

THE INTERWAR YEARS

In this way, it was thus possible for the Weimar Republic to revert to a stricter version of the emigration policy of the empire. In theory, the right to emigrate was still guaranteed by the Weimar constitution, subject to federal restrictions. As long as the main destinations of choice for emigrants were shut off through bans on the emigration of citizens to enemy states, there was no need for the federal regulation of emigration. But as soon as emigration was permitted again, it became clear both that Germans were keen to leave and that they remained desirable immigrants in the racially charged immigration control schemes set up by the United States. As economic crisis tightened its grip on Germany, the number of emigrants rose sharply, reaching 115,000 in 1923.[24]

The Weimar government regarded this development with concern, and bureaucratic procedures were put in place to deter emigrants. The old emigration permit was reborn as official clearance from the emigration authority, which did its best to discourage applicants. In order to obtain a passport, emigrants could be required to show that attempts to find work had not been successful; if they could not do so, they were directed to their local *Arbeitsamt* (job placement bureau) or to domestic settlement schemes. If no work could be found for them and they could not be dissuaded from leaving, they were encouraged to choose destinations where German culture could be preserved in German-only settlements (in South America, for instance). This emphasis on maintaining a German cultural heritage (and the "purity" of the German lineage of emigrants) was a novel development, which was taken up in National Socialist attempts to organize Germans in other states through the *Auslandsorganisation* of the National Socialist Party.[25]

However, National Socialist policy toward emigrants after 1933 did not simply continue preexisting trends. As in many of its policies, the Third Reich combined its perception of so-called racial imperatives with a cynical realpolitik subordinated to its overall aims of expanding German political domination into eastern Europe. Whereas German ethnic minorities there were supported—used as "fifth columns" to undermine the stability of local governments and granted preferential treatment as soon as German troops arrived after 1939—the relationship of the Nazi government toward ethnic Germans in the rest of the world was far more ambivalent and certainly far removed from any attempt to unite all Germans under one government. That there was no attempt to encourage remigration to the Reich before 1938 is indicative of this.[26]

The party leadership did not want to swell the ranks of Germany's unemployed with emigrants; it also did not wish to allow people who had left Germany for political reasons after 1933 to return and challenge the supremacy of Hitler's party. In order to discourage return migration, Germans returning from extended residence abroad received "certificates permitting return" rather than passports, thus signaling them clearly to immigration officials. Anybody with such a certificate was transferred to "education camps" upon arrival. Only as the unemployment crisis eased and the regime stabilized were Germans returning from a longer absence abroad "only" screened by party officials and the secret police, and then classified as more or less suspicious, with the least suspicious escaping automatic internment. The desire to unite all so-called Aryans in one state was thus outweighed by the National Socialist Party's desire to avoid any possible threat to its power. Additional German citizens of the Third Reich were only desirable if they came with additional territory.

In the newly occupied territories in eastern Europe, by contrast, German minorities resident there were treated as "first-class citizens," and such favorable treatment placed German minorities there in an unenviable position after the retreat of German troops. States to the east of Germany no longer wanted to cope with the risk of German minorities proving a pretext for yet another attempt to redraw borders, and they would likely exact revenge for the atrocities committed by the German invaders. This situation—the assumption that being of German ethnicity in eastern Europe per se led to discrimination—led to a continuing emphasis on ethnicity in Germany's relationship with some of its emigrants. The Basic Law of the Federal Republic and subsequent supreme court rulings established a "right of return" for ethnic Germans living in eastern Europe, which was a corollary to the right of immigration granted to non-Germans suffering discrimination—namely, the right to asylum included in the same Basic Law. With the changes in Europe's political landscape and the collapse of the strict East/West divide from the mid-1980s, the return migration of ethnic Germans from eastern Europe became a reality for the first time after 1945. With this, the debate on the *Spätaussiedler* became a different story, because it became part of the immigration debate, which was largely dominated by economic considerations.

CONCLUSION

In sum, over the last two centuries, the relationship of German states to "their" emigrants was mostly a rather distant one. The norm was to expatriate emigrants as soon as possible, which conformed to the view of emigrants as a burden. This attitude changed only at the beginning of the twentieth century, when some attempts were made to strengthen the ties between emigrants and the state. In the Third Reich, for all the rhetoric of an Aryan *Volksgemeinschaft* bound together by ties of blood, the link to ex-patriate Germans was diluted by security concerns. The Federal Republic, finally, limited its attentions to ethnic Germans in eastern Europe. But after eastern European states loosened controls on emigration, the "right of return" for ethnic Germans became a choice to "return" in more cases than had been expected, thus turning this emigration topic into an immigration debate, with the *Spätaussiedler* becoming one group of immigrants along-side guest workers and asylum seekers.

While the concrete developments of emigration policy are a result of particularities or peculiarities of German history, they also give rise to some more general observations on the problems of emigration policy. First, the policy of the country of origin is less important than that of the destination when it comes to determining the legal ties between a mother country and her emigrants. Once the decision to emigrate has been made, there is usu-ally some incentive to seek the citizenship of the state of destination, and to discard the citizenship of the country of origin if this is necessary. Whether emigrants actually do this depends on what advantages they will obtain by becoming citizens, and what losses they may incur by discarding their origi-nal citizenship if this is required. For instance, the policy of nineteenth-century German states to strip emigrants of their citizenship ensured that they had to seek another country's citizenship for complete legal security. But even the later changes in German domestic law did not prevent most emigrants from seeking naturalization in their adopted countries. Unless emigrants want to return to their native states for purposes of business or pleasure, possess or expect to inherit property, or have strong family ties there, any sanctions against voluntary expatriation are powerless to prevent it. The speed of expatriation is thus almost entirely a function of the laws of the receiving state.

Second, emigration is difficult to regulate unless a country is sealed off from its neighbors and prohibits international travel in general. The more hurdles that are introduced to curb emigration, the greater the incentive to camouflage emigration as travel or temporary absence. Unless potential emigrants in their majority decide to abide by the rules, or the countries of destination cooperate by distinguishing emigrants from other travelers (for instance, by the type of visas they receive), it becomes next to impos-sible to control emigration because it is very difficult to distinguish from other types of travel or long-term absence. This explains the peculiar form of the German emigration debate, which focused exclusively on emigration to other continents, not emigration to other European countries. When the destination of travel was America, Asia, or Africa, an intention to emigrate could be presumed; when the destination was France, Britain, or Italy, this was hardly the case. Of course, the presence or absence of large amounts of luggage could also indicate whether the move was to be short or long term. However, regardless of the distance to the destination, travelers would not necessarily carry all of their luggage with them, but send it ahead or have it follow later.

Third, the assumption that migration to far-flung destinations was definitive was a function of class as much as a function of geography. Like the surveillance of travel in general, the surveillance of emigration had a social focus in the nineteenth century, most generally on groups who were extremely unlikely to make intercontinental pleasure trips. It is likely that this class bias changed over time. But this, too, was largely a function of the regulations imposed by the intended destination. As the United States and other countries introduced a "remote control" of immigration,[27] and as this system came to depend less on class than on the country of origin, the easier it became for the country of origin to discern the actual intention of emigrants, depending on the type of visa for which they applied. All these points seem to raise the question whether, in states that are not dictatorships, the politics of emigration are not doomed to fail because they are too easy to evade.

NOTES

1. See Klaus Gerteis, "Auswanderungsfreiheit und Freizügigkeit in Deutschland: Das 18. und 19. Jahrhundert im Vergleich," in *Grund- und Freiheitsrechte von der ständischen zur spätbürgerlichen Gesellschaft*, ed. Günter Birtsch, 330–44 (Göttingen: Vandenhoeck & Ruprecht, 1987); Rudolf Möhlenbruch, *"Freier Zug, ius emigrandi, Auswanderungsfreiheit"*: Eine verfassungsgeschichtliche Studie (Diss. jur., Bonn, 1977); Karl Graf Ballestrem, "Zur Theorie und Geschichte des Emigrationsrechtes," in *Grund- und Freiheitsrechte im Wandel von Gesellschaft und Geschichte: Beiträge zur Geschichte der Grund- und Freiheitsrechte vom Ausgang des Mittelalters bis zur Revolution von 1848*, ed. Günter Birtsch, 146–61 (Göttingen: Vandenhoeck & Ruprecht, 1981); Klaus Gerteis, "Auswanderungsfreiheit und Freizügigkeit in ihrem Verhältnis zur Agrarverfassung: Deutschland, England, Frankreich im Vergleich," in Birtsch, *Grund- und Freiheitsrechte im Wandel*, 162–82.

2. In Germany, the Bavarian constitution of 1818 only granted a right to emigrate to other German states (IV, §14), in line with the provisions of the 1815 Federal Act (*Bundesakte*). The 1819 Baden constitution was more generous (§12), as was the 1820 constitution of the Grand Duchy of Hesse (§24) and the constitutions of the

Electorate of Hesse (1831, §41) and the Kingdom of Saxony (1831, §29). While these texts all made reference to "legal conditions" emigrants had to fulfill, the 1819 constitution of Württemberg ranked the freedom to emigrate together with "freedom of the person, freedom of conscience and thought [and] freedom of private property" (§19). The constitution proposed by the 1848 National Assembly contained the promise of unrestricted freedom to emigrate (§136), and the 1850 Prussian constitution similarly limited restrictions to reasons arising from conscription (art. 11). The constitutions of the North German Federation and the German Empire contained no catalogues of fundamental rights, and therefore did not mention emigration. The Weimar constitution then represented a major step backward, in that it allowed the state to restrict emigration for any reason: "Every German has the right to emigrate to non-German countries. Emigration can only be restricted by federal law" (art. 112).

3. K.-J. Matz, *Pauperismus und Bevölkerung: Die gesetzlichen Ehebeschränkungen in den süddeutschen Staaten während des 19. Jahrhunderts* (Stuttgart: Klett Cotta, 1980).

4. "in einem [!] viel beklagenswertheren Zustand zurücksinken, als der war, dem sie gedachten, für immer entflohen zu sein," Circular of the Bavarian *Regierung* (provincial administration) of Schwaben and Neuburg, Department of the Interior, February 6, 1838, repr. in *"Hier ißt man anstadt Kardofln und Scharzbrodt Pasteten . . ." Die deutsche Überseewanderung des 19. Jahrhunderts in Zeitzeugnissen,* ed. Peter Maindl and Pankraz Fried (Augsburg: Wißner, 2000), 311.

5. Hessisches Hauptstaatsarchiv Wiesbaden, title of file No 211/13443, summarizing observations and legislation from the Duchy of Nassau.

6. Andreas Fahrmeir, *Citizens and Aliens: Foreigners and the Law in Britain and the German States* (New York: Berghahn Books, 2000), 112–15, 128, 139.

7. Ingrid Schöberl, *Amerikanische Einwandererwerbung in Deutschland 1845–1914* (Stuttgart: Franz Steiner, 1990), 190–210.

8. For a detailed description of the procedure, see Sigrid Faltin, *Die Auswanderung aus der Pfalz nach Nordamerika im 19. Jahrhundert: Unter besonderer Berücksichtigung des Landkommissariates Bergzabern* (Frankfurt/Main: Peter Lang, 1987), 218–25.

9. Camille Maire, *En route pour l'Amérique: L'odyssée des émigrants en France au XIXe siècle* (Nancy: Presses Universitaires de Nancy, 1993), 40–41.

10. One example is described in the petition of Franz Brutscher, Immenstadt, March 13, 1853, repr. in Maindl and Fried, *"Hier ißt man,"* 314–17.

11. Joachim Heinz, *"Bleibe im Lande und nähre dich redlich!" Zur Geschichte der pfälzischen Auswanderung vom Ende des 17. bis zum Ausgang des 19. Jahrhunderts* (Kaiserslautern: Institut für Pfälzische Geschichte und Volkskunde, 1989), 225–28.

12. Alexander Müller, *Die deutschen Auswanderungs-, Freizügigkeits- und Heimaths-Verhältnisse: Eine vergleichende Darstellung der darüber in den Staaten des deutschen Bundes besonders in Oesterreich, Preußen und Sachsen bestehenden Ver-*

träge, Gesetze und Verordnungen, zugleich mit literärischen Nachweisungen und Be-merkungen für die Gesetzgebungs-Politik; Zur Selbstbelehrung für deutsche und aus-ländische Staatsbürger jeden Standes (Leipzig, 1841), 1.

13. Fahrmeir, *Citizens*, 50.

14. Ibid., 172–73.

15. Winfried Folz, *Pfälzer Rückwanderer aus Nordamerika: Schicksale, Motive, Re-integration* (Mainz: von Zabern 1992), 119.

16. As a case study, see Renate Vollmer, *Auswanderungspolitik und soziale Frage im 19. Jahrhundert: Staatlich geförderte Auswanderung aus der Berghauptmannschaft Clausthal nach Südaustralien, Nord- und Südamerika 1848–1854* (Frankfurt/Main: Peter Lang, 1995).

17. See the petition of Joseph Anton Heberle, who had left Bavaria for the United States in 1881 and pleaded for amnesty and the granting of Bavarian citizenship in 1901, in Maindl and Fried, *"Hier ißt man,"* 318–21; Folz, *Pfälzer Rückwanderer,* 117–22.

18. See, for instance, Patrick Weil, *Qu'est-ce qu'un Français? Histoire de la nation-alité française depuis la Révolution* (Paris: Grasset, 2002), 187–88.

19. Fahrmeir, *Citizens*, 48–51.

20. Andreas Fahrmeir, "Passports and the Status of Aliens," in *The Mechanics of Internationalism: Culture, Society and Politics from the 1840s to the First World War,* ed. Martin H. Geyer and Johannes Paulmann, 93–119, 112–15 (Oxford, Eng.: Oxford University Press, 2001).

21. Dieter Gosewinkel, *Einbürgern und Ausschließen: Die Nationalisierung der Staatsangehörigkeit vom Deutschen Bund bis zur Bundesrepublik Deutschland* (Göt-tingen: Vandenhoeck Ruprecht, 2001), 278–327.

22. See, for instance, Panikos Panayi, *The Enemy in Our Midst: Germans in Britain During the First World War* (New York: Berg, 1991).

23. Grant Grams, *German Emigration to Canada and the Support of Its Deutsch-tum during the Weimar Republic: The Role of the Deutsches Auslands-Institut, Verein für das Deutschtum im Ausland and German-Canadian Organisations* (Frankfurt/ Main: Peter Lang, 2001), 72–75.

24. Grams, *German Emigration*, 81. In general, see Hartmut Bickelmann, *Deutsche Überseeauswanderung in der Weimarer Zeit* (Wiesbaden: Franz Steiner, 1980).

25. As an example, see Heinrich Volberg, *Auslandsdeutschtum und Drittes Reich: Der Fall Argentinien* (Vienna: Böhlau, 1981).

26. For the following, see Herbert E. Tutas, *Nationalsozialismus und Exil: Die Politik des Dritten Reiches gegenüber der deutschen politischen Emigration* (Munich: Hanser, 1975).

27. Aristide Zolberg, "The Archeology of 'Remote Control,'" in *Migration Con-trol in the North Atlantic World,* ed. Andreas Farhmeir, Oliver Faron, and Patrick Weil, 195–222 (New York: Berghahn, 2003).

PART IV

BORDERS AND LINKS

9

THE UNITED STATES GOVERNMENT AND THE INVESTIGATION OF EUROPEAN EMIGRATION IN THE OPEN DOOR ERA

Dorothee Schneider

The United States, unlike the countries discussed elsewhere in this volume, has been a country of immigration throughout its history. Emigration and emigrants have therefore played a very minor role in the public consciousness and history of Americans during most of that period. Immigrants occupied the public debate, and at the turn of the twentieth century, the imposition of more restrictive immigration policies became a central part of the discussion. Gradually, as this debate widened, immigrants from other countries began to be understood as emigrants in their original national context (conversely, emigrants from the United States were often considered to be former immigrants to this country). This chapter seeks to delineate the efforts made by the U.S. government to understand immigration to the United States as part of European emigration and to align a set of priorities for immigration admission with the existing (or desirable) emigration regulations in European countries. The attempt to understand and control emigration to the United States at the source must be seen as the fourth leg of immigration policy in the so-called open door era. Together with the effort to strengthen restrictive immigration laws, enlarge the administrative capacities of Federal agencies dealing with immigration, and make U.S. citizenship more difficult to attain and retain, emigration control at the source played an important role in the thinking of many officials and some politicians at the turn of the last century. Ultimately, the attempt to change European policies in order to make them conform to U.S. restrictionist legislation was part of the attempt to shape the U.S. immigrant population to conform to ideas of racial desirability, economic self-sufficiency, and cultural conformity.[1]

During the first decades of the twentieth century, European emigration control and American immigration restriction had a set of goals that at times conflicted and at times overlapped. When it came to immigrant admissions, U.S. priorities were relatively clear-cut: immigrants with communicable diseases, paupers, and people of questionable morality and politics were to be prevented from entering the United States. At the ports of entry, inspectors of the Immigration Bureau therefore checked all new arrivals and were empowered to reject them as immigrants if they belonged to an "excludable class." The largest group of rejects consisted of "people likely to become a public charge." Another sizable group comprised those suffering from a "loathsome and dangerous" disease. Prostitutes, criminals, and anarchists, as well as suspected polygamists, were also among those barred from entering. Prospective immigrants who were rejected at the port of entry were transported back to their country of origin (or country of departure) with the cost borne by the transportation company that brought them to the United States. Often, this meant that the transportation company not only had to take back a rejected immigrant but also his or her family. The system accorded the ultimate legal responsibilities to the immigration authorities in the United States, with the risk of rejection borne by the immigrants and the transportation companies. As immigration authorities themselves pointed out, this system split apart families and shattered long-nurtured dreams of a new life; the commissioner general of immigration emphasized time and again that restriction of emigration from Europe would diminish the human cost of rejection at the U.S. border.[2]

European countries' regulations concerning emigration did not mesh well with U.S. laws. Within Europe, governments differed in their approach to emigration. Almost all countries had abandoned the strict control over population movements and the prohibition against emigration that characterized the preindustrial era. Russia was the only country that still maintained a principled opposition to emigration and permitted only its ethnic minorities (Jews, Poles, and Germans, for example) to leave, with permission of the government.[3] Western and central European governments required only adult males of draft age to produce a certificate that they had served in the military (or were exempt from such service) in order to leave the country legally. Such provisions were enforced to varying degrees.[4] In some countries, such as Austria-Hungary, single women needed a police-issued certificate of moral conduct or a "workbook" showing gainful and legal employment. In France, passports were needed to leave the country, though their issuance depended on local authorities' willingness to grant them. Italy required a passport, which was issued to adult men only if their draft requirement had been fulfilled.[5] England had no such rules or laws. Most central European countries thus discouraged the emigration of younger, working-age men indirectly, at least on paper, through their draft laws and passport or workbook requirements. No country prevented the emigration of very poor people; convicted criminals and prostitutes were also not kept from leaving the country. No government checked prospective emigrants for communicable diseases. More important, even if certain laws or regulations were on the books, enforcement was uneven. Russia had practically no enforcement of its emigration prohibition; the state bureaucracies of Italy and Austria-Hungary were often ineffective.[6] France and Great Britain adopted policies encouraging emigration of their citizens to their overseas possessions.[7] Germany, like England—a country of both emigration and immigration (from eastern Europe) at the turn of the last century—tried to regulate immigration from eastern Europe strictly, and supervised emigration agents such as commercial transportation lines or emigration societies regarding regulation and supervision.[8] If the United States wanted to induce European governments to follow a unified set of policies, the realities of different economic and political priorities, as well as the different governmental structures and traditions, were formidable hurdles to this goal and formed a rich field for study by U.S. officials during their investigations in the early decades of the twentieth century.

The systematic investigative efforts related to European emigration began in 1889 (as a result of the passage of the 1886 Contract Labor Law), when U.S. consular officials in Europe were asked by a congressional committee to respond to a catalog of questions relating to the effectiveness of the law. This survey yielded some interesting information on different European labor markets but few insights into the actual causes of emigration and the social and economic conditions in the countries of emigration in Europe.[9] The 1894 European trip of the federal immigration commissioner Herman Stump, the first such trip by a U.S. official, similarly reflected the focus on U.S. border controls that prevailed at the time. Stump had little interest in the conditions of emigration and the origins of immigrants but tried to find means to extend U.S. border control directly into Europe. This reflected the limited perspectives of the Immigration Bureau (founded in 1891), whose powers in the 1890s were circumscribed by its small budget and lack of experience in administering immigrant admissions.[10]

The position of the bureau began to change at the turn of the century, and its importance increased steadily as the number of immigrants grew with extraordinary rapidity and, conversely, the political and legal pressure to limit their admission also grew. One important way to gauge the effectiveness of the bureau at this task is to measure the rising number of immigrants rejected from the port of entry in the early years of the twentieth century. In 1902, almost 650,000 immigrants entered the United States annually via its ports, a number that would increase to over a million per year in 1905–1907.[11] In New York, port of arrival of over 80 percent of all immigrants, 4,203 of 493,262 arriving passengers were rejected (and sent back) in 1902. The percentage of rejected immigrants remained stable (between 0.7 and 1.3 percent) over the next five years. It increased gradually to 1.7 percent in 1907 and crept up slowly thereafter. Immigration officers at other East Coast ports of arrival were more lenient than in New York and had a lower rejection rate during this period. West Coast immigration officers were more stringent, rejecting a large percentage of East Asian would-be immigrants.[12] While overall rejection rates from Europe were low, the commissioner of immigration noted that the rejection rates among immigrants coming from certain areas of Europe or certain ports of embarkation remained quite high. Naples, Marseilles, and Genoa were notorious for the many ill and impoverished emigrants who arrived. Was this because the shipping companies who operated from those cities were particularly negligent? Or was it because the people coming from those regions were particularly "degraded"? Were "racial," social, or political problems to blame, and what could be done about this?[13]

These questions emerged as much through the general discussion on immigration restriction as through the agency itself, and they were fueled by the immigration law of 1902, which authorized more extensive data gathering by the commissioner general of immigration, and by the law of 1907 which authorized the U.S. Commission on Immigration (known as the Dillingham Commission). Theodore Roosevelt's interest in immigration questions and the close personal involvement of his labor secretary Oscar Straus in many immigration debates also stimulated the investigations.[14] To gain a more comprehensive picture of the European situation, the bureau began to send special inspectors abroad after 1902 with some frequency. Altogether, the commissioner general ordered ten investigations between 1902 and 1914: eight in Europe and the Middle East, and two in Mexico and the Caribbean.[15] In addition, the Dillingham Commission, whose members traveled to Europe from May to September 1907, filed an extensive and influential investigation.[16]

All investigations had similar goals, sometimes explicitly formulated in a catalog of questions sent to the investigators by the commissioner general of immigration.[17] The investigations were launched in order to examine the "character" of emigration, the emigrants' impact on their home communities, the attitude of public officials toward emigration and emigration control, and the attitudes and competence of U.S. officials in Europe. In addition, some inspectors were to focus on official policies and laws in European countries, and the administration of these laws. Some investigators were to present themselves as emissaries of the United States government to European officials. Others, however, were to operate more discreetly, sometimes undercover and without contacting European officials. Many of the investigations involved months of travel by one or two inspectors, deputized for that purpose. Some of these men (and one woman) were career officials of the service; others, such as former union leader Terence Powderly, were not. The inspectors usually spoke the language of at least some of the countries visited. Sometimes they were able to blend in with the local scene and even assume false identities, posing as immigrants or labor recruiters. Materials were gathered from official sources but also from countless interviews with prospective immigrants, immigrant smugglers, foreign officials, and American personnel stationed abroad. Investigators took photographs, drew maps, and donned disguises.[18] Depending on the talents and temperaments of the investigators, some reports give a vivid ethnographic portrait of the communities studied, while others focus more on the structure of emigrant flow and the attempts to direct and control it through administrative and legal measures abroad. Some investigators emerge from the sources as keen observers of the human mind, while others remain pale, background personalities. The emigration investigations therefore have to be seen as more than briefings for immigration control policies. In fact, the most vivid and detailed accounts usually had little to offer in terms of remedies for "unchecked immigration"; the driest and most sparse documents set forth a list of proposals.

The first European reports of the early twentieth century were filed by Marcus Braun, a personal friend of Theodore Roosevelt and an immigrant himself; by an unnamed employee of the bureau (probably John Trenor, an inspector who would be sent on two additional trips, mostly to Italy); and, in 1905, by Maurice Fishberg, another special inspector of the Bureau.[19] Their reports focused on the roles of steamship companies and the administration of existing regulations meant to enlist steamship companies in prescreening their customers. Braun, the most thorough investigator, found few open violations of the existing regulations by steamship companies. These businesses made a convincing case that they tried, using medical examinations, to prescreen passengers destined for the United States.

But Braun also noted that some ship companies, operating from England, steered poorer immigrants to Canada first (to ease their transit into the United States), and that in eastern Europe some independent agents who sold tickets on commission from the steamship companies were among the most active emigrant recruiters of poor peasants.[20] The inspector who wrote the second report (on Italy and eastern Europe) also deplored the absence of U.S. officials at most ports of embarkation and argued strongly for a widened role of the immigration bureau in inspecting emigrants at their ports of departure.[21] Open violations of the law were few, but the report recommended that European governments should take a more active role in supervising emigrants from their ports. The report by Maurice Fishberg found much "steering" of poorer emigrants from Le Havre to South America, which, he feared, would only postpone the arrival of "undesirables" in the United States.[22]

The problem, as these three inspectors recognized, was that major ports of emigration often no longer lay in countries whose populations were among the emigrants: ships sailing from Germany, England, France, and Belgium carried few citizens of these countries but, instead, mostly eastern and southern Europeans to the United States. Later American observers, too, noted that the citizens of western European nations had achieved a satisfactory standard of living at home and (unless they were unskilled) felt little pressure to leave.[23] Only Italians and many Greeks still departed from ports in their home countries. Therefore, the countries from which emigrants sailed needed to concern themselves not just with screening their own citizen-emigrants but also with controlling transit migrants who might or might not sail on to the United States.[24]

The inspectors found that, because emigrants were thus usually transit migrants, most of the western European countries investigated considered control of emigrants a pressing matter. Germany and Great Britain were the only exceptions. Great Britain, grappling with an increasing number of poor Jewish immigrants from eastern Europe, made an attempt to control its immigrant population by passing the Alien Act in 1905 soon after the first American investigations had begun. The law, which would severely limit the number of eastern European Jewish immigrants in the years to come, was much applauded by U.S. authorities because the law was expected to have an effect on the transit migration out of Great Britain as well. But before 1905, steamship companies and local harbor authorities had emerged as the sole regulators of emigration in Great Britain, as well as in Belgium. In Great Britain, the transportation companies registered all emigrants as

"English" (much to the aggravation of American observers) unless they had come directly from continental Europe to embark for their overseas trip.[25]

Because of England's traditional role as a country from which emigrants sailed to the United States in great numbers during the nineteenth century, and because of its status as a country of immigration as well as emigration, it was one of the most investigated nations by U.S. immigration inspectors. Terence Powderly, who arrived in 1906, and members of the Dillingham Commission, who traveled in 1907, observed in detail the conditions of emigrants at British ports such as Liverpool, Hull, and London. The shipping lines and the port cities organized most of the emigration procedures.[26] Occasionally, the transportation companies invited American consuls for inspection of immigrants, but this was not the rule. Emigrants leaving from Le Havre and Antwerp also encountered no government regulation or oversight, nor were their governments interested in close cooperation with U.S. authorities on these matters. "The Belgian government is very jealous of any interference on the part of other governments in her emigration affairs," remarked Powderly.[27] Efforts by the United States to induce European governments to produce special exit passports for their emigrating citizens (to certify their good conduct or to provide information about connections to prostitution or crime) met with a chilly rejection from these countries as well.[28] In the eyes of U.S. investigators and immigration officials, the countries whose internal policies regarding migration and civil rights were closest to the United States were the most unsatisfactory when it came to solving the American problem of regulating emigration to its shores.

Only in one nation was there a regulatory apparatus that dealt with immigration, emigration, and transit passengers: Germany. The German example was the polar opposite of England's, and it was much admired (but also misunderstood) by American observers.[29] Most travelers who went to the German interior, such as inspectors Samsey, Dobler, and Fishberg, noted how relatively prosperous Germany had become and how German workers no longer felt the economic pressure to leave that had sent them to the United States earlier in the nineteenth century. By 1905, emigrants leaving from German ports were no longer primarily Germans; they were eastern European Jews, Poles, and other eastern Europeans who chose German ports as their route to America. The migration process through and out of Germany was considered to be particularly well administered, especially in the major ports of departure, Hamburg and Bremen. These cities (and the monopoly of the Hapag and Lloyd lines there that transported passengers to North America) profited handsomely from the good reputation they had as emigrant ports in the late nineteenth and early twentieth century.[30]

"Of all the countries named, Germany is very particular as to who shall immigrate," remarked Terence Powderly, perceptively.[31] Immigrants to the German provinces needed a work permit for the province in which they wanted to work. Southern Europeans who entered the western provinces had relatively few problems obtaining these, but Poles and other eastern Europeans had a difficult time with the Prussian authorities. Migrants from Poland or Russia who wanted merely to travel through Germany on their way overseas were intercepted by German authorities at the border in East Prussia and held for a health inspection by physicians in special transit camps organized and paid for by the overseas steamship companies.[32] Some people were rejected for physical defects (or as paupers) and sent back. Those who passed this checkpoint were then transported on special trains or sealed cars to their emigration port of Bremen or Hamburg.[33] At the embarkation station in Hamburg—which was divided into "unclean" and "clean" areas—passengers and their luggage were disinfected. A doctor hired by the American consul (but paid for by the steamship company) conducted a second medical examination, and German police checked documents once again. The *Auswandererhallen* fed and housed the migrants in accommodations that, according to Powderly, were constructed like steerage compartments of the ships that would take them overseas. Emigrants were taught there the use of public facilities and Western standards of hygiene.[34] Only after these multiple inspections and transition periods were passengers permitted to board the ships. With the cost borne almost entirely by private businesses (in exchange for a lucrative transportation monopoly), the system was, to American observers, a perfect example of the desirable cooperation between government authorities and private companies.

Countries to the east and south of the German empire imposed varying degrees of regulation on population movement, but their economic development also was much more uneven than Germany's. Russia's situation was the worst, as inspector Philip Cowan noted. Poverty among its rural population was endemic; illiteracy and bad health characterized its natives. At the same time, the Russian government made it nearly impossible for anyone except Jews and other ethnic minorities to leave. The vast majority of those who left, as the knowledgeable and Russian-speaking Cowan noted, were therefore Jews (about 60 percent). Cowan and the members of the Dillingham Commission who visited Russia acknowledged the ineffectiveness of the Russian authorities and the absence of any coherent emigration policy. The reasons people left Russia were many, as Cowan documented in impressive detail. But since the Russian government was not facing up to this fact, the large, illegal migration out of Russia, which involved false passports and smuggling operations, and which irritated the Prussian authorities as well, could not be regulated in cooperation with Russian authorities.[35] Nevertheless, the Russian state was effective in other ways: it kept tight control over dissidents and even followed Cowan himself around, intercepting and suppressing his correspondence with his superiors in Washington during his investigations, which he tried to conduct incognito.[36]

As far as American observers were concerned, Austria-Hungary—perhaps because of its geographic location —fell somewhere in between Germany and Russia. Its industrial and urban centers were prosperous enough, but the large, undeveloped countryside harbored many impoverished peasants. Posing as an itinerant foreign laborer, Terence Powderly was struck by the friendliness of Hungarian country folk but also by their great poverty. "Argument is not required to prove why these strong, healthy-looking men left their country to come to us," he mused in his report.[37] The Austrian and Hungarian governments kept track of their populations through police registers and, in theory at least, had to preapprove emigrants, who had to be free of a criminal record and finished with their military service. The authorities had also set up some police checkpoints before emigrants reached their ports of embarkation—at railroad stations, for example. Women who were under 18 and traveling without a relative were detained and sent back, as were men without a military record and those likely to become a public charge.[38] The Austrian government had awarded a transportation monopoly to the Cunard line and obliged emigrants to use that line's vessels leaving from Fiume and Trieste. In return, the authorities received a premium for each departing passenger from the Cunard line.[39] But the system worked only unevenly. While the Hungarian police were avidly pursuing Inspector Marcus Braun as he conducted his investigations (and even had him arrested and imprisoned), their control over Hungary's own emigrant population was tenuous.[40] Indeed, Powderly noted that, indirectly, the Austrian authorities seem to have encouraged temporary migration of its poor, rural citizens to the New World mostly because of the remittances that helped impoverished rural families.[41]

Eastern European emigrants who left from Trieste and Fiume had a high rate of rejection at Ellis Island, and the Cunard line was therefore interested in cooperating with the American authorities in order to minimize the risk of rejection. In Fiume, the American consul, invited by Cunard and tolerated by the local authorities, personally screened all passengers who sailed for the United States prior to their embarkation. He also worked very closely with a medical officer employed by the steamship company. Since the consul's opinion was only advisory, the steamship company did not have to follow his advice. But Cunard obviously did, for almost forty-seven hundred prospective emigrants were rejected in Fiume in one year alone (about 20 percent of those who had already purchased tickets and passed Hungarian government controls). In some cases, when the consul was overruled, he sent telegrams to Ellis Island to warn inspectors there of impending arrivals of suspected prostitutes—triggering a major (though misguided) investigation in the United States.[42] The American consul at neighboring Trieste played a similar role. To inspector John Trenor, the consul "seemed to be imbued with an ardent desire to safeguard the interests of the United States in every way by rigidly excluding all apparently undesirable immigrants. His very energetic action led at times to some friction with representatives of the Cunard Company."[43] Other American consular officials had inspected emigrants and emigrant ships for decades, but in a more cursory way. These men were traditionally commercial agents, responsible to ease the flow of goods, to establish and maintain business contacts in port cities, and to see that U.S. customs rules were followed. Since the second half of the nineteenth century, they had "certified" that the luggage of immigrants on ships followed U.S. customs rules. In some cases consuls were not even U.S. citizens themselves, were not formally employees of the U.S. government, and received their compensation solely from the fees they were paid for their services. Even in cases where consuls were full-time State Department employees, their legal powers did not encompass the screening of persons and in some cases (wherein consuls attempted to gain access to such powers) local authorities in Belgium or Great Britain would not permit it.[44] But even in places where the U.S. consul's role approached that of an official concerned with emigration control, it happened at the behest of private steamship companies who sought the reassurance of an official representative of the U.S. government—even though he could not provide official permits or guarantees of any kind.[45]

Only in southern Italy was the problem of the split authority of American officials circumvented, at least in part. By the early twentieth century, Italians from southern Italy made up a large part of the migration stream to North America, due to the continued economic underdevelopment in their home region. "Your query should have been: why would they not emigrate?"

responded an Italian doctor to Inspector Trenor's inquiry as to the causes of emigration.[46] The Italian government considered this exodus an important social and economic safety valve. In 1902, Marcus Braun had already noted the special eagerness with which Italian authorities were willing to cooperate with the United States. Braun thought that this cooperative attitude resulted from the fear of further American restrictions directed specifically against Italians. After all, emigration to North and South America was an important source of financial support for many rural southern Italian communities.[47] At the port of Naples, three physicians of the U.S. Marine Hospital Service examined emigrants with the approval of the Italian authorities and under contract with the steamship companies (who paid for their services). The American doctors checked all passengers, even first class travelers, for trachoma (an eye infection) and other obvious illnesses according to the same standards that were (presumably) applied in United States ports of arrival.[48] A similar system operated in some other Italian ports at the time.[49] Italian authorities complemented this control with criminal background checks and other measures, or so they stated to members of the immigration commission who visited the port of Naples in 1907.[50]

The Immigration Bureau considered the close cooperation between U.S. physicians and the operators of steamship lines (with the cost and responsibility borne by the companies) to be a model solution. It accommodated the need for stricter and more uniform standards of selection of immigrants. At the same time, it did not involve the federal government directly and did not commit the U.S. authorities to admit anyone before their actual arrival and inspection in the United States. Indeed, despite the rigorous preboarding controls in southern Italy and Germany, the United States Immigration Commission noted in its 1911 report that a particularly high number of arriving passengers from Naples and from German ports were rejected at Ellis Island for health reasons, whereas relatively few emigrants from Le Havre or Antwerp were rejected upon arrival. The high rejection rate of Italian (and eastern European immigrants) pointed to the fact that however much screening took place at the port of embarkation, the poverty of the immigrants still made them vulnerable to exclusion. Emigrants from areas with less economic distress were usually healthier and therefore less likely to be rejected. But although the Immigration Bureau's *Annual Report* made this connection perfectly clear, a racialized view of the problem prevailed.

Congress did not support an increased use of American officials other than the physicians of the United States Marine Health Service in controlling the flow of emigration to the United States, and consuls or foreign service officers themselves did not demand it.[51] Consuls may have welcomed the assistance of American doctors, and the consul in Fiume supported the introduction of visas (issued by the consulate), but many other American consuls in Europe were not interested in serving as emigration control officers, since their interests and their knowledge did not equip them to function this way.[52] It would be another decade and a half before the U.S. consuls became primary screening agents for prospective immigrants. In 1908, they were far from ready to assume that role.[53]

The most cost-efficient and (politically) least controversial tactic to limit the emigration of undesirables from Europe seemed to be increased pressure on transportation companies to screen their passengers bound for the United States more rigorously. Yet, investigators were reluctant to indict ship lines for lax supervision. Only in the hinterlands of eastern Europe and southern Italy did the ticket agents for ship companies recruit potential emigrants actively. In most places no such encouragement was needed to motivate emigrants. Once people had decided to leave for North America, transportation companies were rather diligent in prescreening their passengers in order to avoid the cost of deportation from the United States. Nor could foreign governments be blamed for the exportation of their surplus population. True, public authorities (usually in league with the transportation companies) sometimes encouraged certain types of migration streams to North America, because it fit their population or labor policies.[54] But for the most part, active government encouragement or financial support for emigration to the United States was absent in the early twentieth century.

Within the existing legal and administrative framework for immigration admission, authorities in the United States could do little, short of pressuring European governments to clamp down further on transportation companies and to punish the latter (with fines) if they sent immigrants judged "excludable" to the United States knowingly. (This would continue to be the policy until the introduction of the quota system in 1924.) Such measures would always be imperfect ways to deal with migration control. To restrictionists, the reliance on sanctions against ship and railroad lines demonstrated a weak federal government and an insufficient presence of state power when it came to dealing with mass immigration. But seen another way, this policy was not only cheap and nearly costless politically, but it also—in the end—offered quite an effective way to introduce an apparatus of external control without investing much in its maintenance, politically or financially. In a nation with an ambivalent relationship to central government and an unwillingness to finance an expansion of state power at home and abroad, this provided a way to exert power indirectly over population movements in much of Europe. It would take World War I and the resulting shift in political priorities in Congress and the executive branch to adopt a statist approach to immigrant regulation that required little cooperation from other countries. Ultimately, as the 1920s revealed, immigration policy was not only a national issue but also a way to define the shape of the United States' nationalism. Neither transportation businesses nor foreign governments could be counted on as allies in defining and implementing a policy so central to the nation's identity.

NOTES

1. This chapter focuses only on European immigrants because the Immigration Bureau did not conduct investigations into the background and causes of immigration from East Asia or the Americas. The 1907 investigation of Marcus Braun in Mexico covered primarily Middle Eastern and East Asian migration through Mexico into the United States and focuses on Mexico as a transit country. I am unaware of any investigations taking place in Asia. U.S. Commissioner of Immigration, *Annual Report of the Commissioner General of Immigration to the Secretary of Commerce and Labor: For the Fiscal Year Ending June 1907* [hereafter cited as *Annual Report*, with year of publication] (Washington, 1907), 72–74.

2. Cost savings—both financial and political—were not acknowledged as a motive. *Annual Report, 1904*, 72; *Annual Report, 1905*, 78.

3. *Annual Report, 1904*, 125; Immigration and Naturalization Service, subject correspondence files, RG 86, entry 9, file 51411/56, 4–6 (Cowan report) (all subsequent file numbers are from the same record group and entry at the National Archives, Washington D.C.).

4. *Annual Report, 1904*, 126–27; *Annual Report, 1907*, 62.

5. File 51411/53, appendix; see also François Weil, chapter 5, in this volume.

6. File 52011/B; file 51411/53, 5–6 (Trenor report); Gunther Peck, *Re-Inventing Free Labor* (Cambridge, Mass.: Harvard University Press), 92–93.

7. See Feldman and Baldwin (chapter 6) as well as Weil (chapter 5) in this volume.

8. Michael Just, *Schiffahrtsgesellschaften und Amerika-Auswanderung im 19. und fruehen 20. Jahrhundert* (Stuttgart: Steiner Verlag, 1992). See also Agnes Bretting and Hartmut Bickelmann, *Auswanderungsagenturen und Auswanderungsverein im 19. und 20. Jahrhundert* (Stuttgart: Steiner Verlag, 1991).

9. United States Congress, House of Representatives, *Report of the Select Committee of the House of Representatives to Inquire into the Alleged Violation of the Laws Prohibiting the Importation of Contract Laborers, Paupers, Convicts and Other Classes* (Washington D.C.: Government Printing Office, 1889).

10. United States Immigration Commission, *Report of the Immigration Investigation Commission* (Washington D.C.: 1895), 21–25.

11. *1995 Statistical Yearbook of the Immigration and Naturalization Service* (Washington D.C.: Government Printing Office, 1997), 27.

12. *Annual Report, 1907* (Washington D.C., 1907), 49. The percentage of debarments hovered between 10 percent in San Francisco and 0.5 percent in Philadelphia. New York's rate (1.8 percent) is a bit below the median for that year. Immigrants were aware of the differences in rejection between U.S. ports, and some organized their travel accordingly (*Annual Report, 1905* [Fishberg report], 51).

13. On rejection rates by "race," *Annual Report, 1899*, 31; *Annual Report, 1900*, 41; *Annual Report, 1904*, 42, 123; *Annual Report, 1902*, 59. On Marseilles authorities' attempts to lower rejection rate in the United States, see Camille Maire, *En route pour l'Amérique: L'odyssée des émigrants en France au XIXᵉ siècle* (Nancy: Presses Universitaires de Nancy, 1993), 115–17, and *Annual Report, 1905* (Fishberg report), 51.

14. Elliott R. Barkan and Michael LeMay, *U.S. Immigration and Naturalization Laws and Issues* (Westport, Conn.: Greenwood Press, 1999) 89–92, 97–99. *Annual Report, 1907*, 60–62; Desmond King, *Making Americans: Immigration, Race and the Origins of the Divided Democracy* (Cambridge, Mass.: Harvard University Press, 2000) 58–59. Oscar S. Straus, *Under Four Administrations: From Cleveland to Taft* (Boston: Houghton Mifflin, 1922) 217–34.

15. As early as 1901 the New York commissioner, who had investigated labor migration and assisted immigration in Europe, had urged further studies by other officials of the service abroad. *Annual Report, 1902*, 58. The other reports were published either as part of the *Annual Report*, 1904 (Marcus Brown report on the Near East), 50–52; 1905 (unnamed inspector); 1906 (Fishberg report), 50–56; and 1914 (Kate Waller Barrett), appendix IV; or they can be found in the files of the Immigration and Naturalization Service at the National Archives, RG 85, entry 9, file nos. 51411/54, (Eppler report), 51411/51 (Powderly report), 51411/1 (Seraphic report on Europe and Mexico), 51831/55 (Watchorn investigation), 51411/53 (first Trenor report) 51411/56 (Cowan Report) 51411/52 (Samsey/Dobler Report) 51652/13 (second Trenor report) and 51960/1 (third Trenor report).

16. RG 85, entry 9, file 51411/46; printed report appeared as U.S. Immigration Commission, *Reports*, vol. 4, *Emigration Conditions in Europe* (Washington D.C., 1911).

17. For a published catalog of questions, see *Annual Report, 1903*, 86. Most of the reports listed in n. 15 also include the questions that the inspectors were to answer in the course of their report.

18. For examples of undercover work, see Seraphic report, file 51411/1.

19. *Annual Report, 1904*, 50–52; *Annual Report,* 1905 (unnamed inspector); *Annual Report,* 1906 (Fishberg report), 50–56.

20. *Annual Report, 1904*, 86–96.

21. *Annual Report, 1905*, 127.

22. *Annual Report, 1906*, 51.

23. 51411/41, 22–23 (Powderly report); see also file 51411/51, 24 (Eppler report); file 51411/52, 3 (Samsey Dobler report).

24. *Annual Report, 1905*, 129–30; *Annual Report, 1906*, 50–56.

25. James Walvin, *Passage to Britain: Immigration in British History and Politics* (London: Puffin, 1984), 62–67. See also comments by U.S. inspectors, *Annual Report, 1904*, 129.

26. File 51411/51, 17–18 (Powderly report).

27. Ibid., 18.

28. Files 52483/1–19, 51777/30, 51777/339, 52483/1–18.

29. File 51411/41, 22–35 (Powderly Report); U.S. Immigration Commission, *Reports*, vol. 4, 96–102.

30. On Hamburg and Bremen as ports of emigration: Ulrich Wagner, "Bremen, Bremerhaven und die Auswanderung," in *Hoffung Amerika: Europäische Auswanderung in die Neue Welt*, ed. Karin Schulz, 58–64 (Bremen: NWD Verlag, 1994); Juergen Silemann, "'Haben die Passagiere auch Geld?' zur Geschichte der Auswanderung über den Hamburger Häfen," in Schulz, *Hoffung Amerika*, 81–98. On the competition of French ports, see Maire, *En route.*

31. File 51411/41, 23 (Powderly report).

32. Rene del Fabbro, "Italienische Wanderarbeiter im Deutschen Kaiserreich," in *Fremde in Deutschland: Deutsche in der Fremde*, ed. Uwe Meinders, Christoph Reinders-Duselder (Cloppenburg: 1999), 193–99. For transit migration from eastern Europe, see Michael Just, *Ost und südosteuropäische Amerikawanderung 1881–1914: Transitprobleme in Deutschland und Aufnahme in den Vereinigten Staaten.* (Stuttgart: Steiner Verlag, 1988) 97–125.

33. After the Hamburg cholera epidemic of 1892, Prussian authorities had temporarily halted all emigrant traffic from these harbors. They had reopened the East Prussian border to emigrants only after the ship companies had put in place the elaborate screening system described above. In return for this investment, the ship lines held a monopoly on transportation for emigrants from eastern Europe via Germany, since such passengers were required by the Prussian authorities to purchase tickets for their overseas trip at the East Prussian border. None of the American observers seems to have understood this feature of the Prussian border controls, which obligated eastern European migrants to emigrate to the United States or to England if they wanted to cross the border legally. Because the system was so stringent, illegal border crossings increased at the turn of the twentieth century. Just, *Schiffahrsgesellschaften*, 105–7.

34. File 51411/41, 27–28 (Powderly report); Just, *Schiffahrtsgesellschaften*, 32–38.

35. File 51411/56, 2–30 (Cowan report); file 51411/54, 29 (Eppler Report).

36. File 51411/56, 2–6 (Cowan report).

37. File 51411/41, 48 (Powderly report).

38. U.S. Immigration Commission, *Reports*, vol. 4, 92, 110–24.

39. File 51411/41, 43, 52 (Powderly report); file 41411/53 5–6 (Trenor report).

40. Brown report, file 52011/B,F, 51630/44, B–F. See also Peck, *Re-Inventing Free Labor,* 93.

41. File 51411/41, 53 (Powderly report).

42. Peck, *Re-inventing Free Labor,* 92, 111, 124; file 51411/41, 44–46 (Powderly report); in the rare cases when the steamship company did not agree with the consul's assessment (that a group of women were part of the white slave traffic, for example), he telegraphed Ellis Island officials ahead of time to warn them of the impending arrival of the problem cases, triggering investigation in the United States. See file 51698/7, Clarence Rice Slocum to Dept. of State, n.d. [May 1910].

43. File 51411/53, 7 (Trenor report). See also U.S. Immigration Commission, *Reports,* vol. 4, 111.

44. U.S. Immigration Commission, *Reports,* vol. 4, 129–34.

45. On the Consular Service at the turn of the last century see, Elmer Plischke, *The U.S. Department of State: A Reference History* (Westport, Conn.: Greenwood Press, 1990), 221–23; Robert Ferrell, *American Diplomacy: A History* (New York: W.W. Norton, 1969), 9–12; John W. Foster, *The Practice of Diplomacy* (Boston: Houghton Mifflin and Co., 1906), 216–42; Frederick van Dyne, *Our Foreign Service: The ABC of American Diplomacy* (Rochester, N.Y.: Lawyers' Cooperative Publishing Company, 1909), 117–77.

46. File 51411/53, 3 (Trenor report).

47. *Annual Report, 1904,* 91.

48. File 51411/53, 16–19 (Trenor report).

49. *Annual Report, 1905,* 50–54; the cooperative arrangement was first put in place in various European ports of embarkation in 1899, in the wake of a cholera epidemic in Europe. At that point the U.S. government ordered (and paid for) the inspections as part of the quarantine measures put in place. The system simply continued in Southern Italy after the quarantine measures had been lifted. U.S. Immigration Commission, *Reports,* vol. 4, 77.

50. Ibid., 113–20, 125–26, 210–20.

51. E. P. Hutchinson, *Legislative History of American Immigration Policy, 1798–1965* (Philadelphia: University of Pennsylvania Press, 1981), 108–11.

52. File 51411/53.

53. Hutchinson, *Legislative History,* 108–11, 124–34. File 51411/53 (Trenor report).

54. *Annual Report, 1905,* 78; *Annual Report, 1907,* 60–62; *Annual Report, 1909,* 113.

10

MIGRATION AND NATIONAL CONSCIOUSNESS:
THE CANADIAN CASE

Bruno Ramirez

In 1900, census figures showed that 1,180,000 Canadians (Canada-born) re-sided in the United States—a number corresponding to 22 percent of the Dominion's population. In that same year, foreign-born immigrants con-stituted 13 percent of Canada's population. Despite yearly fluctuations, sim-ilar rates of *out-migration* and *in-migration* continued until 1930.[1]

As both a receiving and a sending society, throughout much of its history Canada has had to confront the issue of migration. As such, Canada has not only produced a variety of policy responses aimed at restraining the flow of immigrants, but also a variety of discursive interventions in the attempt to discredit the behavior of in-migrants while condemning out-migration for its "evil" consequences.

The purpose of this chapter is to focus on a particular conjuncture of North American history that, more than any other period, before or after, forced both French and English Canada to confront the apparently para-doxical issue of receiving immigrants while at the same time losing Canadi-ans to the neighboring republic.

Moreover, to the extent that this conjuncture coincided with a histori-cal effort of national self-definition by both French and English Canada, it provides rare insights into how out-migration shaped Canadian opinion on fundamental issues such as Canadian-U.S. relations, attitudes toward immigrants, and the character of the Canadian nation(s).

During the first three decades of the nineteenth century, out-migration from Canada to the United States underwent yearly fluctuations due to a variety of factors.[2] As a population that was spread largely along Canada's southern border and often concentrated near some of the most impor-tant U.S. centers of economic development, Canadians responded readily to specific economic conjunctures, profiting from the physical proximity, knowledge of conditions south of the border, and the measure of kinship assistance they could rely upon in their migration project. These fluctuations reflected also the diverse socioeconomic realities that marked the Dominion's various regions, making migration a more compelling option for some Canadians than for others.

World War I and its aftermath were the most important of these conjunctures for their immediate impact on population movements, both continentally and transcontinentally. Transatlantic traveling and migration came to a virtual halt at a time when U.S. military preparedness and the subsequent intervention made labor shortages the most acute the country had ever experienced. Along with Mexicans in the Southwest, African-Americans in the South, and women throughout much of the country, Canadian immigrants were crucial in filling significant U.S. employment shortages while at the same time benefiting from the conditions American industries offered them. It should not come as a surprise, then, that during 1915–1918, Canada contributed 31 percent of all immigrants entering the United States despite comparable shortages experienced in its own labor markets.[3]

The war also intensified American restrictionist sentiment toward a variety of European nationality groups, resulting in the 1921 Quota Act. Once again, Canadians could compensate—at least in part—for the fall in the number of immigrants originating from central-eastern and southern Europe. During 1922 and 1923, in fact, Canadians made up nearly 20 percent of the immigration flow into the United States.[4] Inevitably, Canada was drawn into the fierce restrictionist debates that raged in the United States during the early 1920s and that sought, unsuccessfully, to subject the northern neighbor to quota regulations.[5]

The fear of an invasion from the north voiced in the United States had its dissonant counterpart in the denunciations rising from various Canadian milieus that the exodus across the border was doing irreparable damage to their nation. Never before—with the possible exception of the 1880s—had spokespersons and commentators from both English and French Canada been so in tune in addressing an issue of national import.

Up until the surge in out-migration of the early 1920s and the animosity set off by restrictionism, the loss of Canadian population to the south had hardly attracted the same degree of concern in the two sections of Canadian society. Whereas in French Canada this issue kept popping up in public debates, in English Canada—with the possible exception of the Maritimes—it became overshadowed by the more controversial issue of overseas immigration.

In Quebec—where immigration from Europe had been largely confined to the Montreal region—"*le mirage américain*" that pulled French Canadians southward had given rise to a loud chorus of well-concerted voices that had become a permanent feature of public controversy. The strong sense of peoplehood that marked French Canadians—compared to their Anglo counterparts—did much to dramatize the loss of population and provide precious ammunition to those who raised the specter of national extinction.

"If our population keeps on abandoning the land for a few more years"—an editorialist had written in 1892—"the French Canadian nationality will be transported to the United States."[6] As the twentieth century progressed, French Canadians continued to "abandon the land," although at a lower pace, and variants of the alarm kept ringing in the province, often replacing the term "nation" with "race." For every word or sentence that a Henry Bourassa or Lionel Groulx added to their construction of a French Canadian nation, one trainload of Quebeckers headed south across the border.[7]

But far from merely indulging in jeremiads, French Canadian leaders had taken concrete steps to try to contain the problem. They had sent repatriation agents to the United States to try to convince expatriates to return to their homeland. More important, colonization societies—often inspired by the church when not under direct clergy leadership—had sprung up throughout Quebec, sending representatives to New England mill towns to extol the virtues of agrarian life and to elevate colonization to a supreme gesture of nation building. The provincial government had jumped on the bandwagon, creating in 1888 a Department of Colonization that used public money and a staff of newly appointed agents to facilitate the repatriation and settlement of frontier districts.[8] The Franco-American press of New England constitutes a rich and eloquent record of the interminable procession of Quebec prelates and government agents preaching internal colonization to their brothers and sisters living in exile. Despite disappointing results, the flame of colonization was kept alive throughout the era. Eugénie Savoie recalled when, in the late 1920s, "Missionary Fathers" stopped at the Connecticut town where she worked and lived with her family. "They came down to push people to return and settle on the land—they did not want to give up on the land." In this case the message fell on receptive ears, for shortly afterward the Savoies packed up and resettled on a Quebec farm—partly thanks to the dollars they had earned in the United States.[9]

But while French Canada was trying to rescue the race from extinction, much of Anglo Canada was confronted with the dilemma posed by an immigration deemed essential to ensure the growth of its natural resource industries, but whose composition increasingly included nationalities many saw as a threat to the cultural and civic makeup of the Dominion. In many ways, this era of Canadian history stands as an ongoing tug-of-war between two large opposing coalitions: the large railroad companies and immigration authorities on the one hand, a variety of civic groups and restrictionist associations on the other. The former's pragmatism and determination to pursue an open door policy was countered by accusations that special interests and their economic greed were threatening the cultural and social fabric of Canadian society.[10]

As the policies (which made possible the arrival of 3 million immigrants) forced their way through parliamentary debates, political scandals, and fears of invasion, few Canadians expressed their concern over the loss of population to their southern neighbor. Certainly not in Ontario, which received the largest contingent of newcomers; and even less in the prairies and the mountain west, whose growth and expansion became inextricable from the immigration of Europeans and Americans. Though a minority nationwide, American farmers from northwestern states poured into the prairie provinces of Alberta and Saskatchewan in such large numbers that by 1910 they had become the single largest immigrant group.

During the period 1914–1918, immigration to Canada declined sharply (down to 23 percent of the 1909–1913 annual average), a fact that was certainly responsible for taking much of the steam out of the immigration issue.[11] Moreover, the war economies of the two neighboring countries, with the differing roles played by regional labor markets, produced reverse population movements across the border that puzzled even the most attentive observer. Even Marcus Lee Hansen, well-known scholar of migration, saw in those movements "a great variety of often conflicting influences," growing out of "frenzied developments [that] were complicated in the extreme."[12]

Once that frenzy ended, Canada's "return to normalcy" took much longer than in the United States; and the postwar surge in out-migration across the border was accompanied by widespread unemployment and by a renewed activism on the part of the powerful immigration lobby.[13] Despite significant regional disparities, Anglo-Canadian and French-Canadian observers saw similar developments unfolding before their eyes. It was one of the rare contexts in Canadian history that brought the two major opinion movements to converge into a truly pan-Canadian outcry; it also brought to the fore what observers in both sections of Canada saw as a perplexing and nonsensical contradiction: opening the gates to massive immigration while the country kept losing its own population to the south.

John A. Stevenson was one of those writers who sought to tackle this issue head on. When in early 1923 he set out to write about it for one of Canada's leading national magazines, he was immediately confronted with the lack of statistical data. His information on what he called "a southward exodus on an alarming scale" came from reports about "families hurrying in concert from Alberta to California" and parliamentarians who were up in arms because "half of their ridings' populations" had been lost to out-migration to the south, with similar reports coming from Winnipeg, Calgary, Vancouver, and the Maritimes. One report from Edmonton claimed that "the loss of population [had] changed landlords from supercilious tyrants to gracious suppliants."[14]

However eloquent Stevenson may have found those reports, lack of data made it "difficult"—he admitted—"to keep track of our lost citizens because Ottawa, unlike Washington, does not indulge in emigration statistics."[15] He then turned to a report from the U.S. Treasury Department and found "the most disconcerting novelty." It contained figures on customs returns as of December 31, 1922, showing that "the value of imports under the head 'settlers' effects' total[ed] $6,195,569 against a total of exports amounting to $7,832,052." With the aid of other data—and some guesses—he managed to estimate the approximate number of effects-carrying Canadians who had emigrated to the United States in 1922, compared with that of Americans crossing in the opposite direction.[16]

Stevenson lamented the fact that the superior economic and professional conditions in the United States were draining "the flower of our national stock," and he conceded that it was "difficult to blame young men who succumb to the lure." He also warned that if the flow continued, "the results were bound to be disastrous." Among those who crossed the border, however, were significant numbers of European immigrants who had found that conditions were better farther south. Unlike the early Ontario settler who seemed to have a stake in his new homeland, Stevenson explained, the latter-day immigrant was more adventurous and mobile "and too often he moves before he has given the new life a fair trial." So why try to bring over more of these immigrants? His answer was "obvious": "while the exodus on a serious scale is in progress, expenditure on immigration schemes is a sheer waste of money."[17]

The charge against Canadian authorities for wanting to bring over immigrants who would then find their way south of the border was voiced by several other Anglo Canadian critics—as well as in Parliament.[18] But Stevenson must be credited with having been one of the first commentators—if not the first—to apply the term "sieve" to Canada for a role the country had long played in intercontinental migrations. If his article reached the desk of U.S. Secretary of Labor James Davis, it is likely that the latter drew from it precious ammunition to argue his case in favor of quota restrictions.

In Quebec, commentators did not use the corresponding French term but exposed the same paradox—and did it with a barrage of accusations against the government, against big business, and against the immigrants themselves. Much as in English Canada, Quebec readers were treated to articles exhibiting a series of additions and subtractions to estimate the number of out-migrants, the population growth the country would have attained if Canadians had stayed within their border, and the waste of money for importing immigrants. "Cheat" was the term used by Le Devoir's leading immigration editorialist, Georges Pelletier, to characterize the government's record in the area of migration. In surveying the past twenty years of population movements in and out of the country, Pelletier raised a cry that had become a litany in the Quebec press: "We should have encouraged our own people to remain in the country, to established themselves on the land, to multiply themselves, rather than inviting strangers to take that land." Then followed the list of culprits: "the owners of trans-oceanic fleets, of railroads, of land for sale, of factory owners who have sought the cheapest workforce—and the rest. This group then went on making more money by bringing immigrants back to Europe, or by transporting more than half of them to the United States."[19]

Despite the dubious arithmetic contained in the above statement, Pelletier conceded that the government's policy had resulted in a substantial number of European immigrants remaining in Canada. But in Pelletier's misguided logic, they were a sort of human residue, "much of it refuse that ended up in hospitals, in prisons and penitentiaries"[20]—however hard they sought to make Canada their new homeland.

Here, then, was the basic theme of an argument that resounded in the Quebec press, with only slight variations. For the founder of the Société de colonisation de Montréal, for instance, the disastrous immigration campaign was the work of "imperialists" from both England and Canada acting in concert with "international financiers who had no motherland and whose only god was the golden calf." And here, too, the immigrants were the inevitable part of the equation—"the coveted prey" pulled "from the bowels of all the motherlands of the world." The man who pronounced these words in front of the Montreal Chamber of Commerce was also a medical doctor, T.-A. Brisson, and he prefaced his impassioned speech saying that he was going to treat the subject as a "surgeon who must delve deeply into the plague so that he can come up with the necessary remedy." And thus, in his surgical logic, the immigrants could easily turn from "prey" to "plague"; as such, they constituted a grave danger to the health of Canadian society, which was now confronted "with garbage, with despicable leftovers who crowd our courts, our prisons, our hospitals, our asylums."[21]

While applause was filling that sanctuary of civic responsibility and moral rectitude, in another part of Montreal, Michele Marcogliese—illiterate but smart as a fox—was going from house to house, speaking to fellow immigrants from Casacalenda, Italy, trying to convince them to set up a mutual benefits society; they had to find on their own a measure of protection against unemployment, illness, and death—though their immediate deadline was raising enough money so that on the day of their patron saint each villager back in Casacalenda could have "one kilo of meat and two kilos of potatoes." And in a movie theater, not far from the Chamber of Commerce, Antonio Funicelli, his violin tight under his chin, was helping entertain Montrealers while they watched a silent movie.[22]

Moreover, Dr. Brisson, Georges Pelletier, and the others who raised their voices in the public square were smart enough to know that hardly any immigrants went to settle in those agrarian districts that sent out French Canadians across the border, while stubbornly stressing that most of their fellow citizens who left their parishes did so attracted by "luxury, an exaggerated love for enjoyment, and the taste of adventure."[23]

Ultimately, then, the only hope for a remedy was to address the migrants themselves, to make them understand the gravity of their actions, whether departing from the timber district of the Saguenay, the fertile parishes of the Bas-Richelieu, or the recently settled region of Abitibi. And who else had a greater moral authority and power of conviction than the Church? Who else in the province had such an elaborate outreach that made it possible to address the faithful not merely through publications and associations, but directly from the pulpit? And so, on the first Sunday of June 1923, hundreds of thousands of Quebeckers sat on their pews, their eyes turned toward the altar, listening to the pastoral letter sent by Archbishop Bégin and cosigned by the Province's Bishops. The letter could be read in a calm, solemn tone, as part of the liturgical ceremony. But it could also be read passionately, with emphasis on terms and expressions, with fists in the air and fingers pointed to the audience.

It was not the first time since mass migration had begun in the nineteenth century that this medium had been used to call French Canadians to their national responsibility. Now again, in the face of an "intense migration movement that pulls out of our farmland and industrial centers thousands of our fellow countrymen," the Quebec prelates felt they had "to raise [their] voice" and denounce a "danger that threatens again our national expansion." It was not sufficient to remind the faithful that "migration weakens the living forces of our race"; it was necessary to stress that migration amounted to an act of desertion—all the more reprehensible as people were "deserting their place at the very moment when, in order to rescue it, they had to double their sacrifices and their devotion." And deserting one's nation in the face of "circumstances of an exceptional gravity" amounted to "a sort of betrayal and the forfeiting of those duties that bind every citizen to his motherland." It was then the Church's duty to remind every French Canadian that "the land you are deserting is the same one that through sweat and blood your forefathers wrung from barbarism in order to pass it on to you as a sacred heritage."[24]

But 1923 was a record year in the flow of French Canadians to the United States. No one will ever know how many of those migrants represented by that curve crossed the border carrying with them the moral wounds of their act, and how many were able to make the distinction between rhetoric and facts. The *curé* of Manseau, a parish in rural Quebec, certainly knew how to match those words of condemnation with the harsh existence of his parishioners; for, as Bruno Noury recalled, "he did not scream at us for leaving—he was not blind! He saw that there was no work."[25] And so did the prolabor journalist Jean Syndical, who brought to public attention the facts gathered by a lone researcher, which showed that about half the people who lived in Quebec's rural districts were not farmers but *emplacitaires*— rural dwellers who drew from their tiny plots just enough to survive. Why, then, scream that "the land is being deserted, that nurturing farms are being abandoned?" he asked. And what about the half of Quebec's rural population that was made up of "sons of merchants, public employees, store-keepers, craftsmen, and day laborers"? Why wave to them the flag of "colonization, which they don't know; or that of farming, which they know even less and cannot contemplate, not even if they wished to; for they don't have the means to acquire a piece of farmland?" These facts, and others, gave this lone researcher, Syndical, the courage to raise his voice and aim where few cared to aim: "Stop beating on the people who leave; stop telling them that you have forgotten the providential mission of French Canadians, that you have no faith, that you are not patriotic; stop throwing the responsibility on their shoulders," for the real responsibility lies with those who run the government and the economy.[26]

Critical voices such as this—likely submerged by the turbulent tide of patriotism—help us appreciate the distorting effect that nationalism and racialism could have on social and economic realities: how the alleged homogeneity and the sacredness of the "French-Canadian nation" could erase local differences, banalize international dynamics, and drag the migrant's individual struggle for betterment in front of the altar of national purpose.

English Canadian commentators did not slip into these emotional and rhetorical excesses. Their arguments denoted a more rational and calculating frame of mind—one that in later years would be termed a "cost-benefits" approach. Yet, once the "sieve metaphor" took hold in their imagination, the terms of the equation were not much different from those of French Canadians. And immigrants were part of the equation not only because they played the game of misguided politicians and greedy corporations, but also because they forced Canadians out of their country.

Few commentators managed to articulate such logic more fully and scientifically than R. M. Lower—in later years one of Canada's leading historians. In discussing the issue, he did not resort to the supreme design of providence but to "Gresham's Law of Immigration," which he redefined as "cheap men will drive out dear." Lower displayed at length a series of demographic calculations meant to prove that immigration had prevented the Canadian population from growing. By constantly displacing Canadians and pushing them beyond their border, immigrants had prevented the nation from fully exerting its mechanism of natural growth. Using a logic not unlike that of Samuel Gompers, in the competition for economic betterment, Canadians lost out to the aliens, for "the man with the higher standard of living cannot compete with the man with the lower."

"In this sense," Lower went on, "virtually all immigrants are 'cheap' men, for on arriving in this country they are not in a position to bargain for the sale of their labour."[27] But Lower could handle elaborate historical statistics as easily as he could resort to compelling metaphors; and thus he likened Canada to a ship: "[one] that can carry only a fixed number of people, crew and passengers. If she takes a number of passengers in excess of her complement, there is only one way of compensating for it, some of the crew must be left behind. We in Canada for sixty years past have been taking on so many passengers, that is, immigrants, that we have had to keep leaving many of the crew behind. To provide room in the ship of state for immigrants we have had to embark a large proportion of our own children for the voyage of life in another vessel, the good ship *United States*."[28]

In his zeal to apply rigorous demographic and economic laws, Lower did not care to look closer at his country's population, at its ethnic and linguistic composition, at the length of residence that had turned many foreign-born residents into Canadian citizens. His sharp distinction between "crew" and "passengers," between "our children" and "the immigrants," between Canadians and non-Canadians, could only be predicated on an idea of nation he did not spell out, but which ultimately made his argument not so different from the one exposed by French-Canadian nationalists. But unlike French Canadians who could so easily graft the idea of a nation into concrete historical, linguistic, and religious developments, Lower's nation rose by default—by contrasting his ideal Canadian to the foreign and the alien. And his nation, much like that of French Canadians, had to be protected from those who infused in it new blood, for "much evil must come out of this constant renewal of blood generation after generation." Lower's sieve was more complex than the one described by John Stevenson. It kept immigrants within the Dominion, and it let Canadians filter through the border; and as long as this went on, it was difficult "to see Canada [as] a nation and possessed of all best attributes of nationhood."[29]

While Lower and other commentators were deducing and judging through population statistics the behavior of both newcomers and native Canadians, migrants such as Michele Delforno, Eli Mason, and Almira Lusk had long disproved their theories.

Michele Delforno had arrived in Halifax in early April 1913 with the S. S. Campaniello. A 56–year-old married man, he had left his family behind, and like thousands of Italian sojourners he had sought in Canada the wages that could enable him to improve his situation back in Carpino. His stay only lasted six months, for on September 29 he crossed the border at Niagara Falls and headed to a U.S. port city that would take him back across the Atlantic. It is very unlikely that while in Canada, Delforno displaced native workers, for Canadians were hardly interested in the unskilled jobs that laborers like Delforno filled—most often in remote work sites or towns. Delforno's last job was in one of these towns in northern Ontario—Fort William, which largely owed its development to immigrants from Italy, Finland, and several central European countries.[30]

Nor were Eli Mason and Almira Lusk likely to have been displaced by immigrants. Before heading to South Boston in December 1922, the twenty-seven-year-old Mason had worked as a fisherman in his native village of Voglers Cove, a rural district in Nova Scotia few immigrants knew how to find on a map.[31] Almira Lusk headed south of the border leaving from a Canadian city—Toronto—that had attracted large numbers of immigrants. But as a graduate nurse, her professional universe was totally separate from that inhabited by immigrants. Young, single, and educated, Lusk very probably migrated out of professional ambition, heading in 1918 to the New York City's Woman's Hospital, where a job awaited her.[32]

The experience of thousands of migrants like these—however fragmentarily it emerges from our data—reveals the full variety of local and regional contexts that received and sent migrants across the border while helping us to put national and political discourses in their proper perspective. Their study has allowed us to go beyond aggregate population data and reach individual migrants, families, and networks who ultimately were the ones who changed the social and economic geography of North America.

NOTES

This chapter draws on chapter 2 of my book *Crossing the 49th Parallel: Migration from Canada to the United States, 1900–1930* (Ithaca, N.Y.: Cornell University Press, 2001). Used by permission of the publisher.

1. Leon E. Truesdell, *The Canadian Born in the United States* (New Haven, Conn.: Yale University Press, 1943), 10, 16, 57; M. C. Urquhart, ed., *Historical Statistics of Canada* (Toronto: Macmillan Company of Canada, 1965), series A, 133–69, 19.

2. For a detailed analysis of this migration movement, see Ramirez, *Crossing the 49th Parallel.*

3. Calculated from data in Walter F. Willcox, ed., *International Migrations,* vol. 1, *Statistics,* (New York: Gordon and Breach, 1969), table III, 391–93.

4. U.S. Commissioner of Immigration, *Annual Report of the Commissioner General of Immigration, 1924,* 4.

5. Ramirez, *Crossing the 49th Parallel,* 48–57; see also Catherine Collomp, "Immigrants, Labour Markets, and the State," *Journal of American History* 86, no. 1 (1999).

6. *La Gazette de Berthier,* Berthierville, April 15, 1892. (This and all other translations from French are my own.)

7. For the life and thought of these two leading French-Canadian nationalists, see Susan Mann Trofimenkoff, *The Dream of Nation: A Social and Intellectual History of Quebec* (Toronto: Gage, 1983).

8. Paul-André Linteau et al., *Histoire du Québec contemporain* (Montreal: Boréal Express, 1979), 292. For a lengthier discussion of the relationship between colonization and emigration to the United States, see Bruno Ramirez, *On The Move: French-*

Canadian and Italian Migrants in the North Atlantic Economy, 1860–1914 (Toronto: McClelland and Stewart, 1991), 76–86.

9. Bruno Ramirez and Jacques Rouillard, "Projet d'Histoire Orale: Eugénie Savoie," Department of History, University of Montreal (archive).

10. Donald Avery, *Reluctant Host: Canada's Response to Immigrant Workers, 1896–1914* (Toronto: McClelland and Stewart, 1995), especially chap. 1; see also Valerie Knowles, *Strangers at Our Gates: Canadian Immigration and Immigration Policy, 1540–1990* (Toronto: Dundurn, 1992); Reg Whitaker, *Canada's Immigration Policy Since Confederation* (Ottawa: Canadian Historical Association, 1991); Donald Avery and Bruno Ramirez, "European Immigrant Workers in Canada: Ethnicity, Militancy and State Repression," in *Roots of the Transplanted*, vol. 2, *Plebeian Culture, Class and Politics in the Life of Labor Migrants*, ed. Dirk Hoerder, Horst Roessler and Inge Blank, 411–40 (Boulder, Colo.: East European Monographs, 1994).

11. Calculated from data in *Canadian Immigration and Population Study* (Ottawa: Information Canada, 1974), 8.

12. Marcus Lee Hansen (with John B. Brebner), *The Mingling of the Canadian and American Peoples* (New Haven, Conn.: Yale University Press, 1940), 248, 250.

13. Avery, *Reluctant Host*, 82–107; Georges-Marie Bilodeau, *Pour rester au pays* (Quebec: n.p., 1926).

14. John A. Stevenson, "Is Canada an Immigration Sieve?" *MacLean's Magazine*, February 15, 1923, 20.

15. Ibid.

16. Ibid.

17. Ibid., 20–21.

18. See, among others, Duncan McArthur, "What Is the Immigration Problem?" *Queen's Quarterly*, vol. 35 (Winter 1928): 603–14; Agnes C. Laut, "Our Lost Immigrants," *MacLean's Magazine*, January 21, 1921, 13, 54.

19. Georges Pelletier, "La duperie de l'immigration," *Le Devoir*, March 3, 1922.

20. Ibid.

21. "Immigration-émigration-migration," *Le Devoir*, January 18, 1923.

22. Oral History Interviews in Bruno Ramirez, *Les premiers Italiens de Montréal: naissance de la Petite Italie du Québec* (Montreal: Boréal, 1984), 122, 128.

23. "Contre la désertion," *L'Union des Cantons de l'Est*, June 2, 1923.

24. "L'Épiscopat dénonce les désertions," *L'Union des Cantons de l'Est*, June 21, 1923, which reproduced the entire text of the letter.

25. Ramirez and Rouillard, "Projet d'histoire orale: Bruno Noury," Department of History, University of Montreal (archive).

26. Jean Syndical, "Pourquoi ils partent," *Le Devoir*, August 20, 1923.

27. R. M. Lower, "The Case Against Immigration," *Queen's Quarterly* 37 (Spring 1930): 571.

28. Ibid., 569.

29. Ibid., 572.

30. *Soundex Index to Canadian Border Entries*, Record Group M1461: "Michele Delforno," reel 120 (U.S. National Archives).

31. *Index*, M1461: "Eli Mason," reel 260.

32. *Index*, M1461: "Almira Lusk," reel 235.

11

MIGRATION POLICY AND
THE ASYMMETRY OF POWER:
THE MEXICAN CASE, 1900–2000

Jorge Durand

Translated from the French by Amy Jacobs

Mexico is a country of emigrants that does not fully recognize itself as such. The low national awareness of this reality has been due essentially to two factors: the proximity of the receiving country and the fact that emigration is unidirectional. Eighty-eight percent of Mexican emigrants are bound for a single destination—the United States—and nearly 80 percent of them are concentrated in states that were once part of Mexican territory: California, Arizona, Nevada, Texas, and New Mexico.

Most Mexicans who leave do not break definitively with their country, in contrast to emigrants from other countries; the option of return is always there. Mexican emigrants may well go back for the holidays, to bury a relative, to keep an eye on ongoing personal business, or even to attend a soccer match.

Mexicans have been leaving Mexico in great numbers since the late nineteenth century; emigration is thus both a massive and historically deep phenomenon for this country. In 1926, the anthropologist Manuel Gamio noted an emigrant population numbering close to a million (917,000). The 2000 U.S. census reported 9.3 million Mexican-born immigrants.[1]

The migration question is a permanent, fundamental issue in national and bilateral policy. But while over the twentieth century there were both changes and continuities in political discourse on emigration, the Mexican position has always been informed by a fundamental, immutable principle: the constitutional right to freedom of movement. Despite rare exceptions that confirm the rule, the Mexican authorities have never tried to prevent their compatriots from leaving.

Nonetheless, official assessments and arguments with regard to emigration changed several times in the course of the twentieth century, and with them Mexican policy, which I shall review before examining Mexico's current position in greater detail.

THE "DISEASE" OF EMIGRATION (1910–40)

At the dawn of the twentieth century, Mexican emigration to the United States was already a mass phenomenon. The railway line between the two countries, inaugurated in 1884, undoubtedly enabled the supply of Mexican manual labor to meet rising demand from U.S. employers.

The Mexican authorities of the time did not perceive the departure of Mexicans as a desirable development. They viewed Mexico as a depopulated country with enormous natural wealth, a country that was itself in need of immigrants to exploit its resources. "There is work for all in Mexico, Mexicans and foreigners. Work abounds. What is missing is muscle and spirit, hands and brains," affirmed the *Progreso Latino* in 1906.[2] Emigration was also viewed negatively because emigrants were going to former Mexican territories that had been annexed by the United States. After the 1845–1848 war with the United States, Mexico developed a policy encouraging Mexicans "on the other side" to repatriate—with little success, however.[3]

For many early twentieth-century editorialists, the emigrants were traitors to the Mexican cause. The Catholic Church itself was of this opinion, as the then-weekly Catholic magazine *La Epoca* made clear: "The [emigrants'] lack of patriotism swells to enormous proportions when we realize [they] are going to work in, and thereby use their labor to develop, a nation we have always considered our enemy, always thought of as responsible for the greatest misfortunes and sorrows of our nation."[4]

In the first decades of the twentieth century, the Mexican authorities opted for dissuasion and propaganda to rein in emigration. Handbills and posters distributed in villages described the dreadful living and working conditions of emigrants. The worst problem bore the name *enganchadores,* recruiters who paid the future emigrant worker an advance in exchange for his or her pledge to reimburse the sum in work hours. Hiring centers functioned as private businesses, and recruitment was an extremely exploitative system that left matters of hiring, moving, and paying workers, as well as the organization of workers' camps and the assignment of workloads, entirely in the hands of private individuals. The system gave rise to child labor, private militias, extremely one-sided contracts, lifelong debt, and miserable living and working conditions.

The situation worsened with the outbreak of revolution in 1910. Thousands of people fled the dangers and desolation of war in the direction of the northern border. This was the only occasion on which the United States granted Mexicans official refugee status, housing them in military installations until they could find work through a hiring center.[5]

The landscape changed radically in 1917. The Mexican revolution was over, but the United States was entering World War I. America's declaration of war instantly freed up innumerable American jobs. The United States needed manual laborers immediately, so American recruiters began crossing the border to find them, putting pressure on the consuls to facilitate their progress. The Mexican minister of foreign relations declared, "Given that the government cannot put a stop to emigration, they should make all efforts to ensure that their compatriots suffer as little as possible during their stay abroad." In fact, many emigrants without official papers were inducted into the army and sent to the front. An estimated sixty thousand Mexicans found themselves on United States army bases, and nearly fifteen thousand participated in World War I.[6] Once again, the Mexican authorities turned to propaganda and official information to warn incautious citizens dreaming of striking it rich in the North. The government began issuing passports so emigrants could prove their nationality and thereby keep from being conscripted into the United States Army.

After World War I a new phase began, with its own pattern: economic recession resulting in massive deportation of Mexican immigrants from the United States. The Mexican government's posture was once again reactive. It was incapable of controlling the phenomenon, helpless either to discourage or contain the flow, and in no position to refuse to take back deported compatriots. There were three mass deportations: nearly one hundred fifty thousand Mexicans were turned out in 1921; nearly half a million from 1929 to 1933; and almost forty-five thousand workers between 1938 and 1940, including six thousand in conjunction with repatriation programs organized by President Cárdenas. On all these occasions, the Mexican government had to intervene, assisting re-entering emigrants wherever possible with transportation, food, and lodging costs until they returned to their village of origin or could be resettled elsewhere.[7] As part of various settlement projects, the idea was floated of granting returning emigrants land and farming tools, but it never amounted to much.

For analysts of the period, among them Enrique Santibáñez, Mexican emigration had ceased to be a "bloodletting" and become a "hemorrhage" in a "sterile" undertaking: "friendly [relations] with the United States have only helped impoverish our people."[8] For Alfonso Fabila, emigrants were "touched by the sin of emigration," and this called for radical solutions: the government must "make the dangers of emigration known," and if necessary "use the force of the law to prevent emigration." Emigration was an error, and though the Mexican Constitution established the right of freedom of movement, "this law, so just and rational, masks a latent truth: Mexico is losing its peasants, workers, even its intellectuals."[9]

Manuel Gamio had a much more measured view. He acknowledged that, with its emigrants, Mexico was losing "the effort and collaboration of approximately 9 percent of its productive classes," but he believed that transitory emigration of Mexicans reduced social problems and unemployment. He also cited the fact that emigrants abroad received training and sent large sums of money back to Mexico.[10]

Thus, in the first forty years of the twentieth century, Mexican policy with regard to emigration was dissuasive in that it tried to rein in the phenomenon by informing the population of the attendant dangers and difficulties. It was also passive, in that the government did little more than react to situations such as the massive expulsions of the 1920s and 1930s. Some commentators claim that a first, small, *bracero*-like program (see below) was implemented during World War I.[11] In fact, this plan did not go beyond an exchange of consular letters and agreements in which mention was made of certain official arrangements for protecting workers and safeguarding their labor rights. There were no bilateral negotiations or official accords between the two governments at that time.

NEGOTIATED EMIGRATION:
THE BRACERO PROGRAM (1942–64)

Paradoxically, the two states began negotiating conditions for the hire of Mexican workers just two years after the massive 1939 and 1940 expulsions. The specter of deportation was still vivid in the memory of rural Mexicans, but there was now a dearth of manual laborers on U.S. farms and industrial centers. This was therefore a propitious moment to negotiate. For the first time in half a century of emigration, the two states sat across a negotiating table to determine the most effective way of resolving the matter of labor supply and demand. The international context had affected the balance of power; the United States was obliged to adopt a negotiating posture.

The Bracero Program was first negotiated in the context of World War II; it was renegotiated annually over the next twenty-two years. The program led to a significant improvement in the Mexican economy and reinforced the government's populist and nationalist domestic policy approach at a time when nationalizations of the railroad companies (1937) and the oil industry (1939) were having their effect.[12]

In 1942, the United States did not need immigrants as it had early in the century; it needed labor power—"arms" (*braceros*). For its part, Mexico was happy to sign an accord that would attest to its support of the Allied war effort. In this highly particular historical context, Mexico managed to negotiate an agreement that was fairly favorable for its workers, guaranteeing them a work contract, minimum wage, transportation, housing, and insurance. On the other side, the Americans managed to reverse and transform the earlier migration process. These would be male immigrants (to prevent family emigration), of rural origin, whose stay would be both temporary and legal, and who would be employed primarily in farm work.

The first virtue of the Bracero Program was to put an end to the former *enganche* (indentured) system of hiring. Hiring ceased being a private affair; it now had to comply with official, bilaterally determined programs, and the two parties had to follow a signed agreement. The program's second virtue was explicit recognition of the existence of a binational Mexico–United States labor market. Contrary to most American migration laws, which applied to all countries and immigrants, the Bracero Program was a bilateral agreement first proposed by the United States and founded on the mutual interests of the two parties.

For braceros (Mexicans working in the United States), the fundamental problem lay in the contract specification requiring them to stay on a given farm, which prevented them from moving freely and seeking work on the open labor market. Some critics of the program perceived this as a system of semislavery: the worker was tied to a particular employer, and this situation generated abuses.

For the Americans, the main problem was cost and the heavy administrative management the program required. In essence, the Bracero Program amounted to a worker–boss relationship in which two governments intervened and which gave rise to a binational labor market.

Immigration under the Bracero Program also had the advantage of being temporary. Workers could come and go. On this point Mexico and the United States were in full agreement: temporary immigration was the best option for both countries.

The program functioned for twenty-two years (1942–1964) and proved its effectiveness several times. It mobilized an average of 350,000 workers a year, and led to the hiring of a total of 4.5 million persons.

Since both parties were attentive to their prerogatives, this collective bi-national work agreement, with its associated bureaucracy and costs, had to be renegotiated every year. In 1945, for example, twenty-four hundred people were employed in managing the program.[13] On the Mexican side there was a great increase in corruption and influence peddling; of course, this directly affected emigrants, now caught up in practices of bribery, "donations," and favor trading.[14]

Meanwhile, the various governmental agencies involved had their own conflicts, with clashing perspectives, fears, and sympathies. In Mexico, the minister of foreign relations did the negotiating, the interior minister executed the program, while the minister of labor evaluated, intervened, and interfered. In the United States, a conflict developed among the Department of Labor, allied with the trade unions who, for their part, worked in various ways to sabotage the Bracero Program; the Immigration and Naturalization Service, which, paradoxically, became the program's strongest American defender; and the Department of Agriculture, which supported growers' interests.[15]

Another point of disagreement was over where recruiting should take place. The Mexican government wanted it located within Mexico, in zones heavily populated with migrants, rather than on the border, as the U.S. government and American employers proposed, with their eye on transportation costs. Independent of the issue of location, the arrival of thousands of hopeful recruits in one place caused numerous logistical problems that the Mexican government was unable to resolve adequately. For Pedro de Alba, the hiring centers were "one of the most appalling spectacles I have ever seen."[16]

The Bracero Program thus had many negative consequences, but these were not all due to the program itself. A major problem was the concurrent increase in clandestine worker movement, a situation that each party blamed on the other. The American view was that Mexico should prevent "illegals" from leaving, while the Mexican government called on the United States to sanction employers who hired them. In Texas, for example, a judiciary measure known as the Texas Proviso authorized North American employers to hire clandestine immigrants without risking any sanctions.

America's massive hiring of seasonal workers, legal and illegal, affected the labor market in both countries. Governors of certain Mexican states, among them Guanajuato, complained of the lack of manual labor and blamed the Bracero Program.[17] In the United States, the opposite view prevailed: the unions continually complained of an overabundant supply of cheap manual labor that forced local workers to move, brought down wages, and, most important, was used to break strikes.[18]

The most recurrent problem, however, and the one that most complicated annual binational negotiations, was violation of work contract clauses by American employers. The initial wartime agreement proved too costly in a time of peace, and the Bracero accords were definitively terminated in December 1964. Mexico's view was that ending the program would only encourage illegal immigration, and that this was an even less desirable situation.

CLANDESTINE IMMIGRATION AND LAISSEZ-FAIRE POLICY

After the American refusal to renew the Bracero Program, the Mexican government placed its hopes in the possibility of a new accord. The government of President Diaz Ordaz (1964–1970) took the problem to heart, and in 1974 his successor, President Echeverria, made an attempt to reach a migration agreement with the Americans. President Gerald Ford declined, however: "It has been proved that this type of accord does not guarantee the rights of Mexican workers."[19] In sum, the United States refused to re-open the question, arguing that it was for Mexico's own good and the good of the Mexican people.

Above and beyond U.S. government cynicism and rhetoric, Mexican workers themselves were tackling the problem of protecting and winning recognition for their rights. In the 1960s Cesar Chavez, an extraordinary, much-admired union organizer of Mexican origin, set up the United Farm Workers (UFW). On September 16, 1965—Mexican Independence Day— he launched the first of several major strikes in the California vineyards. The struggle was long, but farmworker unionism came out of it greatly reinforced.

Two new types of actors, in addition to the farmworkers, made their appearance at this time: women and urban emigrants. The profile of the Mexican emigrant changed dramatically. As the need for farmworkers fell due to mechanization, the demand for labor rose in industry and the expanding service sector (maintenance, restaurants, hotels, casinos, retail shops). The change was more than a response to new U.S. labor market demands, however; it also reflected radical changes in Mexican social structure. The country was undergoing rapid urbanization, and women, breaking with the traditional propensity to remain in the home, were joining the workforce.

The absence of a specific U.S. migration policy turned any and every

Mexican into a possible illegal worker and placed Mexican workers in the United States in the vulnerable, precarious situation of being fired and deported at any moment. This strengthened the traditional predisposition to return to Mexico, encouraging clandestine workers to invest savings and energy in planning for a better life there. This state of affairs in turn fueled the development of social support and solidarity networks as never before. A bracero had needed neither relatives nor acquaintances in the United States, but both were essential to clandestine immigrants.

The North American labor market now began to be supplied by the workers themselves, and their networks. They were now in charge of recruiting and training new workers, a dynamic that strengthened the system of links with particular communities and regions.[20] Meanwhile and similarly, organized crime networks developed at the border, and border-crossing mechanisms were perfected through the help of compatriots and acquaintances, or the intervention of "coyotes," traffickers of illegal workers. Border controls were sparse at the time, and night crossing was relatively easy.

The Mexican government had ceased to concern itself with the migration issue. Emigrants were left to their fate, left to cross the border, and their employers left to treat workers however they would. "Laissez-faire, laissez-passer" seems to have been the attitude in those years. Only rarely, exceptionally, did the Ministry of Foreign Relations intervene to assist and protect Mexican citizens. Certain commentators have dubbed this period "the policy of having no policy."

In reality, the patent lack of political imagination and vision transformed the border into a lawless, rightless zone. Gangs of thieves loitered around emigrants who were crossing the border, waiting to steal the small amount of money they had on them. Meanwhile, local and federal Mexican police, not to mention customs officials, took charge of collecting *mordidas* (bribes) and extorting money from returning emigrants. Paradoxically, emigrants preferred to be jailed by the American Border Patrol rather than fall into the hands of the Mexican police.

Emigration became a lucrative business. In the 1980s "coyotes" were getting $200 a head for border crossings and offering their services to hundreds of thousands of clandestine workers. North American money-transfer businesses were pocketing about 20 percent of the money sent back to Mexico, which at the time amounted to nearly $3 billion annually. Mexican postal workers systematically stole money orders and the cash in sealed envelopes. Foreign exchange offices and banks lifted another 10 percent when converting dollars into the national currency. And the "policy of having no policy" continued.

The story was different on the American side. In the face of increasing deregulation of the labor market, politicians and the media began displaying concern for the legal status of migrant workers. The Americans were moving toward a profound change in their migration policy: sweeping amnesty combined with strict border controls.

DOMESTIC DAMAGE-REPAIR POLICY

In 1986, the U.S. Congress passed a four-point reform of the immigration law, called the Immigration Reform and Control Act (IRCA).[21] The four points were sweeping amnesty for clandestine immigrants, a special program for farmworkers, much tighter border controls, and sanctions against employers who hired illegal workers.

The first two provisions functioned well enough: 2.3 million clandestine immigrants became legal, and the United States thereby ensured itself a vast pool of cheap labor. The border-control rules worked only moderately well: border crossing became more difficult and risky, but the flow of clandestine immigrants continued as before. The plan to sanction employers, however, was a resounding failure. The Border Patrol's budget tripled, but only 2 percent was earmarked to combat the hiring of illegal workers. In addition, the IRCA had many unexpected effects: a sharp increase in the flow of clandestine workers, changes in the migration pattern, and a significant rise in the number of deaths at the moment emigrants crossed the border.[22]

The American government's unilateral decision and change of pace took the Mexican government, with its wait-and-see attitude, by surprise. This attitude became a problem for Mexico in the 1988 elections, when accusations of fraud were heard from the other side of the border. President Salinas and the Institutional Revolutionary Party (PRI) in power realized that several million Mexicans in the United States were demanding justice, assistance, and guarantees for their civil rights. Celebrations of Mexican Independence Day (promoted by Mexico) in various U.S. cities apparently no longer sufficed to maintain the peace, and during the 1988 celebrations, Mexicans in a number of American cities joined together to accuse politicians in their native country of electoral fraud.

It became urgent for the government to readjust its domestic and foreign policies so as to repair the damage done by its effective abandoning of the emigrants: the latter were considered favorable to the opposition because, after "voting with their feet" by leaving the country, they had been ignored by the Mexican authorities while living in the United States and mistreated upon their return. The PRI had lost its political capital among emigrants. Worse yet, emigrants were no longer showing the traditional patriotism and cultural resistance that had led them systematically to refuse to change nationalities, an attitude that had benefited the PRI.

The Mexican authorities launched several programs to try to repair the damage. In 1990, the Grupo Beta (Beta Group) was founded, a tripartite public safety and law enforcement organization that included some of the country's best police officers. Its mission was to defend emigrant rights on the northern border. The Grupo protected emigrants from attack and police extortion and came to their assistance in the event of problems or danger. Member selection was extremely important, as was evaluation of Grupo Beta's performance. The results were swift and spectacular. Violence in the lawless border zone decreased 90 percent. From 1990 to 2000 there were more than twenty thousand arrests, and the Grupo Beta, which began with twelve people, today employs more than one hundred and operates in seven border cities.[23] The Grupo Beta later extended its activities to the southern border to protect immigrants from Central America. Members have not carried out police functions since 1995 and cannot bear arms. According to press reports, however, certain abuses persist, particularly against Central American immigrants.[24]

Another initiative, the Paisano Program, was aimed at resolving the problems of returning emigrants, particularly the problems arising during the winter holiday season. At first an attempt was made to limit the number of customs inspections and policemen in order to reduce the possibility of extortion. Then the customs "red light" was introduced. A Mexican citizen arriving from abroad has the right to carry $300 worth of merchandise; above that amount, he or she has to make a customs declaration. With the Paisano Program, the traveler had to turn a switch at the customs entrance, which set off either a red or green light, at random. If the light was green, the person passed; if it was red, he or she was searched. The system proved highly effective.

This was not at all true of the Highway Patrol and Criminal Investigation Bureau police in the various states through which emigrants passed. Officers readily identified emigrant vehicles and would stop the driver on any pretext, such as having foreign license plates, or to demand "compensation."[25] The Paisano Program is now limited to running complaint windows, but it still makes information and guidance on rights and obligations available to returning Mexicans.

Consular registration cards did not have the hoped-for results either. Migrants were given an official card to show on demand to the North American authorities. The Salinas and Zedillo governments (1988–2000) issued more than a million such cards, but with no simultaneous support program. The cards were meant merely for identification purposes and looked improvised and amateurish. In some cases they failed to mention crucial information such as education level and sex (the latter was supposed to be self-evident from the first name). Moreover, every consulate kept its own separate database, so the information could not be used for more extensive analyses. And there were serious lapses in security. A number of Central American emigrants managed to obtain consular registration cards so that if they were deported from the United States they would be left at the Mexican border rather than sent back to their country of origin.

The Program for Mexican Communities Abroad was instituted with the purpose of establishing ties with Mexicans living in the United States, supporting educational, cultural, and athletic activities, and acting in the areas of health and business. Another program that proved quite helpful to emigrants and their families validated educational level so that pupils could continue their school year upon return from the United States. Some analysts claim this program was developed for purely political reasons, to improve the government's image, but it has come to fulfill a number of functions. For example, authorities in several Mexican states used the validations to establish contacts with emigrants, and particularly with emigrant associations, which led to the founding of a number of *casas,* such as Casa Puebla and Casa Guanajuato.

The URESA RURESA UIFSA, an interstate program (based on the Uniform Reciprocal Enforcement of Support Act, the Revised Uniform Reciprocal Enforcement of Support Act, and the Uniform Interstate Family Support Act) developed by the Ministry of Foreign Relations, assisted families of emigrants with problems of child and family support after divorce or abandonment. The ministry could transmit a legal complaint against migrant heads of household who failed to return to their families or send financial support, and force them to pay the corresponding alimony or child support. This program has limited application, because it presupposes a legal suit, but it has resolved many migration-linked cases of abandonment.

Last, there is the *Iniciativa Ciudadana* program, better known as "tres por uno" (three for one), which channels emigrant savings into productive investments for their communities of origin, adding contributions from Mexican city, state, and federal authorities. The government has pledged to provide triple matching funds for emigrants' savings; the money is to be used for constructive projects that respond to urgent infrastructure and basic-service needs in the communities of origin. The program, first implemented in the state of Zacatecas, has now been extended to other Mexican states. From 1999 to 2000, Zacatecas emigrants' clubs amassed $2.8 million for their home communities.[26]

Like most development projects, the Iniciativa Ciudadana has experienced success and failure, as well as problems of management, transparence in fund handling, and liaison among the various bodies involved.[27] It has received substantial government support and attracted the interest of international organizations such as the World Bank and the Inter-American Development Bank.

The Mexican government was active in other areas affecting emigrants, reaching an understanding with the United States Immigration and Naturalization Service on "orderly repatriation" of arrested minors and sick persons: they must be turned over immediately to Mexican consular authorities and transferred to reception centers in Mexico, where a relative can come to identify and collect them.

In quite a different matter, the government reacted to the IRCA provision permitting legal residents who so desire to acquire United States citizenship. Growing numbers of Mexicans were being naturalized, and the trend accelerated after passage of the 1996 American immigration law stipulating that only legal residents could receive Social Security payments and other benefits. In December 1996, the Mexican Congress approved a constitutional reform permitting Mexicans to maintain dual citizenship. New American citizens who had already given up their Mexican citizenship were granted the right to request restitution within time limits fixed by the law. This reform was well received by the emigrant population. Emigrants no longer lost their rights as Mexican citizens, and *ejidatarios* or *comuneros* peasants retained their usufructary right to the land. Those who returned to Mexico enjoyed full citizenship rights: the right to vote and be elected; the right to work, buy, or sell goods, etc.

The constitutional reform of December 1996 also allowed for voting "outside voter's electoral district if voter is located elsewhere than in his or her usual place of residence, or abroad."[28] Much remains to be done, however, before the right to vote abroad is fully realized. Although the Federal

Election Institute (IFE) appointed a board of experts to analyze different possible modes for voting abroad, its final report, submitted to Congress in 1998, has not yet been debated.

All in all, the last two PRI governments, headed respectively by Salinas and Zedillo, made some progress in the area of domestic policy (and a little in foreign policy) in protecting and informing emigrants, granting them rights, supervising initiatives involving emigrants, and resolving some of the many practical problems they face daily. After two decades of total abandonment, this represented a major and remarkable move forward. Wrongs against the Mexican community living outside the country were in part redressed by granting rights that had been demanded for decades (such as dual citizenship and the right to vote abroad) and by partially resolving domestic problems of corruption and extortion.

At the bilateral level, however, no new proposals on the migration situation were made during this period.

THE NEW MIGRATION AGENDA

In the last decade of the twentieth century, relations between Mexico and the United States were marked by the "war on drugs." America's enemy was no longer the Soviet Union; it was narcotics.

In the 1970s and mid-1980s, drugs arrived in the United States mainly through the Caribbean; their point of entry was usually Florida. The Colombian cartels in control of production and traffic were hard hit by the war on drugs, and many traffickers turned to Mexico, where cartels made their appearance in Tijuana, Juarez, and the Gulf region. The Mexican border, more than three thousand kilometers long, was ideal for developing new drug routes.[29] Migration routes, especially through border cities, were soon implicated in drug traffic, with narcotics dealers using emigrants and *burreros* ("mules," or drug carriers) to get small quantities of drugs into the United States. Illegal immigration became linked with drug trafficking in the public mind. Fighting drug traffic became as much a part of the U.S. Border Patrol's mission as stopping human contraband.

With drugs and economic accords now at the top of the bilateral agenda, emigrants and their myriad problems placed a distant second, if not third. Even in the case of serious human rights violations, such as the brutal 1996 beating by American police of two immigrants captured in Riverside, California, the Mexican government's attitude was timorous. The Foreign Relations Ministry and the Mexican consulate in Los Angeles protested and sent the appropriate diplomatic memos, but President Zedillo seemed to excuse the conduct of the American police by mentioning that Central American immigrants at times fell victim to the same excesses in Mexico. The affair went all the way to the Mexican Congress, which reacted energetically, demanding that President Zedillo make public the report conducted by forty Mexican consulates in the United States listing human rights violations committed over the preceding five years. The report had remained confidential "so as not to undermine bilateral relations."[30] Clearly, emigrants were seen as an inconvenient matter that provoked discord and got in the way of commercial negotiations.

In the United States, this was the period of the anti-immigrant offensive, particularly in California, where Governor Pete Wilson and his Proposition 187 called for punishing immigrants and their families by denying them access to education, welfare, and health assistance. The Mexican government failed to respond to these moves, which constituted attacks on the emigrant community. In 2000, the arrival of democracy in Mexico gave emigrants some hope. The year began with good news for the Mexican community residing in the United States: the new president Vicente Fox had promised to give new weight and a new direction to the migration agenda. This was not just a campaign slogan. For Fox, originally from the state of Guanajuato, which has a century-long history of emigration, the issue was of great significance and now became a fundamental focus of foreign policy. The new president created a special commission to study the situation of emigrants, and Juan Hernández, a Texas-born Mexican American, was put in charge of the project. For his part, Chancellor Jorge Castañeda was fully familiar with the phenomenon and had good rapport with the Americans. More important still, the language used to discuss the issue began to change. For decades the Ministry of Foreign Relations had used the conventional term "protection" for Mexicans outside the country. Now the official terms became "defense and promotion of the rights of Mexicans abroad."

The Fox government proposed a "complete negotiation of the migration issue with the United States, a negotiation which will examine the roots of the problem, its manifestations and consequences; in which the interest of emigration for our two countries is considered a shared responsibility; and which will establish an ordered framework for guaranteeing adequate legal protection and decent working conditions."[31] The government's democratic legitimacy would allow it to negotiate from a different position. A new phase was under way.

The Mexican president's political will and Chancellor Castañeda's negotiating skill did produce a verbal agreement—on September 10, 2001. According to Frank Sharry, a Washington lawyer for the emigrant cause, such an agreement was virtually unhoped-for.[32] Presidents Fox and Bush publicly declared the political will of the two parties to reach an accord on the migration issue. Mexico's proposal addressed a number of major issues: border security, sweeping amnesty for emigrants living in the United State, a program for temporary migrant workers, extension of the permanent visa program, a project for aiding emigrants' home communities, and a calendar for further discussion to resolve any problems of implementation. The Mexican side went so far as to affirm that the ultimate solution should resemble the European Community, with free circulation among member states.

This promising verbal agreement between the Texas and Guanajuato cowboys also contained crucial points not made public, although their importance was obvious. For the United States, a migration agreement with Mexico presupposed Mexico's control of its southern border to limit the number of illegal Central and South American immigrants crossing Mexico on their way to the United States. The narrowing of Mexican territory at the Tehuantepec Isthmus in the south, an intersection point of highways, roads, and other passageways, was an ideal spot for controlling illegal immigration to the United States. In this connection, Castañeda made a revealing declaration: "In the interests of consistency, but also as a matter of principle, Mexico will ensure that the rights not only of our emigrants but those of Central America and other countries who cross our territory, and who occasionally fall victim to ill-treatment or harassment by Mexican authorities, are fully respected. We will work to guarantee the same treatment for immigrants in Mexico as that which we demand for Mexicans across the northern border."[33] The reality was very different, but here at last was a clear, precise idea of what might be demanded.

Times had changed and the migration issue, taboo during the 1992–1993 negotiation of the North American Free Trade Agreement (NAFTA), reappeared on the horizon. Practice had proven that trade agreements were not enough to reduce migration flows, and border controls had not worked either.

Everything changed on September 11, 2001. Bilateral policy was put on the back burner as the United States prepared to counterattack. The migration agreement was postponed indefinitely. The issue became much more sensitive when the terrorist attacks were linked to illegal immigration. The suicide commando squad was made up of immigrants, some of whom were using false identity papers. They had been granted entry into the United

States on tourist or student visas and stayed beyond the date fixed by the immigration authorities. A lax, inefficient migration policy had let them in. The Immigration and Naturalization Service (INS), which had extended the visas of two terrorists a month after the attacks, was in the hot seat.

Reform was swift. The INS began a process of radical internal reform, and new requirements were added for obtaining tourist and student visas, types used by many emigrant workers in the United States. Use of false information such as a fake Social Security number (no one can work in the United States without one) began to be penalized. Though there was absolutely no connection between Mexican emigrants and the 9/11 terrorists, Mexicans suffered as a result of the general paranoia. Whereas before they had been termed "illegal" and associated with delinquency and drug trafficking, now they were linked in the public mind with international terrorism. Paradoxically, the only logical way out of this in security terms would have been to legalize those residents without proper papers. But this would have meant granting them certain rights and undermining the country's political and economic interest in maintaining a huge supply of cheap manual labor.

The attempts to reach a migration accord thus came to naught. All that President Fox and the Chancellery were able to obtain from the United States were declarations that the international political context had changed and that immigration negotiations were postponed until further notice.

Nonetheless, there was some progress, including a reform of the consular registration card. As mentioned, this had raised serious problems concerning reliability and security. A plan was conceived for modifying and modernizing the card format. The Chancellery negotiated with various banking institutions to get the card recognized as a valid document for opening a bank account. In early 2003, seventy-four banking institutions accepted the registration card; more than a million cards had been issued in 2002. Emigrants now had access to withdrawal accounts, which meant money transfer costs could be dramatically reduced. The Mexican authorities also undertook negotiations with police departments in various American states for validation of the consular registration card. In January 2003, eight hundred police departments accepted the consular card as legal ID; immigrants were less tempted to use false documents.[34] The clearest proof of the impact of the registration card is the fact that the idea has been taken up in other countries, among them Peru, El Salvador, Honduras, and even Poland.

Mexican foreign policy in migration matters has become decidedly more active. The results have not been as good as expected due to the general world disorder. And Castañeda's resignation after two years as chancellor has led to the suspension of the migration agreement and a great number of practical questions. However, progress in terms of proposals has been significant.

CONCLUSION

The historical record shows that Mexican migration policy has been uncertain and oscillating. The asymmetry in the balance of power between Mexico and the United States is extremely pronounced; this continues to affect the pace of negotiations and explains the United States' unilateralist approach. It also seems to explain the PRI's wait-and-see attitude and its readiness to procrastinate instead of doing what should have been done long ago.

In the last century, there have been successive phases of short-lived progress and longer retreats. From 1900 to 1940, Mexico practiced a dissuasion policy in order to keep workers from departing for its northern neighbor, and a reactive policy in response to American unilateralism in matters of inspection, control, and deportation. The period 1942–1964 was characterized by intense negotiation around the Braceros agreement and systematic defense of emigrant workers' rights, though this was rarely effective. From 1965 to 1990, unilateral American action predominated; Mexico kept a low profile. In 1990, the Mexican government became fully aware of the situation of Mexicans outside the country and enacted major domestic policy reforms while making some progress in foreign policy. In 2000, the approach changed radically, and a new phase began.

The periods of Mexican initiative and action coincide with important moments in national life: the rise of nationalism, linked directly to President Cardenas's nationalizing of the railway and oil companies; World War II, which facilitated negotiation of the Bracero Program; and democratization.

The periods of Mexican retreat coincide with particularly difficult or complicated moments in the country's history. Early in the century, these were the end of the Porfirio dictatorship; the 1910–1917 revolution; and the Cristera War (1926–1929), which broke out in regions with a history of emigration. The second major phase coincided with the 1968 student movement, the crisis of the corporatist system, the end of the economic model of import substitution, and the end of the road for the single party.

It took Mexico a century to realize that it is a country of emigrants; at present more than 21 million people of Mexican origin live in the United

States, 10 million of them born in Mexico. And it took the Mexican government decades to learn how to negotiate and demand respect for the rights of their fellow citizens abroad. The asymmetry in power between the two countries must not prevent Mexico from implementing policy that actively supports and defends the human and labor rights of its emigrants.

NOTES

1. Manuel Gamio, *Mexican Immigration to the United States: A Study of Human Migration and Adjustment* (Chicago: University of Chicago Press, 1930).

2. Alvaro Ochoa and Alfredo Uribe, *Emigrantes del Oeste* (Mexico City: Conaculta, 1990).

3. Jorge Durand, *Más allá de la línea* (Mexico City: Conaculta, 1994).

4. Ochoa and Uribe, *Emigrantes del Oeste*, 134.

5. Jorge Durand and Patricia Arias, *La experiencia migrante* (Mexico City: Universidad de Guadalajara, 2000).

6. Fernando Alanis, *El primer Programa Bracero y el gobierno de México 1917–1918* (Mexico City: El Colegio de San Luis, 1999).

7. Fernando Alanís, "No cuenten conmigo: El gobierno de México y la repatriación de mexicanos de Estados Unidos 1910–1928," *Mexican Studies/Estudios Mexicanos* 19, no. 2 (2003): 30–35.; Durand, *Más allá de la línea*.

8. Enrique Santibáñez, *Ensayo acerca de la Inmigración Mexicana en los Estados Unidos* (San Antonio, Texas: Clegg, 1930).

9. Alfonso Fabila, *El Problema de la Emigración de Obreros y Campesinos Mexicanos* (Mexico City: Talleres Gráficos de la Nación, 1932).

10. Gamio, *Mexican Immigration*.

11. Alanis, *El primer Programa Bracero*.

12. Luis Gonzalez, *Los días del Presidente Cárdenas* (Mexico City: El Colegio de México, 1981).

13. Robert C. Jones, *Los braceros mexicanos en los Estados Unidos durante el periodo bélico* (Washington: Unión Panamericana, 1946).

14. José Lázaro Salinas, *La emigración de braceros. Visión objetiva de un problema mexicano* (Mexico City: EDIAPSA, 1955); Durand, *Más allá de la línea*.

15. Kitty Calavita, *Inside the State. The Bracero Program, Immigration, and the I.N.S.* (New York, Routledge, 1992).

16. Pedro de Alba, *Sieto articulos sobre el problema de los braceros* (México D.F.: Autor edition, 1954.

17. Durand, *Más allá de la línea*.

18. Calavita, *Inside the State*.

19. Manuel García y Griego, "The Bracero Program," in *Migration between México and the United Status: A Binational Study,* Mexican–United States Binational Commission, 3:1215–22 (Austin, Tex.: Morgan Printing, 1998).

20. Douglas Massey, Jorge Durand, and Nolan Malone, *Beyond Smoke and Mirrors: Mexican Immigration in an Era of Economic Integration* (New York: Russell Sage Foundation, 2002).

21. Immigration Reform and Control Act, also known as Simpson-Rodino.

22. Massey, Durand, and Malone, *Beyond Smoke and Mirrors.*

23. Javier Valenzuela, "El programa Beta: La protección de los derechos humanos de los migrantes indocumentados desde la perspectiva policiaca, no convencional," in *Migración y fronteras,* ed. Manuel Angel Castillo, Alfredo Lattes, and Jorge Santibáñez, 479–509 (Mexico City: Plaza y Valdés, 2000).

24. *La Jornada,* September 18, 2002, 5.

25. *La Opinión,* January 15, 2003, 7.

26. Rodolfo García Zamora, "Los Proyectos Productivos con migrantes en México hoy," presented at the second conference on international Mexican–Californian migrations, University of California, Berkeley, March 28–30, 2002.

27. Ibid.

28. Leticia Calderón Chelius and Jesús Martínez Saldaña, *La dimensión política de la migración mexicana* (Mexico D.F.: Instituto Mora, 2002).

29. Peter Andreas, *Border Games: Policing the US-México Divide* (Ithaca, N.Y., Cornell University Press, 2000).

30. Rafael Fernández de Castro, "The Riverside Incident," in *Migration between México and the United Status,* 3:1235–40.

31. Internal documents of the Ministry of Foreign Relations, 2000, available at http://www.sre.gob.mx/eventos/fenomenomigratorio/docmigratorio.htm (accessed May 6, 2006).

32. See http://www.immigrationforum.org (accessed May 20, 2000).

33. Internal documents of the Ministry of Foreign Relations, 2000.

34. *Réforme,* January 15, 2003, 5.

PART V

NAMING EMIGRANTS

12

THE "OVERSEAS CHINESE":
THE STATE AND EMIGRATION FROM THE 1890S
THROUGH THE 1990S

Carine Pina-Guerassimoff and Eric Guerassimoff

Translated from the French by Amy Jacobs

Emigration was long prohibited in China. Up until the mid-nineteenth century, the attitudes of successive Chinese governments toward emigration corresponded to their attitudes on maritime trade with foreign countries. Before the advent of the Ming in 1368, there were no severe restrictions; this dynasty, more autocratic than previous ones, prohibited all private maritime trade until 1567. A century later, the new Qing dynasty (1644–1911) proved as mistrustful of emigration as its predecessors once had been and forbade all visits overseas. Chinese living abroad were considered traitors, rebels, or conspirators. In the early nineteenth century, important changes began to develop in relations between China and the European colonial powers pressing on its gates from positions in Southeast Asia, where the Europeans were changing the political economy of the region in ways that affected both the Chinese government and emigrants from the Chinese empire, most of whom were settled in those areas. Over the second half of the century, Chinese emigration attained numbers incomparable to those for the preceding periods, and the process was now being organized under pressure from the foreign powers. It was at this time that a weakened, impoverished China, anxious to defend its sovereignty, came to discover the "Overseas Chinese." At the close of its reign, the Qing dynasty began to formalize its institutional, administrative, and legal relation to emigrants. During the first republic (1911–1949), this interest in emigration manifested in the last years of the empire was continued and expanded. Later, in 1978, the Communist regime re-established contact with Chinese groups living outside mainland China, with the aim of integrating "Overseas Chinese" into its ambitious economic modernization program. It began encouraging and facilitating "returns" and became increasingly tolerant of "departures," turning its back on more than two decades of closed-border policy.

Until the mid-nineteenth century, Chinese living in foreign lands were legally defined as criminals, and the Imperial Court cared little what became of them. In response to the 1740 massacre of the Chinese of Batavia, the Emperor Qianlong (1736–1796) had this comment: "Those people are deserters of the celestial empire, they deserted their ancestral tombs and sought benefits overseas, and the court is not interested in them."[1] Western imperialism would force China to abandon laws prohibiting emigration and lead it to adopt measures for protecting expatriates, measures derived from international law based on a conception of the state as nation.

Coolies and Contracts: The Necessary Recognition of Emigration

China's defeat in the first opium war (1839–1842) opened the Middle Empire's gates to European merchants. In a few years, trade in emigrants along the country's southern coasts became a highly lucrative activity, dominated by Westerners. From 1844 to 1859, vast numbers of Chinese coolies were transported to the "sugar islands" of the West Indies, Indian Ocean, and Southeast Asian colonies to satisfy the pressing need for cheap plantation labor. The first contingent, destined for the Bourbon Islands, left the port of Amoy (Xiamen) in 1844 on a French ship; in 1847, Cuba received Chinese coolies who had left from the Philippines, and after 1850 they continued to arrive from Amoy, Swatow (Shantu), and Macao.

Local Chinese authorities at first closed their eyes to the abuses resulting from this activity. As in the past, departures were tolerated, since they relieved the southern provinces of undesirable elements and helped ease the demographic surplus. Traffickers in migrants bought state functionaries' acceptance and accommodation. Chinese reluctance to intervene may also be explained by the fear of provoking a new conflict with the British. A series of resounding incidents (revolts in embarkation ports, mutinies, xenophobic attacks), along with pressure from Great Britain and France, ultimately forced the Chinese authorities to take charge of emigration.

Britain and France used the conventions signed in Peking at the conclusion of a new opium war (1856–1860) to force acceptance of emigration freedom for Chinese subjects (Article 5 of the Sino-English treaty, Article 9 of the Sino-French). The texts provided for joint drafting of regulations "to protect Chinese who emigrate this way, depending on the situation in the various open ports."[2] For the Chinese government, this soon meant restricting freedom to emigrate to persons who had obtained a work contract. The legal framework for such contracts was drawn up in the following years. In 1866, the government submitted a set of provisions, the "Peking Regulations," fixing conditions for recruitment, passage, employment, and other particulars of coolie contracts. For the first time, the question of protecting emigrants in the workplace was raised. Since there were no Chinese consulates, this task was delegated to foreign diplomats. Neither France nor Great Britain ever ratified these rules, but the texts nonetheless became the reference for emigration in the Middle Empire.

From then on, coolies could lodge complaints of mistreatment and contract violation with the Chinese authorities, which led the state itself to undertake expatriate worker protection rather than leaving it to Western intermediaries. China sent task forces to Cuba (February-May 1874) and Peru (September-October 1874) to investigate the situation of Chinese coolies; shortly thereafter, the Imperial Court negotiated emigration treaties with Spain and Peru that stipulated the creation of consulates designed to protect Chinese laborers.[3] Emigration became one point on which China demanded application of a principle of equality and reciprocity in its relations with Western powers.

Already forced to acknowledge departures, regulate procedures, and ensure protection for its subjects abroad, the Chinese government found itself confronted with a new task in the late 1870s: defending the right to emigrate provided for in the treaties. The Treaty of Burlingame, signed with the United States in 1868, had stipulated freedom to emigrate for Chinese subjects, but in November 1880 the U.S. government, under pressure from certain interests in the Pacific states, imposed a second treaty that allowed for restricting Chinese immigration. The Chinese Exclusion Act of 1882 was a direct consequence of this, and it in turn paved the way for a series of texts that were increasingly unfavorable to Chinese immigration. Discriminatory policies of this sort, implemented in the last quarter of the nineteenth century by Canada, Australia, and New Zealand, as well as the United States, had a twofold impact on the Chinese government: while gradually making emigration problems a national preoccupation (leading, in the imperial age, to the anti-American boycott movements of 1905),[4] they considerably increased Chinese diplomats' knowledge of Chinese communities abroad and radically changed the official attitude toward Chinese expatriates.

Merchants and Mandarins: Implicating Emigrants in the Modernization of the Empire

The career of Huang Zunxian (1848–1905) clearly illustrates the above developments. Poet, reformer, and diplomat, Huang was born in Jiaying zhou, Guangdong province.[5] After debuting a promising career in Japan in 1877, he was named consul general to San Francisco a few weeks before the Exclusion Act vote. This put him in contact with Chinese expatriates and led him to discover both the suffering endured by the coolies and the volume of money and material flowing from them back to China. Alongside the laborers and surely due to exploitation of their labor, a class of wealthy, educated Chinese emigrant merchants had developed. In examining bank account records, Huang observed that the sums emigrants sent back to Guangdong every year ranged between 10 and 16 million taels. Total remittances sent to China over a four-year period from San Francisco alone were evaluated at 11 million taels. Huang estimated that if Chinese emigrants living in Cuba, Peru, Annam, Singapore, and the South Seas were taken into account, the sum could reasonably be multiplied several times. The amount spent by China every year in trade with foreign countries was thus below what it was receiving from Chinese settled outside the country.[6] Huang devoted the next phase of his diplomatic career to convincing expatriate merchants to contribute to China's economic development, and persuading the Chinese government to abandon any measures that would hinder emigrants' return. He soon became consul general in the English colony of Singapore, a good position from which to win over his superiors and a segment of his newly wealthy compatriots to his views. In September 1893, after receiving a report Huang had commissioned, the imperial court issued a decree abolishing all remaining laws punishing either (voluntary) emigration or return. Huang is credited with penning the expression *huaqiao,* "Chinese person temporarily residing abroad," generally translated as "Overseas Chinese."[7]

In the 1880s, the idea of involving emigrants in the reform and modernization process by making use of their financial abilities and familiarity with Western technology took hold in the minds of a number of diplomats stationed abroad and high-level civil servants in China. It was not until the beginning of the twentieth century, however, that China developed a general policy aimed expressly at enabling the empire to profit from emigrant resources. The initiator of the project was a rich emigrant merchant, Zhang Bishi (1840–1908, often designated as Thio Thiau Siat). Zhang was finally granted an audience with the dowager empress Cixi (1812–1908) in 1904, shortly after the Coalition Powers had crushed the Boxer Rebellion. The imperiled imperial power launched a new reform movement and invited Overseas Chinese to contribute to the effort. Zhang, whose participation was requested, proposed two sets of measures for mobilizing his compatriots abroad.[8]

The first was to create a situation favorable to emigrants in China. For Zhang this meant granting Chinese merchants in the South Seas the same advantages and privileges enjoyed by their foreign counterparts. The prerequisite for this was better protection for returning emigrants, who continued to be victimized by unscrupulous state functionaries. In 1904 and again in 1905, imperial edicts were issued, recalling that since 1893 it had been the officials' duty to guarantee the security of all goods and persons re-entering the country. In addition to stronger protection, returning emigrants were also offered incentives such as tax privileges and rewards. The second set of measures the Qing government adopted in the first years of the twentieth century intensified state activity among Chinese communities overseas: "special" task forces were regularly sent abroad to collect funds for various purposes, and Chinese chambers of commerce were established and linked to existing networks of "sister" institutions in China.

By the turn of the twentieth century, China had come to recognize, protect, and value the Overseas Chinese, particularly the wealthiest among them. Use of the term "huaqiao" spread and became dominant in official discourse in China. However, governments of receiving countries and the emigrants themselves did not immediately accept the political and cultural allegiance to China, understood to be a "natural" attribute of the huaqiao.

Chinese Nationality Law:
A Consequence of the Emigration Question

In nineteenth-century imperial China there were no official texts pertaining to Chinese nationality.[9] All persons born of a Chinese father and living on Chinese territory were considered Chinese subjects. When emigrants began returning, China was confronted with the issue of double nationality, as emigrants demanded privileged "foreigner" status and could have recourse, if necessary, to the protection of Western consulates, whereas China still considered them its subjects.

China adopted the 1909 law on nationality for several reasons; the main ones are related to emigration and China's demand to be granted legation rights as recognition of its equality with other nations.[10] The Dutch were opposed to the opening of Chinese consulates in their Asian colonies, affirming on the contrary that Chinese living there were Dutch subjects. For its part, China had no legislation with which to resolve the nationality question. The Chinese authorities did not react until 1907, when the Netherlands extended the benefit of jus soli to inhabitants of its colonies. The Chinese community of Java sent a petition to the Chinese government demanding that it oppose this principle.[11]

The law of 1909, comprising twenty-four articles and a series of special provisions, was drawn up in response to these demands. To "keep the Chinese from falling under foreign domination," the first article laid down the principle of jus sanguinis as the sole valid criterion for automatic possession of Chinese nationality. China recognized as Chinese "all children born to a Chinese father, children of a dead Chinese father, children of a Chinese mother and a father unknown or dead,"[12] regardless of place of birth. Emigrants' Chinese nationality was officially recognized upon their expressing that wish. Possessing another nationality did not preclude or annul Chinese nationality. However, China refused to acknowledge a Chinese subject's foreigner status on its own territory unless the person in question had officially requested to give up his or her Chinese nationality (article 11). Chinese nationality could only be "lost" under certain conditions, and loss implied being stripped of internal rights, namely property rights (article 8, special provision). With this historic text, the Qing government instituted a nationality policy holding that China granted Chinese nationality to all Chinese emigrants, regardless of whether they possessed another nationality. This point became a major source of conflict.

Credit for fully recognizing emigrants and using them in the service of the country—that is, developing an emigration policy—goes to the Manchu government. Overseas Chinese had become assets for the declining empire. Still, because the most dynamic component of the Chinese bourgeoisie overseas had worked in China, these people soon became aware of the incompetence and corruption of the state functionaries with which they were now obliged to have regular dealings. Emigrants quickly became convinced that China had to be reformed in its entirety and came around to supporting the revolutionary opposition, facilitating the fall of the Qing and the imperial regime. In contributing to the rise of the Republic, the Overseas Chinese were propelled to center stage.

Interest in the huaqiao, which only increased after the revolution of 1911, seems due in large part to the ideas and personality of the main republican leader, Sun Yat-Sen (Sun Yixian, 1866–1925). Born near Canton, Sun was sent at age thirteen to join his older brother in Honolulu, where family members had emigrated. On Hawaiian school benches, Sun Yat-Sen discovered democratic, republican, and Christian ideas. In 1895, he turned to activism, founding a secret society whose goal was to topple the Manchu dynasty. The repeated failure of insurrections fomented in China forced him into exile. Like reformist opponents, he took refuge among emigrants and came to appreciate the financial assistance that the richest among them could be relied upon to provide. The funds collected among these Chinese helped finance the insurrections between 1905 and 1911 that ultimately led to the downfall of the Qing dynasty. Support from expatriate communities had been so important that Sun Yat-Sen collectively dubbed the huaqiao "mother of the revolution" (*geming zhi mu*).

Sun very quickly implicated emigrants in development of the new Republic of China. Chinese emigrants helped draft the Constitutional Law, promulgated August 10, 1912. A special electoral college representing Chinese expatriate communities elected six overseas senators. This arrangement remained in place after Sun Yat-Sen was replaced by Yuan Shikai (1857–1916), the first elected president of the Republic. Meanwhile, administrative machinery was put in place to implement legislation for Chinese workers abroad, repatriate them, and handle their investments and their children's education. However, the simultaneous, competing measures in this direction undertaken by the governments of northern and southern China were rendered inoperative in 1916 by the civil war.

The reunified government set up in Nanking in 1927 after the victory of the *Guomindang* (Nationalist Party) established a coherent policy for Overseas Chinese. An Emigrant Affairs Bureau (*Qiaowuju*) was created in Shanghai. Renamed the Overseas Chinese Affairs Commission (*Qiaowu weiyuanhui*), this agency became a full-fledged ministry in 1932. Its organization and functions were defined in the organic law of December 7, 1931. The nationalist government worked harder than previous Chinese authorities to integrate and "acculturate" returned emigrants. The imperial measures of 1909 were reapplied and extended, and in 1929 a new Nationality Law was promulgated (still in effect in Taiwan).[13]

Nanking's emigration policy was part of a wider-ranging project aimed at consolidating the power of the Nationalist Party and its "supreme head," Chiang Kai-Shek (Jiang Jieshi, 1886–1975). The administrative agencies had their counterpart in the Guomindang apparatus known as Section No. 3 (renamed the Overseas Work Committee in 1972). The point was to persuade Chinese emigrant associations to help spread Nationalist Party influence. Numerous branches of the Guomindang became active abroad. After the war, Overseas Chinese communities became the theater for clashes between partisans of the Guomindang and the Chinese Communist Party.

From 1931 to 1948, the nationalist government issued a great number of laws and decrees concerning the education of Chinese abroad, their investments, their movement from one place to another, and the associations to which they could belong. By 1937, there were more than two thousand schools for Overseas Chinese—busy strengthening the emigrants' cultural, emotional, and even legal attachment to their country of origin. The educational programs, developed in China, stressed the ills of imperialism (and its manifestations and effects within the country) and called for a nationalist awakening. They also incited immigrants to revolt against continuing discriminatory measures against them. Overseas Chinese nationalism was further fueled by the wounds inflicted by the Japanese between 1928 and 1938, when Chinese territory was annexed. Emigrants became enthusiastic participants in patriotic activities, either joining up directly to fight against Japan (China officially declared war in July 1937) or massively joining the political organizations set up in expatriate communities. The war also reinforced Nanking's tendency to maintain emigrants in a colonial-type relation of subordination that Overseas Chinese at times found difficult to bear.[14]

"Internal Overseas Chinese": Asset or Obstacle for the New Democracy?

The new People's Republic of China (PRC) announced that it would protect its emigrant nationals and, to ease relations with Southeast Asian governments, it abandoned the formerly aggressive position toward emigrant communities there. However, it soon prohibited further departures. From 1950 to 1966, government policy was focused on returning emigrants and relatives of emigrants within China. This period was comprised of three phases. From 1949 to 1953, the Communist Party continued to allow political representation of Overseas Chinese with the main political institutions (the Standing Party Committee, the National People's Congress) and kept operative the commissions for Overseas Chinese affairs that had been created in the main emigration provinces (Fujian and Guangdong). At first, the point was to reassure emigrant groups and inhabitants with links to migrants, so as to keep remittance channels open. The funds coming in, which often constituted receiving families' main income, were a non-negligible source of hard currency for the government. The various political organs worked to adapt political, economic, and social reforms (such as the agrarian reform, collectivization of business, and re-education) to the specific needs of families of Overseas Chinese. Their real estate was not to be confiscated; business investment was permitted to continue; they were not required to do manual labor. But policy specifications became distorted in the process of implementation. In 1953, provincial Overseas Chinese affairs bureaus signaled excessive property confiscation and too many cases of returned emigrants and their relatives being abusively categorized as "rich peasants."

The beginning of the second period (1954–1958) was marked by a concern to correct these errors, but this plan was undermined by the imperative of implementing socialist reform. In the last period (1958–1966), social reform was intensified to the detriment of returning Chinese and relatives of Overseas Chinese, who now were called upon to do manual labor, develop a more collective spirit, abandon all religious beliefs and superstitions, and adopt a less ostentatious lifestyle. When the radical tendencies that would lead to the Cultural Revolution began to be asserted within the Communist Party, the "ideological" contradiction inherent in party policy with regard to Overseas Chinese could no longer be contained; and during the Cultural Revolution, Overseas Chinese were a select target for ideological criticism. Qualified as "bourgeois capitalists," they and their relatives were forbidden to have ties with the world outside China, including financial ones. The radical changes and turbulence of the Cultural Revolution likewise affected foreign policy with regard to Overseas Chinese. Certain political groups would have liked to use Chinese emigrants to export the revolution. Meanwhile, incidents involving Overseas Chinese broke out in several Southeast Asian countries, events which strengthened the antagonism and mistrust of the majority populations and their governments toward the Chinese communities in their midst. And for many such communities, events in China were a major reason for breaking with the mainland. From that point it was necessary for the Chinese government to establish a more appropriate policy toward them. In the late 1970s, this need became imperative: the government, now led by Deng Xiaoping, wished once again to implicate Overseas Chinese and their descendants in economic reforms.

The PRC now divided migration policy into policy for bringing emigrants back to China (calling on Overseas Chinese to help in economic modernization) and policy for departure (developing new Chinese emigrant communities).

Appealing to Overseas Chinese for Help with Modernization

A preliminary meeting of the Overseas Chinese Commission in December 1977 revealed the will to use Overseas Chinese in the economic modernization of the country: "Developing services to handle Chinese nationals, receiving them among us and enabling Chinese families and nationals and repatriated nationals to express their socialist fervor—all this is important for the realization of our goal to modernize industry, agriculture, national defense, science and technology."[15]

In 1978, after the third session of the Eleventh Congress of the Chinese Communist Party, the call to Overseas Chinese to invest in China grew both more pressing and more pragmatic. The point now was to "bring in capital, intellectual resources, equipment, science and technology from abroad" by means of the Overseas Chinese.[16] Investment from that source was permitted in the same sectors as foreign investment: high technology industries, wholesale distribution, real estate and financial services, and infrastructure. The plan was also for Overseas Chinese to help develop foreign trade. In 1978, Deng Xiaoping named Rong Yiren, leading member of a venerable Shanghai family that had emigrated to Hong Kong in 1949, to head the China International Trust and Investment Corporation (CITIC). If the country was to benefit from Overseas Chinese financial and technological know-how, the authorities had to adopt a specific policy with regard to this group and their descendants. Two sets of measures were devised.

The first allowed for political rehabilitation of Overseas Chinese and their relatives. This gesture was integrated into the general critique of Cultural Revolution-period policy. In November 1977, the Preparatory Meeting of the Overseas Chinese Affairs Commission officially condemned the previous leaders' attitude, together with the persecution endured by descendants of emigrants and their relatives during this period. After acknowledging and denouncing the errors of the past, the Commission declared that the injustices would be repaired.

The policy proposed by the Commission was diametrically opposed to the one used during the Cultural Revolution and was designed to show the error of qualifying emigrants as "bourgeois capitalists." In effect, after 1978, the principle of the class struggle as the driving force of society gave way to that of economic modernization, and this worked to efface any social connotation of the political definition of Chinese emigrants. Today that definition is strictly socio-occupational and pertains to the notion of entrepreneurship.[17] Though emigrants are still depicted as attached to the continent, the ties are no longer political, but cultural.

The second set of policy measures involved restructuring the various institutions that had been dissolved or abandoned during the Cultural Revolution. In January 1978, the leaders instituted the Overseas Chinese Affairs Bureau (*Qiaowu bangongshi*) as part of the State Affairs Council (*Guowu Yuan*), an executive body. This institution at first coexisted with the Overseas Chinese Affairs Commission (*Qiaowu weiyuan hui*)—then, a year later, replaced it. The bureau set up and implemented general work plans and policies for Overseas Chinese; it also handled protection of their rights and interests, as well as those of their relatives in China.[18] It was responsible for the education of returned Overseas Chinese and controlled all press material directed toward Overseas Chinese. Twenty-nine provinces were represented in the bureau, and it was present at both district and autonomous municipality levels.[19] On June 7, 1983, the People's Congress created an Overseas Chinese Committee (*Quanguo renmin daibiaodahui huaqiao weiyuanhui*), in charge of legal questions such as internal protection of returned emigrants' rights. Moreover, the new leaders maintained the Committee for Overseas Chinese of the Chinese People's Political Consultative Conference (*Quangguo shengxie Huaqiao weiyuanhui*) created in 1949, which handled specifically political questions, such as representation for returning emigrants.

Organizations created for Overseas Chinese outside the state apparatus supported the work of the official institutions. In December 1979, the National Federation of Returned Overseas Chinese was re-established to ensure that government policies were implemented correctly. Its purpose was "to develop external economic activities in cooperation with the relevant departments; bring in capital, intellectual resources, equipment, science and technology from abroad; and create a large number of joint ventures of various types with Overseas Chinese and compatriots in Hong Kong and Macao."[20] In 1990, the National Federation was bolstered by the creation of the Chinese National Association for Overseas Exchanges.

Once the Overseas Chinese had been politically and institutionally rehabilitated, they benefited from an economic and social framework well adapted to their needs and interests. The Chinese government chose to emphasize and facilitate spontaneous economic action by Overseas Chinese and their descendants (remittances, donations), and to this end it liberalized family and cultural contacts between emigrants and their relatives in China. During the "ten black years" of the Cultural Revolution, letters and visits to or from the mainland had been condemned and prohibited. They now came to be considered a right of returning Overseas Chinese and relatives of emigrants.[21]

As early as the third session of the Eleventh Congress of the Communist Party in December 1978, the government adopted a more flexible policy with regard to traditional cultural manifestations and religious practices. The emigrants quickly relayed this movement. The major clans began pressing local governments to speed liberalization of practices. In 1979, the International Association of the Guan Clan and the International Longgan Association, representing families from Guangdong, requested permission from the local government to re-establish institutions specific to their clans on Chinese territory. The request was accepted in 1984, and since then the central authorities have encouraged this type of meetings and ceremonies.

The government liberalized family relations to facilitate a quantitative increase in spontaneous economic flows. In the late 1970s the authorities provided direct incentives for sending money, goods, and donations back to China. Money sent back could now be used not only to purchase real estate but also for private economic activities, the authorities' purpose being to foster informal economic cooperation between continental Chinese and the diaspora.

Emigrants' spontaneous economic action has always taken the form of donations to a clan, a village, or a province as a whole. Donations are most often used for investment in infrastructure (roads, bridges), social projects (hospitals and temples), and education. The State Affairs Council published the first official text on gifts from emigrants on September 14, 1979. Current policy grants broad freedom in choosing and managing such projects. The authorities' aim is to reinforce the traditional practices of the Overseas Chinese, eliciting stronger financial and technological commitments from them for improving the economic and social environment in the main development zones in which they are invited to invest.

Since 1978, most legislation on Overseas Chinese investment has been incorporated into legal texts for foreign investment in general. While this measure is fully understandable today because many businesses belonging to people of Chinese descent are legally foreign, it also concerns residents of Taiwan and Hong Kong, and apparently emigrant nationals from the PRC as well. The legislation applies in the designated geographic investment zones and covers modes and time schedules for creating businesses (joint, cooperative, and foreign ventures), relevant business sectors, and tax exemptions. The state's commitment to foreigners not to nationalize investments also applies for Overseas Chinese.[22] These centrally determined regulations are generally completed and made fully operative by local legislation and measures.

Establishing New Overseas Chinese

In the second section of migratory policy, the Chinese government made it easier for nationals to leave while trying to monitor how they used that right. However, it was unable to stop illegal departures.

The first major wave of departures from the PRC began in the late 1970s and early 1980s. This particular "emigré" population was made up essentially of students with state scholarships, since the State Affairs Council had legislated to make state funding for study abroad available to all nationals. In 1984, the number of departures began a continuous rise. Whereas in 1989 the number of self-supported Chinese students studying abroad (*zifei*) was estimated at 18,000, in 1999 it had reached almost 270,000.

The second category of emigrants regulated by the PRC was composed of businessmen, entrepreneurs, workers, officials, and ordinary people wishing to see their families or the world. In 1986, the standing committee of the National People's Congress adopted a law on conditions for entering and exiting Chinese territory for private reasons.[23] In 1999, and again in March 2000, the government further simplified departure procedures for Chinese nationals. Today, anyone who can produce a letter of invitation and identification papers from either a sponsor or a foreign company making a job offer can apply for a passport. While it is still harder to obtain a passport in China than in Western countries, the government has considerably liberalized conditions for leaving the country. The fact that receiving countries continue to impose strict visa requirements made it easier for China to liberalize.

The third category of emigrants is made up of contract workers and job interns, who are present today in both the public and private spheres. Here, China has adopted the equivalent of its 1970s Korean and Philippino policies. This type of emigration has been integrated into current "official" PRC policy, the major goal of which is to reduce unemployment. The last major acceptable motive for leaving China is family reunification, and the government will allow this in some cases—even in the case of prior clandestine migration by a family member.

Since the late 1980s, the authorities have more systematically made available to would-be emigrant nationals information concerning immigration law in the main receiving countries, changes in their immigration policies, visa requirements, immigrant quotas, and conditions for receiving students and workers. In 2002, China agreed to collaborate with the International Migration Organization, particularly in organizing information campaigns on the problems and dangers of illegal emigration.

In the 1980s in China, it was difficult to envision mainland emigration occurring without real government control.[24] Yet the Chinese leaders were not much preoccupied by the first departures, even if they were generally illegal. But certain dramatic incidents, such as the February 1993 shipwreck of the *Golden River* in New York City harbor and the tragic accident at Dover in 2000, drew international attention, and such events are occurring more frequently. Most illegal emigrants come from the provinces of Fujian, Guangdong, and Zhejiang. Having failed to obtain official permission or foreign visas, they turn to professional traffickers for either part or all of the journey. Would-be emigrants pay between $25,000 and $38,000 for transportation and entry into the United States or Japan; for Europe, the price is between $13,700 and $22,900.

States confronted with illegal Chinese immigration have formally complained to the Chinese government. Some European governments did so in June 2003. For its part, China refuses to take full responsibility for the phenomenon: "Illegal emigration is an international problem. China is not the only country to experience it; other states are faced with the problem. ... The Chinese government hopes therefore to obtain cooperation from the other states and territories [i.e., Taiwan] in order to resolve the problem quickly."[25]

Ambiguous Ties among State, Nation, and Emigrants

In 1978, Chinese leaders officially distinguished four categories of Overseas Chinese, still used today (though their contents have changed somewhat). The first consists of "compatriots" (*Tongbao*) in Taiwan, Hong Kong (until 1997), and Macao (until 1999). The second may be called "internal" Overseas Chinese and is divided into *Gyiqiao*, or returned Chinese emigrants, and *Qiaojuan,* persons living in China with family ties to emigrants permanently settled abroad. The fourth category consists of all diaspora Chinese, in turn differentiated by Beijing in 1980 into *Huaqiao,* or PRC nationals, and *Huayi,* foreign nationals of Chinese origin. The legal-administrative term for Chinese nationality—*guoji,* "belonging to the state"—is quite restrictive, and stands in contrast to a broader, more subjective term *minzu,* "belonging to the nation." The latter conception has recently come to dominate in emigration policy.

A Restrictive Legal and Political Definition of Chinese Nationals

The main effect of the legal definition adopted by the PRC was to limit the number of persons abroad eligible for diplomatic protection and Chinese political rights. The fundamental principle of the Nationality Law of 1980 was nonrecognition of double nationality (article 3).[26] To determine who possessed Chinese nationality automatically, the text's authors combined the principles of jus soli and jus sanguinis. Significantly, the text uses the expression "possess Chinese nationality" rather than "is Chinese." As suggested, there are several expressions for "nationality." *Minzu,* used to form the expression "nationalism" (*minzu zhuyi*), denotes membership in an ethnic group. The majority Han ethnic groups and other such groups constitute the different "nationalities" of the "multinational" state: *duo minzu de guojia. Guoji,* the word used in the nationality law, refers to legal membership in a state. A Chinese citizen (*gongmin*) possesses Chinese nationality (*guoji*) while being of Han, Hui, or other nationality (*minzu*). Article 2 of the Nationality Law may be translated in this way: "The People's Republic of China is a united multinational country. Whosoever is a member of one of its nationalities (*minzu*) possesses Chinese nationality (*guoji*)."

The code indicates two ways of losing Chinese nationality. As was the case earlier, those wishing to renounce their Chinese nationality to acquire a foreign one must make an official request to the Ministry of Public Security. Article 10 cites residence abroad as a legitimate reason for this request. Article 9 decrees that Chinese citizens residing abroad who have willingly been naturalized or otherwise acquired foreign nationality automatically lose their Chinese nationality. The 1980 law was established both to reassure receiving states and satisfy a vast number of Overseas Chinese, either long-term emigrants or descendants of emigrants. The loosening of legal ties has gone together with a loosening of political ones, including for new Chinese emigrants.

Another manifestation of the will to efface political ties between China and Overseas Chinese is the abandoning of any political representation for emigrants. In contrast to the first years of the regime, Overseas Chinese no longer participate in Chinese political life. The constitutional texts of the National People's Congress (the Constitution and the organic law) and the Chinese People's Political Consultative Conference no longer provide for political representation for Chinese expatriates. In 1978, it was still possible to think of emigrants as participants in the political life of the People's Republic of China.[27] Article 34 of a 1982 law making political rights contingent on residency eliminated that possibility. However, the decrease in the number of nationals recognized and represented in the PRC does not mean that the government has ceased to be interested in its emigrants. On the contrary, that interest has been extended more fully than ever to all diaspora Chinese.

A Cultural Definition of the Link between Chinese Emigrants and China

The current definition of the ties uniting diaspora Chinese to the mainland, based on a cultural conception of those ties, is largely effected through local-level policies and action.

The official texts on Overseas Chinese confirm what the leaders declared in 1978: "By taking another nationality, a national ceases to be a Chinese citizen, but nonetheless remains our relative and friend."[28] As Wang Gungwu showed in 1979, it is not the essential aim of this rhetoric to establish distinctions among overseas Chinese, but to designate them all "Overseas Chinese" and declare that they are all part of the Chinese nation.[29]

While official Chinese discourse has grown considerably more tolerant since 1978, so the idea of transnational ties based on culture and even ethnic group is now very favorably received. In 1994, Xiang Daoyou, member of the Overseas Chinese Affairs Commission of Guangxi, declared: "The Chinese mainland is the ethnic foundation of the Asian Chinese. China's descendants, descendants of Yan and Huang, whether inside or outside the country, have the same nationality, the same blood ties, the same language, and an identical culture consisting in similar feelings/emotions."[30]

For his part, Sun Xingcheng of the Overseas Chinese Affairs Office, part of the State Affairs Council, took up the metaphor first used by Prime Minister Zhou Enlai: the ties between China and Asian Chinese are like the relations between mother and daughter: though the daughter belongs to her husband (a foreign country), she nonetheless remains attached to her mother (China).[31]

The regions of Fujian, Guangdong, Zhejiang, and Hainan, from where most Overseas Chinese left, have made considerable efforts to develop institutions and activities capable of attracting people of Chinese origin. The same institutions present at the central level have been established at provincial administrative echelons all the way down to the canton. In turn, local associations based on shared canton and/or clan membership (*Qiaoxiang hui*) support these agencies, and the two types of institutions work closely together.

A main policy concern of local government institutions, seconded by the associations, is to establish and maintain links with highly reputable Overseas Chinese and to set up active networks. Many such persons have been solicited to become honorary presidents of local associations, and they are regularly contacted by delegations sent abroad, which then arrange protracted visits for them in their home cantons where they are solemnly and lavishly received. The festivities are organized around three traditional holidays or types of holiday (Chinese New Year, the PRC national holiday on October 1, local festivals such as the Putian lychee festival) or around sports or cultural themes. In 1995, the Qiaoxiang associations of Fujian received more than seventy thousand visitors, including five hundred major delegations, among them the General Clan Association for people originating from Jinjiang in the Philippines.

Finally, Qiaoxiang associations and local political authorities have been working together in the last few years to further internationalize local clan association meetings. In 1994, Guangdong provincial authorities organized world conferences of the Mei clan, the Panyu, and the twelfth world conference of the Hakka. For the Chinese authorities, a policy in which priority is given to informal ties based on clan and/or local membership means it can circumvent direct dealings with receiving countries. The classic definition of the link between the state and its emigrants (in terms of nationality/citizenship) has thus given way to a broader definition, based on cultural (i.e., clan) allegiance, confined to a portion of the national territory, the Qiaoxiang. Today it is primarily around the notion of emigrants' canton of origin that relations between the Chinese state and its emigrants and their descendants are conceived and organized.

○ ○ ○

The interest in emigrants manifested by the Chinese authorities since the mid-nineteenth century has given rise to several definitions of the ties existing between China and Overseas Chinese. These ties as variously defined have in turn been activated through different measures. State attention to the phenomenon, at times considerable, but often minimal, has ultimately produced a utilitarian, virtually instrumentalist vision of the state–emigrant relation. Chinese governments have regularly perceived emigrants and their descendants as a means of furthering and strengthening economic modernization in the country, bolstering political change, and supporting war efforts or revolutionary aims. Today, PRC authorities are working to implicate emigrants in their vast economic modernization plans. Studying how the state has conceived of emigration leads logically to evaluating the impact of government measures on the people they concern most: Overseas Chinese. Reflection on this matter is particularly relevant now, when immigration states and regional organizations such as the European Union are officially turning to emigration states for assistance in managing international migration flows.

NOTES

1. Yen, Ch'ing Hwang, "Ch'ing Changing Images of the Overseas Chineses, 1644–1912," *Modern Asian Studies* 15 (1981): 97.

2. "Convention of Peace and Friendship between Great Britain and China, Signed in Peking, 24th October 1860," in *Treaties and Conventions between Great Britain and China; and between China and Foreign Powers; and Orders in Council, Rules, Regulations, Acts of Parliament, Decrees, &c affecting British Interests in China,* 2 vol., ed. Godfrey E. P. Hertslet, 48–53, 50 (London: Harrison and Sons, 1908).

3. *Chinese Emigration, the Cuba Commission: Papers Relating to the Commission Sent by China to Ascertain the Condition of Chinese Coolies in Cuba, 1874* (Shanghai: The Imperial Maritime Customs Press, 1878).

4. There is a vast literature on the subject. See, for example, Charles A. Price, *Restrictive Immigration to North America and Australasia, 1836–1888* (Canberra: ANU Press, 1974).

5. For a brief overview of Huang's career, see A. W. Hummel, *Eminent Chinese of the Ch'ing Period, 1644–1912* (1943; repr. Taipei: Ch'eng Wen Publishing Company, 1972), 350–51. For greater detail, see the first part of Geneviève Barman's "L'expérience occidentale et l'évolution intellectuelle d'un lettré chinois: Huang Tsun-hsien (1848–1905)," doc. diss. (3rd cycle), École des Hautes Etudes en Sciences Sociales, 1979, 1–105.

6. On other aspects of his California period, see Noriko Kamashi, "American Influences on Chinese Reform Thought: Huang Tsun-hsien in California, 1882–1885," *Pacific Historical Review* 47 (May 1978): 239–60.

7. Wang Gungwu, "A Note on the Origins of Hua-ch'iao," in *Community and*

Nation: Essays on Southeast Asia and the Chinese, ed. Anthony Reid, 118–28 (Sydney: George Allen & Unwin, 1981).

8. See also, Michael R. Godley's classic text based on the figure of Zhang Bishi: *The Mandarin-Capitalists from the Nanyang: Overseas Chinese Enterprise in the Modernization of China, 1893–1911* (Cambridge University Press: 1981).

9. The only legislation concerning nationality during the Qing dynasty concerns the marriage of "Bannières" girls, that is, women belonging to certain noble classes of the Manchou. Their marriage with Chinese (Han) men meant exclusion from the Bannières group. Chu Kuing Chang, "Essai sur la nationalité chinoise," doc. diss. (law) (Paris: Université de Paris, Faculté de droit et des sciences économiques, 1941), 49.

10. Chutung Tsai, "The Chinese Nationality Law, 1909," *The American Journal of International Law* 4 (1910): 404–11.

11. Chiu Hungdah, "Nationality and International Law in Chinese Perspectives," *Chinese Yearbook of International Law and Affairs* 9 (1990): 29–65, 31.

12. "Loi chinoise sur la Nationalité, 1909," *Revue Indochinoise* 11 (August 1909): 812–18, esp. 813 and 814.

13. "Loi du 5 février 1929," *Répertoire de droit international* 9 (1931): 588–89. The 1929 law introduced the principle of equality between men and women with regard to nationality. This rendered a woman's nationality independent of her marital status. Jus sanguinis remained the principal method of acquiring Chinese nationality; an authorization from the Ministry of Interior was necessary to lose it (Art. 11).

14. On the problems of Chinese emigrés in Singapore with the Nationalist Party before and after the war, see E. Guerassimoff, "Tan Kah Kee et le *guomindang* (1910–1940): Aux origines du ralliement à la RPC," *Approches Asie* 17 (2000): 9–46.

15. "Les ressortissants chinois et les politiques adoptées à leur égard," *La Chine en Construction* (Beijing: Ed. en langues étrangères, no. 17–f-1183, 1983), 4.

16. "Le congrès des Chinois d'outre-mer rapatriés," *Beijing Information*, April 23, 1984, 5.

17. "Les ressortissants," 1.

18. "Guowuyuan Qiaowu bangong shi" (Overseas Chinese Office of the Chinese State Affairs Council), in *Shijie huaqiao huaren cidian* (Dictionary of Ethnic Chinese and Overseas Chinese in the World), 500 (Beijing: Beijing daxue chubanshe, 1993).

19. Ibid.

20. Ibid.

21. Quanguo renmin daibiaodahui changwu weiyuanhui (Overseas Chinese Committee), "Zhonghua renmin gongheguo guiqiao qiaojuan quanyi baohu fa shishi banfa, 19 juil. 1993" (Law on the application of the protection of the rights and interests of returned Overseas Chinese and the families of emigrés), *Qiaoguo* 12, no. 5 (1993): 44. The 1993 law had been preceded by a more general legislative text in this regard in 1991.

22. *Shijie huaqiao huaren cidian*, 516.

23. "Law of the People's Republic of China on the Control of the Exit and Entry of Citizens, 1st Feb. 1986," in *The Laws of the People's Republic of China, 1983–1986*, comp. Legislative Affairs Commission of the Standing Committee of the National People's Congress of the People's Republic of China, 197–200 (Beijing: Foreign Language Press, 1987).

24. Carine Guerassimoff, "Legal and Illegal Mainland Chinese Emigration during the 1990s," in *New Developments in Asian Studies*, ed. Paul van der Velde and Alex McKay (London: Paul Kegan Publisher, 1998), 135–52.

25. "Feifa yiming shi guoji wenti" (Illegal emigration is an international problem), *Fujian Qiaobao*, July 4, 1993, 3.

26. "Zhongguo renmin gongheguo guojifa" (Nationality Law of the PRC, September 10, 1980) in *Zhonghua renmin gonheguo guojifa jianghua* (With Regard to the Nationality Law in the PRC), ed. Mousheng Jin, 48–50 (Beijing: Qunzhong chubanshe, 1981).

27. Article 44 of the 1978 Constitution provided that "all citizens over 18 years of age [had] the right to elect and be elected, with the exception of those who had lost that right."

28. Guofeng Hua, *Rapport sur les activités du gouvernement présenté à la 1ère session de la Vème APN* (Beijing: Ed. en langues étrangères, 1978), 118.

29. Wang Gungwu, "China and the Region in relation to Chinese Minorities," *Contemporary Southeast Asia* 1 (May 1979): 40.

30. Xiang Dayou, "Lun Zhongguo gaige kaifeng yu hua zitou xiang qushi" (Reforms and the opening of China and the Investments of Overseas Chinese), *Bagui qiao shi* (History of the Overseas Chinese of Bagui) 1, no. 1 (1994): 5.

31. Sun Xingcheng, "*Guanyu mingan wenti*" (Concerning sensitive issues), in *Huaren jingji nianjian 1997–1998*, 226–27 (Beijing: Shehui kexue wenxian chubanshe, 1997).

13

TRACING THE GENESIS OF BRAIN DRAIN
IN INDIA THROUGH STATE POLICY
AND CIVIL SOCIETY

Binod Khadria

Brain drain, which implies emigration of the highly educated, skilled, and experienced—including students of higher learning—from relatively less developed to more developed countries, is a recent phenomenon, although migration (immigration and emigration) in general is much older.[1] Emigration per se, it has been said, has drawn little scholarly attention in the debates on citizenship and state policy formation; and within emigration, the particular aspect of brain drain has drawn even less attention. For the sending country, the focus in the literature remains more on the theoretical possibilities of loss/gain from the brain drain and their quantitative estimations, and even these concerns of researchers waned by the end of the twentieth century. It is from the threshold of the twenty-first century, with increase in high-skill emigration in areas such as information technology (IT) wherein professionals from developing countries like India move to the developed West, that the paradigm of brain drain is brought to the forefront again.

The term "brain drain," a concept initially connected with the emigration of British doctors to the United States in the late 1950s and early 1960s, became applicable to the Indian and other Asian doctors who, in turn, emigrated to the United Kingdom to fill the vacuum there. Today, India almost tops the list of another category of brain drain: that of IT professionals moving to developed countries like the United States, Canada, Australia, Germany, France, Japan, as well as the United Kingdom. The Indian state polity had, however, become conscious of the negative implications of the brain drain long before the United States itself became, by 1970, the preferred destination for Indian "knowledge workers."[2] In fact, immediately after India's independence in 1947, the phenomenon had drawn the nation builders' attention in the context of the science policy formulation,[3] and later it was evident in the Report of the National Commission on Higher Education (or the Kothari Commission) in 1964–66, which explicitly mentioned "brain drain" as a policy issue to be tackled by the Indian state.[4]

The *World Employment Report 2001* of the International Labour Office (ILO) highlights the brain drain of skills from India in the twenty-first century as follows:

> In India the brain drain of its highly trained manpower is a major problem. . . . The rise of the software industry now offers greater opportunities at home which could alleviate the outflow of manpower, but as a result of the global demand for skilled ICT [information and communication technology] workers, a large number of countries have been planning to import software engineers from India. In addition to the U.S. increasing the cap for its H-1B visas, Germany is offering 20,000 "green cards" for software workers, Japan is seeking 10,000 IT workers from India over the next three years, Ireland is proposing to bring in 32,000 by 2005, France wants 10,000, Italy needs 8,000 and the Republic of Korea another 10,000. Other countries such as Belgium, Iran, Singapore, Spain, and Syria, have also shown an interest in importing Indian talent, although not indicating precise figures. When the total supply of IT engineering graduates is just over 90,000 per annum, it is clearly going to be a major problem for India to retain its best talent.[5]

The *Human Development Report 2001* says, "About 100,000 Indian professionals a year are expected to take new visas recently issued by the U.S. The cost of providing university education to these professionals represents a resource loss for India of $2 billion a year."[6] The *World Competitiveness Yearbook 2000* has ranked India forty-second out of forty-seven countries, and a significance score of 3.291 on a ten-point scale in a survey of brain drain, where the low score and high ranking both mean that India has a high degree of brain drain.[7] A number of Indian institution-based studies present brain drain estimates for various institutions of excellence. These have ranged from a low of 23 percent to a high of 31 percent in the Indian Institutes of Technology, and a very high of 56 percent from the All India Institute of Medical Sciences.[8] (See table 13.1.)

Among the main recipient countries of skilled Indian immigrants, the United Kingdom traditionally ranked first until the end of the 1960s. Later, it was overtaken by Canada and eventually by the United States, the latter continuing to be the destination country for permanent emigration of the largest number of highly skilled people from India—as from many other developing countries during the remainder of the twentieth century.[9] According to unconfirmed estimates, 80–90 percent of India's brain drain was U.S.-bound at the close of the twentieth century. In the United States, the share of Indian immigrants has ranged between 5 and 6 percent among all immigrants coming to the country for permanent residence every year since 1996.[10] In broadly rounded figures from U.S. Immigration and Naturalization Service data, the number of Indians being given immigrant visas (i.e., permanent residency) is in the range of 35,000–45,000 per year between 1996 and 1998, with 75 percent of those becoming American citizens in the long run.[11]

As part of the shift from demand for specific occupational skills (like those for doctors, engineers, etc.) to that for generic skills (like IT professionals possess) in the twenty-first century, some developed countries in western Europe, Australasia, and East Asia have opened up their labor markets to Indian professionals, and the United States and Canada have increased their intake not only through permanent immigration but also from streams of temporary "visitors" who stay for seven to ten years.[12] India thus stands to be the single largest contributor to the world from a purely high-skill labor market point of view.

It is in this context that this chapter attempts to trace the genesis of brain drain in India through its political history and the perception of the phenomenon in the Indian civil society.[13] The beginning of brain drain from India may be traced in what the very term "brain" signifies: investment in education, training, and experience embodied in the human capital of the emigrant. We will look at the evolution of the education policies, first in British India (in terms of the English and Oriental learning replacing the Persian) and then in independent India (in terms of expansion of Western education)—both eventually paving the way for linking higher education of Indians with the labor markets in the primarily English-speaking countries of the world. We also attempt to link education policies to the phenomenon of educated unemployment in India in the 1960s, the main cause and origin of brain drain in India.

THE BRAIN REACH: THE QUALIFYING ROLE OF THE ENGLISH LANGUAGE AND WESTERN EDUCATION

Knowledge of the English language is a passport for reaching a large part of the modern world. The impetus to India's transition from the medieval to the modern age is said to have come from the introduction of English education in the first century of British rule (1757–1858). The new spirit of this age was Raja Rammohan Roy, who in 1828 founded an organization for social reformation that ultimately developed into the Brahma Samaj. Rammohan was a great pioneer of English education, and his reform movement was based on the belief that the people of India had the same capability for progress as any other civilized people.

When the British first took over the administration of the country in mid-eighteenth century, in Bengal, higher education in India was confined to a study of classical Sanskrit, Arabic, and Persian in *tols* and *madrasas,* to the neglect of vernaculars, natural sciences, and subjects like mathematics, history, political philosophy, economics, and geography as separate areas of study. Educated Indians had little knowledge of the world outside India, or about the great strides Europe had made since the Renaissance.[14] The idea of setting up a network of schools for teaching English was accomplished ultimately by the Christian missionaries in Madras and Bengal. The example of William Carey, a Baptist missionary who came to Calcutta in 1793, was followed by other missionaries and liberal Indians, the most notable being David Hare and Raja Rammohan Roy, respectively. These two were instrumental in establishing several English schools, including the Hindu College in Calcutta, which afterwards developed into the Presidency College.

The transition from the traditional classical medium and curriculum to the new one was not smooth. Even at the policy level, the Committee of Public Instruction was gradually divided into two parties known as the "Orientalists" and the "Anglicists," or the "English party," which advocated the famous "filtration theory." The Anglicists held that public funds should be devoted only to the imparting of liberal education along Western lines *through the medium of English.* Although this could naturally reach only a limited number of pupils, it was argued that ultimately this knowledge would spread through them to the masses by means of vernacular literature. The Anglicists scored their first triumph when the first medical college was established in Calcutta. In 1835, the Council of Education (the successor of the Committee of Public Instruction) decided that henceforth the available public funds would be spent on English education, though the existing oriental institutions like the Sanskrit College and *madrasa* were to continue alongside.[15] The cause of English education was further advanced by the regulation that all public services were to be filled by an open, competitive examination, preference being given to those with knowledge of English. English education was made the only passport to higher appointments that

Indians could reach in terms of eligibility, and hence its popularity and rapid progress were equally assured.[16] The advantages of knowing English were reaped initially by the middle-class Hindus, while the Hindu aristocracy and the Muslim community kept aloof from it.

A structured foundation for the education system in British India was, however, laid through the famous Despatch of Sir Charles Wood, president of the Board of Control, in 1854. Wood called for the creation of a properly coordinated system of education, with an adequate number of efficient teaching institutions at primary, secondary, and higher levels of education. Merit scholarships were made available, and private educational institutions received government grants. For coordinating higher education, a university was to be established in each presidency town, with professorships in law, civil engineering, vernaculars, and classical languages. With regard to religious instruction in the government institutions, the Despatch clearly stipulated that the education conveyed in them should be "exclusively secular," an approach which could perhaps be said to have prepared the Indian middle-class elite to adjust in any society abroad.[17] The first university in India was founded in 1857 in Calcutta; over the next thirty years, four new universities (Bombay, Madras, Lahore, and Allahabad) were added. The expansion of the modern education in its first phase was, however, halted by the great Revolt of 1857, which brought the governance by the East India Company to an end. However, the Despatch of 1854 continued to be the basis of education policy in India even after its governance was transferred to the Crown, and there was a steady increase in the number of schools and colleges, although primary schools lagged behind.

The opening of the teaching section of the University of Calcutta contributed much to the expansion of higher education, not only in Bengal but also in other parts of the country. In 1910, the government of India established a Department of Education. The growth of communal consciousness and provincial patriotism helped the establishment of new universities during the period 1906–38 in places such as Patna, Lucknow, Aligarh, Benares, Agra, Delhi, Nagpur, Waltair, Dacca, Mysore, Hyderabad, Chidambaram, Trivandrum, and Rangoon. The Indian Women's University at Poona was started in 1916. Rabindranath Tagore founded the Viswabharati, a unique educational institution famous for its holistic and cosmopolitan outlook, at Santiniketan in Bengal in 1921. In the wake of the Swadeshi Movement, which led to a boycott of English goods during the early phase of the Indian National Movement at the beginning of the twentieth century, there also arose many progressive indigenous institutions to propagate "national education," though higher education was still being largely imparted in the English medium.[18] Growth of institutions, together with the spirit of nationalism, led to a reasonable progress in the study of science, philosophy, and politics by Indians in the twentieth century.

Any review of the progress of education, however, showed that between 1931 and 1941, literacy rose from 8 percent to only about 12 percent. A postwar plan of educational reconstruction, submitted by the Central Advisory Board of Education at the beginning of 1944, not only prescribed universal compulsory and free education for boys and girls ages six to fourteen, but it also contemplated the provision of nursery schools and classes for one million children below age six. The board further recommended the provision of secondary schools for the spread of technical and vocational education. As a corollary, it also stressed the need for adequate and improved arrangements for higher education, both in universities and in professional and technical institutions at the university level. Following the board's recommendations, the central and provincial governments formulated plans and schemes for their implementation. While debate arose over the question whether to replace English with regional or state languages as the medium of university education, instruction in English continued to provide highly educated Indians an easy reach to the world labor market.

THE "DRAIN THEORY"

The formulation of "drain of wealth theory" as a systematic critique of the economic aspects of British rule (propagated by nationalists like Dadabhai Naoroji, M. G. Ranade, G. V. Joshi and R. C. Dutt)[19] constituted a significant contribution to Indian nationalism in the last quarter of the nineteenth century. From roughly 1870 on, a gradual but still extremely important shift was taking place within the whole universe of discourse and activities of the intelligentsia toward various forms of nationalism. The nationalists' early attempt to explain this onset of nationalism in terms of growing unemployment of the educated, which historians have not accepted as entirely satisfactory, differed conceptually from the theory of drain advocated by some of the post-1870 generation of Indian intellectuals. It is true, Indian newspapers as well as many official reports repeatedly complained of diminishing prospects for the educated. It has also been said that the very slow growth of industry, combined with the humanistic bias given to English education right from its beginnings, made overcrowding of the liberal professions and government services inevitable.[20] Starting with Naoroji, a whole tradition of nationalist economics began developing in 1870 and found expression through a vast literature of books, newspaper articles, speeches, and memorials. The nationalist critique directly related the abysmal and growing poverty of India to certain deliberate British policies, more particularly to *drain of wealth* through an artificial export surplus, destruction of handicrafts followed by hindrances to the development of modern Indian industry, and excessive land revenue burden.[21] The remedies repeatedly suggested were a reversal of these policies and an all-out Indian effort at industrial development.[22]

Such moderate economic thought would provide the core of the Indian critique of foreign rule throughout the later phases of nationalism, whether extremist, revolutionary-terrorist, Gandhian, or even socialist. The drain-of-wealth theory did provide a rough approximation to the underlying realities of colonial exploitation. In an immediate sense, it served as the theoretical underpinning for the demands and activities of the early moderate-led Congress. As late as 1905, Gokhale's presidential address had asserted that the educated were "the natural leaders of the people," and explained that political rights were being demanded "not for the whole population, but for such portion of it as has been qualified by education to discharge properly the responsibilities of such association." Among demand for administrative reforms, pride of place went to the Indianization of services through simultaneous Indian Civil Service (ICS) examination in England and India—a demand raised not really just to satisfy the tiny elite who could hope to get into the ICS, as has been sometimes argued, but connected with much broader themes. Indianization was advocated as a blow against racism.[23]

THE BRAIN FACTORY: ROLE OF THE QUANTITATIVE EXPANSION OF HIGHER EDUCATION

An obvious, necessary condition for brain drain would be the availability of many highly qualified personnel. India had established a moderate number of universities by the time of independence in 1947. However, it lacked highly trained scientific and technical human resources and an institutional base in science and technology (S&T) to embark immediately upon the industrialization and modernization programs planned under the political leadership of Jawaharlal Nehru. Nehru presided over the important science agencies and is said to have recurrently monitored their workings. He forged a close alliance with a group of elite scientists such as Homi Bhabha,

S. S. Bhatnagar, D. S. Kothari, and P. C. Mahalanobis, granting them considerable autonomy to promote the development of higher scientific research and education. One of the first priorities of the Nehru government was thus the expansion of the university sector's engineering, agriculture, and medical sciences. The first systematic effort in this direction was the constitution of a Scientific Manpower Committee (SMC) in 1947, which submitted its report in 1948. The same year another important report was submitted by the Sarkar Committee (established in 1946), which recommended the setting up of no less than four higher technical institutes. The recommendations came into effect when the parliament passed the Indian Institutes of Technology (IIT) Act of 1956 and set up the first IIT in Kharagpur the same year. The next was opened in Bombay in 1958; Madras in 1959; Kanpur in 1960; and Delhi in 1963—with aid from the United States, the Soviet Union, Germany, and the United Kingdom. The five IITs together trained between one thousand and thirteen hundred basic engineering graduates every year during the 1960s. The historical growth of other S&T institutions and the expansion of the university sector, legitimized by various committees set up by the government during the 1940s and 1950s, demonstrate the extent to which the development of high skills occupied the policymakers' attention. The close and easy alliance between science and policy planning in the Nehru era was further strengthened by the Scientific Policy Resolution passed by the Parliament in 1958, which legitimized and charted out higher education infrastructure in S&T and the state support to S&T.

In 1963, the official concern for loss of "brains" came out in a speech by Dr. Humayun Kabir, minister for scientific research and cultural affairs. A roundtable conference called by the prime minister in 1967 recommended making every possible effort to evolve institutional mechanisms to ensure the return of Indian scientists living abroad. The Council for Scientific and Industrial Research (CSIR), which had instituted a National Register of Scientific and Technical Personnel in the late 1940s, had added a special "Indians Abroad" section in the national register in 1957, creating a database of persons holding postgraduate degrees in science, engineering, medicine, agriculture, and social sciences. In an effort to create avenues for attracting Indian scientists and technologists from abroad, the CSIR in 1958 launched a scheme called "Scientists' Pool," for providing suitable temporary employment to persons returning from abroad. Even though the Scientists' Pool scheme was specially designed for scientists and technologists returning from abroad, 25 percent of the slots were reserved for persons from within India who had outstanding academic achievements and were potential emigrants. Because there were not many takers from abroad, however, the focus of the scheme changed, by the 1970s, from being an institutional mechanism of facilitating "brain gain" to that of checking the "brain drain" to the extent possible.

The enthusiasm of the early post-independence years had resulted in a somewhat lopsided growth of higher education as compared with primary education. To Blaug et al., who took stock of what had happened in India over the first three Five-Year Plans, the most striking feature of the post-independence scenario was the general tendency for the higher level of the system to grow faster than the lower levels in all quinquennia, whether one looked at the boys alone, the girls alone, or the totals.[24] An analysis of the extent to which these trends were the outcome of planning in India showed that without a single exception, the plans gave top priority to the achievement of universal primary education in accordance with the provisions of Article 45 of the Indian Constitution, but the quantitative targets for primary, secondary, and tertiary education belied this avowed preference.[25] The plans sometimes also advocated restricted growth of secondary and higher education. But if one looked at the pattern of growth of educational expenditure, one would have found the same story as with enrollments. Total educational expenditure from all sources had risen faster than national income since 1950, rising from 1.2 percent of income in 1950–51 to 2.9 percent in 1965–66.[26] However, if one compared the concurrent growth of expenditure among the different levels of education, one would find the fastest rate of growth in higher education, and the slowest in the middle and primary schools.[27] The differences were much the same as for enrollments, for the simple reason that costs per student increased at very similar rates at the three broad levels. The result was that the proportion of expenditure going to higher education had grown sharply, from about 23 percent in 1950–51 to 29 percent by 1965–66. In other words, although the total pie was getting bigger, university expansion had eaten into the share going to school education.[28]

Maulana Azad, the union minister of education, emphasized in 1953 that the most important policy reform for university education appeared to be *limiting the number of students,* particularly when the desired expansion of elementary and secondary education cold result in an inordinate increase in their numbers too. K. L. Shrimali, the union minister of education in 1959, reaffirmed this policy, as did C. D. Deshmukh, chairman of the University Grants Commission, in 1957.[29] It is clear from these observations, that leading educational planners in India had long felt the need for a restricted expansion of the higher levels of the education system, which was desirable at least until the goal of universal primary education was achieved.

This imbalance at different levels of education was, however, not a completely new phenomenon; review committees had noticed the trend even earlier. The Sargent Report of 1944 had described the Indian educational system as "top heavy," with too few students enrolled at the lower stages compared with the higher stages. The First Five-Year Plan repeated the phrase of a "top-heavy school system" and defended the principle of selective admissions to the universities. The Second Five-Year Plan did not establish any quantitative targets for university education, although it did stipulate targets in certain kinds of professional and technical schools. Despite the fact that it acknowledged the plight of unemployed matriculates, the plan refused to place any restrictions on the growth of enrollment in secondary schools providing general education. The Third Five-Year Plan estimated that the backlog of "educated unemployment" totaled one million. Nevertheless, it did not advocate any change in the growth rate of the secondary education, merely remarking that "with the expansion of education at the secondary level, greater attention should be put on absorption of the educated persons into gainful employment." Graduate unemployment was simply not mentioned, and nothing more was said about tightening up admission policies at the university level. The working group that prepared the draft Third Five-Year Plan for education paid lip service to the early provision of universal primary education—but then admitted that "it is neither right nor feasible to arrest expansion at these post-primary stages—to some extent, it is inevitable and follows from the pressure of the objective situation." On higher education, it remarked: "It has been suggested earlier that admissions should be regulated on the basis of adjudged capacity of students to benefit from education, but this would be possible only after the techniques of guidance, examination and selection have been perfected and this alone may take years of planned effort. It will not be realistic to expect that admissions will be regulated right from the start of the Third Plan and allowances will, therefore, have to be made for the normal expected increase."[30] The working group made no concrete suggestions for improving selection procedures. In the draft Fourth Five-Year Plan, a target date for achieving universal primary education—to cover all children up to age 14—was fixed for 1981, but the target was never achieved. Plan after plan set new (similarly unrealized) target dates, the latest target announced being 2015.[31]

Thus, despite the declarations of intent by planners over fifteen years, the actual targets put forward always embodied a more rapid rate of increase at the higher levels than the lower levels, turning the education system into a "brain factory." It boils down essentially to the question of why the Indian planners have been unable to control or resist the private demand for secondary and higher education. The answer provided has always been essentially political. The clients of the educational system are said to be the politically turbulent lobby. In addition, the organization of education at the higher levels made it intrinsically difficult to put brakes on its expansion. Only one in five of the arts and science colleges, which provided the bulk of higher education, were owned by central or state governments or by local authorities, and only one in three secondary schools were government schools. Even within the government sector, since politicians routinely tried to please their constituents by founding or helping to open a school or college in their areas, the difficulties of controlling the growth of higher education grew out of proportion. Moreover, added to the expansion in the number of institutions of higher education came the expansion in the capacity of the existing ones in general education.

In a nutshell, planning targets for secondary and higher education in India have been based on projections—not on what was considered desirable, but on what was considered likely.[32] The 1966 Education Commission report is undoubtedly the most comprehensive examination of the ills of Indian educational planning ever attempted. A year later, a parliamentary committee considered the report and set out to identify a program of action. Contrary to expectations, the committee—which included Dr. Triguna Sen, the new minister for education who had also been a member of the Education Commission himself—took grave exception to the attitude of the commission toward the post-primary population explosion and rejected the commission's proposal that the government should adopt a system of selective admissions at the higher secondary and undergraduate stages.[33]

Thus, the caution on the part of the Education Commission followed the way of all previous attempts at restraint in post-Independence India. The state governments were never willing to resist the rising private demand for upper secondary and higher education. Commenting directly on the issue of brain drain, however, even the Education Commission itself did not put the problem in a visionary perspective. Rather, taking a neutral view, it observed: "Those who go abroad generally obtain far better emoluments than available in the country, and in general also better research facilities. However, not all who go out of India are necessarily first-rate scientists, nor are they of critical importance to the country's requirements. We recognize that the seriousness of the 'brain drain' is often exaggerated, but even so, the problem is of sufficient importance to merit a close and systematic study. Talent attracts talent, and even within a country, this often leads to dangerous anomalies in the geographical distribution of outstanding scientists and engineers. This is becoming quite a serious problem even in the U.S.A."[34]

The Education Commission took note of the global dimensions of the issue: "The total number of foreign citizens in the U.S. colleges and Universities was 91,000 in the academic year 1964–65. Of this, 82,000 were students (46 percent were undergraduates) and 9,000 were teachers or persons holding research appointments. Canada provided the largest number of foreign students (9,253) and India came second with 6,813 students. The U.K. provided the largest number of faculty members and research appointments (1,166), Japan stood second, and India third (1,002)."[35] It also mentioned the British problem of brain drain: "The U.K. Royal Society Committee which examined this question some time ago reported that 'the emigration of scientists has created some serious gaps in the scientific effort.'" The Education Commission thus tried to take solace by finding parallels with what was happening in developed countries like the United States and the United Kingdom, and did not reflect any immediate concern for brain drain through emigration of the highly skilled Indians.

THE DRAIN FACTORY: UNEMPLOYMENT IN INDEPENDENT INDIA

One of the major causes of emigration of highly qualified Indians in independent India has been identified to be mass graduate unemployment. The declared goals of development policy in independent India were to bring about a rapid increase in living standards, provide *full employment at an adequate wage,* and reduce inequalities arising from the uneven distribution of income and wealth. Yet, in 1967 there were about half a million "educated unemployed," a number equal to 6–7 percent of the total stock of Indian educated labor in 1967, or to one in fifteen of all matriculates and graduates who were working or looking for work. It was also equal to nearly two-thirds of the annual output of matriculates and graduates. Furthermore, if one included (as looking for work) all the educated people registered with employment exchanges—some of whom had part-time or full-time jobs—the figure was 900,000, nearly twice as high. It was, however, not a new problem. Long before independence in 1947, official committees had drawn attention to the phenomena of "unemployment in the learned professions."[36] What was new was that the Indian economy was growing more rapidly than ever before since 1947, but educated unemployment did not come down. On the contrary, there is evidence that it remained more or less at constant proportion of the rapidly growing stock of educated labor.[37]

That a poor country suffered from a chronic pool of unemployment is hardly surprising. Educated unemployment was, however, not exactly the same as unemployment of labor in general. As a poor country, India was committed to an ambitious growth program and, therefore, needed a growing number of highly educated people with the requisite administrative skills. It was obviously strange that an economy that grew at about 3.5 percent annually for fifteen years failed to absorb one out of every fifteen of its best-educated people into gainful employment. After all, educated manpower with matriculate and graduate qualifications numbered to less than 4 percent of the entire labor force of India: it is only the apex of a vast pyramid, and yet even at this apex the unemployment rate exceeded anything that was experienced in advanced countries since the Great Depression.[38] One of the arguments has been that students in a country like India attached so much prestige to a degree that they continued at school regardless of career prospects or job opportunities. The market forces failed to eliminate unemployment under such a social environment, so the brain drain became a safety valve for the economy.

CONCLUSION

Expansion of western education through the English medium at higher, technical, and professional levels could be said to have been at the root of mass graduate unemployment both in colonial and independent India. Complemented by the theory of drain of wealth, it gave impetus to the spirit of nationalism in the pre-independence Indian civil society, leading in turn to pressures on state polity for recruitment of India's human resources (e.g., in the Indian Civil Service and the army, and eventually employment generation through industrial development on the Indian soil). In the post-independence period, the same phenomenon of mass graduate unemployment led to brain drain—emigration of the highly skilled human resources from India to developed countries of the West. But, unlike in the colonial period, it did not generate any pressure from the civil society on the state for creating suitable employment opportunities at home. This was despite the recognition of a continuing surplus in educated manpower and the need for the state to curtail enrollment in higher education. There was a fair understanding of the magnitude of the problem of brain drain among statesmen and scholars of the time, though no concrete measures emerged to check the exodus of talent during the 1960s and 1970s. A partial explanation may lie in the fact that, in sharp contrast to the times of the "drain of wealth," India, when faced with the phenomenon of brain drain, was no longer the colony of an alien state but a sovereign, independent nation. There was neither a nationalism-like objective nor any force toward formulating a "theory of brain drain" akin to the "theory of drain" (of wealth), although the element of national loss through neocolonial exploitation of resources would have been, in a sense, common to both.[39] Rather, by the early 1990s, the perception of "brain drain" had gradually given way to that of "brain bank" abroad, a concept dear to the then Prime Minister Rajiv Gandhi.[40] In the past few years, the emigration of Indian IT professionals is being perceived as the complete reversal of the "brain *drain*" into "potential *gain*" through globalization of India's human capital embodied in the Indian diaspora.[41] This, however, need not belittle the significance of the phenomenon of high-skill emigration as a problem, because it has been responsible for the perpetuation of a low-level productivity trap[42] for the average Indian worker who did not emigrate. The setting up of a Royal Commission on Indian Labour as far back as in 1929 "to enquire into the health, efficiency and standard of living of the workers" lends credence to the essence of this important argument.[43]

Table 13.1. Comparative overview of Brain Drain estimates of graduates of various Indian institutes

Institution	Indian Institute of Technology Bombay, Mumbai	Indian Institute of Technology Madras, Chennai	All India Institute of Medical Sciences Delhi	Indian Institute of Delhi New Delhi
Indicators				
Year of Study	1987	1989	1992	1997
Period Covered	1973–77	1964–87	1956–80	1980–90
Population Size	1,262	5,942	1,224	2,479
Sample Size	501	429	402	460
In India	179	184	200	316
Out of India	322	245	202	144
"Brain Drain"	30.8% (+/−2%)	25–28%	56.2% (+/−1.3%)	23.1% (+/−1.5%)

Source: Various institution-based surveys sponsored by the Government of India, Department of Science and Technology, as cited in Binod Khadria, *The Migration of Knowledge Workers: Second-Generation Effects of India's Brain Drain* (New Delhi: Sage, 1999).

1. "The 'brain drain' issue moved from scholarly analysis and newspaper recriminations onto the floor of the United Nations' General Assembly in late 1967. The UN community feared that the brain drain was jeopardizing fulfillment of the UN's Second Development Decade. Resolutions were adopted with a view to obtaining reliable facts about the magnitude, causes, and consequences of the brain drain." See U.N. General Assembly resolutions 2320 (XXII) (1967) and 2417 (XXIII) (1968), and other citations in W. Glazer, *The Brain Drain: Emigration and Return* (Oxford, Eng.: Pergamon Press, A UNITAR Study, 1978).

2. See Binod Khadria, *The Migration of Knowledge Workers: Second-Generation Effects of India's Brain Drain* (New Delhi: Sage, 1999). The term "knowledge workers" (and its counterpart "service workers") was coined by Peter Drucker in the 1960s (Peter Drucker, *Post-Capitalist Society* [New York: Harper Collins, 1993]). In the Indian context, knowledge workers include doctors, nurses, engineers, architects, economists, scientists, IT professionals, etc.

3. The initiatives Prime Minister Nehru announced in the Science Policy Resolution of 1958 were intended to woo the Indian scientists who were abroad into returning to India and enriching the scientific laboratories the Council for Scientific and Industrial Research (CSIR) were setting up.

4. See Government of India, *Education and National Development: Report of the Education Commission* (The Kothari Commission) 1964–66, vol. 3: *Higher Education* (New Delhi: National Council of Educational Research and Training, 1970).

5. International Labour Office, *World Employment Report 2001* (Geneva: International Labour Office, 2001), box 7.8, 68.

6. United Nations Development Program, *Human Development Report 2001* (New York: Oxford University Press, 2001), 91.

7. International Institute of Management Development, *The World Competitiveness Yearbook 2000* (Lausanne: IIMD, 2000), 500, table 8.13. In terms of these rankings of brain drain, India is better off, relatively speaking, than Venezuela, Philippines, Russia, Colombia, and South Africa, but worse off than Argentina.

8. Ignoring the margins of error given in the brackets in the table. For reference to the relevant studies on brain drain from IIT Madras, IIT Bombay, IIT Delhi, and the All India Institute of Medical Sciences, see Khadria, *Migration of Knowledge Workers*.

9. A small annual quota of one hundred immigrants was set in 1946 for Indian citizens to settle permanently in the United States, and this comprised mainly the unskilled and semiskilled "service workers." It was later, when the U.S. Immigration and Nationality Act Amendments of 1965 raised this quota to twenty thousand—on par with the individual quota of every other country—that the United States started welcoming (at least) the Indian "knowledge workers" in significant numbers. Subsequently, even larger number of Indians in various categories of knowledge occupations and skills (doctors, engineers, architects, scientists, teachers, nurses, etc.)

were absorbed into the U.S. labor market. The Education Commission Recommendations of 1966 in India coincided with the new American legislation—the former laying the foundation of higher education policy in India and the latter determining its emigration pattern until the dawn of the twenty-first century.

10. For the United States, India's ranking has varied within the first seven countries of emigration from 1996 on. However, all other six countries had non-high-skill considerations as primary motives for emigration to the United States: Mexico sent mainly the unskilled and semiskilled labor; China received priority for student immigration in the post-Tiananmen Square massacre; the Philippines as a former American military base; Vietnam for war reparations; the Soviet Union due to the fall of socialism; and the Dominican Republic as practically a dominion of the United States.

11. U.S. Immigration and Naturalization Service (INS), *Statistical Yearbook of the INS 1996* (Washington, D.C.: Department of Justice, Immigration and Naturalization Service, 1997).

12. Khadria, *Migration of Knowledge Workers;* and Binod Khadria, "Shifting Paradigms of Globalization: The Twenty-First Century Transition towards Generics in Skilled Migration from India," *International Migration, Quartely Review* 39, no. 5 (1/2001): 45–72.

13. The selected literature includes primarily R. C. Majumdar, H.C. Raychaudhuri, and K. Datta, *An Advanced History of India* (London: Macmillan, 1967); Government of India, *Report of the Education Commission;* Mark Blaug, R. Layard, and M. Woodhall, *The Causes of Graduate Unemployment in India* (London: Allen Lane and Penguin Press, 1969); Dharma Kumar, *The Cambridge Economic History of India, Vol.II: c.1757–c.1970* (Cambridge/Hyderabad: Cambridge University Press and Orient Longman, 1982); and Sumit Sarkar, *Modern India 1885–1947* (Madras: Macmillan, 1983).

14. According to V. S. Naipaul, the India-born expatriate Nobel laureate in literature for 2001, it is only at the end of the twentieth century that India has come out of its medieval intellectual stagnation.

15. Cited in R. C. Majumdar et al., *Advanced History,* 812.

16. The reasons for the government's promotional policy toward English education were obvious: rapid political expansion and administrative control led to a high demand for clerical staff, and this could be fulfilled much more economically through training the Indians.

17. It was perhaps this that prompted many an Indian voyager in the late nineteenth and early twentieth centuries to get over the taboo of "crossing of the seas," which was forbidden by popular belief in the traditional Hindu society. Examples in contemporary literature of the time could be found in the writings of the celebrated Hindi novelist and short-story writer Munshi Premchand.

18. See Sumit Sarkar, *The Swadeshi Movement in Bengal 1903–1908* (New Delhi: People's Publishing House, 1973), 174.

19. See Sarkar, *Modern India.*

20. Ibid.

21. Sarkar (in *Modern India*) calls them the three recurrent themes of R. C. Dutt's *Economic History of India (1901–03).*

22. As Tilak's *Mahratta* echoed, "We must become capitalists and enterprisers . . . a nation of traders, machine makers, and shopkeepers . . . ." (Feb. 13, 1881), and, by implication, emigrate to other parts of the world.

23. Raja Rammohan Roy had earlier advocated a reduction of the rent on land. The consequent loss of revenue, he suggested, should be met by a tax upon luxuries or by employing low-salaried Indians as collectors, instead of high-salaried Europeans. He also advocated Indianization of the British-Indian army. See R. C. Majumdar et al., *Advanced History,* 809.

24. Blaug et al., *Causes.*

25. Ibid.

26. Government of India, *Report of the Education Commission,* 859.

27. Blaug et al., *Causes,* 47, table 2.5.

28. "It is easy to understand how this happened when one extra student in an arts and science college cost Rs.328 a year and in a professional college Rs.1,167, compared with only Rs.30 in a primary school. . . . If resources were limited, one more college student meant ten less pupils in village schools. To direct more funds into primary education would have required comparable restriction of higher education" (Blaug et al.).

29. See note 13.

30. Draft Third Five-Year Plan document of Government of India, as cited in Tapas Majumdar, "Education: Uneven Progress, Difficult Choices," in *Independent India: The First Fifty Years,* ed. H. Karlekar, 293–313 (Delhi: Oxford University Press, 1998).

31. Majumdar, "Education."

32. In the words of J. P. Naik, the member-secretary of the Education Commission, as cited by Blaug et al., "The test of a real 'plan' is that its programme cannot be implemented under 'natural' circumstances and it is only the support provided by the planning mechanism that pulls it through. In so far as expansion (except in technical and professional education) is concerned, we have simply anticipated what is anyhow going to happen and dubbed it as 'targets.' If the anticipation is understood—and we usually do it on financial grounds—we claim the honour of having exceeded the targets."

33. The targets laid down by the Education Commission, like 6 percent of the National Income to be spent as public expenditure in education (or even the earlier one of universalization of primary education up to age fourteen by the Indian Constitution), have continued to elude India even until the beginning of the twenty-first century, when the dates have been shifted to 2015. For intervention of the apex judiciary in this, see Majumdar, "Education."

34. Government of India, *Report of the Education Commission,* 761. According to Blaug et al. (*Causes,* 157), "Of the relatively high quality of the brains drain there is no doubt, at least if 'quality' is defined in terms of education achieved. (But), according to the Indian vacancy statistics, the skills in extremely short supply in 1966 were management, medicine, nursing, pharmacy, agricultural and electronic engineering, accountancy, and secondary school teaching, but not civil, mechanical, electrical and chemical engineering, and not middle and primary school teaching, at least in the country as whole."

35. Government of India, *Report of the Education Commission,* 762.

36. The fact that ten commissions were set up between 1927 and 1937 in British India to study acute unemployment among the educated testifies to the existence of unemployment before Indian independence. See Walter M. Kotsching, *Unemployment in the Learned Professions: An International Study of Occupational and Educational Planning* (London: Oxford University Press / Humphrey Milford, 1937), 79–80, 129–32; and the Report of the Departmental Committee Appointed to Suggest Solutions for the Prevalent Unemployment Amongst the Middle Classes in the United Provinces (1930) under the Chairmanship of Sir Tej Bahadur Sapru.

37. This applied only until 1967. By 1968, the proportion had grown further because of prolonged recession.

38. Blaug et al., *Causes.*

39. See Binod Khadria, "Brain Drain—The Missing Perspective: A Comment," *Journal of Higher Education* 4, no. 1 (1978): 101–5; Binod Khadria, "Contemporary Indian Immigration to the United States—Is the Brain Drain Over?" *Revue européenne des migrations internationales* 7, no. 1 (1991): 65–96; Binod Khadria, "The Divides of Development-Underdevelopment Relationship in Higher Education and the Policy for Brain Drain" in *Education, Development and Underdevelopment,* ed. Sureshchandra Shukla and R. Kaul, 175–98 (New Delhi: Sage, 1998); and Binod Khadria, "Embodied and Disembodied Transfers of Knowledge: Geo-Politics of Economic Development, " in *The Knowledge Society,* ed. M. Carton and J.-B. Meyer, 191–203 (Paris: L'Harmattan, 2006), for elements of neocolonial exploitation and various socioeconomic linkages to brain drain.

40. Binod Khadria, "Brain Drain or Brain Bank? Aspects of Professional Indian Immigration to U.S.A.," International Conference on Indian Diaspora, organized by the UGC of India and the Rajiv Gandhi Foundation, University of Hyderabad, November 1–2, 1994.

41. Khadria, *Migration of Knowledge Workers;* and Khadria, "Shifting Paradigms." See, also ICWA, *Report of the High Level Committee on the Indian Diaspora* (New Delhi: Indian Council of World Affairs, 2001).

42. For elaboration of this argument and empirical evidence on contemporary average labor productivity in India vis-à-vis other countries, see Khadria, *Migration of Knowledge Workers* and Khadria, "Shifting Paradigms."

43. R. C. Majumdar et al., *Advanced History,* 949.

14

ISRAELI EMIGRATION POLICY

Steven J. Gold

ISRAEL'S ORIGINS: INGATHERING OF THE EXILES

Israel was envisioned as a homeland for the world's Jews in the 1890s, and brought into being in 1948, following the Holocaust. The movement for a modern Jewish state was conceived by a secular Jewish journalist named Theodore Herzl as he reported on a series of anti-Semitic incidents culminating in the Dreyfus Affair. Convinced that "the Jewish problem was intractable, emancipation had failed, and that a new approach was urgently needed,"[1] Herzl led Jews in Russia and Romania in the formation of a movement called *Hovevei Zion* (Lovers of Zion), whose goal was to establish a political entity in the land of Israel. The founders of Zionism were influenced by the political ideals of their time and place—especially socialism and nationalism—as they sought an opportunity for Jews to build their own lives on their own land. A half century later, in 1948, their dreams were realized, and the state of Israel had been formed. Its presence is justified by the Balfour Declaration of 1917, the League of Nations, and the United Nations.

Over the next fifty years, Israel would overcome a variety of political and economic obstacles, and survive several wars. Its Jewish population would swell from about 500,000 in 1948 to over 5,243,000 in 2001—the result of natural growth and in-migration from many nations. In addition to these 5.2 million Jews (which, ironically, includes about 250,000 recent immigrants from the former Soviet Union "who are not regarded as being Jewish"), there are 1,215,000 Israeli Arabs.[2] While other countries have sought to be the symbolic homeland of diasporic peoples, Israel seeks the actual migration of Jews—the ingathering of the exiles—as the basis of nation building.[3] Because the state of Israel is based both politically and demographically upon encouraging the immigration of Jews, its emigration policy has to be understood in light of its broader policies of immigration and re-migration.

As is the case with many aspects of Israeli society, the nation's emigration policy is an outcome of its dualistic status as both a Jewish state and a democracy with non-Jewish Arabs comprising about 19 percent of its population.[4] The emigration of Jews is strongly discouraged, while Jews living abroad are encouraged to return, and to this end they are given citizenship and resettlement benefits.[5] Zionism holds that Israel is the homeland of all Jews, including those who cannot trace known ancestors there. Accordingly, when Jews migrate to Israel for the first time, they are considered by national ideology to be returnees.

Arabs who left Israel upon its 1948 founding are not entitled to citizenship and often had their property confiscated. Arabs who remained in Israel are Israeli citizens but are excluded from various opportunities and benefits provided by governmental, quasi-governmental, nongovernmental, and religious/ethnic organizations that service the Jewish majority.[6] Israel's official policy encourages the return of Jewish emigrants but not Arabs. It "provides hefty economic benefits to its Jewish citizens returning from a stay of over two years abroad, but until 1985, has denied its Arab citizens the same benefits."[7]

Arabs living in the occupied territories are ineligible for citizenship, and more than one thousand who have been defined as security risks have been deported.[8] The two hundred thousand Palestinian refugees of the 1967 war have not yet been allowed to return to the territories. According to Israeli demographer Yinon Cohen, with regard to residents of the territories enumerated by Israel in September 1967, "no official policy on their emigration and return can be found."[9] Furthermore, "a former advisor on Arab affairs has confirmed that 'no government in Israel has ever formed any plan or any comprehensive policy towards [Israeli Arabs].'"[10] In official publications, Israel denies responsibility for the problems of Arab refugees and suggests that they should be resettled in Arab countries. Israel's Ministry for Foreign Affairs asserts that while "Arab countries claim that UN General Assembly Resolution 194 offers the [Palestinian] refugees a 'right of return' to Israel, it is not legally binding," and "Israel believes that the Resolution is not an appropriate solution to this complicated humanitarian issue."[11]

Summing up the current position of Jewish Israelis on Arab emigration, an article published in the leading Israeli newspaper *Ha'aretz* stated, "Not that all that many people would go into mourning if the Palestinians (on both sides of the Green Line) agreed to pack their bags and register for 'voluntary transfer.' ... But by now most Israelis realized that the neighbors have no plans to move."[12] In fact, seeking to retain their claim to the region, Arab and Palestinian organizations often discourage the emigration of co-ethnics.[13]

THE COMPLEX CONTEXT OF ISRAELI POLICIES

While Israel is regarded as a strong and centralized state, at the same time it is often difficult to characterize its policy actions with regard to emigration and other realms. It has no written constitution, its government is made up of many disparate branches and parties, and its polity includes groups with a particularly wide range of ideological positions and interests, including religious and secular, leftist and rightist, and nationalist and cosmopolitan, many of which are seated in the Knesset (parliament) due to proportional representation. In many cases, government officials, agencies, and parties engage in complex negotiations and compromises with numerous interests and constituencies, and thus avoid openly confronting controversial issues or establishing precedents that could yield opposition in local, national, or international arenas.[14] Contradictory policies may simultaneously reward and punish the same action; for example, while government spokesmen are condemning the emigration of Israeli Jews, consular officials encourage Diaspora communities to provide services to Israeli emigrants.

Finally, many services and functions that in other countries would be conducted by the national government are carried out, in Israel, by quasi-governmental and nongovernmental organizations and agencies created and supported by the world Jewish community as a means of supporting ethnic and religious goals. Many of these are funded and influenced by non-Israelis (Diaspora Jews).[15] Several of these Jewish organizations "predate the state and are conceived as strictly Jewish institutions, in which Arab participation is not seriously proposed."[16] Hence, while such organizations shape Israeli emigration and treat Jews and Arabs in a distinct manner, these are not always part of the government of Israel. Consequently, it is difficult to identify their origins, bases of action, and guiding rationale.

WHY HAVE ISRAELIS BEEN SO CONCERNED WITH EMIGRATION?

The justification for Israel's existence is the immigration of Jews. Hence, their emigration to reside elsewhere clearly presents an ideological and demographic problem. Nevertheless, Israelis continue to emigrate. According to the *Israel Bulletin of Statistics*, between 1948 and the end of 1992, 438,900 Israelis were living overseas and had not returned.[17] This group includes persons born abroad as well as native Israeli Jews (*sabras*). The largest fraction resides in major Jewish communities, including New York, Los Angeles, Paris, London, and Toronto.[18]

The 1990 U.S. census enumerated 144,000 people living in Hebrew-speaking homes, "almost all of which can be assumed to be Israeli."[19] According to the British census, there were 12,195 Israel-born persons in the United Kingdom in 1991. However, because Israel's population includes numbers of people who were not born there, the number born in Israel accounts for only a fraction of all Israeli Jews in England. Using the ratio of Israeli-born individuals to all Hebrew speakers determined in the U.S. census, Marlena Schmool and Frances Cohen estimate that approximately 27,000 Israelis live in England.[20] Drawing from South African census data, Allie Dubb estimated that the legal-resident Israeli population of South Africa in 1991 was 9,634.[21] France has a significant population of Israelis, many of whom trace their ancestry to former French colonies in North Africa. Because of their possession of French citizenship, or their birth outside of Israel, only a small fraction of these are enumerated as Israelis in the French census. Based on official national population censuses, the figures for Israeli citizens permanently living in France were 3,500 in 1981 and 2,900 in 1990.[22] According to the 1996 Canadian census, 21,965 Canadian residents indicated that they possessed Israeli citizenship, regardless of their country of birth. Finally, the 1996 Australian census enumerated 5,923 Hebrew-speaking people. Observing a general lack of data on the emigration of Israeli Arabs, Yinon Cohen notes that 25,600 emigrated between 1949 and 1979, and that Israeli Arabs settling in the United States are highly educated and skilled, often Christian, and unlikely to return.[23]

It is a standard principle of demography that every nation populated by immigration will reveal a considerable flow in the opposite direction.[24] While the rates of emigration by Jewish Israelis have been less than those in many other countries of settlement, the government and people of Israel have nevertheless been extremely concerned with emigration. There are three possible reasons for this: population growth is considered essential for Israel's political, military, and economic survival; Jews' history of persecution makes them obsessed with security; and because of Israeli Jews' cosmopolitan outlook and access to international networks, their potential for emigration is considerable.

286   STEVEN J. GOLD

Population growth is essential for Israel's political,
military, and economic dominance.

As a developing, settlement-based society, Israel needs workers to build its economy and citizen-soldiers to achieve military and demographic security in a world region surrounded by hostile neighbors. Reflecting on Israel's concern with security, Alan Dowty writes, "Ironically, the state founded to solve the perennial problem of Jewish security has itself been plagued by constant insecurity. During its entire history, the country has been involved in numerous wars. Until 1967, the bulk of the population was within artillery range of hostile armies." The surrounding countries outnumber Israel by a range of 20:1 to 50:1 in population, 8:1 in armed forces, and 3:1 in tanks and combat aircraft.[25]

Prior to 1967, the population of Arabs was relatively small and not a major concern of Israeli politicians. (Excluding Arabs in the West Bank and Gaza Strip, the fraction of Arabs in the Israeli population has grown from 12.2 percent in 1950 to 17.3 percent in 1984, and to just under 19 percent in 2001.[26]) However, following the Six Days' War and capture of the West Bank and Gaza in 1967, several hundred thousand Arabs came under Israeli control. Even if relations with Arabs were far better than they currently are, projected growth of their population would mean an end to the Jewish majority in the Jewish state. According to an Israeli government website: "The influx of millions of Arabs into the State of Israel would threaten the existence of Israel as an independent Jewish State."[27]

Further, as a result of the Holocaust, high rates of Jewish assimilation into gentile societies of the Diaspora, and a low birth rate, the size of the world Jewish population is small and growing slowly, if at all. Despite efforts to recruit Jewish immigrants, Jews in affluent democratic countries have shown little propensity to move to Israel permanently. This means that most significant sources of Jewish migration to Israel have been all but exhausted.

In addition to the military and demographic reasons for restricting emigration, Israel also seeks to retain its Jewish population in order to foster economic growth. This is especially true with regard to highly skilled persons who generate the income and technology upon which the country relies for both military and civilian purposes.[28] At the same time, like other affluent countries, Israel also requires numerous low-level service workers and laborers. As Palestinians from the occupied territories are no longer permitted to perform these jobs for political and security reasons, Israel now employs over 150,000 migrant workers—from eastern Europe, the Philippines, Thailand, and Africa—a large fraction of whom are undocumented and have little hope of permanent incorporation.[29]

The Jews' history of persecution and genocide makes Israelis defensive, fearful, and especially concerned with security.

With their personal experience as refugees, Jewish Israelis tend to be especially concerned with security. Moreover, as Alan Dowty writes, "Security cannot be measured simply by the objective threats that a nation faces. In the end, it is a matter of subjective feeling of safety in the minds of individuals, which is more difficult to achieve among a Jewish generation that passed through successive waves of twentieth-century anti-Semitism culminating in the Holocaust."[30]

Facing shared threats, Israelis developed a culture and way of life that emphasized cooperation as a means of insuring survival. The threats that Israeli Jews faced from hostile neighbors were not perceived as new; rather, they evoked Jews' collective memories of risk and victimization (four major Jewish holidays—Passover, Purim, Hanukkah and Tishah b'Av—commemorate a threat to Jewish existence), of which the current situation was merely the latest instance.

Observers see the concern over security as one of the most basic elements of Israeli society, and as playing a fundamental role in the formation of Israeli values, culture, and patterns of interaction. For example, the need for security has caused Israelis to reject the anti-authoritarianism ubiquitous in Jewish culture in favor of a strong state. Moreover, noting the cultural, national, ideological, and religious diversity that exists in Israeli society, writers describe the need for security and mutual defense as holding this fractious society together.[31] As Dowty notes, "The ongoing conflict with the Arab world has mitigated intercommunity tensions between religious and nonreligious Jews, improved the climate of industrial relations and attenuated internal conflicts regarding policies on the West Bank and Gaza Strip" and generally increased social consensus among Jewish Israelis."[32]

Israeli sociologist Zvi Sobel—who admits his own "recognition of the threat—personal and communal—suggested by large scale 'desertion' on the part of thousands of countrymen," describes Israelis' anxiety about emigration: "While a demographic emergency in a purely objective sense might not exist, it is clear that a psychological emergency does. Whatever the 'facts' of the matter, large numbers of Israelis—the man in the street as well as establishment figures—*perceive* emigration as a problem and one of serious dimensions."[33] Accordingly, because emigration imperils Jewish Israelis' sense of security on both practical and ideological levels, it is treated as a serious threat indeed.

Israeli society is made up of recent immigrants who have extensive links elsewhere and, hence, a high potential for exit.

Israel is a young nation of immigrants, and many of its citizens are recent arrivals. As of 1999, approximately 40 percent of the country's population was born overseas. Consequently, Israelis have relatives in numerous countries, and a significant fraction possesses citizenship or legal residence in countries beyond the Jewish state. Most of their ties to family members abroad can be traced to a time prior to their families' settlement in Israel. However, a fair fraction of *sabras* (Israeli-born Jews) have themselves resided abroad in order to travel, study, or work. Even those who have not been overseas meet visitors from other countries and hear stories of their friends' and relatives' lives in London, Vienna, New York, or Paris. Since the propensity to migrate is transmitted along family networks, having relatives abroad is often correlated with ones' own emigration.[34] According to the owner of one of Israel's largest international shipping companies, "Israelis are considered people who adapt to new surroundings with record speed. They learn new languages quickly, they are mobile, and there is an Israeli community in every large Western city that helps them acclimatize. The Israelis are migrants in their souls."[35]

While personal or family experiences may encourage travel abroad, so do a number of macrosociological and historical factors. In *Jewish History in Modern Times,* Joseph Goldstein writes that geographic mobility is a fundamental element of the Jewish experience. "Jewish migration and the establishment of Jewish communities all over the world have existed since the emergence of the Jewish people as a religious and ethnic identity." Moreover, "the dispersion of the Jews throughout many countries was a major factor in ensuring their continued existence."[36] Similarly, demographer Sergio DellaPergola sees migration as so central to the Jewish situation that he refers to a "World Jewish Migration System." While noting that Jewish migration is a "product of a complex chain of explanatory determinants" rather than a primordial disposition toward travel (as suggested by the stereotype of "the wandering Jew"), DellaPergola nevertheless concludes "the

Jewish case [with regard to migration] appears to extend over a longer time span and is geographically more complex and articulated" than that associated with "other ethnoreligious or sociocultural groups."[37]

An examination of the origins of Israel's population since 1948 suggests that most came because Israel offered immediate asylum for Jews who lacked other options. Consequently, their numbers include potential candidates for further movement if advantageous circumstances become available. The largest fraction of Israelis hails from eastern Europe, North Africa, and the Middle East. They came because political developments in their countries of origin forced them out. As a result of centuries of oppression, the Holocaust, and anti-Jewish hostility following the formation of Israel, Jews felt that they had no future in these settings. In contrast, relatively few of the millions of Jews in the more secure and affluent nations of North America and western Europe made *aliyah* (moved to Israel). Of the approximately 3.1 million Jewish immigrants who settled in Israel between 1919 and 1997, 95 percent came from eastern Europe, North Africa, the Middle East or Asia, while only about 5 percent (160,000) came from the United Kingdom, France, Australia, New Zealand, the United States, and Canada.[38]

Further suggesting Israel's status as a location of temporary residence is the steady stream that has left the Jewish State for other countries. This group accounts for about one-fifth the number who have entered Israel from 1948 to 1976.[39] Finally, the post–World War II emigration of Jews from North Africa, the Middle East, the Soviet Union, South Africa, and Argentina reveals "significant sociodemographic self-selection," according to DellaPergola. "In broad aggregate generalization," he notes, "more of the culturally more traditional and socially lower strata emigrated to Israel; more of the better educated, entrepreneurial and professional strata preferred France, the United States and other Western countries."[40] As some of these economically disadvantaged Israelis increase their ambitions and resources, they too may follow co-nationals abroad to what appear to be greener pastures. Hence, both theoretical and empirical evidence indicates that Israelis would be likely candidates for emigration to Western countries. Accordingly, on both practical and symbolic levels, emigration is seen as presenting risks to the physical survival and ideological justification of the Jewish state.

ACTIONS TO DISCOURAGE EMIGRATION

Faced with the threat of exit by its Jewish population, Israel has undertaken a series of actions to counter emigration. Unlike those societies that prohibit emigration as a crime against the state, Israel, as a liberal democracy, has not closed its borders to the departure of Jews.[41] Rather, it generally relies on moral and ideological pressure, speeches by prominent officials, and the creation of anti-emigration cultural productions (such as books, articles, news reports, and films) to discourage exit. This agenda has been fomented in four ways: by repudiating the Diaspora as a setting for Jewish life, by condemning emigration as immoral, by describing actual emigrants as unhappy and unsuccessful, and by discouraging host-country Jews from assisting emigrants. In addition, Israel has also developed policies that punish exit and reward return.

Repudiating the Diaspora as a setting for Jewish life

Early Zionists hoped to create among Israeli Jews a "New Zionist Person" with character traits distinct from those associated with Diaspora Jews. In order to recruit and retain Jewish citizens, Zionists redefined the meaning of diaspora. Before the formation of the Jewish State, the Diaspora was largely a religious concept. The desire to return home involved a spiritual rather than a geographic journey. Residence in the Diaspora was the Jewish reality, good, bad or indifferent. It was simply the place were the vast majority of Jews lived.[42]

The early Zionists proclaimed a radically different view. "In the case of the Jews, the term diaspora itself—which essentially and neutrally means a dispersion of an ethno-national group—acquired an utterly negative meaning and became synonymous with detested 'exile.'"[43] Zionists depicted the Diaspora as a place of isolation, degradation, and suffering—"Jewish life in exile constituted a recurrent history of oppression, punctuated by periodic pogroms and expulsions, of fragile existence imbued with fear and humiliation."[44] Moving from the Diaspora (or *golah*, exile) to Israel was "making aliyah," or going to a higher place. In nation-building texts and rituals, the achievements of Jews in the Diaspora were denigrated or repudiated by early Zionists. In Israel, it is widely believed that "diaspora Jews are plagued by a *galut* (exilic) mentality that precludes them from freely expressing themselves as proud, self-confident and self-respecting Jews."[45] According to Oz Almog, author of *Sabra: The Creation of the New Jew,* "Zionism condemned those who deviated from its precepts and castigated schismatics and heretics—in this case Jews who chose to remain in the diaspora . . . the person who emigrated from the country was called a *yored,* or 'descender,' that is, an apostate and a traitor."[46] The impact of this ideology was so deep-seated and pervasive that even the biographies of heroes of Israel's War for Independence were recast to obliterate their "life as a child and adolescent in eastern Europe,"[47] thus separating Israelis from the millions of Jews who continued to reside outside of the Jewish state.

As a consequence, some forms of Israeli culture denigrate the Diaspora as a place unfit for Jewish life, and Israelis frequently hear messages about the undesirability of existence outside of Israel. While this cultural and ideological practice was intended to transform people inside Israel, it had the additional consequence of inhibiting emigration, even among those who had never considered living abroad.

Condemning emigrants as immoral

If general messages about the undesirability and degradation of life in the Diaspora do not discourage Israelis from emigrating, then the moral consequences of emigration further emphasize the negative connotations of going abroad. Summing up this position, two psychologists write: "There is an implication that the citizen who has left Israel is guilty of a subtle form of betrayal of the shared obligation to protect the land of Israel."[48] During the 1970s, Israeli politicians such as Prime Minister Yitzhak Rabin were especially vitriolic on this issue, calling Israeli emigrants "moral lepers," "the fallen among the weaklings," and "the dregs of the earth."[49]

The problems of emigration are also addressed in popular culture. Israeli emigrants are the subject of novels, films, comedy sketches, and political speeches, as well as scholarly, journalistic, and official inquiries (often featuring wildly exaggerated estimates of their numbers, indicating the seriousness with which this social problem is treated).[50] Illustrating the content of such accounts, an opinion piece in the *Jerusalem Post* described Israeli emigrants as imprinted with "The Mark of Cain." The article went on to condemn "the almost 400 Israeli-born persons" who, during the previous year, had settled in Australia, and asserted that "as every yored knows only too well, he has simply deserted, abandoned the defense of his country and the shared responsibility for it."[51] In a highly collectivist society, this characterization can be quite powerful. "The country is still small enough and intimate enough for this kind of informal condemnation to be more than most individuals can take."[52]

If negative characterizations of the moral implications of emigration fail to discourage would-be leavers, then media accounts, academic writings, and popular discussions suggest another reason for remaining in Israel: migrants' inability to achieve personal success or otherwise enjoy life overseas. Since statistical data and comparative research depict Israeli emigrants as successful, writings critical of Israeli emigration often focus on the individual and communal troubles of the group, namely, disillusionment, loss of Jewish identity, family breakdown, poverty, unethical behavior, alienation from host-country Jews, and loneliness.[53] This line of argument often assumes that Jewish Israeli emigrants have been affected by their socialization in the Jewish state to the extent that they are ill suited for life outside it. As a textbook on Israeli social problems asserts, "*Yordim* [Israelis who have left] are described by the media in negative terms, and where failure to adjust overseas can be cited, this is reported with great relish."[54]

For example, Israelis are described as more collectivist, less materialistic, more outspoken, and less willing to tolerate life as a minority group than Diaspora Jews. "It is often suggested that for most Israelis individual identity is embedded in their national identity, so that separation from the nation may result in identity conflict."[55] In a letter to the editor, a reader scolded a prominent Israeli newspaper for publishing an article on Israelis leaving the Jewish state due to worsening conditions associated with economic recession and the Al Aksa Intifada beginning in 2000: "If you wanted to be truthful, perhaps you'd publish a cover issue about the miserable life of yordim . . . about their estrangement from their environment, about the pain they and their children feel at being cut off, a pain that doesn't heal with time, about the pseudo-Israeli lifestyle in a foreign and alienating city, a pathetic way of life built entirely on ambivalent ties with Israel."[56]

Countering the image of affluence and career advancement available to Israelis who go abroad, Israeli scholar Naama Sabar describes former Kibbutzniks in Los Angeles who speak broken English, live in squalor, and support themselves as archetypical middleman entrepreneurs—by selling shoddy, overpriced remodeling services to slum-dwelling African-Americans and Latinos.[57] As well, while Israeli emigrants settle among Diaspora Jews, observers often note the tension and conflict that characterizes relations among the two groups. Israeli anthropologist Moshe Shokeid illustrates emigrants' difficulty in establishing social ties in the United States: "As noted by many Israelis, not only did American Jews make no effort to facilitate the Israelis' entry into American society, but they themselves appeared to be no less reserved and unapproachable than gentile Americans."[58]

Suggesting the unwelcoming environment in another point of settlement, Rina Cohen and Gerald Gold report that Canadian Jews portray Israeli emigrants with the same stereotypes that Canadian gentiles see Jewish Canadians: loud, dishonest, arrogant, and rude.[59] (Israelis respond by describing Jewish Canadians with the identical platitudes that Canadian Jews attribute to their non-Jewish neighbors: formal, lazy, naive, and beer-drinking). These reports generally conclude that emigrants' feelings of guilt and disorientation with regard to being outside of the Jewish state prevent them from creating viable and supportive ethnic communities—a pattern associated with immigrant adaptation in general and especially with non-Israeli Jewish migrants.

All told, from the Israeli perspective, Israeli emigration is fundamentally unlike other forms of migration. Several studies make this point explicitly. "Israelis in the homeland and Jews in the Diaspora exhibit attitudes towards Israeli emigrants that are markedly different to those that other homeland societies have shown towards their emigrants."[60] For example, in his book on Israeli emigration, Zvi Sobel asserts that existing models of migration are of little use for examining the experience of Israeli emigrants: "Thus, from the starting point of our analysis [of Israeli emigration]—defining and labeling the act or process as well as the actors—we are confronted by a rather singular situation with little parallel material to provide guidance."[61]

Discourage host-country Jews from assisting Israeli emigrants

The Israeli government has also used its leverage with host Jewish communities and their communal organizations to withhold aid from Israeli emigrants. Until the 1980s, the Israeli government either ignored or actively condemned its citizens abroad. During the 1970s, "one top Israeli government official referred to the emigrants as *zevel* (garbage) and urged consulates world wide to have little if anything to do with them." In order to discourage further emigration and impede settlement of those abroad, from the early 1970s until the late 1980s, the Israeli consulate in New York "repeatedly urged the (Jewish) Federation to provide no special services to Israelis."[62]

Following the lead of the Israeli government, Diaspora Jewish communities offered little of the support that they have customarily extended to immigrant Jews from other lands. In her report "The Israeli Corner of the American Jewish Community," Sherry Rosen asserted that the communal response has been to approach Israeli emigrants as "anything but Jewish settlers seeking to build new lives for themselves and their families in the United States."[63]

In 1986, the U.S. government instituted the Immigration Reform and Control Act (IRCA) that allowed undocumented immigrants residing in the United States to normalize their migration status. Because of Israel's instructions, some American Jewish community organizations were reluctant to assist Israelis who sought to become legal residents. Israeli emigrants in the United States who felt rebuffed by Jewish agencies sometimes relied on the assistance of Catholic organizations, thus furthering their alienation from U.S. co-religionists. An employee of a Jewish communal agency working with Israeli emigrants described the climate of hostility during the 1970s and 1980s:" I wouldn't call it [American Jews' attitude toward immigrants] hostility, but I would say that there was a real discomfort. For the Americans, it wasn't an individual thing but a global phenomenon that is, 'How could they come here? They belong *there*. I mean, they're beautiful Israeli *sabras* [Jews born in Israel]. *Sabras* belong in Israel, and you know, we help them and they could fight in the wars.' That was the American perception."[64] Reflecting the anti-emigration mindset of the era, Israeli policy of the 1970s and early 1980s extended benefits (financial and otherwise) for returnees, while discouraging overseas representatives from assisting or even socializing with long-term emigrants.[65]

FROM CONDEMNATION TO OUTREACH

Although Israeli emigration reached an all-time low in 1983, the Israeli government continued to be concerned with the problem and began a new initiative to address it during the 1980s.[66] Toward this end, the Israeli government appointed Simcha Ehrlich, deputy prime minister at the time, and Schmuel Lahis, the director general of the Jewish Agency (an international organization that assists Jews migrating to Israel), to investigate the subject. The Lahis Report, published in 1980, declared that up to a half million Israelis (a figure now considered to be highly inflated) lived in the United States, and that this loss of many citizens (most of whom were young and skilled) was bound to have disturbing implications for Israel's demography, economy, morale, and defense of the country. The report went on to assert that the emigrants "were greatly attached to Israel and that this feeling should be nurtured."[67]

The findings of the Lahis Report alarmed the Israeli Jewish public when the media publicized them; the government reacted by transferring the activities to the Office of the Prime Minister to provide better oversight. By the mid-1980s, the prime minister's office, along with a special appointed committee consisting of the directors general of the Ministries of Defense, Education and Culture, Finance, Housing, Labor and Welfare, and chaired by the director general of Immigrant Absorption, adopted recommendations to deter emigration, which included offering services and benefits, and an intensification of education in Zionist values. These measures were to be aimed at young persons nearing the age of military service, since they were those most likely to go abroad. However, the government implemented relatively few of the proposed financial incentives intended to discourage emigration—such as educational, housing, and employment benefits, and income tax reductions—because of the bureaucratic complexity and political opposition that would have had to be overcome to grant them.[68]

A decade after the publication of the Lahis Report—and in spite of a last major spike of anti-emigrant editorializing in Israeli newspapers—a shift in attitudes and policy began to occur. On the international level, during the late 1980s, the Israeli government encouraged its consular officials to initiate the development of relations between Jewish Israeli immigrants and host-society Jewish institutions. Yossi Kucik of the Jewish Agency reported that he attended a 1985 meeting wherein "it was agreed that State could no longer afford to ignore these citizens abroad."[69] During a 1989 trip to Los Angeles, Israeli Absorption Minister Yitzhak Peretz claimed that Israel should change its attitude towards emigrants if they cannot be convinced to return. "Israelis," he said, "should be encouraged to be part of the Jewish community and become integrated because it offers them, and particularly their children, some chance of retaining their Jewish identity."[70]

In 1991, Prime Minister Yitzhak Rabin recanted his famous condemnation of Israeli emigrants during an interview in the Israeli-American newspaper *Hadashot LA,* saying, "What I said then doesn't apply today . . . the Israelis living abroad are an integral part of the Jewish community and there is no point in talking about ostracism."[71] Because of "the importance it attaches to the re-emigration of Israelis to Israel,"[72] the Israeli government, in 1992, took responsibility for "*re-aliyah*" and offered an enhanced package of benefits including cash assistance, low-cost air fair, suspension of import duties, education, assistance in finding jobs and housing, financial aid for school tuition, and reduction in military duty requirements for Israelis and their family members who return.

In accordance with this evolving Israeli policy toward expatriates, Jewish communities in settlement countries established outreach programs for recently arrived Israelis that were intended to facilitate both their maintenance of Israeli culture and their successful integration into the local Jewish population. At the same time, the Israeli government itself has sponsored various emigrant outreach programs intended to preserve ties with Israeli expatriates. These include the Israeli Scouts (Tzofim), summer in Israel programs for emigrant children, and Israeli Houses that provide Israeli-oriented social, cultural, and political activities for emigrants in major points of settlement.

Israel's new attitude toward Israeli emigrants developed within a context of unprecedented demographic and economic growth, and significant improvements in Israel's political situation that enhanced national security. In 1989, Israel was suffering economic stagnation, had a rate of inflation near 20 percent, experienced an ongoing fear of war, and suffered from an inability to retain many of its best and brightest.[73] However, by the late 1990s, Israel had signed the 1993 Oslo Peace Accords with the Palestinians and had seen a relaxation of the Arab economic embargo. In addition, due to the massive Soviet aliyah, the Jewish state's population had increased by close to 20 percent—almost one million people, many of whom were highly educated. Its inflation rate was below 3 percent, and it had the greatest number of engineers per capita in the world (almost double that of the second-ranking United States).[74]

Moreover, during the 1980s, Israel's economy was plagued by stagflation, and its major export was citrus; by 2000, however, Israel had become a center of high tech and was viewed as among the world's top growth economies. As such, it could offer its more affluent citizens a standard of material life equal to that of the industrialized West.[75] These political, economic, and demographic developments transformed Israeli society, making it better able to tolerate demographic losses to emigration. Furthermore, Israel's recent economic transformation creates an ever-increasing need for a globalized, peripatetic workforce to facilitate the continued growth of its economy.[76]

Another reason Israel became less hostile to Jewish emigration is that policy makers realized not all exits were permanent. While common-sense thinking and popular ideology often assume that migration is forever, the actions of contemporary Jewish Israeli migrants suggest that it is not. Many studies of Israeli emigration report that Jewish migrants—including those who have spent a decade or more in the host society—continue to "sit on their suitcases" and refer to their imminent return to Israel.[77] Several Israeli emigrants I interviewed expressed this outlook. Ilan, a London restaurateur, told us "I make a living here—I don't really live here." I asked, "Do you feel any change in your identity? Do you feel more or less Israeli or Jewish since you came here? Do you feel English?" And he replied, "No change at all. I'm an Israeli and I will go back to Israel. I do not see myself living here, and we made no such decisions to stay here. We have no plans to emigrate. It's a rolling snowball. We will go back eventually. When I'm 40 years old—I'll go back home."

Such sentiments are often put into action. Data suggest that a significant fraction of Israeli emigrants eventually return.[78] In fact, Israeli demographers assert that the "failure to consider Israeli's high rates of return migration" is a major reason for the controversy surrounding Israeli emigration.[79] During much of the 1990s, the number of Israelis returning did increase substantially. During 1985–1991, the annual average number of returnees was 5,500; during 1992–1994, there were 10,500 returnees annually, and 14,000 returned in 1993 and 1994.[80] Since migration is not always permanent, the presence of Israelis abroad is not as threatening as it might first appear to be. In fact, former Israelis are much more likely to make aliyah than other segments of Diaspora Jewry, a fact not missed by Israeli officials, who have altered policies toward emigrants to further encourage return.[81]

THE CURRENT SITUATION

Most recently, the economic decline of 2000–2001, coupled with the Al Aksa Intifada, has re-ignited the debate about emigration within Israeli society. From the fall of 2000, when the uprising began, to the fall of 2001, applications for travel abroad increased about 13 percent. For example, requests for permanent residency in Canada's Tel Aviv embassy increased 50 percent during that time. (However, the overwhelming portion of these—over 90 percent—came from recently arrived Russian Jews and Palestinians; only 4 percent were requested by veteran Jewish Israelis.) Moreover, the rate of Israelis returning from overseas fell by almost 24 percent between 2000 and 2001.[82] It is possible that the ongoing social and economic effects of the second intifada may increase emigration while discouraging immigration and tourism.

According to several respondents and newspaper reports, a fraction of the Israeli population is now more tolerant of emigration than ever before. A survey on emigration conducted by Israel's *Ha'aretz Magazine* during 2001 found that only 37 percent of respondents had a negative opinion of emigrants. Sixteen percent had a positive reaction, while 43 percent were indifferent. A commentator added: "[I]t is also clear that the Israelis who are leaving the country have liberated themselves from the stigma of being a yored . . . once derisively hurled at emigrants. In a world where flights out of the country are available and cheap, and moving from one land to another for employment is a routine matter, leaving is not necessarily forever." Supporting this assertion, the owner of one of the largest international shipping companies in Israel noted that the word *yeridah* (the process of Jews leaving Israel) has been erased from the lexicon of his clients.[83]

Just as Jewish Israelis have new reasons to leave, so do some Palestinians. A recent *Ha'aretz* article asserted, "Palestinian communications channels have been reporting a resurgent interest in obtaining immigration visas for the West."[84] *Migration News* more generally reports that violence, economic stagnation, and political conflicts in the West Bank and Gaza are encouraging Palestinians—especially those with residence permits in North and South America and Australia—to emigrate.[85]

While some indicators suggest that Israeli Jewish emigration is increasingly tolerated, going abroad remains controversial. "More than two decades after Yitzhak Rabin disparaged emigrants as 'droppings out of parasites,' emigration is still a major taboo in Israeli society. Israelis who are thinking about leaving the country don't usually think out loud."[86] When a thirty-five-year-old tour guide posted his intention to leave Israel with his family on the Internet in June 2001, he was ferociously attacked. One respondent stated, "Jewish history is filled with losers and cowards like you, from Josephus all the way to the *yordim* in Los Angeles who have become car cleaners."[87]

Reflecting the security implications of emigration, the Web site for the Israeli newspaper *Yediot Ahronot* reported that during August 2001, the Israeli Defense Forces were preparing recruitment stations in numerous locations in Europe, Asia, North America, and Africa to airlift "Israeli reservists sojourning abroad" if their services were required by the Israeli Army. Los Angeles-based Israeli consul for communication and public affairs, Meirav Eilon Shahar, explained, "Israel, over the years, has expressed varying degrees of interest in the mechanics of reaching, recruiting and returning the many battalions of young Israelis who wend their ways around the world." Despite the fact that the standing army now has more recruits than it wants or needs, it still seeks the ability to access these reservists, largely because their experience is of special value.[88]

Israel's emigration policy must be understood in terms of its dualistic im-migration policies, which emphasize and encourage the in-migration of Jews while offering limited options for immigration by non-Jews. Israel discourages Jewish emigration for demographic, economic, and ideological reasons. Most commonly, these policy goals are enforced through informal social pressure. However, due to Israel's recent economic and demographic growth and the increasing globalization of production and consumption, the Jewish state has now become somewhat more tolerant of its citizens traveling abroad and encourages host-society Jews to assist them. This is largely because Israel realizes that its sojourners may provide economic benefits for the Jewish state and eventually return to it.

Israel's dualistic policy with regard to emigration is a central issue in the ongoing conflict between Jews and Palestinians, and one of the most difficult to resolve. As a consequence, issues of both emigration and immi-gration will likely remain central to Israeli political and cultural life for the foreseeable future.

NOTES

1. Joseph Goldstein, *Jewish History in Modern Times* (Brighton, U.K.: Sussex Academic, 1995), 111.

2. "Population Reaches almost 6.5 Million," *Jerusalem Post*, September 16, 2001, http://jpost.com (accessed September 16, 2001).

3. Nina Glick-Schiller, Linda Basch, and Cristina Blanc-Szanton, "Transnationalism: A New Analytic Framework for Understanding Migration," in *Towards a Transnational Perspective on Migration: Race, Class, Ethnicity and Nationalism Reconsidered*, ed. Nina Glick Schiller, Linda Basch, and Cristina Blanc-Szanton, 1–24 (New York: New York Academy of Sciences, 1992).

4. *Jerusalem Post*, "Population Reaches almost 6.5 Million"; Israel Ministry of Foreign Affairs, *Frequently Asked Questions about Israel* (1999), http://www.israel-mfa.gov.il/mfa/go.asp?MFAH0kdfo.

5. Ministry of Immigrant Absorption (Israel), *Returning Residents*, November 27, 1998, http://www.moia.gov.il/klita-last/english/types/return/return1.html.

6. Yinon Cohen, "Economic Assimilation in the United States of Arab and Jew-ish Immigrants from Israel and the Territories," *Israel Studies* 1, no. 2 (1996): 75–97; Calvin Goldscheider, *Israeli's Changing Society: Population, Ethnicity and Development* (Boulder, Colo.: Westview, 1996).

7. Cohen, "Economic Assimilation," 83.

8. Alan Dowty, *The Jewish State: A Century Later* (Berkeley: University of Califor-

nia Press, 1998); Permanent Observer Mission of Palestine to the United Nations, *Israeli Occupation of the Palestinian Territory* (1999), http://www.palestine-un.org/info/occ.html.

9. Cohen, "Economic Assimilation," 83.

10. Dowty, *Jewish State*, 188.

11. "No attempt was made to integrate them [the Palestinians] into the various countries and communities in the region. Thousands of refugees remain today in a number of Arab countries with no political, economic or social rights." Ministry of Foreign Affairs, *Frequently Asked Questions*.

12. Akiva Eldar, "It's Good to Die for Their Country," *Ha'aretz*, September 3, 2001, originally accessed at http://www.haaretz.co.il/hasen/objects (September 2, 2001); currently available through the Ha'aretz archive at http://www.haaretz.com/hasen/pages/arch.

13. Cohen, "Economic Assimilation," 77.

14. Dowty, *Jewish State*, 73–74.

15. Dowty, *Jewish State;* Gallya Lahav and Asher Arian, "Israelis in a Jewish Diaspora: The Multiple Dilemmas of a Globalized Group," paper presented at the annual meeting of the International Studies Association, Washington, D.C., February 16–20, 1999, available at http://www2.hawaii.edu/~fredr/lahav.htm.

16. Dowty, *Jewish State*, 192.

17. Israel Central Bureau of Statistics, *Israel Bulletin of Statistics* 6 (Tel Aviv, June 1994).

18. Steven J. Gold, *The Israeli Diaspora* (London and Seattle: Routledge and University of Washington Press, 2002); Gabriel Sheffer, "The Israeli Diaspora: Yordim (Emigrants) Are the Authentic Diaspora," in *The Jewish Year Book,* ed. S. Massil, xix–xxxi (London: Valentine Mitchell, 1998).

19. Sue Fishkoff, "Don't Call Us Yordim," *Jerusalem Post,* March 4, 1994. According to the 2000 U.S. census, about 125,000 Israel-born persons live in the United States. This figure includes non-Jewish Palestinians. At the same time, about 40 percent of the Jewish population of Israel is foreign-born, and a fraction of these Israeli citizens have also made their way to the United States but are not enumerated by the U.S. Census as Israeli (U.S. Bureau of the Census, 2000, 2003 5% PUMS data).

20. Marlena Schmool and Frances Cohen, *A Profile of British Jewry: Patterns and Trends at the Turn of a Century* (London: Board of Deputies of British Jews, 1998), 30.

21. Allie A. Dubb, *The Jewish Population of South Africa: The 1991 Sociodemographic Survey* (Cape Town: Kaplan Centre Jewish Studies and Research, University of Cape Town, 1994), 17.

22. Council of Europe, *Recent Demographic Developments in Europe* (Strasbourg: Council of Europe, 1998); Sergio DellaPergola, personal communication, March 12, 2000.

23. Cohen, "Economic Assimilation," 77.

24. Goldscheider, *Israeli's Changing Society*, 57.

25. Dowty, *Jewish State*, 86.

26. Yinon Cohen, "War and Social Integration: The Effects of the Israeli-Arab Conflict on Jewish Emigration from Israel," *American Sociological Review* 53 (December 1988): 909; *Jerusalem Post*, "Population Reaches almost 6.5 Million".

27. Ministry of Internal Affairs, *Frequently Asked Questions*.

28. Returning scientists receive special benefits. Ministry of Immigrant Absorption, *Returning Residents*.

29. Larry Derfner, "Israel's Alien Nation," *Jerusalem Post*, January 28, 2001, http://cgis.jpost.com (accessed January 30, 2001); "Israel, Migrants, Palestine," *Migration News* 8, no. 7 (2001), http://migration.ucdavis.edu/mn/more.php?id=2419_0_5_0.

30. Dowty, *Jewish State*, 87.

31. Ibid., 87–89.

32. Yinon Cohen, "War and Social Integration," 909.

33. Zvi Sobel, *Migrants from the Promised Land* (New Brunswick, N.J.: Transaction Publisher, 1986), 8 and 14; italics in the original.

34. See, for example, Douglas S. Massey, Luin Goldring, and Jorge Durand, "Continuities in Transnational Migration: An Analysis of Nineteen Mexican Communities," *American Journal of Sociology* 99, no. 6 (1994): 1492–1533.

35. Uriva Shavit, "Westward Ho!" *Ha'aretz Daily*, August 22, 2001, currently available through the Ha'aretz archive at http://www.haaretz.com/hasen/pages/arch.

36. Goldstein, *Jewish History*, 6.

37. Sergio DellaPergola, "World Jewish Migration System in Historical Perspective," paper presented at International Conference Human Migration in a Global Framework, University of Calgary, Alberta, Canada, June 9–12, 1994, 3.

38. Israel Central Bureau of Statistics, http://www.cbs.gov.il, tables 5.1, 5.3.

39. Harold Greenberg, *Israel: Social Problems* (Tel Aviv: Dekel, 1979): 49; *Migration News*, "Israel, Migrants, Palestine."

40. DellaPergola, "World Jewish Migration System," 12.

41. Lahav and Arian, "Israelis in a Jewish Diaspora."

42. Etan Levine, ed., *Diaspora: Exile and the Jewish Condition* (New York and London: Jason Aronson, 1983): 3.

43. Sheffer, "Israeli Diaspora," xix.

44. Yael Zerubavel, *Recovered Roots: Collective Memory and the Making of Israeli National Tradition* (Chicago: University of Chicago Press, 1995), 18.

45. Steven M. Cohen, "Israel in the Jewish Identity of American Jews: A Study in Dualities and Contrasts," in *Jewish Identity in America*, ed. David M. Gordis and Yoav Ben-Horin, 122 (Los Angeles: Wilstein, 1991).

46. Oz Almog, *The Sabra: The Creation of the New Jew* (Berkeley: University of California Press, 2000), 21–22.

47. Zerubavel, *Recovered Roots*, xv.

48. Ruth Linn and Nurit Barkan-Ascher, "Permanent Impermanence: Israeli Expatriates in Non-Event Transition," *The Jewish Journal of Sociology* 38, no. 1 (1996): 7.

49. Paul Ritterband, "Israelis in New York," *Contemporary Jewry* 7 (1986): 113; Shaol Kimhi, "Perceived Change of Self-Concept, Values, Well-Being and Intention to Return among Kibbutz People Who Migrated from Israel to America," PhD diss. Pacific Graduate School of Psychology, 1990.

50. Pini Herman, "The Myth of the Israeli Expatriate," *Moment* 8, no. 8 (1983): 62–63.

51. Alexander Zvielli, "The Mark of Cain," *The Jerusalem Post*, September 26, 1989.

52. Greenberg, *Israel: Social Problems*, 55.

53. Steven J. Gold and Bruce A. Phillips, "Israelis in the United States," *American Jewish Yearbook*, 1996, 51–101; Y. Cohen, "Economic Assimilation."

54. Greenberg, *Israel: Social Problems*, 55.

55. Linn and Barkan-Ascher, "Permanent Impermanence," 7; S. M. Cohen, "Israel in the Jewish Identity."

56. Amir Shor, "The Miserable Truth," *Ha'aretz Daily*, letters to the editor September 5, 2001, http://www.haaretz.com (accessed September 10, 2001).

57. Naama Sabar, *Kibbutz L.A.* ([Hebrew] Tel Aviv: Am Oved, 1996); Naama Sabar, *Kibbutznicks in the Diaspora* (Albany: SUNY Press, 2000).

58. Moshe Shokeid, *Children of Circumstances: Israeli Immigrants in New York* (Ithaca: Cornell University Press, 1988), 39–40; Natan Uriely, "Rhetorical Ethnicity of Permanent Sojourners: The Case of Israeli Immigrants in the Chicago Area," *International Sociology* 9, no.4 (1994): 431–45; David Mittelberg and Mary C. Waters, "The Process of Ethnogenesis among Haitian and Israeli Immigrants in the United States," *Ethnic and Racial Studies* 15, no. 3 (1992): 412–35.

59. Rina Cohen and Gerald Gold, "Israelis in Toronto: The Myth of Return and the Development of a Distinct Ethnic Community," *The Jewish Journal of Sociology* 38, no. 1 (1996): 22.

60. Sheffer, "Israeli Diaspora," xix.

61. Sobel, *Migrants*, 223.

62. Steven M. Cohen, "Israeli Émigrés and the New York Federation: A Case Study in Ambivalent Policymaking for Jewish Communal Deviants," *Contemporary Jewry* 7 (1986): 159; Tom Tugend, "Peretz: Integrate Yordim into Jewish Community," *Jerusalem Post*, November 29, 1989.

63. Sherry Rosen, "The Israeli Corner of the American Jewish Community," Issue Series #3, (New York: Institute on American Jewish-Israeli Relations, The American Jewish Committee, 1993), 2; see also Gold and Phillips, "Israeli."

64. Gold, *Israeli Diaspora*, 156.

65. Ibid., 149.

66. Y. Cohen, "War and Social Integration," 914.

67. Lahav and Arain, "Israelis in a Jewish Diaspora"; Gold and Phillips, "Israelis."

68. Lahav and Arain, "Israelis in a Jewish Diaspora."

69. Rosen, "Israeli Corner," 3.

70. Tugend, "Peretz."

71. Rosen, "Israeli Corner," 3.

72. "For Those Returning Home" [Hebrew], Supplement to *Yisrael Shelanu* (1995); Ministry of Immigrant Absorption, *Returning Residents.*

73. Shlomo Moaz and Avi Temkin, "Olim and Yordim," *Jerusalem Post,* May 9, 1989.

74. Matt Richtel, "New Israelis Get Computers to Aid Assimilation," *New York Times,* January 21, 1998.

75. Michael A. Hiltzik, "Israel's High Tech Shifts into High Gear," *Los Angeles Times,* August 13, 2000; Yarolslav Trofimov, "Booming Economy Lures Israelis Home from U.S.: Jewish State Now More Inviting," *San Francisco Examiner,* October 8, 1995.

76. Galit Lipkis, "Business Envoys Whet U.S. Appetites," *Jerusalem Post,* November 26, 1991.

77. Shokied, *Children;* Mittelberg and Waters, "Process of Ethnogenesis"; Uriely, "Rhetorical Ethnicity."

78. Y. Cohen, "Economic Assimilation"; "For Those Returning Home"; Michele Chabin, "Behind the Headlines: Israelis Living Abroad Wooed to Return by Government Firms," *Jewish Telegraphic Agency On Line,* March 2, 1997, available at http://www.highbeam.com/doc/1P1:3633469/BEHIND+THE+HEADLINES~C~+Israelis+living+abroad+wooed+to+return+by.html?refid=SEO

79. Yinon Cohen and Yitchak Haberfeld, "The Number of Israeli Immigrants in the United States in 1990," *Demography* 34, no. 2 (1997): 200.

80. Gold and Phillips, "Israelis," 63–64.

81. *Yisrael Shelanu,* "For Those Returning Home."

82. Mary Curtius, "Tech Slump is Just Leading Edge of Israel's Misery," *Los Angeles Times,* June 22, 2001; Larry Derfner, "Waiting for a Better Home," *The Internet Jerusalem Post,* August 26, 2001, http:// cgis.jpost.com (accessed August 27, 2001); Shavit, "Westward Ho"; Nina Gilbert, "Immigration Rising Only from Argentina and France," *Internet Jerusalem Post,* May 6, 2002.

83. Shavit, "Westward Ho."

84. Eldar, "It's Good to Die for Their Country."

85. *Migration News,* "Israel, Migrants, Palestine."

86. Shavit, "Westward Ho."

87. Ibid.

88. Sheldon Teitelbaum, "L.A.'s Hidden Battalions," *Jewish Journal* (Los Angeles edition) 16, no. 24 (August 10–16, 2001): 14.

CONTRIBUTORS

M. PAGE BALDWIN received her master's degree in later modern British history from King's College, London, and her PhD in British history from Birkbeck College, University of London, in 2003. Her research interests include issues of American concepts of belonging as they relate to the continuing debate between U.S. state and federal powers.

CAROLINE DOUKI is a graduate of the École Normale Supérieure (Fontenay-Saint-Cloud), where she subsequently taught for several years. Douki is currently an associate professor of European studies at the University of Paris-8. She was a member of the École Française de Rome (Italy) from 1993 to 1996. She specializes in the social and political history of international migrations in southern Europe and is currently working on relationships between migrants and institutions in southern Europe and in the Mediterranean region during the nineteenth and twentieth centuries. She is the editor-in-chief of the quarterly *Revue d'histoire Moderne et Contemporaine*.

JORGE DURAND is a professor of anthropology at the University of Guadalajara, Mexico, and codirector, with Douglas S. Massey, of the Mexican Migration Project and the Latin American Migration Project sponsored by the University of Princeton and the University of Guadalajara. He is a member of the Mexican Academy of Sciences and a foreign member of the National Academy of Sciences. His publications, as author or coauthor, include *Return to Aztlan; Más allá de la línea; Miracles on the Border; Migrations mexicaines aux Etats-Unis; La experiencia migrante; Beyond Smoke and Mirrors; Clandestinos: Migración mexicana en los albores del siglo XX*.

CORRIE VAN EIJL received her PhD in 1994 (*Het werkzame verschil: Vrouwen in de slag om arbeid, 1898–1940*), and is a senior researcher at the University of Leiden. She has published on women's work and migration history. Her latest book, *Al te goed is buurman's gek: Het Nederlandse vreemdelingenbeleid 1840–1940,* is on Dutch immigration policy from 1840 to 1940.

ANDREAS FAHRMEIR is a professor of nineteenth- and twentieth-century European history at the University of Frankfurt. His publications include *Ehrbare Spekulanten: Stadtverfassung, Wirtschaft und Politik in der City of London (1688–1900); Citizens and Aliens: Foreigners and the Law in Britain and the German States 1789–1870;* and *Migration Control in the North Atlantic World: The Evolution of State Practices in Europe and the United States from the French Revolution to the Inter-War Period* (co-edited with Olivier Faron and Patrick Weil).

DAVID FELDMAN is a reader in history at Birkbeck, University of London. He is an editor of *History Workshop Journal.* In 1994, he published *Englishmen and Jews: Social Relations and Political Culture, 1840–1914.* He has also published essays on the history of migration and immigration in Britain and co-edited (with Leo Lucassen and Jochem Oltmer) *Paths of Integration: Migrants in Western Europe (1880–2004).*

DONNA R. GABACCIA is the Rudolph J. Vecoli Professor of Immigration History and director of the Immigration History Research Center at the University of Minnesota. She is the author of many books and articles on Italian migration around the world and immigrant life in the United States, most recently *Immigration and American Diversity; Italy's Many Diasporas;* and *We Are What We Eat.*

STEVEN J. GOLD is a professor and associate chair in the Department of Sociology at Michigan State University. He has published articles on qualitative research methods, visual sociology, immigration, ethnic economies, race, and ethnic community development. He is past chair of the International Migration Section of the American Sociological Association; co-editor of *Immigration Research for a New Century: Multidisciplinary Perspectives* (with Rubén G. Rumbaut and Nancy Foner); and the author of four books: *Refugee Communities: A Comparative Field Study; From the Worker's State to the Golden State; Ethnic Economies* (with Ivan Light); and *The Israeli Diaspora,* which won the American Sociological Association's award for the best book on international migration in 2003.

NANCY L. GREEN is directrice d'études (professor) at the École des Hautes Etudes en Sciences Sociales (Paris), where she teaches comparative migration history. Recent publications include *Repenser les migrations* and *Ready-to-Wear and Ready-to-Work: A Century of Industry and Immigrants in Paris and New York* (Chinard Prize of the Society for French Historical Studies). She is currently at work on a book concerning elite migration: American expatriates in France in the first half of the twentieth century.

ERIC GUERASSIMOFF is a professor of modern Chinese history at the University of Paris-7 and the current director of the SEDET (a research unit on Developing Societies of the CNRS and the University of Paris-7). His research focuses on the history of Chinese migration since the nineteenth century. He has published books on Chinese migrants and education in Singapore and has edited a volume on migration dynamics in southern developing societies. He is currently researching the position of French citizens in the Chinese coolie trade and their consequences on Sino-French diplomatic relations up to the early twentieth century.

DIRK HOERDER teaches North American social history and history of migrations at Arizona State University (formerly at the University of Bremen, Department of Social Sciences). His areas of interest are European labor migration in the Atlantic economies, history of worldwide migration systems, and the sociology of migrant acculturation. He has been director of the Labor Migration Project (Bremen) and has taught at York University (Toronto), Duke University, and the University of Toronto. His publications include *Labor Migration in the Atlantic Economies: The European and North American Working Classes during the Period of Industrialization; European Migrants: Global and Local Perspectives* (with Leslie Page Moch); *Creating Societies: Immigrant Lives in Canada; Cultures in Contact: European and World Migrations, Eleventh Century to the 1990s* (Sharlin Prize of the Social Science History Association); and *The Historical Practice of Diversity: Transcultural Interactions from the Early Modern Mediterranean to the Postcolonial World* (co-edited with Christiane Harzig and Adrian Shubert).

BINOD KHADRIA is a professor of economics at the Zakir Husain Centre for Educational Studies, School of Social Sciences, Jawaharlal Nehru University, New Delhi, India. His book *The Migration of Knowledge Workers—Second-Generation Effects of India's Brain Drain* is acclaimed for addressing a paradigm shift in migration research and policy. In addition to migration studies, he teaches economics of education and human resources. He is currently a visiting senior fellow at the Asia Research Institute and the Department of Economics at the National University of Singapore.

LEO LUCASSEN is chair of social history at Leiden University and an associate professor of social and economic history at the University of Amsterdam. His most recent publications include *The Immigrant Threat: The Integration of Old and New Migrants in Western Europe since 1850* and (co-edited with David Feldman and Jochem Oltmer) *Paths of Integration: Migrants in Western Europe (1880–2004)*.

CARINE PINA-GUERASSIMOFF has her doctorate in law and development studies, and she is an affiliated researcher at the SEDET, a research unit of the CNRS and the University of Paris-7. She was a fellow at the Institut für Asienkunde (Hamburg) with a Clemens Heller Grant of the Frantz Thyssen Foundation (2005–6). Her research focuses on the Chinese state's relations to Chinese overseas, transnationalism, new Chinese migrants to Europe, and Chinese asylum seekers. She has published a book on Chinese state migration policies and numerous articles on the subject in French, English, German, Dutch, and Chinese reviews. She is currently writing a study on Chinese women in migration.

BRUNO RAMIREZ is a professor of history at the Université de Montréal. His books and articles have dealt with labor and migration history in a variety of national contexts such as Canada, the United States, and Italy. Among them are *Les premiers Italiens de Montréal; On the Move: French-Canadian and Italian Migrants in the North Atlantic Economy, 1860–1915;* and *Crossing the 49th Parallel: Emigration from Canada to the United States, 1900–1930.* He has also authored and co-authored the screenplays for several long feature films that recount the experience of Italian immigrants in Québec.

DOROTHEE SCHNEIDER teaches at the University of Illinois at Urbana-Champaign. She has published on the history of citizenship and naturalization and is the author of *Trade Unions and Community: German Trade Unions in New York City*. She is currently completing a study on immigration and U.S. borders in the twentieth century.

JOHN TORPEY is a professor in the PhD program in sociology at the City University of New York Graduate Center. He is the author of *The Invention of the Passport: Surveillance, Citizenship, and the State* and of *Documenting Individual Identity: The Development of State Practices in the Modern World* (co-editor with Jane Caplan). He has also edited, with Daniel Levy and Max Pensky, *Old Europe, New Europe, Core Europe: Transatlantic Relations After the Iraq War*, and is the author of *Making Whole What Has Been Smashed: On Reparations Politics*.

ADAM WALASZEK is a professor of history in the Institute of American Studies and Polish Diaspora, Jagiellonian University, Rynek Glowny, in Krakow, Poland. He specializes in international migration movements and Polish ethnic history in the United States and is the author of three books, editor of five others, and author of over ninety scholarly articles published in Poland and abroad. His latest works include *Identity, Conflict and Cooperation: Central Europeans in Cleveland, 1850–1930* (co-author) and *Diaspora polska* handbook (editor). Walaszek was awarded the Haiman Award for outstanding contribution to the field of Polish American Studies by the Polish American Historical Association in 2004.

FRANÇOIS WEIL is directeur d'études (professor) and director of the Center for North American Studies at the École des Hautes Etudes en Sciences Sociales in Paris. His publications include *Les Franco-Américains, 1860–1980* and *A History of New York*. He is currently at work on two books, one about French emigration to the Americas in the nineteenth century, and the other on the cultural history of genealogy in the United States.

ARISTIDE R. ZOLBERG is Walter A. Eberstadt Professor of Political Science at the Graduate Faculty of New School University in New York City and is the director of its International Center for Migration, Ethnicity, and Citizenship. He held the University-in-Exile chair there from its founding in 1984 to 2002. Zolberg has published broadly in the fields of comparative politics and historical sociology in both English and French. After his initial specialization in African studies, he has written extensively on state and nation formation in Europe and the United States. His works in the field of immigration and refugee studies include *Escape from Violence: Conflict and the Refugee Crisis in the Developing World* (co-author with Astri Suhrke and Sergio Aguyao); *Global Migrants, Global Refugees* (co-editor with Peter Benda); *Shadows over Europe* (co-editor with Martin Schain and Patrick Hossay); and *A Nation by Design? Immigration Policy in the Fashioning of America.*

INDEX

Buenos Aires, 82, 117, 122
Bush, George W., 238
Byelorussians, 78

Calcutta, 268, 269
Calgary, 215
California, 224, 236–37
Canada, 5–6, 37, 46, 47–49, 55, 65, 76, 115, 123, 137, 146, 147, 156, 158, 185, 200, 211–21, 247, 265, 266, 267, 276, 286, 294, 298
Canton, 251
Cape of Good Hope, 137
Cárdenas, Lázaro, 226, 240
Carey, William, 268
Carpi, Leone, 71, 73
Castañeda, Jorge, 237, 238, 239
Castlereagh, Lord (Robert Stewart), 39
census, 41, 125, 211, 224, 286; in Italy, 70, 93, 95
Chandèze, Gustave, 115–16, 122
charity, 55, 136, 140
Chavez, Cesar, 230
Chiang Kai-Shek, 252
Chile, 123
China, 2, 6, 25–28, 245–62. *See also* China, laws
China, laws: Directive Concerning Establishment of a Permanent System of Household Registration (June 22, 1955), 25; Law on the Control of the Exit and Entry of Citizens (1986), 257; Nationality Law (1909), 7, 250; Nationality Law (1929), 251; Nationality Law (1980), 259; Peking Regulations (1866), 247; Regulations on Household Registration (1958), 26; Regulations on the Criteria for Defining Urban and Rural Areas (1955), 25
Chinese National Association for Overseas Exchanges, 255
Churchill, Winston, 149
Ciemieniewski, Jan, 75
citizenship, 21, 24, 27–28, 34, 51–52, 170, 182, 188, 235, 286; and China, 249–50, 259; and Germany, 66, 68–69, 81, 182, 183, 184–85, 188; and Great Britain, 140, 143–46; and Israel, 284, 289; and Italy, 72, 74, 81, 104; and the Netherlands, 156, 160–61, 162; and Poland, 81; and the United States, 144, 195

Cixi, Empress, 249
Clarendon, Lord (George William Frederick Villiers), 145
Cobbett, William, 42
Cockburn, Lieutenant Colonel (Francis), 137
Cohen, Frances, 286
Cohen, Rina, 294
Cohen, Yinon, 284, 286
Coletti, Francesco, 102
colonial emigration, 6, 35, 43, 46, 67, 157; and Great Britain, 139–51; and the Netherlands, 158; and Italy, 70–71, 72–73
Colonial Land and Emigration Commission (CLEC, Great Britain), 48–49, 141, 142, 146, 147
colonies. *See* colonial emigration; colonization
colonization, 80–81, 213, 217, 218; and France, 119, 123; and Great Britain, 135, 137, 140–43. *See also* colonial emigration
Commissariato Generale dell'Emigrazione (CGE), 102, 103, 108
Committee on Emigration (Great Britain), 45
Communism, 28; in China, 7, 8, 25–28, 245, 252–62; in Russia, 20–21, 23–24
Confederate States of America, 49
Congress of Vienna, 17
Constitution of 1791 (France), 13, 15, 28, 51
consulates, 2, 7, 17, 126, 166–68, 182, 197, 201, 202, 204, 205–6, 236, 237, 247, 248, 249–50, 285, 294, 296, 298
contract labor, 117, 197
coolies, 246, 247, 248
Corradini, Enrico, 73
Cowan, Philip, 202–3
"Coyotes," 231
crime, 72, 179, 180, 182, 196, 197, 201, 203, 205, 231, 236, 239, 246, 248
Crispi, Francesco, 73, 100
Cuba, 246, 247, 248
Cultural Revolution (China), 7, 8, 253–55, 256
Cunard line, 203–4
Czechs, 69

Danes, 69
D'Annunzio, Gabriele, 73

prostitution, 67, 196, 197, 201, 204
Prussia, 16–17, 66, 159, 160–62, 167, 178, 179.
    See also Prussia, laws
Prussia, laws: Edict, October 1807, 16; Passport 1817, 16
Przeglad Wszechpolski, 76
Pufendorf, Samuel, 34

Qianlong, Emperor, 246
Qing Dynasty, 245, 249–50
Quebec, 213, 216, 218, 220. *See also* Canada

Rabin, Yitzhak, 292, 296, 299
race, 81, 186, 195, 198, 213, 219
recruiters, 52, 67, 71, 104, 114, 117, 158, 197, 200, 225. *See also* emigration agencies
Reichskommissar für das Auswanderungswesen, 67
remittances. *See* transfer payments
repatriation, 6, 185, 226, 235, 296. *See also* return migration
restrictions (emigration), 13, 212
return migration, 5, 6, 52, 69, 97, 102, 163, 164, 165, 167, 168, 170, 177, 181–82, 183, 186, 187, 188, 246, 255–56, 284, 296, 298
Revolution of 1848 (Germany), 66
Rong Yiren, 254
Roosevelt, Theodore, 198, 199
Rosanvallon, Pierre, 115
Rosen, Sherry, 294–95
Rotterdam, 167
Roy, Raja Rammohan, 268
Royal Commission on the Laws of Nationality and Allegiance (Great Britain), 145–46
Ruhr, 157, 177
Russell, Lord John, 138
Russia, 17, 18–21, 65, 66, 68, 75, 156, 169, 196, 197, 202–3. *See also* Russia, laws
Russia, laws: Collection of Statutes on Passports and Runaways (1857), 19; Declaration of the Rights of the Working and Exploited People (1918), 20; Edict (1719), 19; Emancipation Decree (1861), 19; Legal Code (1649), 18
Russyns, 75
Ruthenians, 75

Sabar, Naama, 293
Salinas, Carlos, 232, 234, 236
San Francisco, 248
Santibáñez, Enrique, 226
Saskatchewan, 214
Savoie, Eugénie, 213
Say, Jean-Baptiste, 52
Scandinavia, 51
Schmool, Marlena, 286
Scotland, 39, 42, 44, 46, 136
Scottish Highlanders, 39, 42
Scrope, George Poulett, 139
Sen, Triguna, 275
serfdom, 2, 16, 18–20, 28, 36, 177
Seward, William H., 145
Shahar, Meirav Eilon, 299
Sharry, Frank, 238
shipping, 5, 18, 39, 44–45, 51, 55, 65, 103, 121, 141, 142, 151, 177, 180, 196, 198, 199–201, 202, 204, 205, 206, 289
shipping laws, 38–40, 45, 67. *See also* Great Britain, laws: Passenger Act of 1803, Passenger Act of 1828, Passenger Act of 1842
Shokeid, Moshe, 293
Shrimali, K. L., 273
Siemiradzki, Józef, 76
Singapore, 248, 266
slavery, 2, 14, 19, 21–23, 28, 35, 39
Smith, Adam, 43
Sobel, Zvi, 288, 294
Sorbs, 65
South Africa, 286
South America, 51, 63, 64, 67, 69, 73, 76, 78, 79, 80, 81, 116, 123, 186, 200, 205, 238, 299
South Seas, 248, 249
Soviet Union, 2, 18, 20–21, 23–24, 25, 27–28, 69, 236, 283. *See also* Russia
Spain, 51, 63, 72, 122, 247, 266
Stanley, Lord (Edward), 140
State Office for the Problems of Returning Prisoners, Refugees, and Workers (JUR, Poland), 77, 78
statistics: France, 4, 120, 121, 124, 125; Israel, 286; Italy, 3, 71–72, 73, 93–99, 102; Poland, 78
Statistique générale de la France (SGF), 120, 124, 125, 126

STUDIES OF WORLD MIGRATIONS

The University of Illinois Press
is a founding member of the
Association of American University Presses.

———————————————————————

Composed in 10.5/13 Adobe Minion
with Meta display
by Jim Proefrock
at the University of Illinois Press
Manufactured by Sheridan Books, Inc.

University of Illinois Press
1325 South Oak Street
Champaign, IL 61820-6903
www.press.uillinois.edu